The *Antelope* and the *James M. Donahue* at Donahue's Landing. NATIONAL MARITIME MUSEUM.

This is a limited edition
consisting of five hundred copies.
Of these signed and
numbered copies this is
copy number 205.

R. H. Dillon

IRON MEN

A stalwart survivor of the April 1906 earthquake and fire was the Mechanics' Monument, sculpted by Douglas Tilden, dedicated to mechanics in memory of Peter Donahue. SOCIETY OF CALIFORNIA PIONEERS

CALIFORNIA'S INDUSTRIAL PIONEERS

IRON MEN

PETER, JAMES, AND MICHAEL DONAHUE

BY RICHARD H. DILLON

CANDELA PRESS

Candela Press
P.O. Box 134
Point Richmond, California 94801

Produced by Total Book Source
Designed by Abigail Johnston
Typesetting by Curt Chelin
Printed and bound by Braun-Brumfield, Inc.

Manufactured in the United States of America.
ISBN: 0-9613530-7

FOR ANNIE

CONTENTS

FOREWORD

IN THIS EXHAUSTIVELY RESEARCHED, well written triple-biography of the pioneering brothers Donahue—James, Peter, and Michael—historian Richard Dillon, one of the pre-eminent chroniclers of the Far West, has made an important contribution, not only to the history of California and the story of the Irish in America, but also to the largely untold history of technology on the frontier. Here is a rich and satisfying story, replete with detail that is presented with a novelist's eye and capacity for narrative. Masterly writer that he is, Dillon manages the specifics of his history so that they at once tell an immediate story—the saga of three enormously talented and energetic Irish immigrants in mid-nineteenth century America—while at the same time suggesting through these lives a complexity of social, economic, financial, and technological forces. This, ultimately, is what biography is all about: the employment of individual lives both as ends in themselves and as embodiments of larger experience.

Iron Men is primarily the story of three brothers—the inventive Michael, Peter the entrepreneur, James the idea man—who, born to Irish parents, came from Scotland to the bright promise of America itself, which unfolded for the Donahue family, as it did for millions of other immigrants in this era, "the fresh green breast of the new world" to use the phrase of a later Irishman, novelist F. Scott Fitzgerald. Obviously, the Donahue brothers were atypical. Their talent and energy raised them far above the level of the majority of their peers; yet even extraordinary immigrants were forced to endure a representative experience of dislocation, a dangerous trans-Atlantic voyage, the stepping with so little preparation into a new country, in which many of the older residents violently resented them for both their race and their religion. In the story of the Donahues' rise from foundry days to commanding positions as manufacturing entrepreneurs is contained the cumulative drama of the nineteenth-century immigrant aspiration, as men and women struggled in both the cities and on the land, first to survive in their new surroundings and then to gain some measure of the material and psychological prosperity that motivated them to emigrate in the first place. Beginning their lives near Glasgow, the Donahue brothers—Peter at least—survived to see daughters married to young American men of background and education and in one instance, European nobility. Richard Dillon tells a story of dynasties established and estates built in the wilderness, of dreams made real through heroic struggle and canny good judgment more than the traditional luck of the Irish.

It is this Irishness which provides the context and primary premise of Dillon's narrative; for in their single lifetimes the Donahue brothers passed through every successive phase of Irish-American experience: from genteel poverty to factory, from modest enterprises to vast undertakings, from impoverishment to industrial aristocracy. All this was done, moreover, without loss of identity, without undue pretense or repudiation. In the midst of their prosperity, the Donahue brothers never forgot where they had come from; nor did they forget their fellow Irish immigrants, many of them their longtime employees, who had helped them get there. How remarkably do these brothers move by their own efforts from simplicity to elegance, while all the while remaining in their deepest identities mechanics, iron men, working with their hands such as praised by their contemporary Walt Whitman. The Donahues were democratic men for a democratic era, iron men for an age of iron, which is to say, an age of beginnings in which neither background, nor education, nor previous status was necessary for major careers.

The collective experience of the Donahue brothers also distilled within itself virtually every phase of "Manifest Destiny" and the opening of the Far West as experienced by the men and women who made this history happen. Donahues were present in Mexico during the Mexican War, which constituted the logical extension of the Manifest Destiny imperative that the Mexican territories of the Southwest and the western edge of the North American continent were, by force of destiny, to be enfolded into the American Union. All three Donahue brothers were involved in the Gold Rush, which accelerated settlement of the most significant territory ceded by Mexico in 1848, California. Two came by sea, experiencing that great odyssey; and one of them came overland, experiencing the hardships of that long journey—hunger, thirst, fatigue, dangerous encounters with hostile Indians, Dillon's management of this portion of his narrative is a *tour de force* of both research and story telling. I can recall few accounts of military campaigning by Americans in Mexico that are comparable to Dillon's treatment. Once the Donahue brothers arrive in California, moreover, Dillon treats us to an extraordinarily rich narrative of Gold Rush days, the rise of San Francisco, the beginnings of manufacture, the coming of the railroad, the age of silver bonanzas and high finance. In these events, Michael played some part until his removal to Iowa, James played a major role until his untimely death in 1862, and Peter, the survivor, saw it all through to the much different world of the 1880s. *Iron Men* is thus a selective, which is to say a properly biographical, history of California as reflected in the experiences of three important protagonists; but it is also the history of all the others that came as well, for what the Donahue brothers experienced, all Californians experienced, albeit to a lesser degree.

In this book, Richard Dillon captures the importance of technology in the development of California and the Far West and the major role played by the Donahues in bringing technology to the Pacific Coast. Trained as mechanics, as iron men, the Donahues got right to work after their dramatic reunion in San Francisco: they repaired ships. They melted down iron and remolded it for maritime use. They created an ingenious form of stove. They devised and constructed San Francisco's first gas plant. They established the state's first iron works. And in 1865, Peter Donahue was on hand to see *The California,* the first locomotive to be constructed on the Pacific Coast, roll down the tracks to San Jose. From this bold beginning, Peter Donahue went on to become a pioneering railroad developer in the San

Francisco Bay Area and Northern California; and but for the untimely death of Theodore Judah, he might have beaten the Big Four in the race to construct a railroad across the American continent. Dillon's story of technology as associated with the Donahues recounts something very important about California and the Far West. In California, the technology of mining established the socio-economic disposition and the supporting infrastructure for the ensuing era of irrigation and agriculture. The twin principles of technology and environment, the machine and the wilderness becoming the machine and the garden, is in many ways the inner story, the real history, of California and the Far West. The brothers Donahue helped make this so.

In choosing *Labor Omnia Vincit,* Labor Conquers All, as his motto, Peter Donahue elegantly summarized the lives of himself and his brothers. *Iron Men* is above all else a celebration of labor, real work in a real world, and the good gifts that purposeful work can bring. Conspicuous in their success, the Donahue brothers, Peter especially, maintained a life-long association with the working men and women of America. Their enterprises, after all, created jobs—in foundries, gas plants, on the railroad—and these jobs in turn made other lives possible. True, the brothers grew rich in the process; but so did many others as well. They also created work for two generations of Americans in the West, many of them Irish immigrants like themselves.

Labor Omnia Vincit. Truly, labor did vanquish all in the Donahue story; vanquished the Glasgow poverty, and the perils of fierce combat in Mexico, and the disappointments of not finding gold, and the prejudices extended to the Irish as they arrived in America. Labor conquered the raging Atlantic, across which they sailed; labor conquered the continent itself; labor overcame the notion that California did not have within itself the maturity necessary to create a fully integrated commonwealth. James, perhaps weary of this labor, died before forty years of age; Michael and Peter carried on; and then there was Peter alone, the last of the brothers, visiting Europe in his autumnal years, then passing on with the dignity with which he had lived his life: universally mourned, but not forgotten, as these following pages so eloquently suggest.

Kevin Starr
San Francisco

IRON MEN

INTRODUCTION

THE LUCK OF THE IRISH is proverbial. In the nineteenth century the phrase called to mind a picture of merry Celts, drunk or sober, blundering into good fortune.

But California's industrial pioneers, James and Peter Donahue, with their lesser-known brothers, Michael and Thomas, did not fit the stereotype. These strong "Men of Iron"—the punning term was so often applied to them by their contemporaries—*made* their luck. And they did so by hard work, technical skill, business acumen and vision, and personal integrity. Fortuitous happenings and chance played small roles either in the daily drama of their lives or in their rise from genteel poverty to the status of captains of industry and millionaires.

The impact of the Donahues on San Francisco and, indeed, California, proves, for once and for all, that truth can be stranger than fiction, even the rags-to-riches, pluck and luck, moral tales of Horatio Alger. The hard work and subsequent success of the Donahues is also a double-barreled refutation of G.K. Chesterton's old saw that if you get two Irishmen together, you have a quarrel; assemble three and you have a riot.

None of the Donahue boys had "the Devil's own luck," the extraordinarily easy success by which everything that one touches is turned, Midas-like, into gold. No observer of the lads ever ascribed their success to luck. All have emphasized the factors of application and diligence in their bootstrap rise to prominence.

If anything, the Donahues seem to prove the very opposite of the old Irish saying that "Good luck beats early rising." Each brother epitomized the best sort of emigrant Celt, the Irish-American artisan, not the lazy or bumbling stage Irishman. Without forfeiting his Catholic religion, each seemed to adopt the so-called Protestant work ethic.

Like others of their stripe, the Donahues were fascinated by the opportunity, the potential offered them by America. They were thrilled, too, by the social mobility of "the States." The United States was very much of a melting pot, altogether different from the stratified class society of the old world.

In 1888, California's greatest historian, Hubert Howe Bancroft, assigned Alfred Bates to the task of compiling notes on Peter Donahue's career. The resulting biographical sketch was never included in Bancroft's *Chronicles of the Builders* as planned, but the notes, preserved in the University of California's Bancroft Library, show that Bates ranked Peter Donahue as one of the most successful men ever to land on the Pacific shore. Bates described Donahue as a self-made man of vast energy and uncommon talent who was hard-working until the very end of his life. "His wealth was in no sense the result of accident," Bates reported to Bancroft, "but was acquired by hard work, honest toil."

Peter Donahue, himself, agreed. He once said, "I have worked hard, and my success is due to hard work . . . I have always known how to direct my employees and held myself ready to throw off my coat and show them how to handle their tools." It is understandable that the Irishman and his San Francisco contemporary, Adolph Sutro, a Jew, chose the same motto—*Labor Omnia Vincit,* "Labor Conquers All."

Alfred Bates was also struck by the fact that Donahue, the "presiding genius" of so many enterprises, not only acquired his wealth the hard way—through the exercise of prudence, foresight and sound common sense—but expended it where he had gathered it, among the artisans and laborers of his adopted city of San Francisco. For example, wrote Bates, "Although his railroad enterprises, in common with others, were undertaken in part for personal gain, they have also contributed in no small measure to the common good, and there are none whose projects have been more instrumental in developing the resources of the state."

Bates contrasted Donahue as a railroad builder with the Central Pacific's Big Four. Peter was reluctant to imitate them and use "Crocker's pets"—Chinese laborers. So-called coolie labor would save him thousands of dollars each month, but he saw this pool of cheap labor as a threat to American workers.

The editor of the *San Francisco Mail Bag,* contributed a profile of Peter Donahue to Oscar T. Shuck's collective biography, *Sketches of Leading and Representative Men of San Francisco,* published in 1875. He stressed the fact that his subject was a self-made man. "Mr. Donahue had to forego, to a degree, the advantages of a thorough education in early life and trust to a clear, sound brain, seconded by a vigorous physical constitution, to his advancement in life. His present position shows that these have not failed him."

Just seven years later, and only three years before Peter's death, Alonzo Phelps, in a similar book titled *Contemporary Biography of California's Representative Men,* reiterated the fact that the capitalist's great wealth was not "the result of brilliant speculations or lucky strikes, but the gradual accumulation of industry and business thrift."

Many decades later, Julia Cooley Altrocchi in her appropriately-named book, *The Spectacular San Franciscans* (1949), was still echoing these Victorian writers. She wrote that much of the sturdy substance of San Francisco was created out of the brain and brawn of Peter Donahue. And, she might well have added, that of James Donahue.

Almost a full century after Alfred Bates wrote of Peter Donahue, radio station KABL saluted him as San Francisco's First Man for All Seasons. In the 1980s, Kevin Starr, the brilliant young California historian, aptly described the 1840s as a time of both "muscle" and democratic possibilities. The Donahue boys were as ambitious as any men of their day, eager for advancement by means of hard work. But to Starr, they were also perfect examples of the kind of self-made men who developed the West in the Age of Iron that followed on the heels of California's Gold Rush. They were the archetypes of the Mechanics idealized by Walt Whitman.

It has been said that the Donahues—like the Floods, Fairs, Mackays, and O'Briens—moved from shirt sleeves to white tie and tails in a single generation. Maybe so. But Peter Donahue, to the day of this death, obstinately saw himself not as a capitalist but as an honest and diligent artisan; a machinist, not a millionaire. "Once a Mechanic, Always a Mechanic" might have served him as a motto just as nicely as *Labor Omnia Vincit.*

If luck entered into the lives of the Donahues, it was in the happy decision of their parents to move from Ireland to Scotland and from there to America. In each move there followed a rise in opportunity. The choices of their cities of adoption were "lucky," too, but hardly accidental. And, finally, the young Donahue boys were very fortunate in their choices of role models. They emulated American industry's Hugh Beggs, Thomas Rogers, and William Swinburne.

None of the places which they chose to live and work—Paterson, New Jersey; Davenport, Iowa; and San Francisco—was rife with prejudice and hostility toward Irish immigrants as were such larger and older cities as Boston, New York and Philadelphia. These were already crowded with famished, sickly, and unskilled Irishmen, mostly peasants-turned-slum dwellers. Many of them were crushed in spirit by the bigotry surrounding them as well as by their own illiteracy, self-pity, and alcoholism. Small wonder that placards appeared in these old cities to warn job-seekers that "No Irish Need Apply." Or that in these cities the old Manx saying was no longer a jest—"Hit him again, he's Irish!"

Emigrant Irish who settled in smaller, newer cities and especially, in San Francisco, suffered almost none of the despair or alienation they would have experienced in New York's Hell's Kitchen. This was particularly the case if they were of the artisan class, with marketable skills in this time of labor-intensive industrial beginnings and a shortage of skilled workers.

San Francisco's Irish community was unlike that of the squalid tenement cities of the Middle Atlantic states. Almost all pioneer Irish-San Franciscans, an incredible 95 percent, were so-called trans-migrants. They were not directly from the Old Sod, but were making a second pilgrimage. They moved to the West after a seasoning stay on the East Coast. Few were farm boys; most were either skilled or, at least, ambitious artisans ("mechanics" as all kinds of craftsmen were called) as were the Donahues. Some of them were mature Mexican War veterans, like James and Michael Donahue; a few had even accumulated some capital before migrating to the West Coast, as had the three brothers.

Luckily for the Donahues, San Francisco was, of all American cities, the most tolerant of ethnic, racial, religious and social diversity—in spite of its early anti-Oriental bias. The city was founded and built up by Mexicans, Germans, French, Jews, Chinese, Chileans, and Hawaiians in addition to Anglo-Saxons. This made the Irish, by comparison, practically "mainstream."

But San Francisco's record was in marked contrast to that of the Eastern cities. The Donahues arrived in America just in time for anti-Irish and anti-Catholic riots. An Ursuline convent was burned in Charleston in 1834. The Donahues were about to move west, a decade later, when the worst riots erupted in 1844. Ironically, the violence exploded in the City of Brotherly Love. Twenty people were killed and a hundred injured in Philadelphia.

The American Party (called the Nativists, and also the Know-Nothings because of their reticence) made a secret society into a briefly-powerful party whose main plank in its political platform was hostility to Irish Catholics. Even in California, Know-Nothings were able to elect justices to the State Supreme Court, put a governor, J. Neely Johnson, into office, and influence the Vigilance movement in San Francisco. But in the face of the goodwill of most of the electorate, their power waned as quickly as that of the anti-Chinese radical demagogue, Denis Kearney. The major legacy of the anti-Papist All-Americans was the folk rhyme of street urchins. This durable bit of doggerel contrasted the "Micks" unfavorably with even the "Dutch" (i.e. *Deutsch,* German):

"The dirty, dirty Dutch
They don't amount to much.
But they're a damned sight
Better than the I—rish!"

If the Donahues had any strong feelings against the Nativists, they kept them to themselves and shrugged off their yelping bigotry. There is certainly no record of the Donahues being slowed a whit in their chosen careers by prejudice.

Like Paterson in the East, San Francisco was infected much more with a boom town get-up-and-go philosophy than it was with bigotry. It was just this spirit of the ante-bellum decades that would transform the Young Republic into an industrial giant and a world power. A sketch of Peter Donahue in the San Francisco *Post's* "Pen

Portraits'' series (April 7, 1877) suggested the milieu in which the Donahue brothers found themselves in the early 1850s:

> We of California believe it is quite possible to do quickly and to do well; to stride *a grand pas* over the country and yet see the wild flowers as well as its engineering possibilities. We believe in towns and cities that go ahead, and not in those that stand still, in the smell of new mortar rather than the moldy air of long ago. . . . It is astonishing how quickly the newcomer is converted. Working, working, working, he becomes proud in the knowledge that his own history will form that of a place he is living in.

Irishmen accommodated beautifully to the bustling, liberal and cosmopolitan overnight-metropolis on the far edge of the Western frontier. They made San Francisco, even with its strong Italian and Chinese neighborhoods, into an ''Irish town'' until about the time for World War I. They liked the city's civic pride, its remarkable sense of freedom. As Irishmen, they were impressed by the questioning of authority that would become almost a trademark of the city. As early as St. Patrick's Day 1851, Thomas D'Arcy McGee noted in his *History of the Irish Settlers in North America*, ''The recent emigration of Irishmen to California has, of course, much increased the resources of the diocese. Judging from the support they have given to their Bishop, and the fervor with which they celebrate the festival of St. Patrick, they seem to be truly zealous and steadfast in their faith.''

Many San Francisco Irish remained blue collar laborers (like the Donahues, in a sense), but many others became white collar workers. Many gravitated to police work; in time, virtually dominating the force. With their gift of blarney, many went into local politics. The sky seemed the limit in this area. For example, within just two years of his arrival in town, the Donahues' friend, Irish-born Frank McCoppin—not yet a citizen—was a city supervisor. Proof positive that the Irish had arrived was McCoppin's election as mayor of San Francisco in 1867, the first native of Ireland to reach the top office in a major U.S. city.

Social and economic progress were as common as political rewards. So it was that the swift progress of the city on the Pacific brink of the continent fostered the growth of the most prosperous and successful of all Irish settlements in America. The Irish of San Francisco were, by any measure, a full generation ahead of similar immigrant communities in the rest of the country. By 1880, San

Francisco had the highest percentage of foreign-born population of any large American city, with the Irish forming its largest ethnic group. It was rich soil into which the Donahues could sink their roots.

What was said of Peter Donahue could also be said of his younger brother. James lacked only Peter's much remarked-upon "vigorous physical constitution." As a youth, James had to flee from New Jersey to the South in hopes of improving his health. But he was highly successful in San Francisco industry and apparently he, rather than Peter, took the lead when they went into business together at the end of 1849.

Alfred Bates wrote of James, as well as of Peter. "No shattered fortunes, no lucky speculations have helped to rear the monument that their enterprise and foresight have erected on this Coast." He compared the blind luck of other rich men with the way in which the hard-working James and Peter had seized opportunities and followed up on them. Bates was probably thinking of the Bonanza Kings of the Comstock Lode—James Fair, James Flood, John Mackay, and William O'Brien. "To gather riches by gambling in stocks or grain, or by the discovery and development of mines, requires no special ability; for a fool may become wealthy by speculation, and the strike of a miner's pickax may lead to the unearthing of a bonanza."

None of the Donahues had time for a proper education. Their main academy was the traditional School of Hard Knocks, into which all self-made Americans of their day matriculated. Even in middle age, Peter's habits of hard work were so ingrained that he had little or no time for reading, much less study. Thus, he was almost certainly unfamiliar with the great English essayist, Joseph Addison. Yet the latter's words seem almost addressed to Peter and to his brother James: "I never knew an early-rising, prudent man, careful of his earnings and strictly honest, who complained of ill luck . . . ."

Another Addisonian maxim was even more apropos of the Donahue brothers. "A good character, good habits, and iron industry are impregnable to the assaults of all the ill luck that fools ever dreamed up."

Addison's phrase, "iron industry," with its delightful double entendre in terms of the Donahues, seemed to serve as a watchword for these pioneers of California's industrial era.

I

APPRENTICESHIP

THE IRISH HISTORIAN, Hugh Quigley, has described the nominally Glaswegian Donahue family as actually representative of the Ulster and Leinster branches of the ancient O'Donahue/O'Donahoe clan. Peter Donahue (Senior) and his wife, Mary O'Kane Donahue, may have left their Ulster birthplace as early as 1796, but it is more likely that they migrated to Scotland after the Wolfe Tone rebellion in 1798, to escape persecution in their homeland. As Quigley observed, the Catholics there had little protection from biased local magistrates; their property, and sometimes their lives, were in danger from the harsh reprisals of the Scots-Irish faction. In just five years, 1798-1804, the Donahues were joined by 30,000 Irish fleeing to Scotland for a better chance to gain a livelihood. Curiously, Quigley's "Irish Race" was welcomed in Scotland once the Catholic Relief Act of 1778 had eased the worst restrictions placed on those of that faith. However, full socio-religious freedom had to wait for parliamentary acts of 1792 and 1829, and even today "No Popery!" graffiti can still be found on the walls of buildings in hardshell Scotland.

Scotland was not only a more peaceful part of the British Empire than the Emerald Isle, it was a far more enterprising place. The greatest number of the voluntary exiles settled in Glasgow because it was on the cutting edge of the frontier of industrialization, which by the early nineteenth century was building in progressive momentum as had enlightenment in the eighteenth.

Scotland held the promise of new jobs and the possibility of steady advancement.

Within just a few decades, the Irish formed an important and industrious section of Glasgow's population. It was an ironic exchange; peaceably, Ireland sent Scotland about as many of her children during the nineteenth century as there were Scots transplanted into Cromwellian Ulster via conquest and "plantations" in the previous century.

The Industrial Revolution itself can be said to have begun in Scotland, with the perfecting of English inventor Thomas Newcomen's steam engine by James Watt of Glasgow in 1769. Other factors which gave Scotland, and Glasgow, a headstart were the deep-dredging of the Clyde in 1770 that made Glasgow a world port; and the digging of the first canal in 1779.

Irish immigration to Glasgow surged after 1792 when Scotland's first cotton mill was built; and again around 1810-1812 when power looms were introduced, and the first steamship appeared on the Clyde. In 1828, there was another surge of immigration after Glasgow's James Nelson invented the hot blast furnace. (The first railroad did not come till about 1840, by which time the Donahues were long gone.) Thanks to the attraction of the Industrial Revolution, Irish immigration to Glasgow compensated considerably for the depopulation of both Lowlands and Highlands by Scots emigration to America.

* * *

Peter and Mary O'Kane Donahue settled in Blantyre parish, Lanarkshire, a small town in a coal mining district south-east of Glasgow. In 1785, a cotton spinning factory had been established there, and the Falls of the River Clyde (which drop two hundred-fifty feet in four miles) were a source of water power, which encouraged new industry to locate nearby.

Their first child, Ellen, was born in Blantyre on March 2, 1809. Tradition has it that the rest of the Donahue children —Michael, born February 9, 1816; Roseanna, born 1819; Anne, born 1821; Peter, destined to become the most famous of the clan, born January 11, 1822 (some sources incorrectly give the date as June 22); James, 1824; and Thomas, 1829—were born in Glasgow, but they all may have been born in Blantyre. The Donahues, for simplicity and convenience, may have given their birthplace as the recognizable Glasgow rather than as a little-known village.

Blantyre was also the birthplace of David Livingstone, the great missionary and explorer of Africa. He was born in 1813, and there is a good chance that some of the Donahues knew him. It has been said that Livingstone's strict Scots upbringing sharpened both his mental and physical gifts; many years later, the California press liked to suggest that the younger Peter Donahue, though Irish by blood if not birth, had the same Scots sharpness, picked up—perhaps by osmosis—during his first dozen years of life. The San Francisco *Post's* 1877 "Pen Portraits" sketch, for example, stressed his supposedly parental-environmental hybridization:

> Though he first saw the daylight through a Scotch mist, both his father and mother claimed a greener, fairer, land as home, and it is this peculiarity of birth and parentage . . . (and) that combination of North British canniness and Irish humor which has proved so useful as a makeweight to him on his way through the world.

Professor Quigley also attributed the Donahue success to a combination of Irish genes and Scots environment. "Scottish thrift and industry, as a groundwork to build upon by Irish genius, led generally to successful results. Hence the early training of the Donahue boys in Scotland was favorable to their subsequent splendid success in California."

The San Francisco *Chronicle* (in its 1885 obituary of Peter) picked up this theme as well. "In his childhood days, he acquired those habits of industry, shrewdness and perseverance which are characteristic of the Scottish character."

Certainly, the tough-minded Peter was a wee bit more Scots in manner than easy-going James, a "pure" Irishman who lacked the no-nonsense bluffness of his older brother.

Young Peter Donahue may have attended a common school, possibly the same school attended by Livingstone, for a short time, but he had to work in a factory in Glasgow or Blantyre (some traditions say that it was a grim sweatshop) when he was barely nine years old. An early child labor reform law, the Factory Act of 1819, prohibited the employment of children under nine years of age in the mills. Peter's genteel poverty thwarted all hopes of receiving a substantial education. However, Glasgow proved to be the ideal training ground for a quick-witted lad with an interest in technology.

The anonymous compiler of the *Pioneer Record* of the Society of California Pioneers (over which Peter presided in 1872-73) put the case for Peter's early "schooling" this way:

> Even in his childhood, he acquired those habits of industry, shrewdness and perseverance so eminently characteristic of the Scotch, and it is not strange that the idea of becoming a mechanic should have suggested itself to him in early life, for the city of his nativity fairly bristled with foundries, forges and factories, whilst on the Clyde the building of steamships and construction of engines and machinery for every department of mechanical industry have long stamped Glasgow as a great manufacturing center.

Nevertheless, The Donahues were not satisfied with their lot in booming Glasgow. The true land of opportunity was America and the family determined to improve its situation by migrating there.

By 1830, Americans seemed more dynamic and innovative to Peter Donahue (Senior), readier to risk their fortunes in the new economic future. Unable to leave Scotland himself right away, he chose to send his oldest son, Michael, to join Michael O'Kane (Mary O'Kane Donahue's brother, young Michael's uncle) who had already made the move to the United States.

* * *

Before the American Revolution, Great Britain had tried to prevent the outflow of machinery and mechanics to its Thirteen Colonies—to "keep them in their place" as a source of raw materials and a market for finished products, rather than encourage them to become an industrial rival.

Of course, Britain failed in this effort. Following the War of Independence, the spread of technology was astonishingly rapid, thanks to leaks, smuggling, and what would today be called industrial espionage. Quickly a muscular and independent young American adopted—and adapted—European inventions and innovations. Thanks to its rich natural resources and a growing pool of skilled wood and iron workers, the new United States of America was turning into an industrial power in its own right.

There was one major difference between the Industrial Revolution in Great Britain and that in the early United States. The Britons geared themselves to produce fine goods; American industry, while imitating British milling, also found a great market at home—and elsewhere—for heavy goods, culminating in railroad locomotives and steamships in the 1850s.

New England pioneered in New World industrialization, but soon the mid-Atlantic states were just as productive. By 1820, New York's mills were producing one-fifth of America's cotton goods (only the mills of Rhode Island exceeded New York's output, and New Jersey was not far behind, with Paterson the jewel in its industrial crown). By the time Michael Donahue joined his uncle, Michael O'Kane, the young nation was well on its way to surpassing Great Britain and other European countries as an industrial leader.

Michael O'Kane had entered the cotton milling business in Scotland, along with his three brothers Peter, James, and John. He was the most skilled and progressive of them all, so he was engaged to go to America as a master cotton manufacturer and had settled in the Hudson River Valley town of Matteawan, in Dutchess County, New York, near Newburgh and not far from West Point.

Soon he sent for his sister and brother-in-law, Hawkins, and for Michael Donahue, the oldest son of his other sister, Mary. They all came over on the same ship.

Within a short time, Michael O'Kane enticed all of the extended Donahue clan to the United States. According to a nephew, Michael Hawkins, the families of Michael O'Kane's sisters were always "singularly and closely united, more like brothers and sisters than cousins." (Hawkins, first cousin of the Donahue siblings, described the emigration of the family many years later to the younger Peter's daughter, Mamie. Hawkins himself was "more like a brother than a cousin" to the Donahues, and this account of the "Iron Men" they were to become contains many of his recollections.)

In about 1833-1834, Mary O'Kane Donahue, together with young Peter, came to the United States; and a year or so later, the family was almost completely reunited when Peter (Senior) arrived with the younger children, including James. Ellen, the eldest child, who was by now married to Patrick Edward Dougherty and living in Glasgow, came later.*

The Donahues joined Michael O'Kane in the oddly named hamlet of Matteawan (sometimes spelled Mattewan, Matewan, or Mateawan). Matteawan meant "creeks join," indicating that it was at a fork in a stream. The early Dutch settlers had named this creek *Friskill* (Freshskill, or Fresh Creek), because it was at the point, two hundred feet above sea level, where the Hudson River turned from brackish to fresh water. It was also the best fishing point on the entire river and it soon earned the name of *Viskill* (Fishkill) or Fish Creek. When the Donahues arrived, it was still a great place for netting shad.

Matteawan proved itself to be a good choice for an immigrant family. New York was beginning to flex its muscles as the Empire State, thanks to its early leadership in the Industrial Revolution. Ever since Colonial times, there had been a modest industry "upstate." In 1751, a charcoal blast furnace making anchors and anvils began operating in Dutchess County. In the 1760s, rich deposits of iron ore were found in the area. During the revolution, Peter Townshend's Sterling Iron Works, across the river in Orange County, had forged in just six weeks a great chain that was stretched across the Hudson to block British warships.

The iron industry grew particularly in such upstate towns as Albany and Troy, spreading west along the Erie Canal to Amsterdam, Utica, Syracuse, Auburn, Rochester, and Buffalo; and south down the Hudson to little Matteawan. At first, the products were nails, horseshoes, and railway spikes, but soon the factories were turning out stoves, mill gears, coaches and carriages, as the dawn of truly heavy industry approached with the building of the first railway locomotives.

Young Peter Donahue's first job in America was as a manual laborer in a Matteawan cotton factory, where it is believed he

---

*The Donahues never completely cut their ties with Ireland and Scotland. One of Ellen Donahue Dougherty's daughters, Annie, returned to Scotland from Petaluma, California, and lived in Hamilton, a town near Blantyre, until her death in 1925. (Another of Ellen's daughters, Mary, married Alexander Keenan. Their granddaughter, Patricia, is the informal archivist of the Donahue clan today.)

James's daughter, Margarete, lived with her husband, Richard Burke, in Ireland as well as in California, as did his grandson, Richard James Burke.

worked for two years, circa 1835-1837 (according to Thomas F. Prendergast, who cited the records of the Society of California Pioneers in his *Forgotten Pioneers: Irish Leaders in Early California*, published in 1942).

Then Peter went to work on the farm of Isaac DePeyster Teller. The Teller Homestead* in Fishkill, a low, rambling wooden structure with siding of overlapping, scalloped (fish scale) cedar shingles, was built between 1708 and 1713 by Roger Brett and his wife Cathryna Rombout Brett, and had been occupied by the Bretts and their descendents ever since—Teller being married to their great-granddaughter Alice Schenck.

Peter and his brothers learned that Matteawan and nearby Fishkill Landing (now combined to form Beacon, New York), along with upstream Fishkill Village, were all part of the great Rombout Patent, named for Cathryna Brett's father Francis Rombout who (in partnership with the scholarly Gulian Verplanck) received 85,000 acres from the Indians in 1683—by straining his eyes. The Indians had agreed to let him have as much land as he could see. So Rombout climbed the 1,500-foot Mount Beacon for the best view in the county. (From there, and from the slightly higher South Beacon, one today can pick out the distant Empire State Building, *if* the weather is extraordinarily clear.)

Within a few years of the building of the house on the portion of the Rombout Patent that was left to her when her father died, Cathryna's husband died also. She ran the large estate—still in the first stages of development—so well (though women of her day were thought to be incapable of such management skills) that she was known by the complimentary title of "Madam." In fact, she had established industry in Matteawan by building a flour mill near the mouth of the creek above Plumb Point.

By 1800, other grain mills had been established including the largest of them all, the Schenck Mill, run by Abraham Schenck, Isaac Teller's uncle-in-law, who was soon shipping large amounts of flour to New York City. As the textile industry began to boom, some

*Visitors to the historic house in the 1890s were regularly told that the noted California capitalist and railroad president, Peter Donahue, began his remarkable career there as an errand boy. According to the San Francisco *Call* of March 31, 1895, "Thousands of people visit this remarkable house every year and the occupants never fail to tell the story of how Peter Donahue made his start."

of the flour mills were converted to cotton milling. In 1841, the first bona fide factory was built in Matteawan. It was a stone cotton mill owned by another Schenck, Peter, and Philip Hone (a former mayor of New York City), together with John Jacob Astor, the king of the American fur trade. In 1845, the pioneering company built a machine shop and foundry for the production of cotton mill machinery; and, circa 1848-1849, it even began to turn out locomotives, setting the pace for New York's manufacture of machinery.

Isaac Teller, however, was not interested in his relatives' factories. He devoted his life to agricultural pursuits, though he did hold several local offices and was briefly (1845-1855, long after Peter knew him) a Democratic New York Congressman.

A friend of Peter Donahue's from the New York days recalled, many years later, an incident involving Peter when he was (very temporarily) a farmboy on the Teller Homestead. The account appeared in the Colusa (Calif.) *Sun* of February 11, 1871 and was reprinted in the San Francisco *Daily Alta California*.

While working Teller's farm, Peter was close enough to West Point to hear the roar of cannon as cadet gunners of the United States Military Academy practiced for an Independence Day celebration. As he listened to the gunnery, Peter was approached by his employer. Teller spoke. "Well, Peter, I suppose you wish to celebrate the Fourth."

"Yes, sir," replied the young farmhand, thrusting his fists deep into his empty pockets. "Well," said the farmer, smiling, "You shall do so." He then took nine pennies from his own pocket and put them in the hand of the grateful boy.

Peter tusseled with his conscience, his habit of thrift, but he finally did spend the money.

As the anonymous old friend put it, "He squandered the nine copper cents in his reckless moment, when his patriotism overcame his sense of economy."

It is unlikely that Peter had much leisure time, either as a factory worker or as a short-term farmhand, for strolling along the Hudson. But surely, a youth of his inquiring mind must have appreciated the spectacular setting of the little mill town. Matteawan's altitude was hardly more than one hundred-fifty or two hundred feet, but the views of the broad Hudson and the fast-running Fishkill were as beautiful then as they are today. There were smaller watercourses on the slopes of Mount Beacon—like little Dry Creek, running through Matteawan itself, and the cascading stream in the glen called the Melzingah—that Peter might have explored.

Probably, Peter fished from Long Wharf (built between 1811 and 1812), dropping his line near the old frame inn on the pier. Perhaps he climbed Mount Beacon and South Beacon; or took the ferry to Newburgh on the west bank, with its fine views of the North Portal of the Hudson Highlands, Bannerman's castellated island (once Polipol's Island), and the mighty Storm King Mountain (which had been called *Boterberg*—Butter Mountain—by the early Dutch, until a man named Nathaniel P. Willis, inspired by its rugged, romantic setting, renamed it).

* * *

By 1838, Peter's family had moved to new Jersey's Passaic Valley where the industrial city of Paterson was already being called the new Pittsburgh. Soon he joined them there, leaving farming behind for good.

Some historians (including Barry J. Brady writing in the September-October 1981 issue of *Archeology*) now consider Paterson to be the real birthplace of America's Industrial Revolution, a Yankee Glasgow that set in motion changes that have permanently transformed this country's landscape and society.

Peter's cousin, Colonel Michael Hawkins, recalled this move for Peter's daughter, "After a few years, my uncle Michael [O'Kane] was sought out and engaged as a manager to take charge of a cotton factory in Paterson. The two sisters with their husbands and families moved to Paterson with their able and progressive brother, who was as generous and gentle as he was able. . . . Your father and his brothers served their apprenticeship in Paterson to the branches of the iron trade—one a molder [Michael], one a boiler maker [James], and one a machinist [Peter]."

Or, as the "Pen Portraits" sketch put it, sixteen-year-old Peter was soon busy learning "the mysteries of cogs, ratchets, eccentrics and bearings in the smoky New Jersey town of Paterson."

* * *

Paterson was already well-established when the Donahues arrived. In 1791, the New Jersey legislature had chartered the Society of Useful Manufactures (the S.U.M.), the brainchild of Secretary of the Treasury Alexander Hamilton. The lawmakers had granted it "perpetual" tax exemption (which lasted a decade), and permitted it to hold property, improve rivers, build canals, and raise $100,000 by lottery. The society was also given the power of eminent domain to condemn and seize land for mill raceways.

The S.U.M. made only a short search before selecting Hamilton's favorite site, Great (Passaic) Falls, for its factory settlement. There was then only a Dutch hamlet of ten houses and a tavern that took its name, Bocht (Bend), from a curve in the Passaic River at the base of Garret Mountain. The waterfall there dropped almost a hundred feet into a chasm of basaltic bedrock.

The site (soon renamed for William Paterson, New Jersey's governor at the time of the founding) seemed perfect for industry, but the S.U.M. was able to build just one factory. Major Charles Pierre L'Enfant, who had laid out Washington, D.C. so handsomely, was the planner. He not only envisioned a great system of raceways, but also a ship canal from the coast to town. His grand design almost plunged Paterson into bankruptcy.

Paterson had been virtually abandoned several times during business recessions; one, in 1816, occurred when a flood of cheap English textiles swamped the local market. But Paterson persevered, and the Lower, Middle, and Upper Raceways were all finally finished by the late 1820s. By 1830, the town was securely established, and for several decades it was among the fastest-growing cities in the United States, its population almost doubling every ten years.

Industrialization in Paterson was given a big boost by the 1838 canal above Great Falls which fed water efficiently to a growing number of mills and factories via the three main raceways. Eventually, the original S.U.M. factory was able to send cotton, linen, and silk textiles to the huge New York City market. Garments, yarn, even mosquito netting were produced, but the bestseller was Paterson's famous cotton duck or sailcloth.

Before long, Paterson was crowded with workmen, many of them foreign-born, especially Irish. As early as 1826, well before the great influx of "Paddies," there was a district just east of the Great Falls called Dublin.

In the 1820s, Paterson had been called the Cotton City; but within the next twenty years it was becoming a great iron center and railroad engine builder. Here, circa 1838, Peter Donahue became an apprentice millwright and engineer in the factory of Thomas Rogers.

The move of the Donahues to Paterson was a natural progression. They were part of a steady flow of talent to that town from just such smaller industrial centers as Matteawan. L.R. Trumbull in his *History of Industrial Paterson*, 1881, wrote, "It is wonderful how many of those great pioneer mechanics and successful manufacturers came to Paterson by the way of Matteawan."

In a sense, the words of the dedication in Trumbull's book apply to the Donahues (as well as to mentors such as Thomas Rogers), for the author extended his dedicatory inscription to include "the bold and enterprising men who followed, and to the skillful workingmen and working women who rendered possible the realization of the grandest industrial achievement."

*   *   *

In the Passaic Valley town, the Donahues also learned much about labor relations that would stand them in good stead later. There was a great deal of unrest among the workingmen. At first, mills and factories employed more women and children than men. They were made to work up to sixteen hours a day, starting at 4:30 a.m., and for low wages. As early as 1794, the S.U.M. was complaining about "disorderly" (i.e. restive) calico workers, and in 1828 the mill hands struck. They lost, but they made history with their strike. For the first time in the history of the country, a sympathy strike was called. Mechanics, masons, and carpenters joined the strikers in a show of solidarity.

In 1832, the population of Paterson was 9,085. Folks in Jersey City and Newark looked down their noses at it as just an uppity up-country hamlet next to a powerful waterfall. They saw it as a place of mixed population, little wealth, and less refinement. But by the time that the Donahues arrived, Paterson was already off and running, industrially speaking. It was well on its way toward renown for its milling machinery and locomotives.

The completion of the Morris Canal (1831) and the Paterson and Hudson Railroad (1832) also boosted the city's prospects, which continued to be rosy despite some setbacks. Samuel Colt's revolver factory in the Gun Mill failed (1836), as did his brother's silkworks. (After Sam Colt's Paterson six-shooters proved themselves in the Seminole and Mexican Wars, Colt reestablished his factory, but in Hartford, Connecticut, not Paterson.)

In 1837, Paterson produced one of America's first locomotives, the *Sandusky*. By the time of the Paris World's Exposition (1855), the little city (in historian Trumbull's words), "wrested the prize of merit from the astonished European builders of that triumph of modern mechanics, the locomotive." During Paterson's forty-some years of locomotive production, the city turned out 5,871 railroad engines that were shipped all over the Americas.

The life-long interest of Peter Donahue in railroading was born in Paterson, where he and James fell under the influence of American industrial pioneers Hugh Beggs, Thomas Rogers, and William Swinburne.

The production of Paterson's first railway engine took a dozen years, and each of the Donahue's three mentors played a part in its development.

Around 1825, Hugh Beggs and his partners established a machine shop, and in 1830 moved it to a new site where his brother William began to build a locomotive. The plant burned in 1835, and the engine was destroyed with it, along with certain priceless mill gear patterns. After the disastrous fire the partnership was dissolved, and William left town to become the master mechanic of the New York Central Railroad. Hugh Beggs then built his famous Union Iron Works (which he ran until his death in 1844) where the Donahue brothers, in part, were to learn their trades so well. Begg's business was now mainly millwrighting. Workmen from his plants were sent to all parts of the country to install wheels and gears and other Union Works machinery in grist, cotton, and woolen mills. There were few capable millwrights around, and Beggs was one of the best of them. His factory was kept busy by orders even during the recession that began in 1837.

Thomas Rogers, a descendent of a *Mayflower* pilgrim and a War of 1812 veteran, had come to Paterson from Connecticut as a house carpenter during the post-war depression of 1815. His carpentry was so distinguished that he soon rose to positions of greater responsibility, making patterns for wooden power looms used for manufacturing cotton duck and then working for John Clark in his machine shop where he later became a partner. In 1822, Godwin, Rogers & Company were the town's major makers of machinery.

In 1831, Rogers sold out to go into business for himself. Shortly thereafter, however, he joined with New York capitalist Morris Ketchum and Jasper Grosvenor to make cotton, wool, and flax machinery exclusively in their Jefferson Works. In 1836, they added locomotive building, and this line of work made Rogers, Ketchum and Grosvenor world-famous.

Rogers and his associates learned to build locomotives almost by trial and error. They built bays with recessed floors (for drainage during boiler testing, not for easy access to undercarriages) and ran the locomotives' wheels on rails mounted on the walls of the bays, with the engines' parts lowered in place by swing cranes. The *Sandusky* was "launched" in October, 1837, and this system of assembly continued, almost unchanged for decades afterward.

For twenty years, the Rogers Locomotive Works on Paterson's Spruce Street at the west end of Market Street, was the largest manufacturer of railroad engines in America. Between 1837 and 1881, Rogers (and his successors) built 2,926 of the 5,871 engines produced in Paterson, making the Rogers name second only to that of Baldwin in American locomotive-making. Its most famous locomotive was the *General*, built in the late 1850s, which figured in the dramatic "Great Train Chase" during the Civil War. In the last quarter of the 1800s, the Rogers supremacy was overtaken by Philadelphia's Baldwin Locomotive Works as interest in Paterson shifted increasingly to silk manufacture.

The greatest actual *builder* of Paterson locomotives was not Rogers himself, but William Swinburne. Born in Brooklyn in 1805, he like the Donahues had come to Paterson via Matteawan where he had married a local girl and made machinery patterns on the Fishkill until 1833.

Swinburne worked as a patternmaker for Rogers, Ketchum and Grosvenor, who in 1835 took over the burned-out shell of Begg's first plant and added a stone millwright shop on the southeast corner of Spruce and Market streets where Swinburne made all of his patterns.

But soon, Swinburne's services were needed elsewhere. The builder of the *Sandusky,* an Englishman, was proving to be incompetent. The Briton's calculations were off by 25 to 30 percent; the boiler did not have sufficient space in its shell for the furnace.

Rogers, normally a man of remarkable good judgment as well as force of character, was in despair at his poor choice of an engine-builder.

"Lay the whole business up! Put it away!" he exploded to the Englishman's assistant, William Swinburne. Swinburne protested that there would be no difficulty in completing the engine. "Who'll do it?" asked Rogers. "*I* will," said Swinburne. "You?" "Yes, I," said the New Yorker. Rogers persisted, "And *can* you?" "I am sure of it," was Swinburne's assurance. He carefully studied the English-built locomotive the *MacNeil*, down at the depot, that was the *Sandusky's* model. Being a natural engineering genius, Swinburne finished the *Sandusky* in just six months.

William Swinburne thereafter served as general factotum of Roger's locomotive works. He was the only foreman for the smithy, machine shop, and foundry. He supervised construction, drew all plans, and made the patterns.

Because Swinburne was so busy with his new work, Rogers had to replace him in the mill machinery end of the business. Naturally, he went right back to that nursery of machinists, Matteawan, and chose Watts Cooke to succeed Swinburne.

The young Donahues profited from Paterson's manufacturing climate. They were indoctrinated in the importance of *quality* in workmanship. Historian Trumbull stressed another important aspect, and the Donahues would have agreed with him. With regard to Roger's line of locomotives, he wrote, "The style which marks their engines. . . . Wherever one travels and meets one of splendid engines from Rogers, he may know at a glance, its builders. . . . Perhaps no concern in this country has done so much to popularize the locomotive and make it the easily-managed and powerful motor that it is today—the veritable 'iron horse,' a servant that yields as ready obedience to its driver as its fleshy namesake."

No railway engine in the United States (as late as 1882, at least) failed to use the principles in boilers, levers, wheels, and smokestacks that were first introduced in the workshops of Rogers, Ketchum and Grosvenor, and which were familiar to the Donahue lads.

When Peter Donahue returned to Paterson for a visit in 1876, he granted an interview to a New York *Sun* reporter. "It is true that I began life [*sic*] as a poor boy here in Paterson. I had no hope of a great inheritance and I knew I must learn to work. I became, when a good-sized lad, an apprentice to the Rogers Locomotive Works and faithfully endeavored to learn all that I could of a machinist's work during my apprenticeship. Soon afterward, I became a journeyman."

Peter left Rogers, Ketchum and Grosvenor to enter employment with Hugh Beggs. Testimony to his maturing skills was his rate of pay. As a journeyman in Begg's millwright shop, circa 1843, he received $1.50 a day, very high wages indeed for a young fellow who had just reached his majority and who was barely out of his apprenticeship. The quick-learning Peter was soon a master mechanic and millwright to boot, though he probably worked for Beggs for only a year.

Again, one wonders if Peter Donahue was able to take the time to enjoy his surroundings, "workaholic" that he was. Did he climb to the top of Garret Mountain to see one of New Jersey's great panoramas—the Passaic Valley—spread out before him? Was he familiar with the legends about Passaic Falls (old Totowa—"To be forded beneath water"—to the Indians)?

Probably the Donahues *had* heard the story of Sarah Cummings, bride of Reverend Hooper Cummings of New York, who fell to her death near the falls in 1812. Although some said that the cleric had to be restrained from jumping into the chasm after her, local old Dutch *volk* stoutly clung to the belief that he had shoved his wife over the side. (Nasty verse to that effect even circulated in Paterson's streets, though it may have been forgotten by the Donahues' time.) Perhaps supersititious Patersonians show Peter and James the site of the old tree overhanging the cliff with the "evidence of struggle" on its bark and limbs, and told the boys how the tree mysteriously "wilted" from the hour of Mrs. Cummings's strange death. And maybe they told them that when the Reverend had preached at the Totowa church on the Sunday prior to the tragedy, a strange bird, black as a raven but no manner of crow ever seen by humans before, entered by a window. After flying three times around the inside of the church, it had perched on the high pulpit over the minister's head, an omen, then had flown out the same window after making "an ominous noise."

No longer a so-called student machinist or apprentice, Peter returned to the banks of the Hudson around 1844. This time, the young journeyman took up work at Cold Spring, Putnam County, New York in Gouverneur Kemble's foundry. Named for a refreshing spring where Hudson River boats went to fill their butts with drinking water, Cold Spring was downstream some eight miles by road from Matteawan, across the river just north of West Point, and directly opposite mighty Storm King and Crow's Nest, the site of Captain Kidd's Cave and the pirate's legendary lost treasure. To the south lay Sugar Loaf; and to the north the twin hills of Mount Taurus (Bull Mountain to the locals) and Breakneck Ridge, named for a notorious bull that used to trample crops until farmers, armed with pitchforks, chased him over one hill and up the other where the ugly beast fell and broke his neck.

Cold Spring had become well-known in the Revolution because one of the first mass inoculations for smallpox had been administered there (1781). The foundry where Peter worked for about two years (circa 1844-1846) was to make it even more famous during the Civil War, when it produced the Union's great Parrott rifled cannon. Colonel Robert Parrott, bursting with pride, once demonstrated his giant field-pieces to President Lincoln by firing them at targets across the river. Honest Abe, tired and bored as well as half-starved, merely said, "I'm confident that you can hit that mountain over there, so suppose we get something to eat. I'm hungry."

While Peter was gaining skill as a machinist in Paterson and then on the banks of the Hudson, his brothers James and Michael worked at Begg's Union Works in Paterson where they were apprentices in the related trades of boiler making and molding.

Although he was not strong as a boy (unlike his husky brothers), James Donahue shared their great potential as skilled industrial craftsmen. The *North Pacific Review* in 1862 observed, "He was remarkable, even at this period, for his faculties of observation and for the readiness with which he applied himself to his tasks. As a child is said to be father of the man, so did the boyhood of James Donahue give early promise of the triumphs that awaited his maturer exertions in the fields of industry."

The oldest of the Donahue brothers, Michael, was soon seized by an attack of wanderlust. He just could not settle down to his trade, the making of molds or matrices for casting iron. Instead, when he finished his apprenticeship, Michael became a sailor. He shipped before the mast as an ordinary seaman on a merchantman. His first passage was down the Atlantic coast to the West Indies, then to Rio de Janeiro, and from Brazil back to the Antilles, calling at Barbados.

Michael's voyaging lasted fourteen months. When he got home to visit his family, he jumped ship and "swallowed the anchor" (that is, gave up the sea) for good. But his brothers soon found out that he was not yet content to settle down to a non-adventurous life.

Michael followed Peter to the Cold Spring iron works. There he was given an important job, that of molding sections of huge water mains and machinery parts for the Croton Aqueduct, New York City's water supply. These were believed to be the largest such parts ever manufactured in the United States. The experience was prophetic for the man who would later build in Davenport, Iowa, one of the greatest waterworks in the Midwest.

* * *

During the 1840s, perhaps around 1845, while her husband Peter (Senior) was in Scotland settling up some business affairs, Mary O'Kane Donahue died in Paterson. The closely-knit Donahue family began to unravel; the three oldest boys, though still close friends, scattered.

Michael left Cold Spring and Peter, and went to Cincinnati where he found employment, first in the molder's trade, next as a first-class workman in a large machine shop. Like Peter, he was by now a skilled machinist.

Michael enjoyed life in Cincinnati; ever afterward he loved to recall his happy days on the Ohio River. This was partly because he was a fire buff, and in Cincinnati he became a volunteer fireman. For more than a year he was not just one of the "fire bhoys," but assistant foreman of a proud engine company. As the Davenport *Daily Democrat* remembered him in 1884, "He used to say with pride that he did not fool away his time and neglect his work while he was a fireman; but when there was a summons to duty, he was on hand as soon as anybody."

James, suffering from poor health, could no longer endure the rigors of freezing New Jersey winters. He fled to the sunny South in hopes that a softer climate would build up his constitution. He apparently went to New Orleans, which was already receiving (even before the Potato Famine of 1848) a second wave of immigrants from Ireland. Before 1850, New Orleans (then the third-largest city in the United States) would be one-fifth Irish, Protestant Ulstermen as well as Roman Catholics.

The "Old Irish" of the first wave of migrants to New Orleans were of the so-called Lace Curtain variety, genteel folk who had come between 1803 and 1830 to a Franco-Spanish Catholic city with refreshingly anti-British traditions. There was a Hibernian Society and a Shamrock Benevolent Society. St. Patrick's Day was celebrated, and special all-Irish militia units, like the Republic Greens and Emmet Grays, proudly tramped through the streets in military uniforms.

Many "Old Irish" had prospered in business by the time of the arrival of the proletarian wave of "New Irish" between 1830 and 1850. James had much more in common with the established Irish of Louisiana than with the rough newcomers. Many of these new immigrants were victims of the potato blight, and many were ignorant, illiterate, and desperately poor; some became the hard-drinking brawling "Wild Irish" of New Orleans who earned the particular emnity of the American Party Nativists or Know-Nothings in the 1850s.

James was becoming interested in steamships, and surely he knew Gregory Byrne (the shipyard founder of Algiers, the town across the river from New Orleans) and steamboat owner Nicholas Burke. Perhaps he met James McKenna too, charter member and president of the New Orleans Mechanics Society. In any case, James soon found work as a steamboat engineer on Lake Pontchartrain, east of the city.

Soon opportunities drew James to the Alabama port of Mobile where he worked in a boiler shop. According to David Sessions, historian H.H. Bancroft's assistant, "It was not long however before his skill and character were perceived and he was appointed assistant-engineer of a steamer engaged with the Gulf ports." Shortly thereafter, James became the owner of a coasting vessel which sank. The safe that went down with her was rumored to contain a large sum of money, but when it was raised the strongbox was found to be empty.

* * *

The outbreak of the Mexican War signalled another move for the Donahue boys, one which was as natural a progression as had been their move to Paterson.

As Colonel Hawkins remembered, "While they (the Donahue boys) were still apprentices, their maternal uncle and mine, Michael O'Kane, went to Mexico (in 1840) under contract to start cotton factories and teach the Mexicans how to manufacture cotton into cloth." It was probably Uncle Michael's Mexican adventure that made the three brothers interested in Latin America.

II

THE MEXICAN WAR

AFTER TWO YEARS in Kemble's Cold Springs foundry, Peter Donahue went to Stillman, Allen & Company's Novelty Iron Works in New York City to help build the first steam warship for the Peruvian Navy. (H.H. Bancroft's assistants were incorrect in assuming that Michael and James also worked in the Novelty plant.) At the time, Novelty was America's leading manufacturer of marine steam engines. Its only rivals were Joseph P. Allaire's works and the plant of Theophilus Secor, later the Morgan Iron Works of Charles Morgan. (Between 1860 and 1867, Novelty built eleven engines for Pacific Mail Steamship Company vessels; and it is said that twenty-two of a total of sixty-four engines made, over the years, for these Panama steamers were from the iron works where Peter worked.)

In 1845, rumors that Chile was buying a steam war vessel frightened Peruvian Grand Marshal Ramón Castilla (who was also Peru's President) to vow to modernize his navy too. He wrote General Pedro Cisneros on February 17, 1845 that, in just three years, he would give the nation three war steamers capable of earning for Peru the respect that it deserved on the seas. The Marshal was so pro-navy that his critics sarcastically dubbed him "El Nelson del Pacífico."

On April 13, 1846, Frigate Captain Domingo Valle Riestra left Callao at the head of a naval commission charged with securing a warship in the United States. A New York paper of March 3, 1847, (reprinted by Lima's *El Comercio* on June 9) reported that the

Rimac (named for the river flowing through Lima), a 683-ton sidewheeler with handsome lines—"a beautiful steamer"—was being built for Peru at the shipyard of Noah Brown and Thomas Bell.

Brown and Bell were shipwrights who ranked with Isaac Webb, Smith and Dimon, Donald McKay and Henry Eckford. They were turning from the clipper ships that they had helped perfect to work on steamships, and already they had an international reputation for their advances in naval architecture and construction. At the same time, Stillman and Allen were fabricating the warship's machinery with the help of Peter Donahue and others. The Peruvian officers closely supervised each step of construction, and took a course in steam engines from Professor James Renwick at Columbia College.

Castilla wrote on April 12, 1847, "Soon we shall complete our squadron, which will be the strongest in South America. The steamer *Rimac*, which is being finished in New York and is very advanced, will dominate our seas. With this vessel alone, we shall make ourselves respected, and guarantee peace for Peru."

On August 20, the *Rimac* was launched and, shortly, her machinery was installed. She was armed with two 68-pound cannon and four 24-pounders, all of English manufacture. The cruiser was capable of a speed of thirteen knots with her 200-horsepower engine. Her ultimate rival, Chile's *Esmeralda*, thought launched seven years later, could only count on making seven nautical miles per hour.

Peter Donahue was appointed assistant engineer on the *Rimac* in December of 1847. She left New York on February 1, 1848. Although her captain, Valle Riestra, complained of an incomplete crew and bad weather (mostly strong winds), she made her first one hundred miles at an eleven-knot speed. The *Capitán* had to admit that she both sailed well and handled well under steam. He reported that both vessel and engines had proved their "solidity and excellent qualities."

Peter arrived at Río de Janeiro in the engine room of the *Rimac* on March 2 and departed on April 6. The warship entered the Straits of Magellan on May 11, in stormy weather, and left that tortuous passage on May 30, being the first American-built steamer to pass through the Straits. When she reached Talcahuano on June 8, the steamer was in good shape except for wave-battered wheel boxes. As for Donahue's engine room, Valle Riestra reported, "The engines are found to be in the best of order also, not even the most minor defect having been noted in the entire voyage."

After repairs by her crew, the *Rimac* steamed to Callao, arriving on July 27, 1848. President and Field Marshal Castilla sailed out to welcome his new flagship as crowds shouted "*Viva el Rimac!*"

* * *

According to Michael Hawkins, Michael Donahue was a soldier (of sorts) already when the Mexican War was declared on May 12, 1846. He was captain of a company of Cincinnati militia, quite likely Irishmen of that city's Montgomery Guards. The unit volunteered to enlist, en masse, in the U.S. Army, then changed its collective mind. Hawkins offered no explanation. He only wrote, "When it came to sign the articles, the company backed out. So my cousin [Michael], ashamed of his men, enlisted as a private, saying that he was no coward. He was made a sergeant and in that rank fought until the war was over."

Actually, Michael was promoted to corporal soon after volunteering, but did not make sergeant until his unit's baptism of fire at Monterrey, September 19-24, 1846. And he left the service, like most of his Ohio friends, when his one-year enlistment ran out long before the war's end. He then joined his brother, James, who was working for the Army as a civilian at Point Isabel, Texas, until at least February 2, 1848 when the Treaty of Guadalupe Hidalgo ended the Mexican War.

Major Luther Giddings was a veteran of Michael's Ohio regiment, so the experiences of the two men were parallel. He stated that the first requisition of volunteer soldiers for the war was the recruiting of three regiments—thirty companies—in Ohio, the state called "The Young Giant of the West."

Ohio's Adjutant General, Samuel R. Curtis, established a rendezvous at Camp Washington, Cincinnati. In less than a fortnight's time after the War Department's call for volunteers, 3000 Ohioans were marching on the Queen City of the West. By mid-June, there were tents enough for forty companies and latecomers were already being sent back home.

Michael Donahue was one of the 838 men mustered into the First Volunteer Regiment of Ohio Infantry on June 23, 1846. Most of the men were from rural areas of southern Ohio, but every trade and profession was represented. There was one all-Irish company and two German companies. The commanding officer of Michael's First Regiment was Colonel Alexander M. Mitchell. Colonel Sturgis, himself, commanded the 3d Regiment. The 2d Regiment's C.O. was G.W. Morgan. Donahue served in A company of the 1st, so the *History of Scott County, Iowa* could be correct in stating that he was the very first volunteer to enroll from Ohio.

Giddings, author of a popular 1853 book *Sketches of the Campaign in Northern Mexico in 1846 and '47,* had the highest of motives in going to war. Probably, Michael was of the same mind. Major Giddings considered his service to be a kind of patriotic, almost sacred, duty, part of the country's "Manifest Destiny" to fill the continent from sea to sea. He quoted Secretary of War Edward Everett's prediction that victory would bring to the conquered such benefits as free speech and press, trial by jury, religious equality, and representative government. "Every addition to the territory of the American Union has given homes to European destitution and gardens to European want. . . A march of immigrants has been taken up such as the world has never before seen." It was all very apropos for Michael, with many of his comrades German or Irish immigrants.

At Camp Washington, clergymen among the crowd of well-wishers handed out Bibles to the uniformed young men, who later joked that these were "the only rations of religion issued during the campaign." (General Zachary Taylor would have no time to honor the Sabbath while in the field.) There was little sickness in the Ohio camp and only one man died during the first month of the regiment's existence.

After drawing clothing and camp gear, the 1st Ohio struck its tents and marched proudly through the cheering streets of Cincinnati while artillery salvoes saluted its departure. At the bank of the Ohio River, *La Belle Riviere* of history and tradition, the young soldiers embarked on steamers.

July 4 found the new warriors afloat on the broad Mississippi, listening to patriotic speeches by officers. Brigadier Thomas L. Hamer was judged to be the best orator of the lot. Arriving in New Orleans in early July, the Ohioans sailed for Brazos Santiago on the south Texas coast near the mouth of the Río Grande.

Major Giddings was attacked by fever, probably malaria, while on the Mississippi. He was laid up in New Orleans for two weeks, and thus was later in getting to the front than Michael Donahue. But, unwilling to miss out on any action, he decamped from the hospital and boarded a steamboat to chase down his regiment.

By the time that the major's steamboat dropped her hook off Brazos Santiago on July 29, Michael Donahue must have become thoroughly acquainted—and disgusted—with the place. It is unlikely that he had as easy a time there as did Giddings. The latter's steamer, *Alabama* took only three days from New Orleans. But the passage by sailing vessel, thanks to Gulf calms, sometimes ran to more than two weeks. The passage was called Purgatory by the troops because it lay between Heaven (the United States) and Hell (Mexico). An officer who had been becalmed for ten days on a dirty little schooner told Giddings how his men had trained for combat with the Mexicans by battling the rats for possession of the cabin's dining table.

Doubtless, Michael Donahue had a similar reaction to Giddings's when he first saw the low-lying, almost treeless, flat South Texas coast. The major termed it "a dreary waste, expanding to the sky." When he arrived, there was not a breath of breeze to ruffle the glassy surface of the Gulf of Mexico. It was intensely hot. Between the vessels at anchor offshore and the mainland proper lay a narrow strip of sand stretching northward and southward to the horizon and, presumably, on to infinity. It was broken only by the shallow channel of the Brazos Santiago (The Arms of St. James) leading to a great lagoon, *Laguna Madre,* inside Padre and Brazos islands, two vast sandbars running to the north and south. The principal camps for the Army's 5,000 troops ashore by July were on the southernmost tip of Padre Island. Directly across the broad lagoon, on a low bluff of the mainland, was Point Isabel, today's Port Isabel.

Transports (called "hog pens" by the suffering soldiers), even when they drew only five feet of water, had to lay off Padre Island either in whipping winds or dead calms. A mosquito fleet of small, shallow-draft steamers and schooners lightered men and equipment and supplies to flatboats for the last of the four or five miles to the Point Isabel depot and Fort Polk. Stevedores were non-existent and laborers scarce, but Captain Robert B. Lawton, superintendent of the port, did the best he could. Still, the Brazos base was overwhelmed by the influx of Volunteers. General Zachary Taylor had far too many men for the horses, mules and, especially, wagons on hand. He reported in August that the Volunteers injured his forward movement "by engrossing all the resources of the Quartermaster Department to land them and transport them to healthy positions."

West Pointer Lt. George B. McClellan (who later commanded Union troops as a general in the Civil War) had a low opinion of citizen-soldiers such as Michael Donahue. The Volunteers had to supply their own clothing, although they were given a six-month advance on their $3 per month pay, and also a clothing allowance of $21 upon being mustered. The money went quickly, and some Volunteers whose boots had worn out wore Mexican *huaraches* in combat. McClellan commented, "Falstaff's company were Regulars in comparison to these fellows—most of them without coats; some would have looked much better without any pants than with the parts of pants they wore; all had torn and dirty shirts." Congress did not get around to providing clothing for them until it was too late, the war was over. But General Taylor, on his own hook, outfitted them, as well as his Regulars, from the Point Isabel clothing depot.

* * *

Major Charles Thomas, who founded the Point Isabel depot, advised General Thomas S. Jesup on May 15, 1846 that several of his steamers were so worm-eaten as to be worthless, but that "It is not worth the expense of building ways at this place." He either changed his mind or was overruled.

At the outbreak of the war, according to the *North Pacific Review* of 1862, James Donahue's Gulf steamer was chartered as a troop transport and sent to Brazos Santiago. "While there, his capacity to make the best of adverse circumstances in repairing, without the necessities and conveniences, the boilers of a steamer (the use of which could not have been dispensed with by the Government without serious inconvenience) attracted the notice of the Commanding Officer. This led to his being appointed to start a Government foundry and machine shop at the mouth of the Río Grande, although only 22 years old. He remained as Superintendent of this establishment during the war, keeping in running order the machinery of the fleet of transport steamers used on the river, and filled the position with credit to himself and satisfaction to the Government."

James Donahue was shortly running the Point Isabel repair shop and yard, almost certainly with marine ways, as winter weather began to disable vessels crucial to Zachary Taylor's advance into Mexico. By January of 1847, however, not only was the main Quartermaster depot, including Donahue's workshops, shifted to the very mouth of the Río Grande, but a dry dock was built there to repair the Army's own twenty-three river steamers, plus those chartered by the government.

As early as November 1846, Jesup lamented, "Had we seen the nature of the navigation of the Mexican coasts and harbors, and of the Río del Norte (Río Grande) and built suitable steamboats several month ago, a million dollars might have been saved by this time." He urged that ten miles of railroad be built from the Brazos Santiago to the Río Grande's mouth. This was not feasible, but he organized direct communication between the two points with a train of two hundred wagons and suggested that the lagoon en route be bridged instead of ferried.

Major Giddings described the Padre Island that both Michael and James came to know all too well during the Mexican War. "Two or three months previous, the island had been a wild and uninhabited ridge of sand, whose solitude was broken only by the melancholy dirge of the great waves that broke on its shore. Now it was alive with busy men; soldiers, sailors, artisans (including James Donahue) and others, who were running about like ants on sandy hillocks."

Four or five regiments were camped in the hot dunes of south Padre Island, awaiting transportation by General Zachary Taylor's too-few wagons. They were destined for the mouth of the Río Grande, less than ten miles away. The only building at the tip of the long island was a small frame shed, just yards from the water's edge. It was to become familiar to Michael and James because it was the Quartermaster's office (they worked for him). It was elevated three feet against flooding by palmetto logs. Under it always lay a dozen sick Volunteers, enjoying its scant shade.

The only hospital was a small one at Point Isabel. Most Volunteers ill with fever or measles just lay half-buried in the drifting sand. Giddings saw "many a poor fellow . . . choked with sand, parched with fever." The major was able to buy ice from a Boston ship for only $1.00 a pound to relieve his own feverishness.

Giddings was too weak to ride to the camp of Donahue's First Ohio on the Río Grande's left bank some three Spanish leagues (nine miles) above its mouth. He hitched a ride on a small vessel going there for water to supply the Padre Island bivouacs. Río Grande water was not very palatable, however, so there was a humming business in steep-priced liquors of all kinds. There was no fresh water, at all, on the sandy islands.

Even Giddings's shallow-draft vessel grounded on the treacherous Río Grande bar. Surf broke over her and a schooner, stranded nearby, lost most of her cargo. But the morning flood lifted the craft free and she entered the 300-400 yards wide *Río Bravo del Norte,* as many of the Mexican fisherman and *vaqueros,* or cowboys, still called the Río Grande. The only settlement at the river's entrance was Resguardo which, in Spanish, meant something like "Anti-smuggling Post." The whimsical Yankees redubbed it Baghdad, using the Spanish spelling *Bagdad.*

The Ohio Volunteers spread their canvas amid scrubby mesquite trees on the Texas bank of the Río Grande at Camp Belknap. Donahue found this base to be opposite the village of Burrita, about fourteen miles from Matamoros. (The score of mud hovels in Burrita had been described in newspaper headlines as a stronghold of the Mexican nation.) The Buckeyes were thankful for even the slight protection of the brushy mesquite against clouds of scorching sand rolled over the campsite by the often stiff Gulf breezes. They likened the blasts of dust to "pillars of fire."

The Ohioans had no wagons, so Donahue and his mates had to wade a mile of swamp to reach the commissary tent, or to carry back drinking water in barrels slung on poles. They had to trudge, knee-deep, through the bog because their well water was too bitter and their pond water too salty to drink.

Even though many of Michael Donahue's comrades were now sick with fever, the Ohio encampment was full of bustle and cheerful excitement. The *esprit de corps* was remarkably high, thanks to able, industrious and attentive officers—a rarity in Volunteer regiments officered by political preferment, as Lt. McClellan would have stressed. The enlisted men were of good stuff, too, and Giddings dedicated his book to such soldiers as Mike Donahue. "To the non-commissioned officers and privates of the First Ohio

Volunteers." He stated that he wrote his book of reminiscences "out of justifiable state pride and a desire to pay tribute to the constancy and courage of gallant men."

Still, the miserable conditions at Camp Belknap sparked the silly "Catfish War." A fight broke out between the 1st Ohio and the Baltimore Battalion over right to a single "cat." It was a stupid quarrel, yet ill feelings between the two units lasted a long time as a result of it.

After only a fortnight at Camp Belknap, one hundred men of Donahue's outfit were on sick call as a result of the hot, humid weather, the over-flowed ground, and the anopheles mosquitoes in residence. Many men were already disabled by illness and some were discharged on the spot. Giddings later recalled, "I do not think we could have mustered more than 600 bayonets at Camargo and scarcely 500 at Monterrey, so rapidly did the climate, like a skillful anatomist, designate and discard the unsound men. . . . The groans and lamentations of the poor sufferers during those sickly, sultry, nights were heart-rending."

It is unlikely that Donahue adjusted to his situation any better than Giddings. It rained every day from July until September, not steadily, of course, but at intervals—"in sudden, drenching showers, each followed by a burst of melting sunshine."

Camp Belknap, so hostile to humans, was a paradise for vermin and vipers. It was infested with snakes, including venomous rattlers, also biting ants, tarantulas and other spiders, centipedes, scorpions and fleas; even a few non-belligerent lizards and horned toads. The tarantulas, because of their hairy appearance, were most feared, but the ants were the most vicious attackers. Giddings saw an assistant surgeon (apparently violently allergic) bitten so badly that his spasms required several men to confine him to his tent.

Many of the Volunteers, possibly Michael among them, visited the bloody battlefields of Palo Alto and Resaca de la Palma, where American light artillery had won the day for Taylor over General Mariano Arista.

On July 6, General Taylor—still bitterly complaining about inadequate transport—advanced on Camargo. He planned an advance base there to attack Don Pedro de Ampudia in Monterrey, capital of the state of Nuevo León. The American general commanded only six thousand men, half of them Volunteers. He had no siege training and Monterrey was a walled city of stone. His artillery was too light to do much damage to stone fortifications. He possessed hardly any land transport, either wagons or pack mules. But he had guts.

Taylor, called Old Rough and Ready by his men, assigned Brigadier General Hamer to command the Ohio Brigade, or Buckeye Brigade, of the three regiments. But he left the 3d at Matamoros, taking along Mitchell's 1st and Morgan's 2d Regiments, with Michael Donahue marching in the former.

Sending their heavy baggage and a few companies of men ahead by woodburning steamer, the Ohioans began the ascent of the Río Grande on August 8, 1846. By July, there were a dozen under-powered steamers fighting the swift current to Camargo. It is not known whether Donahue hoofed it or rode in what Giddings called the "frail and filthy little steamboat" which took a week to make the run to Camargo. Since there were no woodlots and few trees, troops had to be sent ashore to pillage fences to keep the boiler hot.

Navigation of the muddy Río Grande was less dangerous than tedious. Since there was no real timber on the stream, only low, evergreen and thorny brush and mesquites the size of peach trees, there were not even snags to dodge in the river. There were no tributaries below the San Juan River, but the Río Grande over-flowed into broad *lagunas* during the worst floods in thirty years. So pilots had to sound their way, by day, to find a channel. They laid up their steamers at night. A steamboat was still a very rare sight on the Río Grande, so the people of the little *ranchos* gathered on the banks to watch the slow progress of the Buckeyes' "tea kettle."

Giddings was not happy with the Río Grande, writhing across a hot, treeless plain to its delta, like a rattlesnake with a broken back. "It fails to charm," he growled. The monotony of travel was broken only by the sight of great flights of waterfowl and the scattered turkey vultures that scouted the stream for bloated carcasses of drowned cattle. As for the metropolis of the Río Grande, Matamoros, the major dismissed it as a collection of "cowpens" and contemptible mud huts on narrow, mirey streets. Only the main plaza was made respectable by a few two-story adobes with barred windows. The town was jammed with soldiers, three thousand Mexican citizens, and camp followers—"adventurers of every description." They drank smuggled *pulque* despite the emphatic anti-liquor edict of General Taylor. Giddings could hear them smashing glasses and bottles in various dives. Even some of

Donahue's fellow Ohioans were a.w.o.l. from overindulgence in the century plant liquor when the regiment left the area.

The *Gringos* or *Yanquis,* Americans, called the Mexicans "Greasers" because the cowboys, *rancheros* or *vaqueros,* all wore leather pants and jerkins as protection against the thorny chaparral and mesquite thickets. Correctly, Giddings called their costume "leather armor, shiny from grease and long usage."

Reynosa was a decayed town, with only a few substantial stone houses, garrisoned by a few regulars. Off Reynosa, the waterborne Buckeyes slept on the steamer's main deck, with their greasy haversacks over their faces as ineffectual protection against the voracious mosquitoes. Occasionally, the restless soldiers mounted to the hurricane deck in hopes of catching a night breeze, laden with fragrance from the Texas shore.

On Sunday, August 16, the Ohioans' steamboat reached Camargo, captured by Zachary Taylor on Bastille Day. It lay on the Río San Juan's right bank, a league above its junction with the dark and muddy Río Grande. Taylor received the Volunteer officers under an awning in front of his tent. He was wearing a linen coat and trousers and twirling a straw hat in his fingers. There was not the slightest trace of pomp about him. He was kindly, naturally gracious. To Giddings's surprise, he spoke with a stammer. He told the newcomers to report to General William J. Worth, who was in command of the camp.

The steamboat Ohioans pitched their tents to await the arrival of their comrades marching overland. They filled their kettles from the clear-running San Juan and waded out, to their knees, to launder their dirty shirts.

Michael Donahue found Camargo to be abandoned by its Mexican population of about two thousand people. It had recently been flooded, and many of the town's adobes were dissolving piles of straw-filled clay. No wonder the punning troops promptly dubbed the place Quagmire. Only a little church and a few other buildings around the *Plaza Mayor* were in "tolerable preservation," to borrow Giddings's words.

In contrast, Donahue's camp was in apple pie order. Tents were pitched in regular rows on a vast and smooth parade ground outlined by breakfast fires, mesquite trees, the dragoons' horses, and the muzzles of Captain Braxton Bragg's cannon, peeking out from under their tarpaulins.

General Worth marched to Cerralvo, but soldiers continued to arrive in camp by boat and on foot. Dragoon General David E. Twiggs, a rival of Worth's, joked that patriotism was oozing out of the Volunteers' toes and that their officers had to buck them up with three stirring speeches a day. This was the usual nonsense expected of Regulars, but even Giddings had to admit that it took time for such independent "cusses" as his men to become accustomed to the yoke of military discipline.

The 1st Ohio was finally reunited on August 23 when Lt. Colonel Weller brought up the last six companies. It had been a very trying march for green troops under a hot sun. Several wagons were laden with sick men, some of whom were dying. Donahue found the mortality at Camargo to be appalling. Even the natives called the town the sickliest spot in the whole Río Grande Valley. Giddings wrote, "The Dead March was always wailing in our ears." The large hospital tents were always full to bursting, although the dead were removed at sunrise and sunset to make room for the dying. Burials were out in the mesquite thickets.

Once Worth secured control of Cerralvo, Taylor reduced his regiments to five hundred men; as he did not have sufficient transport for even all of his healthy men. The shrunken 1st Ohio joined the Kentuckians to form Taylor's First Field Brigade, under Hamer. The other brigade of Major General William Butler's division of four regiments was commanded by John A. Quitman. Butler was an aging Irishman who had survived the terrible Raisin River Massacre of Kentuckians by British-allied Indians in the War of 1812.

No one was sad at leaving Camargo's malarial plain, the bitter oranges sold by Mexican peddlers, or the mustangs palmed off, over and over, on gullible officers. The half-wild horses seemed trained to stampede for the brush at the first opportunity. Anyway, Michael Donahue and his friends were itching for a "*fandango*"—a fight—at Monterrey. Giddings remembered how pleased his men were to be going into action. "We of the First Ohio were much rejoiced at our good fortune."

Hamer's brigade crossed the San Juan on September 4 and began its march to Cerralvo via the town of Mier on Sunday, the 6th. The weather continued dry and intensely hot. After the downpours of the Gulf, it rained only once during Donahue's stay in Camargo.

The colonel had not provided a water wagon, so there were many delays on the first day's five-league march, as men tried to find water to refill their canteens. At one abandoned ranch, some men broke into a run to a well, in spite of their fatigue, only to find it gone dry. The dense cover of chaparral blocked any vagrant breeze from reaching the road, which generated dense clouds of flour-fine dust to half-suffocate the thirsty marchers. Giddings noted that even the handful of black servants, supposedly heat-proof, were drooping from the sun, thirst and dust.

Shortly, the weakest stragglers, with their empty canteens rattling, began to reel away from the dust-covered ranks, to sink down at the roadside. Threats and persuasion by officers, and non-coms like Donahue, were equally ineffective. In their stupor, the fagged-out men were indifferent to both. They were a sorry sight. Soon, wrote Giddings, "All order was lost. . . . Had we been attacked at the time by a resolute enemy, our troops would, inevitably, have been cut to pieces." Fortunately, no Mexican *lanceros* charged the ragtag column.

For the first time, men cussed their officers, for failing to bring a water wagon along. The officers' neglect to do so was due to the fact that the first day's march was "only" five leagues long.

By the second day, however, the enlisted men were in better spirits. They were toughening up; they got an early start; their route lay across a level, if dry, grassland and mesquite country. Suffering less from thirst this time, they were safe in camp by noon and not terribly fatigued. By the third day's march, Donahue and his buddies were footsore but strong and cheerful as they began to harden up in the field. They stepped off six leagues by 11 a.m. Giddings was surprised how the arduous marches improved both the health and the spirits of most of the men.

The footsoldiers did not leave the road to enter Mier, a pretty village of whitewashed walls, They pressed on into broken hills until the mountains around Cerralvo came into sight. The countryside was rugged, but the soil was fertile enough to support a bright display of wildflowers, and the air was cooler. At night, piled-up dark clouds were fringed "fantastically" with moonlight. By day, the men marched under clear blue skies while lightning blazed just to the south of them.

On the fourth day, Donahue marched right through Punta Aguda (Sharp Point). Probably, like many of the men, he bought some fine dried figs there before camping on a clear and rapid stream. The land, except for stream banks, was now stony and poor. Stratified limestone lay so close to the surface of the soil that it was difficult to peg down tent ropes. A night storm carried away a lot of Ohio canvas, and flying tent pins on the end of whipping ropes lashed sleepers awake in a rain squall. Horses broke loose, mules kicked, and soldiers swore vile oaths as they fell over knapsacks and cook pots in their rush to save the tents.

Most of Donahue's fellow infantrymen were making as good time as veterans as the vanguard reached the regimental campsite at a pond near Cerralvo, twenty-five Spanish leagues (seventy-five miles) from Camargo. Some of the men ("noble fellows" Giddings called them) hurried back with water to help some of their friends who had fallen by the way. Only half of the column reached the bivouac by dusk but, at morning roll call, only two men of the entire five hundred men were absent and unaccounted for. These two had been given permission to search for water en route. Once that they left the route of march, they were never seen again, dead or alive. Donahue assumed that they had been picked off by skulking "*guerrillas*" *(guerrilleros),* for these irregulars were shadowing the American force.

Michael Donahue must have liked the looks of Cerralvo, often spelled *Seralvo* by the Americans, which he reached on September 10. Everyone else did. Giddings found it to be a "smiling place." Charles J. Peterson, author of *The Military Heroes of the War With Mexico* (1848), said of the volunteers, "When they reached Cerralvo, they realized their dreams of an earthly paradise." The air of the town was as balmy as if it were spring. Every house had a garden, fragrant with flowers. A limpid river ran through the town, murmuring in cascades and spanned by stone bridges. In the center of town rose a cathedral-sized church, in the eyes of the strangers, whose "half Saracenic" architecture reminded Peterson of romantic old Spain.

Benjamin F. Scribner, a soldier in the Spencer Grays from Indiana, wrote a volume in 1847 titled *Camp Life of a Volunteer.* To him, Cerralvo bore "the impress of an antiquated fortress, and reminds one of the dilapidated castles we read of in romances. The houses are built of gray stone, with loopholes for windows. Through the center of the town runs a beautiful clear stream, spanned by bridges and arches. There is also a large cathedral [*sic*] with chimes and a towering steeple."

Cerralvo was sited in such a beautiful region that the Indianan quite forgot his toilsome journey to get there in the "exalted excitement" of the mountain grandeur of the Sierra Cerralvo and the greater Sierra Madre Oriental beyond. When the Hoosier left the town, it was daylight. He recalled the moment when the sun began to light the mountains. "I think I never beheld anything so beautiful and sublime. The whole chain, as far as the eye could reach, appeared like piles of burnished silver, shaded out in delightful golden tinges."

The one incident in the uneventful and pleasant stay in Cerralvo was the height of absurdity. The captain of one of the two German companies was so ignorant that, when given a mustard plaster for his pleurisy, he ate it! Naturally, he became deathly ill and had to be left behind.

General Butler's Field Division of Volunteers marched out of Cerralvo on September 15 to join the Regulars at Marín on the 17th. Marín lay barely twenty-five miles away from the blue mountains surrounding Monterrey. Each man carried eight days of rations and forty rounds of ammunition. General Torrejón's cavalry, 1,000 of them, fell back without attempting to stop the *Gringos,* only destroying some Army property that fell into their hands.

The march to Marín took Donahue's unit over rough, bare hills in distressingly hot weather, then through a somewhat better landscape, though still a rough country of generally barren and desolate aspect. Brush and cactus covered dreary and forbidding ridges. Hills and mountains seemed to glow with heat. Only a few narrow belts of green clung to the banks of streams. In these favored spots, Donahue and the others could see fig, olive, lemon, and orange trees. Ranches were scattered and often abandoned. Sometimes, Michael did not see a Mexican all day long, only their "wretched" shacks on the borders of *arroyos.* But he did see many crosses on the wayside, marking the graves of people killed by *bandidos.* Giddings thought it to be a dismal landscape, perfect for warfare since, away from the streams, there was neither life nor beauty.

The now-weary troopers marched through Marín. Donahue found it to be a village of only one hundred people picturesquely perched on the edge of an extensive elevated plateau with a view of the land stretching toward the capital. The soldiers then dropped into a charming valley at Marín's feet and joyfully stacked arms on the grassy banks of a silvery creek. All were given a blessed hour's rest before being posted as guards or assigned such camp chores as kindling campfires. The officers lazed about, smoking their cigars. Most of the enlisted men chatted in groups as they soaked their blistered, hot and swollen feet in the stream.

Some of the grass-green soldiers from the Buckeye State refused to believe that there was any enemy about, though the Mexicans had just quit Marín ahead of Taylor's Pioneers, or Engineers. The Texas Rangers showed off a lance head they had found on the road, however, and, finally, Taylor's vanguard exchanged fire with some Mexicans. Next, the Volunteers picked up copies of an offer of General-in-Chief Pedro Ampudia. He promised protection and kind treatment to all American soldiers who would lay down their arms in this unjust, illegal and anti-Christian war of aggression against Mexico.

Ampudia's psychological warfare did not work with the Ohioans. The war was unjust enough, a simple fit of imperialistic aggression. But the Buckeyes' patriotism was unshakable. However, some Catholic Irish would later succumb and desert the American Army for the Mexican Army, where they formed up the San Patricio Battalion for General Santa Ana. Ultimately, a few were executed for treason.

Ampudia planned to make a stand on the Cerralvo Road. The country from Marín to Papagallo was a plain favorable to maneuvering by his calvary. But when he called a *junta*—a council of war—of his brigade chiefs, only General Mejía supported his plan. So he pulled out, all the way back to Monterrey.

Taylor's sleeping camp at Marín was awakened before dawn of September 18th by a drum and bugle reveille. At 5:30, the first troops crossed the stream and headed for the peaks standing like sentinels over the capital, only eight leagues away.

Hamer's brigade, with Donahue, was the last to move out. It was 9 a.m. when their bright bayonets flashed in the sun. They had a bit of excitement when a fat Mexican muleteer for the Army goaded his swaybacked mount into a galloping retreat with whip and spurs. He was shouting "Canales! Canales!," the name of the feared guerilla leader, General Antonio Canales. The drummers pounded out their "beat to the colors" and Donahue joined a line forming up to fight the leader that Giddings sarcastically called "the Bayard of the Greasers." It was a false alarm. The nervous muleteer had mistaken some of Jack Hay's uncouth Texas Rangers for mounted Mexican partisans.

The American Army nooned at the village of Agua Fría and finished its regular five-league march by tramping briskly into the nearly-deserted village of San Francisco, Nuevo León, at sunset. The men were jesting and singing ballads taught them by the few old-timers in the ranks.

En route, Donahue and his companions had to take in stride a muddy swale, badly cut up by those in front. A sergeant described the road through it as being like the slimy trail of an army of turtles. A rugged Irishman hung onto Giddings's stirrup as he slogged along through the muck, the officer carrying his musket for him. "That's first-rate mud, sir," the Irishman commented, "It's patched all the holes in me trousers."

Michael Donahue found San Francisco to be only a hamlet of a few streets, gardens and green fields. There was no more of the kids and chickens that foragers had earlier confiscated, but after a hearty supper of coffee, hard biscuits, and tough stew, some of the men (possibly Donahue included) climbed to flat rooftops to enjoy the evening breeze from the mountains. The view in the clear, dry weather compensated for all of the bruises and scratches that they received clambering up by the footholes and handholds left in the walls by the masons.

San Francisco was surrounded by a broad, flat and uncultivated valley between the huge Sierra Madre and the Sierra Cerralvo. The vale descended slightly toward Monterrey, situated between Saddle Mountain and Miter Mountain. The capital was a mass of whitewashed buildings on the Santa Catarina River. It was backed by the huge bulk of the Sierra Madre Oriental which, from a distance, had looked like floating clouds. Now, close-up, rugged peaks reared up above the gorge, or pass, guarded by Monterrey. Giddings termed the peaks "massive palaces of nature." Of the great sierra, he later wrote, "I have gazed upon it at all hours and seasons, and always with increased delight—glowing at midday; at lingering twilight; or under a silvery moon."

The lower and less-well known Sierra Cerralvo was striking in its own right. The scenic range rose abruptly from the plain like a great wall. Although only lightly forested, with a scatter of pines and cedars fringing the summit and crowning crags and pinnacles, the rough, weather-stained and mossy rocks were half-overgrown with vines, shrubs and bright-flowered cacti.

The First Ohioans grumbled on the 19th when Taylor posted them in the rear of the march on Monterrey. Their disgust was relieved when they heard cannon fire from the city and the cries of their battalion officers, "Column forward! Quick march!"

To impede Taylor's march, the enemy had broken up the Cerralvo Road near Monterrey and flooded it by damming the streams that crossed it. Old Rough and Ready's soldiers fell to with enthusiasm, however some pushing wagons through the mire while others dashed forward through the dry chaparral in order of battle, eager to get a look at the capital.

The heat and the extraordinary pace soon took their toll and the faltering Army had to camp near Santo Domingo, two miles from the city of 12,000 people. The campsite was a beautiful grove of trees watered by a clear gushing spring. It was called Walnut Grove, but was actually a hundred acres of live oaks and pecans. Most of the men were without tents. That night, they rolled up in their blankets under a roof of branches bearded with Spanish moss.

Taylor's Pioneers led an extensive reconnaissance of the capital, which resembled the walled cities of Europe, probing for a soft spot. They could get little information on its artillery batteries and other defenses because of the orange trees and acacias masking them. Texas Rangers galloped close enough to draw musket fire, yet officers disagreed over Monterrey's strength. Most anticipated a bloody fight. One old-timer insisted that a battering train was necessary. But all were confident that they would gain a victory that would be worthy of their arms and country.

The proximity of the enemy excited the green Volunteers. They were completely inexperienced in warfare, but they trusted—almost blindly—in the military genius of their leader, Zachary Taylor. So curious were the men about Monterrey that many of them casually strolled, unarmed, to a hill (really a swell of the plain between camp and city) for a look-see. Giddings was aghast. A single rush of lancers would have slaughtered them to a man. Taylor became alarmed, too. On the 20th he established a picket line on the road to arrest all such sightseers. The guards did not pick up all of them, however, and those who escaped their vigilance finally drew a few artillery rounds from the Mexican guns. The spectators scattered like quail at the flash and smoke and thunder of the cannon on the city's battlements. Casualties were few or nil, but Giddings noticed that "the excellence of the enemy's guns and the skill in which they were served were the subjects of mingled admiration and regret."

Taylor then placed his mortar battery, for effect, on the knoll. It was a single 10-inch piece. To Giddings, at least, it was useless at such a distance. He noticed a disgusted, gray-haired old sergeant of artillery give the mortar, which looked like a witch's soup pot, a contemptuous kick—which almost dislodged it from its platform—after it proved incapable of lobbing an explosive shell as far as the city's walls.

Taylor's men were unusually quiet as breakfast fires dissipated the darkness of the grove on Sunday, September 20. The men clearly heard the church bells pealing in the city. The general took no offensive action that day, not because it was the Sabbath and his Jesuit chaplain, Father Anthony Rey, was meeting with such Catholics as Donahue. No, Taylor's Pioneers, under Major Joseph K.F. Mansfield, were still reconnoitering the defenses of Monterrey, seeking out a chink in its armor.

Peterson later recalled, "Through the blue morning haze, palace and hill, steeple and fort seemed floating in the air." Monterrey, largely spared by revolutions, was a long north-south parallelogram of hewn-stone buildings covered with white stucco. It boasted regular, intersecting, streets and wide plazas, the whole dominated by a grand cathedral. On the Santa Catarina were gardens and rural cottages.

Reconnaissances were important. Taylor's original army of 9,000 men (on paper) had shrunk to 6,400 effectives after sickness and the garrisoning of Matamoros, Camargo, Cerralvo, Marín and other points on his badly over-extended line of communications with the Gulf at Point Isabel. And he was aware of Ampudia's strength—about 7,000 Regulars reinforced by 3,000 militiamen.

Mansfield studied particularly the *Obispado,* the Bishop's Palace (or Castle) on a steep and bare hill rising from the western suburbs. Between it and a spur of the Sierra Madre, the latter crowned by two more fortifications, ran the river and the Saltillo Road to the mountain pass.

The only other approach was the Ohioan's Cerralvo Road from the north, which entered the city proper on its east side. It was commanded by the guns of the presumably impregnable Citadel, supported by small batteries. The Citadel itself was a great strongpoint, a 270-yard square fortification with an unfinished church in it that was almost as strong as the fort, per se. This bastion commanded the suburban dwellings and gardens, where tall hedges and rows of fruit trees held sharpshooters waiting for *los Americanos.*

The Americans realized that even when they got inside the city, their peril would not be over, not by a long shot. The parapeted houses formed continuous lines of defense, and every plaza or square held a ten- or twelve-foot high barricade with embrasures for guns. As Peterson put it, "The streets had been trenched, the house tops loaded with missiles, and artillery placed in every possible position." By some Americans and by virtually all Mexicans, Monterrey was considered to be unconquerable.

A gentle evening shower brought a sparkling clear dawn on September 21. Taylor had already sent Worth to carry the Saltillo Road's pass and heights, including the *Obispado.* Worth told him that he would either "win a grade (promotion) or a grave." Now, Taylor's force made a necessary diversion to relieve pressure on Worth before storming the capital via the Cerralvo Road, itself. This route crossed several small streams before entering the city by the bridge called *Puente Purísima.* In the city, it became the main thoroughfare. The *Purísima* Bridge was protected by infantry and artillery grouped in and around massive stone buildings that flanked the bridgehead. To "turn" these works seemed impossible to Taylor, so he searched for a more vulnerable spot.

As Michael Donahue and his comrades left the shelter of the copse of trees and advanced on the hillock holding their mortar, they heard a dull report from a Mexican battery, followed by the hissing roar of a cannonball overhead. The crucial Battle of Monterrey was begun.

Clouds of dense smoke soon obscured the gaudy flags flying on the Citadel as gunners sent round shot crashing into the American ranks. A long-barreled gun on a barbette of the city's northeast battery appeared to have the exact range. A friend of Giddings said, "It seems to carry death in every discharge." Men began to fall, and surgeons scrambled to assist them. This deliberate fire against the frontal line was returned by Major Lucien Bonaparte Webster, but if any of his howitzer or mortar shells managed to drop inside the city walls, their effect was not evident. As for the light field pieces of Braxton Bragg and Randolph Ridgely, at such a distance they were, in Giddings's words, "as useless as muskets."

Taylor advanced his left wing past a sugar canefield to strike at a five-gun redoubt called *La Tenería*, The Tannery, from its locale, a tanyard. His men were met with a deadly rain of grapeshot and musket balls. But the Volunteers, including Donahue, were not yet involved in the action; they were in a quiet zone. Soon, the leading companies of badly cut-up regulars broke into small units. Some kept up an annoying fire from the shelter of cottages on the outskirts of town, but others reeled back and collided with the Volunteers. They were bloody and groaning and the greenhorns realized that Taylor's first attack had shattered against the tough *Tenería*.

Now the Citadel opened a brisk fire on the Ohioans. The lone mortar tried to reply, its shells exploding high in the air, but short of their target. Taylor ordered Butler's three regiments, including Donahue's unit of about four hundred men now, to the left flank to support the battered regular Army men. But before they advanced very far, the hurrahing Buckeyes were ordered to the right, to a more central point near the Citadel. Peterson recorded how gallantly they met the galling fire. "For a full mile before they reached the suburbs, the Volunteers were exposed to the batteries of the enemy. They were welcomed to the city's edge by a tremendous crossfire of musketry and artillery . . . . A portion of this force dashed forward against the redoubt, but was received with such a withering fire as to be compelled to withdraw . . . . The air above us was turbulent with whizzing and bursting shells and, more than once, we distinguished a sharp cracking as of balls driven violently in contact."

The Ohio regiment advanced in excellent order in spite of losses from flanking fire and managed to save Bragg's battery near the edge of town. It was a total wreck. Somewhere between a dozen and twenty horses were down, dead or dying. A few of the artillerymen were also sprawled on the foamy, bloody ground. But some of Bragg's men, exposed to the killing fire, were struggling to refit teams, or to strip bridles from dead or disabled animals. They were determined not to leave a strap or buckle on the field for the Mexicans, should the latter prevail.

Now the defenders poured all of their fire on the volunteer companies instead of against the torn-up artillery. The Buckeyes, entering the suburbs, found them to be a labyrinth of lanes and gardens. Virtually all of the metal thrown, so far, was by Mexican cannons. In fact, the Volunteers had hardly been able to "burn a single cartridge" because their foes were so well-hidden.

Major Mansfield urged Hamer to withdraw, telling him of the failure of Brevet Colonel John Garland and his regulars. He added that a short advance would bring the Volunteers into the very focus of concentrated enemy crossfire. Giddings paraphrased Mansfield's warning, "There could be no longer any object in advancing farther. . . . If he advanced, he must meet a fire that would sweep all before it."

Hamer now halted his Ohioans in a broad street at the stream, parallel with and two hundred yards from the enemy strongpoint. Though they were somewhat screened by pomegranate trees, the Americans were being cut up by canister or case shot. It was here that H Company lost to the shrapnel its acting C.O., Lieutenant Hett, who was filling in for the foolish mustard-eating German captain.

This was the most trying moment of the battle for Donahue and his fellow soldiers. Giddings put it well. "To stand still and be thus tamely and unresistingly slaughtered was a severe trial for the Volunteers. Had the order been given, they would willingly have cleared the hedge and stormed the barricades in front, with indomitable fury."

Fortunately, at this moment Quitman seized Fort *Tenería* and the redoubtable Ridgely turned its cannon on the other battery, *El Diablo,* The Devil, which was playing hell with the Ohioans. Butler now tried a second assault as grapeshot whistled over Donahue's head. It was in vain, though Peterson reported, "The Volunteers advanced with heroic intrepidity."

Peterson's description of the second advance by Donahue and his comrades was graphic and dramatic, and more detailed than that of Giddings.

> Raked by batteries in front, and torn by others on each flank, his [Butler's] soldiers advanced, nevertheless, with the firmness of veterans and, buffeting the iron whirlpool, struggled manfully to gain a foothold in the town. But the Mexicans, posted behind house walls and barriers, possessed every advantage and could, unseen, pick off their assailants. In

vain, the Volunteers passed garden after garden and surmounted ditch after ditch, hoping finally to gain some open space where they could, at least, view their enemy; that withering crossfire from concealed marksmen still continuing, the soldiers falling beneath it like rye beaten down by hail.

Yet still the officers, pressing to the front, cheered on the men; still, as they dropped, dead or wounded, other leaders sprang to their places, and still the men, answering their superiors with hurrahs, rushed on, firing where ever they supposed a foe to be hiding, resolute to conquer or die.

At last, some of the foremost, mounting a wall, perceived a corps of the enemy just in front and bursting upon it like tigers first maddened and then let loose from their dens, they drove it before them until it sought shelter behind an impregnable battery. For a few minutes, there succeeded a tremendous conflict between the Volunteers and the occupants of this battery, the Mexicans firing grape and canister as well as musketry, and the Americans replying with the latter. But a contest so unequal in the arms employed, and one, moreover, in which one party was sheltered and other exposed, could not continue with any prospect of success.

Butler was unwilling to retire but Taylor, informed of Mansfield's information, ordered the Volunteers to fall back. According to Giddings, "The movement was accordingly commenced, but in no very good humor."

When he heard of Quitman's seizure of the *Tenería*, Taylor countermanded his order to retreat. He sent the Buckeyes back to attack the devilish fort, El Diablo, again. The boys reentered the streets on the left, to strike at the fort and the *tête-du-pont* of *Purísima* Bridge. It took them half an hour to even get within range of the bridgehead, thanks to the concentrated fire of the gun batteries. Butler's reconnaissance found the fort even stronger than expected. It was flanked by a ten-foot high stone wall with a deep ditch forming a moat in front of it; its rear was covered by defensive works.

As the *Gringos* left their first position, Mexican troops sallied out to fill the vacuum, pursuing the advancing (not retreating) Buckeyes with a hot fire. However, when the Americans counterattacked, the Mexican skirmishers fell back in such haste that volunteers officers had to keep the companies in good order for the struggle ahead, restraining their impetuous men from bolting from the line to chase the withdrawing enemy.

The Volunteers now passed through the area fought over by Twiggs's Regulars. Wounded and dying men groaned for water. A soldier of the 1st Ohio's G Company climbed a shot-torn tree to pick oranges for the thirsty victims.

But for the wall that now sheltered them, the Ohio infantry could not have held its position for five minutes. As it was, a number of men were wounded in the head and shoulders. Mexicans who leaped atop barricades to shoot down on the Americans were soon put out of action by Ohio sharpshooters, but not before they shot a soldier named Majors in the mouth. Luckily, he had his mouth closed at the time. The ball smashed through his teeth and, its power spent, lodged in his palate. He coughed and spat out the bloody lead slug, along with broken teeth and a lot of gore, growling bravely about the "pill that had saluted him."

The Americans now learned why the enemy had left them the shelter of the rock wall in the garden. It was a trap. The street and wall were raked by enfilading fire from the right flank, from General Mejía's battery at *Purísima* Bridge, often hidden by wreaths of thick smoke. Looking back, Giddings shook his head and wrote, "The escape of the regiment from utter destruction seems now, in a calm retrospect, almost miraculous."

Nevertheless, the Volunteers remained cool in their untenable position, taking what shelter they could find from the raking fire that swept along the wall. The Mexicans did not expose themselves to view, and the sulphurous smoke was so dense that many a volunteer just fired his musket blindly at flashes in the haze. Most of the musket balls glanced harmlessly off the stone walls.

The din of battle was so deafening that hoarse officers had to pantomime their orders, even to men standing in the street alongside them. But over the pall of gunsmoke, the silken standard of the regiment, repaired by its color guard, still "streamed like a rainbow o'er a cloud," as Giddings put it.

At noon, the battle was at its height. The city was ablaze with musket fire and artillery salvoes as Webster's howitzers, in the captured *Tenería* with Twiggs and Quitman, pounded Fort Diablo, Ampudia's headquarters, and the powder magazine in the beautiful, but almost bombproof, cathedral.

General Butler prepared to order a third and final charge of his Ohio boys against the "Devil Fort." But, recalled Giddings, "It was, wisely, unattempted." It would have been the most useless of forlorn hope tactics. With the regiment being decimated, both Butler and Colonel Mitchell were wounded. The former was so incapacitated by a leg wound that, bleeding profusely, protesting loudly, he was carried from the field of battle. Reluctantly, he ordered Hamer, who succeeded to his command, to abandon the attack.

Hamer was in complete agreement with Butler's new order. The last hundred yards in front of the Mexican bastion were so swept with gunfire that he would lose half of his men even if survivors could make it to safer ground beyond. Giddings was even more dubious that Hamer of success with Butler's prior order. He guessed that only ten percent, thirty out of the three hundred being readied for the charge, would even reach the walls of the fort. And that Diablo could not possibly be held by them even if they should, somehow, manage to seize it.

Butler later admitted to doubts about a successful storming of the Mexican stronghold. His men were falling fast under the converging fire of three batteries, and the fort itself was covered by musket fire from the rear. "There is a *possibility* that the work might have been carried," he later wrote, choosing his words carefully, "but not without excessive loss and, if carried, I feel assured that it would have been untenable."

Hamer broke off the action and pulled his now-scattered companies back in a withdrawal to less-exposed positions. Throughout the fight, the Ohioans were fortunate to be aided by two regulars attached to the regiment. Both would soon earn much military renown, Colonel Albert Sidney Johnston of Butler's staff, and Colonel Joseph (Fighting Joe) Hooker of the First Artillery, of Hamer's staff.

Lt. Colonel Weller extricated his battalion of Volunteers under heavy fire, retiring them eastward in good, if extended, order. They moved down a street and across some plazas into the suburbs again. But Colonel Pedro García Conde charged them with his elite corps, the 3d Lancers. The horsemen, with flags flying and sunlight gleaming on their polished blades, were no "elite" to Giddings. He termed them "fiends from hell." For they deliberately galloped their horses over fallen Americans and the unarmed surgeons and corpsmen attending them. They then swung in their saddles to spear the helpless men, pinning them to the ground. A number of *lanceros* left the charge in order to murder wounded *Gringos* as the medics fled for their lives with the Mexican cavalrymen in hot pursuit.

A bitter Giddings later noted that Mexican historians claimed proudly that the 3d Regiment lanced more than fifty of their enemy—without mentioning that many were already-wounded men in the care of doctors, or were non-combatants of the medical corps. When Mexican apologists for their defeat at Monterrey spoke of a brave sally by "*Viva!*"-shouting artillerymen at *Puente Purísima*, Giddings was also disgusted. He scornfully retorted that the only such sortie must have been the besieged who "charged the dead and bayoneted the wounded."

Still, the major considered the ancient lance to be a much-underrated weapon, especially in the hands of such skilful graceful, if brutal, horsemen as the Mexican cavalry. But, unlike the animals of the American dragoons, their horses were small and wiry mustangs. They lacked the necessary strength and weight, the sheer impact, to smash through lines of footsoldiers.

An orderly retreat under fire is the most difficult maneuver that green troops can perform, yet Donahue and his fellow amateurs pulled it off. They even formed up, instinctively, in the proper defensive square behind a brush fence. There had been no time for the one-year enlistees to be drilled in such formations. The lancers' charge slackened as it neared the defensive line of Americans. The latter, enraged at the butchery of their wounded friends, opened a hot fire on them. In fact, they discharged their muskets too soon, because of their anger. Their officers, in vain, ordered them to hold their fire until the cavalry were closer. Only a few shots emptied Mexican saddles. Giddings remarked, "Had they waited but a few minutes, their vengeance would have been ample."

The brisk musketry sent the Mexican horsemen reeling in flight—and fright—save for a few brave officers who galloped forward in hopes of reviving the charge. One of them fell only twenty paces from the American line and a "Lieutenant H——" of Donahue's own A Company, who had lost his shoes scrambling for cover in the ditch, confiscated the dead man's boots, saying, "There never was a better fit."

Once that the lancers were repulsed, Donahue's company was moved, with other units, to support Bragg's artillery. The volunteers remained largely unemployed in their new position, but they were still targets for enemy cannoneers. In fact, they were pin-ned down there for the balance of the day. As evening approached, Taylor pulled all of his men back to the oak and pecan grove, except for the regulars in captured *Tenería* and their reinforcements of the fresh Kentucky Volunteers.

Worn-out with fatigue and excitement, Donahue and his fellow-infantrymen retired to the *Bosque de Santo Domingo* as Monterrey's church bells rang out—very prematurely—in rejoicing at the repulse of the hated *norteamericanos.* Although many of the latter now realized how badly they had underestimated the fighting ability of the Mexican Army, and although the camp was a gloomy one, sodden and virtually tentless in the drizzling rain, few doubted that the city would fall. For Worth held two forts on the west and Quitman the key one on the east side of Monterrey.

General Taylor visited all wounded officers and paid a call on the crowded, dimly-lit hospital tent where surgeons were amputating limbs and dressing wounds. The enlisted men rebelled momentarily because they were expected to eat their dinner on the same table on which the doctors had been performing surgery. But when the gory table tops were simply flopped over, the soldiers sat down to rest and eat before dropping off into the sleep of exhaustion.

During the night, fatigue parties brought in wounded men. Others straggled in on their own. One of them caused an alarm, with pickets firing shots at imaginary attackers. It is not known if Donahue responded to the "long roll" of the drummer, as did the regimental surgeon who stood guard over the tent of the wounded C.O. with pistols and a captured lance, or whether he slept right through the "stampede," like so many of his worn-out buddies.

The Ohioans did not go into action on the 22d, but rested and guarded prisoners in the grove. Early Wednesday morning, September 23d, they were delighted to find that the enemy had abandoned *Fuerte Diablo,* along with all exterior works on the north end of the city except for the Citadel.

Now the Volunteers made a cautious advance, but soon were cheering loudly as they fought, house by house and plaza by plaza, against the now-silent defenders pinched between them and Worth's force. The Mexicans were finally squeezed into the barricaded *Plaza Grande,* which was now being pounded by Taylor's heavy mortar. That afternoon, as Taylor and Worth planned the final push on the main square, Hamer's boys relieved Quitman's brigade. Night then closed down all activity except that of the wolves which, attracted by the stench, tore at the bodies of the unburied dead.

As the Ohioans prepared to renew their assault on the 24th, a cease-fire was called to arrange for Ampudia's capitulation. The Buckeyes breakfasted in captured forts *Diablo* and *Tenería*. Giddings never forgot that historic meal. It was a tin cup of a liquid facetiously called coffee, slapjacks, and crawdads—crayfish tossed up on *Tenería's* walls by shells exploding in the moat.

General Butler was proud of his green soldiers. The Kentuckian wrote in his final report, "It is with no little pride and gratitude that I bear testimony of the gallantry and good conduct of my command. Were proof wanting, a mournful one is to be found in the subjoined return of casualties of the day. That part of my division properly in the field did not exceed 1,100, of which number one-fifth were either killed or wounded."

The Mexicans claimed that the U.S. loss on that first critical day of the Battle of Monterrey, alone, was 1,000 men. It was actually 394 dead and wounded. This figure amounted to most of the total for the entire siege—120 dead and 368 wounded. Mexican losses were unknown.

Butler continued. "The fact that troops for the first time under fire should have suffered such loss without shrinking in a continuous struggle for more than two hours, and mainly against a sheltered and inaccessible foe, finds but few parallels, and is of itself a eulogium to which I need not add. That there were some more prominent for skill and gallantry than others, even in a contest where all were brave, there can be no doubt; and I leave to those better qualified from their situations than myself the pleasing, though delicate, task of reporting upon their respective merits."

Butler's wound was more serious than he knew. He was invalided home, where he remained until the close of 1847. (He then succeeded to the chief command of Mexico City when General Winfield S. Scott was recalled.) Hamer replaced him in command of the Volunteer regiments. Of his successor's efforts in battle, Butler said, "General Hamer was placed in a position where nothing brilliant could be achieved but which, at every moment, imperatively demanded prudence and calm, unbending, courage. It is but justice to him to say that I found him equal to the emergency."

Zachary Taylor now permitted the Mexican troops to withdraw with their small arms, even some cannon. He agreed to an eight-week armistice, during which he promised not to move further south than Rinconada Pass, Linares, and San Fernando de las Presas. Taylor was roundly (and properly) condemned for his leniency toward the defeated enemy after a victory of such cost. The "bloodthirsty" Texans (Giddings's term) were especially after his scalp.

Taylor's excuse was his lack of supplies and transportation. He reported that he could not move south for six weeks, in any case. He had only ten days' rations. "The task of fighting and beating the enemy," he reported, "is among the *least* difficult we encounter. The great question of supplies necessarily controls all the operations in a country like this."

Not till November 2 did Taylor receive the first wagons since those of July in Corpus Christi. By the time that he was ready to move on Saltillo and San Luís Potosí, his jealous rival, General of the Army Scott, had reached Brazos Santiago. It was New Year's, 1847. Scott promptly took away most of Taylor's best troops for his own invasion of Mexico via the port of Vera Cruz, with the capital, Mexico City, as his target.

It was on September 25 that American troops marched into Monterrey and took over the Citadel. The Mexican troops withdrew, accompanied by many civilians. Most of the people had to remain, of course, and some described the *Voluntarios* as the very picture of the barbarians against whom their priests had warned them. All were shabby-looking fellows in worn pants and jackets. With their long hair and unkempt, straggly beards, they seemed not to be soldiers but "ragged vagabonds who looked like Comanches in manners and ferocity."

The occupying Americans were astounded by the strength of the city's defenses. They would have strongly disagreed with their commander's "least difficult" comment about fighting, versus transport, if asked. It was commonly said that a garrison of only two thousand Yanks (even Britishers!) could have held Monterrey against thirty thousand besiegers.

Michael Donahue and his comrades-in-arms had attacked the Nuevo León capital at its strongest point. Historian Peterson, who called the action "the most dangerous day of the siege," remembered that "especially were the conquerors amazed that they had been able to penetrate, even for an instant, into the eastern half of the city, which was a perfect network of defenses. Worth, on the west, had but to carry the heights in that quarter to find the route comparatively open to him. But Taylor, at the corner of every street, was met by a fort or a masked battery."

* * *

Colonel Michael Hawkins wrote his titled cousin, Mamie Donahue, Baroness von Schroeder, in 1906.

There was a very interesting and romantic meeting of my two cousins on the field of Monterrey two days after that historical battle. . . . After the battle, the Volunteers were stationed in the city. . . . The Regulars remained in the field. [This situation was shortly reversed.] Two days after the battle, Cousin Michael [Donahue] visited the field to look over the ground he had fought over. While conversing with some of the men, a Regular soldier came up, extended his hand and said, "Cousin Michael, how do you do?"

Michael, always reserved and dignified, as you will remember, replied, "Sir, you have the advantage of me." The Regular answered, "Why, don't you know me? I am your cousin, Peter O'Kane."

Michael grasped his hand, saying, "Are you the long-lost Peter," and was rejoiced to meet him. This cousin of ours was the son of our mother's brother, James O'Kane. The boy had disappeared years before and, after the family had searched for him for two years, they mourned him as dead, thinking his employer, to whom he was an indentured apprentice, and who was very cruel to him, had murdered the boy. This meeting on the battlefield of Monterrey was the first news that anyone had that he lived, and no other member of the family, except Michael Donahue, knew of his existence from that time for years, owing to the fact that the regiment he was in was [later] cut to pieces at the bloody battle of Cerro Gordo. Cousin Michael made an earnest search, but could not find his name among the killed, wounded or missing, so he concluded not to write his father, who had so long mourned him as dead, of their meeting on the field of Monterrey.

Inaction was not good for the *Voluntarios.* There were "turbulent spirits" in the ranks, as Giddings put it. The regiment, now half strength at four hundred men after convalescents were sent home for discharge, began to suffer losses from disease and even murder. The first courts-martial were held. Officers as well as enlisted men went a.w.o.l. Giddings blamed a *fonda* tavern run by a rascal who called himself Hindoo John. The Major added, "To the lasting honor of my own regiment, be it recorded that, while several of its number were treacherously murdered, it never sought for blood save on the battlefield." One of the Buckeye victims was killed in the company of Chaplain Anthony (Antonio) Rey. Brigands used lassos and knives to murder the men on the main road between Camargo and Monterrey. The entire population of Marín went out to claim the body of the priest they had grown to admire. Reverend Rey was buried in Marín.

In the garrison in the *bosque* (grove), the Ohioans cleared away thickets of aromatic shrubs and thorny brush for a parade ground. The ax, spade and pickax men took many "prisoners"—tarantulas, scorpions, and non-combatant armadillos and chameleons. Most of the troopers were still without tents, so they made bizarre wigwams of poles and Spanish moss. These strange structures, at least in Giddings's eyes, enhanced the picturesqueness of the campsite. The romantic officer pictured the woods—"The lofty arches of the grove, adorned with waving banners of moss, and illuminated by the ruddy glow of many fires." Alas, many of the fine trees were cut down by the Ohio "barbarians" during their stay of two months, to make quarters and to build a bombproof powder magazine in the Citadel.

To fill the time and maintain discipline, there was much guard duty, drill and instruction in infantry tactics. At sick call, even Mexican citizens were welcomed. This is not so surprising, since they often brought in poultry, sweet corn, fruit, and pumpkins. The German volunteers sang in harmony; others played on the banjo. The commissary had the companies build ovens so that freshly-baked bread might replace the tiresome diet of flapjacks or pancakes, weevily ship's biscuits or hardtack, and "pandy mice"—*pan de maíz,* "Mexican cornbread," that is, tortillas.

Since they were paid regularly, the troops gambled and drank too much for their own good. This was over the opposition of their officers. But many of the enlisted men were not only sober but devout. Catholics received permission to attend mass at Monterrey's cathedral. Some officers, liking exercise, hiked up steep 5,000-foot *Sierra Silla* (Saddle Mountain), east of town, for the view. There, after a sweltering day, they were unhappily caught in one of the area's infrequent northers and lashed by what seemed to be a freezing hurricane.

The Volunteers were saddened by the deaths in camp of some brave officers and men, especially Hamer, whose frank manner had won him many friends among the enlisted men. The general died in camp on December 2, 1846 after a very brief illness. Giddings wrote, "Never was a general more beloved by his troops." Zachary Taylor said, "I have lost the balance wheel of my Volunteer Army."

Washington had ended Taylor's unfortunate armistice on November 3, as all hopes of a negotiated peace with the wily president, General Antonio de Santa Anna, vanished. That *generalísimo,* in fact, was rallying a new army at San Luís Potosí during the truce, to drive the *Gringos* out of his homeland. Taylor countered him now by taking Saltillo on November 16, without a fight, and shortly added Victoria.

Rumors of an advance by Santa Anna kept Monterrey nervous, and the Ohioans were ordered to reinforce Saltillo. They set fire to their strange huts in the "bosky" (woods), then cooked their breakfast over the coals before marching out at 2 a.m. on December 17. Since they still had not a wagon or packhorse, they had to travel light. Even so, many carried bird cages holding parrots that they had caught in the woods.

The Buckeyes marched to Saltillo through the streets of Monterrey and thence over the Sierra Madre passes of *La Rinconada* and *Los Muertos.* The latter was named "The Dead" because of the many white crosses, rooted in piles of rocks, over the graves of murdered travelers. Giddings recalled the trek, "Crossing the Sierra Madre was one of the most fatiguing (marches) of the campaign, but full of interest and excitement."

The rumors of Santa Anna's move were just that, rumors not facts, so the Ohioans went into camp outside Saltillo near a real *rara avis* for northern Mexico, a cotton factory. Donahue, with his interest in technology must have visited the two-story adobe, with its forty looms and two hundred spindles. Since they were made in New Jersey, probably in his own Paterson, he may have wondered if his old boss, Thomas Rogers, installed them in the late 1820s, or his own kin, Michael O'Kane, in the early 1840s.

Winter weather turned inclement and the Ohio boys, still without tents, dug deep foxholes in order to escape the raw night winds. Fuel was even scarcer than water, for only a single wagonload of wood arrived each day, brought twenty-two miles to the company cookfires. Still, Christmas Eve was celebrated with band music and songs, bonfires and rockets. The cotton mill's little chapel was illuminated, and the peal of Saltillo's church bells echoed over the countryside.

Even a false alarm, the sound of pack mules being mistaken for the drumming of Mexican cavalary hooves, could not dim the spirits of the officers at the assistant surgeon's eggnog party, though some of them had to buckle on arms while their moustaches were still white with froth from their drinks. Hopeful of another "stampede" like the fight at Monterrey, the enlisted men were sleeping on their weapons as Christmas dawned. But New Year's Day of 1847 found them still at Camp Butler, the fort six miles out of Saltillo, with everything quiet.

Even Taylor knew that he had lost the confidence of the government by his lenient armistice. He fully expected to have to abandon Saltillo in order to hang onto Monterrey. The capital was now garrisoned by most of the 1st Ohio under General Marshall, while Kentuckians held the Citadel itself.

When fresh word of an advance by Santa Anna spread to Monterrey, Donahue and his unit were back in the city. By February 21, when Taylor chose to meet Santa Anna in battle at Buena Vista beyond Saltillo, Monterrey was like a ghost town, a city of the dead. Giddings claimed that he did not see ten Mexican citizens within its walls. The brush telegraph had warned the civilians of a crucial battle. The Ohioans, of course, were placed on an alert. Donahue did not take his shoes or clothes off for a full week. The drumroll of alarms—all false—called him to his post several times.

Even the great victory by Taylor at Buena Vista on February 23, 1847 did not end the war of nerves around Monterrey. On the 24th, Lt. Colonel Irwin reported the 2d Ohio under siege at Marín. The 1st Ohio rushed two companies to scatter the enemy. The very next day, word arrived of a terrible defeat of Lt. (Brevet Major) Philip N. Barbour's escort and the murder and mutilation of fifty of his wagonmen on the 21st by General Jośe Urrea's Regulars and the *rancheros* of General Antonio Canales.

Next, word reached Monterrey that Colonel Morgan was trapped near Agua Fría. In just ten minutes, two hundred First Infantrymen were on the quick-march to relieve him. By now, Marín, Cerralvo and Punta Aguda were all abandoned, while the Ohioans, ironically, were celebrating Taylor's victory at Buena Vista by ringing Monterrey's church bells.

On the night of March 3, three 1st Ohio companies joined two Kentucky companies to form an armed escort for dispatch-bearers for the U.S. They carried Taylor's report on the Battle of Buena Vista. Unfortunately, the Buckeyes were also ordered to guard a slow, two-mile long wagon train of 150 vehicles, with 700 animals in harness. Also along were some panicky *Gringo* civilians. One of the Ohio units was Donahue's A company, commanded by Captain Kenneally. (The gallant Irishman would be killed in action, at Vera Cruz, in only a few months' time.)

In Agua Fría, the Volunteers found plunder from Barbour's shattered train. But this did not prepare them for the horrors of the battlefield itself. Everywhere were evidences of atrocities. They found fifty naked corpses of teamsters, blackened by sun and fire. Some had been smeared with tar and set afire while alive. Some were beheaded; some had their hearts torn out.

On the third day of escorting the cumbersome train, March 7, 1847, the Ohioans and "Kaintucks" marched twenty-eight miles from Papagallo to the outskirts of Cerralvo via Robber's Rancho. They made the hike in scorching heat and with little water. They walked smack into a trap, perhaps the one pictured in a woodcut frontispiece illustration of Peterson's book, *Military Heroes,* if it did not depict the beginning of the tragic Barbour action. The cut, showing Mexican lancers, was titled "Mexicans Watching a Train of Army Wagons."

A few horsemen in the vanguard of the train galloped back across the plain to report Mexican troops swarming out of recaptured Cerralvo. Soon, a long array of lancers was seen. The Volunteers placed their four-pounder in a clearing on a slight elevation and gave the enemy a dose of canister shot. Then the infantry fired its muskets and the Mexicans fled in disorder.

But now firing came from sharpshooters hidden in the thick chaparral flanking both side of the road. More fire came from the rear of the train, which the Mexicans had infiltrated. So strung out was the long line of vehicles that the rearguard of Howe's and Kenneally's companies were fully two miles back from the van.

Unaccountably, Howe moved his men to the front, stranding the all-Irish Company A of Kenneally—and Michael Donahue. It now had to defend itself and the most vulnerable part of the caravan, alone. Giddings said of the situation: "Had the latter company been composed of less resolute material, [this] might have seriously endangered the whole command. But the commander of the escort was not apprehensive that the rear guard would be captured so long as one gallant Irish heart was left to bleed in its defense." The Cincinnati-Irish company dug in its heels.

At the first gunshot, many drivers in the center of the train ran to both front and rear, or scrambled off into the dense brush on either side of the narrow road. The whole column came to a halt. More than a dozen teamsters were quickly lanced to death by the *caballería*. Wagons were abandoned. About forty were lost when their unattended mules stampeded into enemy hands, But another one hundred twenty were saved by the escort and the more courageous drivers.

If the infantrymen had been accompanied by one hundred dragoons—even fifty—most of the wagons could have been saved On foot, the Americans could not stop the mounted Mexican irregulars of Canales from unhitching animals and driving them off, after setting vehicles afire.

The worst loss was that of the ammunition wagon of the escort. It was in the care of the two most dependable teamsters of all. But it was taken and fired. When it blew up, it killed three looting Mexicans and wounded others. Sergeant Donahue must have gritted his teeth at the loss, while telling his men to husband their few cartridges. Giddings was guilty of gross understatement when he wrote, "It was no easy matter to prevent the loss from having a depressing effect upon our troopers."

Luckily, the steadiness of the escort whilst under fire, and Sergeant Howell's round shot, some of which skipped into Cerralvo to scare the wits out of the citizenry, held back the vastly superior enemy force.

Mexican footsoldiers now entered the fray. They charged the front of the column, were driven back, but charged again. Horsemen dismounted and fired on the caravan from the brush, too, until a four-pounder opened up on them and flushed them like a covey of birds. At this moment, some Yankee's pet gamecock fluttered up to the bow of a wagon and crowed lustily. The Americans took this as a good omen and gave the rooster applause and loud cheers.

Giddings was fascinated by a beardless youth, a spunky civilian clerk, who fired rapidly at the Mexicans with a small brass pocket pistol. He would drop down into a wagon bed to reload, then pop up and blaze away, long after the soldier's cease-fire signalled that the enemy had fled far out of range. His driver, shaking with laughter, continued to point out fast-disappearing targets to him.

Another man who caught Gidding's attention in the battle, and very likely Donahue's as well, was a survivor of Barbour's debacle. He jumped into a twenty-foot clump of brush alongside the road during the ambush. In the brush, he had to dodge lance thrusts. He escaped, torn by thorns but uncut by lance heads, to jump and sing in joy, "Hurrah for Bill Robbins! Hurrah for Bill Robbins! Run over by Lancers, two times, and a'living again!"

A gray-haired man, identified by Giddings only as Mr. R——, was separated from his family by the ambuscade. He tried to get back to his kin in the rear, but could not manage it even though he killed a Mexican soldier in hand-to-hand combat in the attempt. Tearful and bloodied, he pleaded with the column's commander, Major Andrew Jackson Coffee, for help. "At the earliest possible moment," the embattled C.O. promised.

Lieutenants Edward Pierce Fyffe and Augustus Moor offered to bear orders to the cut-off Kenneally, and to take the civilian along with them, but the Major declined. Actually, the man's family proved to be safe already, though some of his friends with them had been killed. When R——'s wife and children begged for mercy in Spanish, the Mexicans spared them and let them join Kenneally.

Familiar with the ground, the enemy was able to attack all along the line of stalled wagons. Coffee could not spare any men to help the rearguard. He did not know it, of course, but they did not need it. Kenneally, Donahue, *et al*, had already forced their attackers into a disorderly retreat, with some losses. But he reassured Mr. R—— by saying that he had ample confidence in the Cincinnati Irish. "Company A certainly is not one to withdraw from danger and thereby involve their comrades in greater danger."

When the Mexicans in front were thrown back, Coffee ordered Captain Edwin D. Bradley to take eighty men back to join Kenneally and to bring up all surviving wagons. However, before Bradley could set out, who should ride up, as sprightly and cheerful as ever, but Captain Kenneally. And on a handsome, caparisoned Mexican horse, to boot.

The Irish Captain reported that his company was still surrounded, but quickly showed his superior his reason for leaving his men, even temporarily, in such a spot. It was a communication in lead pencil on the large sheet of foolscap, given him by the Mexicans under a flag of truce. It read, "The Colonel Langberg offers to all the soldiers life and security, if you surrender yourself." It was signed "Emilio Langberg, Foreign Officer."

Kenneally had asked for and received an interview with the German. He found him in General Romero's large force at the midpoint of the besieged caravan. Langberg, fluent in English, told him that further resistance was useless. The Mexican force, led by three generals, totalled 1,600 men. (So fierce was the attack on the train that some of the besieged guessed that their opponents numbered as many as six thousand men.) Langberg was honest, too. When the Irishman asked if the remainder of the American contingent had surrendered, he answered truthfully, that it had not. Kenneally then requested permission to consult with his superior officer. He was given a horse and an hour of truce.

Coffee sent Kenneally back with words of encouragement for his men and a suitably-couched negative reply to Langberg's offer. He also promised the captain some reinforcements under Bradley. When Kenneally notified Langberg that the truce was terminated, he courteously advised the Teuton to move his troops since they were in a dangerous position—they might get hurt by his Irishmen!

Bradley's men, accompanied by the worried but brave New Englander, Mr. R——, were fired on by cavalry. But their own hot fire drove the horsemen away. The reinforcements joined Donahue's Company A and, together, had little difficulty in bringing up the unburnt wagons to reconcentrate the train.

General José Urrea, himself, sent a flag of truce to Major Coffee. The C.O. was careful to meet the bearer halfway, so as not to reveal how few men he had in the escort. The General-in-Chief complained to him that the *norteamericanos* had twice violated the earlier truce by shooting at him. Coffee explained that he had understood that Langberg's truce applied only to Kenneally's Company A. Anyway, he argued, he believed that Urrea was only using the trucial flags to gain time and information. He warned that he would personally fire on the next one. Naturally, he spurned Urrea's reiterated demand that he surrender.

A few more shots were exchanged as Kenneally and Bradley joined Coffee, but Urrea's force withdrew toward Cerralvo around dusk. Coffee closed up his remaining wagons. He had lost forty of them, along with fifteen dead drivers but, miraculously, had had only two soldiers killed. He placed the vehicles in a tight mass, a "park" that covered several acres, and placed his force on all four sides of the square. Slowly, he moved toward Cerralvo. It was dark when he arrived, so he halted outside, posted strong pickets, and waited for daylight. He planned to fight his way into Cerralvo, but Urrea evacuated the town and the Ohioans retook the 161-year old community without a fight at 8 a.m.

The Volunteers were welcomed back warmly by the citizens. Naturally, the Ohioans were suspicious of them, but two wounded Americans in town reported that the people had been kind to them while Urrea held Cerralvo. So the *alcalde* (mayor) was promised U.S. protection in return for his humanity.

On March 9, 1847, the C.O. ordered the wagons to resume their progress to Camargo. But the wagonmaster told him that his teamsters flatly refused to drive. Langberg had promised safety to the soldiers, not to the U.S. Army's Mexican teamsters. Twice, wagonmen had been horribly butchered by their fellow countrymen. Nor were they convinced that Urrea and Canales had really pulled out. Coffee could not force them to move. He had no authority to courtmartial civilians.

Major Coffee now decided to split his force. He would use half to escort the important despatches and leave the rest in Cerralvo to guard the wagons. But his men had only ten to twelve cartridges left, each, and the cannons had even fewer rounds. So, after a council of war with his officers, he decided to sit tight, instead, and wait for aid from Camargo.

Coffee took the precaution of sending a messenger to Camargo, to ask for ammunition and supplies. The man, an experienced Mexican smuggler, refused to carry a written communique. He would only convey oral messages. He was back in just a few hours. He and the nervous teamsters had been right. Canales still had a ring of guerrilla-soldiers around Cerralvo. He had stopped the man and searched his clothes and saddle for papers before letting him go.

The smuggler was game enough to try again, via a roundabout route down the Texas side of the Río Grande. A brave Volunteer, whose name is not known today, shaved off his beard, "painted" his skin a darker hue to disguise himself as a Mexican, and accompanied him. They both got through.

The Americans were trapped in Cerralvo for four more days before General Samuel R. Curtis broke through Canales's lines with his force of one thousand two hundred men. He had been alarmed about the fate of the 1st Regiment. Fugitives from the wagon train fight had met him in Mier to report that the unit was being "cut to pieces." Taylor, at Monterrey, got the same disturbing, and erroneous, news. Actually, as Peterson stated in 1848, "After a desperate conflict, the Americans proved victorious, with a loss of seventeen (including 15 wagon drivers), the enemy losing forty."

After Cerralvo, Michael Donahue always had a soft spot in his heart for General Curtis. He never forgot that March day, telling friends, "The sight of the reinforcements, and the scattering of the besieging Mexicans, was one of the happiest scenes of my life."

Resupplied by Curtis, Donahue's 1st Ohio continued its march to Camargo. It next took a hundred loaded wagons on March 20 on the dry and dreary road back to Monterrey, with the escort beefed up to five hundred men, including Texas Rangers, to prevent a recurrence of the Cerralvo attack.

At the site of the butchery of Barbour's wagoners, between Marín and Ramos, "Mustang" Gray and his Texas Rangers left the Volunteers, bent on vengeance. Giddings later heard that the *Tejanos* had put to death every male that they found, twenty-four of them, in a village. Zachary Taylor expressed regret at the reported outrage, but he reminded Mexican officials of the atrocities responsible for such a bloody revenge. As for the Rangers, they denied that the rumored massacre of townspeople ever took place.

Now the terms of service of the citizen soldiers were expiring. Giddings noted, "No great number of old Volunteers could be induced to re-enter service until they had once again seen their homes." Michael Donahue, like many, had apparently had a bellyful of "sojering." There was no pressing need for his services, in any case. Scott had shifted all action far to the south. The north was quiet. Word of the fall of Vera Cruz reached Monterrey in mid-April, followed by news of the American victory at Cerro Gordo. A few patrols of tough Texas Rangers were sufficient to put down both *guerrilleros* and *ladrones* (bandits) in the north. Wagon trains moved safely with only small escorts.

Soon, Volunteer companies began to head for Brazos Santiago en route to New Orleans and mustering out. Benjamin F. Scribner noticed the 1st Ohio as it left the Buena Vista area for the Río Grande on May 18, 1847. Giddings remembered that last long walk. "Our homeward march was a joyful one, though over a road then numerously dotted with skeletons of men and animals."

It was the hot season again and the Río Grande was low. To Giddings, it looked like a mere creek. Steamboats could not be used as troop transports. The Ohioans marched overland, paralleling the river, past roofless and ruined *ranchos* to Reynosa and Matamoros. En route, they met new recruits, their replacements. The contrast was striking—fresh complexions and new uniforms versus bearded and burnt visages above tattered rags.

On a June evening, the veterans from Ohio spied the blue water of the Gulf, and soon pitched camp on a breezy beach. They gazed with bewitched delight at the rolling billows and the stout transports lying offshore. To Giddings, they seemed to be chafing at their anchors in their impatience to bear the boys home.

The 1st Ohio was mustered out of service on June 5, 1847. The regiment lost twenty-four men killed in actions and forty-two dead of disease, and had many men wounded. One of the luckier ones was Sergeant Michael Donahue, who came through the campaign without a scratch. He was anxious as any of his buddies to secure his discharge, but he was not going home, like most of them. He had decided to stay on at Brazos Santiagos as a civilian employee of the Army, working alongside his brother, James, superintendent of the Río Grande shipyard machine shop that kept the steam transports in operation.

The Brazos Santiago ship repair operation is virtually unknown today, even to historians of the Mexican War. But it was a remarkable feat, planting a foundry, shipyard and machine shop in a howling wilderness. Perhaps General Thomas S. Jesup, head of the Quartermaster Department, was thinking of James Donahue's operation, in part, when he wrote in 1847 that, "With our depots farther from the sources of supply than Algiers is from Toulon or Marseilles, we accomplished more in the first six months of our operations in Mexico than France, the first military power in Europe, has accomplished in Africa in seventeen years."

Donahue's operation was part of the depot at Brazos Santiago run by officers like Lt. Col. Henry Whiting, Captain George Crosman, and Charles Thomas. Donahue recalled, particularly, serving with Quartermaster officers (Majors) Edmund Augustus Ogden, Edmund Brooke Alexander and Thomas B. Eastland. He became a close friend of the latter. The quasi-shipyard was not on the pass, or inlet called "Brazee San Diego" by many *Yanquis* but (in 1846) on the high ground of Point Isabel and, in 1847, at the mouth of the Río Grande itself.

At Point Isabel, on *Laguna Madre,* were the remnants of the little Mexican settlement of Frontón (1788), which became a sort of summer resort after 1800. Its few inhabitants had destroyed the place before abandoning it at General Taylor's approach in late March of '46. But it revived and boomed under the Americans, as Point Isabel, during the Mexican War, 1846-48. It boomed again, to some extent, during the California Gold Rush (1849-50) as Texas Argonauts headed for the placers of the Mother Lode via the Gila Trail. The only other Mexican settlement nearby, a tiny village on the tip of Padre Island, had been swept away by a storm long before the war.

During their long stay on the Texas Gulf Coast, James and Michael found themselves on a genuine frontier, anything but "The Magic Valley" of citrus, oleanders, date, onions, and fan palms that it would become. Cotton would become king, but long after the brothers left the scene. only a little *algodón* (cotton) was being tried by local Mexicans. In time, lonely Point Isabel (now Port Isabel) grew into a major port for "cotton wool" as well as the base of a shrimping fleet rivaling that of Key West itself.

The Donahues found the lower Río Grande Valley near its mouth to be a plain—actually a 4,200-square mile flat delta— not a valley. It was an exotic place of shell beaches, sand dunes, swamps and marshes, rivers of grass like Florida's Everglades and groves of bizarre mangroves with aerial roots wading in the water. The young Irishmen found the only "forests" inland to be thickets of spiny mesquite, scattered palmettoes, and a rank undergrowth of weeds and prickly pear cactus, all tied together with briars. The soldiers defined coastal south Texas with a little ditty:

All bushes have thorns,
All insects have horns.

Adding to the discomforts were the dank river fogs which at night reduced visibility to zero. Isolation, bad food, and illness led to frequent fights among the bored troops stationed at Brazos Santiago, fights reminiscent of Michael's Catfish War. James must have seen the scuffle between different companies of Georgia Volunteers in September 1846. Illinois and Indiana regiments had to intervene to quell the riot, and courtsmartial followed.

Many Americans were not as lucky as the Donahues in escaping the ravages of disease. Even a deadly plague of measles swept the Río Grande country. Luckily, the breeze-swept Brazos area was healthier than the river itself. General Taylor, (as unkempt in appearance as Generals William T. Sherman and George Crook) was almost indifferent to hygiene and sanitation at first, but finally moved sickly men from Fort Brown (Brownsville) to the Brazos in hope that the fresh, salt atmosphere would improve their health.

James Donahue's Texas home was a bleak and barren place. When Benjamin Scribner first took in the sights under a ninety degree sun (July 31, 1846), he found them to be almost nonexistent. There was the armory, the hospital, the grave of brave Major Samuel Ringgold, hero of the Battle of Palo Alto, and the Quartermaster's depot, including James's operation. Only the hospital impressed Scribner, with its large, clean and airy rooms. The overall air of the Brazos and the point was unimpressive. "I never was more disappointed with the appearance of a place than I was with Point Isabel. The Government houses are built principally like barns with canvas roofs. There are in the place only three or four old Spanish huts with thatched roofs; the rest are tents and canvas-covered booths."

When Scribner returned to the Brazos on October 23, 1846, he was dumfounded by the changes he saw. "It appeared more like the levee at New Orleans than the desert island on which we first encamped. The Government had about 150 teamsters and laborers employed, and whole acres were covered with baggage wagons and Army stores." There was apparently no shortage of work for James Donahue, either, for Scribner added, "The harbor is filled with hundreds of vessels."

Army grub still ran to moldy crackers and fatty ham, rancid junk so blubbery that soldiers joked about "living off the fat of the land." But the local waters teemed with fish, the shallows and beaches with oysters, clams, crabs, and turtles. In the mesquite and chaparral, one could hunt deer, wild cattle, plover, prairie chickens, and wild turkeys. (The soldiers, of course, ate anything that moved. One mess even cooked up a seven-foot rattlesnake.) As civilian employees, and friends of officers, the Donahues had a better diet—flour (unspoiled), pickles, and six-bits-a-quart molasses, and did not have to stoop to fried rattlers. There was the luxury of sea bathing in the Laguna and surf bathing on the "outside" of Padre Island, only a short run by sailboat from James Donahue's shipyard. For sport, the brothers could chase coyotes in make-believe "fox hunts," or try to lasso mustangs. Beachcombing and "shelling" on the strands was limitless.

Scribner and a companion found a hotel in Point Isabel by late '46, the Palo Alto House, also a post office and even a theater. There was an inn, now, the Greenwood Hotel, on the tip of Padre Island. Perhaps the two men jostled James Donahue's elbow in the crowd watching Major Ringgold's remains being ceremoniously disinterred that October for transfer home to Baltimore. The Army band played *Adeste Fidelis* and 18-pound cannon roared in salutes to the fallen hero.

James had to endure a storm which hit the Brazos in the fall of '46. The winds almost swept the islands clean, the gales driving everything before them on the mainland, too. Soldiers bet on which flying item would win the race—a hat, a barrel,or the old smokestack of a steamer. (The sombrero won.) The wind-driven water swept right across the long sandspit that was Padre Island. Scribner and a friend had to wade through the invading high tide to their battered lodgings.

Perhaps James (and, later, Michael) caught a glimpse of the most famous camp follower in U.S. Army history. She was Mrs. Sarah Bowman-Phillips, universally known by her nickname "The Great Western." She was also called "The Heroine of Fort Brown" for her bravery under fire in the bombardment that cost Major Jacob Brown his life. Scribner wrote, "Quite an excitement! She has every appearance of an Amazon, being tall, muscular, and majestic in her expression. She won laurels at the bombardment of Matamoros. She issued coffee to the men while the bombs were falling around her."

The Donahues became good friends of Quartermaster Thomas B. Eastland, and his son, Joseph Green Eastland, while at the Brazos.

(The latter would become a business associate later in San Francisco.) Still a youngster, Joseph accompanied his father to Mexico City, where he enjoyed his role as probably the youngest *Gringo* in the occupied capital. He was barely sixteen years of age. On his way back home to Nashville to attend school, young Eastland stopped off at Brazos Santiago.

Between the time that the Mexican War was ended by the Treaty of Guadalupe Hidalgo, February 2, 1848, and news of the discovery of gold in California reached Texas, circa January 1849, the Brazos Santiago-Point Isabel complex began to dwindle away. By February 20, 1848, A.B. Clarke found little there besides major William Warren Chapman's quartermaster's building, some run-down shanties, and an old steam boat (one that had defeated the best efforts of the Donahues, apparently) run up on the sand and used for a hotel and post office.

John W. Audubon, son of the great ornithologist, was there at about the same time as Clarke. He, too, was dismayed by his first view of Brazos Santiago. Aside from a handful of government buildings, there was nothing but "the glaring beach, broken here and there by the dark, weather-stained wrecks of unfortunate vessels."

Neither Clarke nor Audubon noticed the repair yard of the Donahues if, indeed, it was still in operation either at the Río Grande's mouth or where transferred back to the settlement Point Isabel.

After the war's end, General Jesup ordered Quartermaster (Major) David D. Tompkins to get rid of the Army's excess steamboats. Of the twenty-three government steamers (plus other charter boats) on the Río Grande during Taylor's invasion, only three were still running in 1849. The rest were sold off and James bought one of the surplus vessels. Joseph Eastland told David Sessions that "James owned a steam boat on the Río Grande before he came here." The river was ordinarily navigable up to Roma.

Apparently, James Donahue's riverboating predated that of the acknowledged pioneers of Río Grande steamboating, Captain Mifflin Kenedy and Captain Richard King, later of the enormous King Ranch. The two Texans did not form Kenedy & Company to run their steamers till 1850, long after James Donahue pioneered civilian steamboating on the Río Grande.

III

ALCHEMISTS IN IRON

News of California gold reached "the States" at the end of 1848. Some of the very first Argonauts, including Isaac Duval and Benjamin Butler Harris, set out from the mines from Texas in early '49. Not far behind them was James Donahue. No one knows why Michael did not accompany him overland through Mexico. His only known companion on the trail was J.Y. McDuffie. According to the October 1862 *North Pacific Review*, James had lost his wartime profits by shipwreck. "His earnings he invested in a [Río Grande] steamboat and a sailing vessel, both of which were wrecked, leaving him but sufficient means to reach California.

It was long believed that James accompanied his Point Isabel friends, Thomas and Joseph Eastland, to California because the *North Pacific Review* stated that "James joined a party crossing northern Mexico to the port of Mazatlán, where they took a vessel which arrived in San Francisco in April 1849." But it was not the ex-quartermaster's company. The elder Eastland, Thomas, did not resign his Army commission until April Fool's Day of '49 to join the Gila Trail party of Colonel John Coffee Hays, greatest of Texas Rangers (and future sheriff of San Francisco and surveyor general of California).

Hays had just been appointed Indian Agent for the Gila River country of Arizona. The lower part of that tributary to the Colorado River formed the boundary between American territory and Sonora until the Gadsden Purchase of 1853. Hays was to open a road from San Antonio to El Paso before continuing on to the Gila where, he hoped, privately, to find more gold than redskins. General Worth, with whom Michael Donahue had soldiered at Monterrey, was to command Hays's escort, but he died of cholera in 1849 before the party set out. Worth was replaced by Colonel Joseph E. Johnston of the Army's Corps of Engineers. Years later, the Donahue boys' friend, Joseph Eastland, recalled. "It was an entirely unknown country, but from what was reported about it, it was interpreted that gold 'diggins' would be found there, such as had been found in California."

If the various given dates are correct, it is impossible for James Donahue to have marched to Mazatlán with the Eastlands. James's cousin, Michael Hawkins, stated that James was the first of the brothers to arrive, beating Peter who sailed in during June of '49. According to James O'Meara, and the *North Pacific Review*, James was in San Francisco by mid-April of '49. The Eastlands, who were in Galveston in April, finally left Hays's slow-moving party at El Paso and reached Chihuahua City in September and Mazatlán in November. There they squeezed aboard the *Oregon* and reached San Francisco in December. Although they were his dear friends, the Eastlands at no time ever mentioned James Donahue as being a member of their party, though they did refer to others, like James Nugent, later editor of the San Francisco *Herald*, and Major John Caperton, who accompanied them at least part of the way across the continent.

Nor could James have traveled with Jack Hays after the Eastlands pulled out. The former Texas Ranger did not leave San Antonio till late June and took ninety days to survey, map, and build the road to El Paso. While lodging at the Adelphi Hotel in San Francisco, a barracks-like hostelry of many-tiered bunks, the Eastlands were rejoined by Hays, Nugent, and Caperton who now arrived, a month behind them, in early 1850.

The Eastlands ran a store in the city; then pioneered the town of Oso at the mouth of Bear River and prospected for gold on the Feather River. They returned to San Francisco on October 29, 1850 but, according to Joseph, their paths did not finally recross with those of the Donahues till March of 1851.

Meanwhile, Michael Donahue had also struck out overland for El Dorado, but his desert crossing was interrupted. According to the Scott County, Iowa, history, it took him nearly two years to get to California and he and his friends "had to fight their way through."

He was captured by Indians. These may have been the Comanches of west Texas, northern Mexico and New Mexico, the Yavapai of the Gila River or the Apaches of Arizona. In any case, his captors tied him to a tree preparatory to torturing him to death. With just a bit o' the luck of the Irish, he had placed a bottle in the carpetbag that the Indians ransacked. Already aware that whites put all kinds of liquids into the strange containers, some unpalatable and others downright poisonous, the redskins forced the Irishmen to drink from the bottle. Michael was happy to oblige, since it was whiskey. The Indians quickly snatched the bottle back and drained it. Their savage natures were softened up enough by the grain spirits for them to untie their prisoner.

According to family tradition, after Michael demonstrated his skilled marksmanship and his prowess as a horseman, the Indians adopted him into their tribe. It took him six months, but the captive finally made his escape. Michael crossed Mexico to the coast but, instead of going to Mazatlán like the Eastlands, he headed for the port of San Blas.

(Michael's 1884 obituary notice badly garbled both history and geography in describing his route to California. "From New Orleans by steamer up the Red River to Alexandria, Louisiana, via El Paso to Santiago on the Pacific Coast." There he supposedly took passage with thirty companions on the *Oregon*, bound for Panama and then back up to San Francisco. Of course, the Iowa paper confused Brazos Santiago on the Gulf of Mexico with San Blas on the Pacific coast. It *is* possible that Michael reached El Paso from Alexandria, but a more direct route across Texas from Brazos Santiago is more likely.)

While Michael was delayed en route, Peter Donahue set out for the gold country. The wooden sidewheeler *Oregon*, a three-masted two-decker of 1,050 tons, was built by Smith and Dimon in New York and launched on New York's East River on August 5, 1848. She left New York on December 3, 1848, the second Pacific Mail Steamship Company vessel sent to San Francisco. She was commanded by Captain R.H. Pearson, appointed by owner William H. Aspinwall, though technically he was not qualified since all of his experience was in sail. But he was trusted as much as were the captains of the *Oregon's* sister ships *California* and *Panama*, whose skippers' experience with steam was only with ferryboats in New York harbor.

With only some trifling repairs to her machinery being necessary, the *Oregon* reached Río de Janeiro safely to take on coal. She negotiated the Straits of Magellan in the fast time of thirty-six hours and made Valparaíso through rough weather. On February 12, 1849, she reached Peru at the port of Callao. The "Peruvian" marine engineer, Peter Donahue, naturally went aboard her. After all, the *Oregon's* two boilers and 208-horsepower side-lever engine had been made in his own Novelty Iron Works.

But Peter did not go aboard just to look the vessel over. He had become infected with gold fever, just like his two brothers. As the San Francisco *Post* put it in 1877, "The yellow glare of California was too attractive, and he flew toward it." When the *Oregon* sailed from Callao on February 18, 1849, he was a passenger.

The steamer reached Panama on the 23d, where Peter, like so many Argonauts, fell ill with "Isthmian" fever, or malaria. The sidewheeler paddled away from the island of Taboga on March 13 without him. He stayed on the isle to recuperate.

Many selfish gold-seekers were pleased to see Donahue and others detained in Panama by fever. Their absence meant more room on California-bound ships. Tickets were scalped, with some greedy individuals ready to pay $1,000 for a miserable steerage passage to San Francisco on any overcrowded ship. The *California*, for example, was built to carry fifty to sixty cabin passengers and one hundred fifty to two hundred people in steerage, but many, many more bodies were always crammed aboard her.

Arriving in San Francisco Bay on April Fool's Day of 1849, Pearson ran his vessel under the guns of the U.S.S. *Ohio.* He requested, and was granted, help should his crew mutiny and desert to the mines. (This is exactly what happened to the *California* when she arrived in port on July 15. Every last crewman, save one oiler, jumped ship and headed for the diggins, leaving Captain T.A. Budd stranded.)

Even under the watchful eyes of the Navy, some of the *Oregon's* complement, including some officers and the engine room "black gang," deserted her. But Pearson managed to take her back to Panama with a short-handed crew, putting the one loyal fireman in charge of the engines. He planned to sail much of the way, in any case, since only seventy tons of coal were left in the bunkers. Pearson left San Francisco on April 12 with seventy-nine passengers—and $165,000 in gold dust. He reached San Blas, under canvas, on April 26. He had removed enough buckets from her paddle wheels so that she sailed well. He took on coal in the Mexican port and reached Panama safely on May 5, though her boilers failed on the passage. So the *Oregon* made the first San Francisco-Panama round trip by steamer, but Pearson had to "cheat" by substituting sail for steam during part of the run.

By now, Peter Donahue had regained his health on Taboga. The island, twelve miles out in the bay from Panama City, was cooler, because it caught more vagrant ocean breezes than the sweltering, disease-ridden port city. It also boasted springs of good water to fill ship's tanks. Small wonder that the Pacific Mail Steamship Company shifted its base from Panama City to Taboga.

On Taboga, company officials sought Peter's expertise to superintend the repairs to the *Oregon's* boilers and engines. He tackled the work and did it so well that he was offered the post of chief engineer on the steamship, although a new set of engineers had been sent out from New York. He accepted the post, but only for the run north to San Francisco.

When the steamer sailed on May 23, Peter was in complete charge of her engine room. Pearson brought the *Oregon* past the heads of the Golden Gate on June 13, 1849, twenty days from Panama. She was jampacked with 323 passengers. Agents of Pacific Mail urged Peter to return with the *Oregon* to Panama. But he had come to California to dig gold, so he declined.

During his Peruvian stay, Peter had saved $3,500, so that when he arrived with his Pacific Mail windfall he had nearly $6,000. This was no mean sum in '49, even in inflated California. But not all of his capital was in coin. When the *Oregon* halted at San Blas, Peter bought a large load of onions, guessing that vegetables would be in short supply in the mines. He was right and, moreover, even potatoes and onions were believed to be anti-scorbutics, like citrus, and many miners were suffering from scurvy as well as general malnutrition because of inadequate diets. He promptly sold his Mexican *cebollas* for a neat profit in San Francisco. The buyer, a Sacramento merchant named Moses G. Leonard, took the onions upriver and resold them for a dollar apiece.

Peter's relative affluence in 1849 was in marked contrast to his brother James's financial state. Thanks to his multiple shipwrecks, James arrived in San Francisco with hardly a farthing to his name. James O'Meara wrote in 1877, "He had come here at the age of 25 years, alone, and with no other capital than his industry, his energy, his integrity, and his active mind and stout heart, to carve and hew his way to fortune and a name to be honored and revered."

In San Francisco, Peter Donahue immediately joined a party of prospectors. He did not identify them by name, but he later said that some of them became prominent in California affairs. Peter acted on the adage that an idle day was a day lost. How he must have hated the nine "wasted" days on the schooner that crawled its way through the maze of sloughs of the Sacramento Delta and then up the river to the city of Sacramento. From there, the party drove an ox team across the hot plains of the Sacramento Valley to reach the gold country of the Sierra Nevada foothills.

Peter spent about four months in placer mining around Auburn and then at Kelly's Bar near the junction of the Middle and North forks of the American River just above Calf Bar in Placer County. The camp was recorded in county records on October 23, 1851 and appeared on two 1851 maps of the mines by B.F. Butler and Charles D. Gibbes, so Peter was a very early pioneer of the camp. Otherwise, little is known of the latter diggings, long since a ghost town, except that it was, temporarily, quite rich. Also, according to Silas Weston's *Life in the Mountains* (1854), "an awful slaughter of Indians" took place there, but in May of 1853, well after Peter left the place.

For all of his innate diligence, Peter could find little gold, and he paid heavily for the time he spent prospecting. Not only in the time that he hated to lose, but also in ill health and the wasting away of his hard-won capital. The San Francisco *Chronicle* later explained Peter's decision in late '49 to abandon gold mining. "His thrifty nature would not allow him to be content with taking his chances in the lottery of the mines." The San Francisco *Post* said much the same thing. "He was no moth . . . but a working bee, bound to build houses and lay up stores, so it was that '49 had not slipped by when he threw away the pick . . . and proceeded to make gold by working in iron." (Thomas Prendergast put it this way in 1942—Peter was "not contented with the uncertain recompense of the gravel mines.")

Peter's cousin, Michael Hawkins, wrote that the three Donahue brothers met in San Francisco during the Gold Rush "without preconceived action." He saw their reunion as a fortuitous circumstance, a sample of God's will. "I have always had a profound gratitude to God for the distinction conferred upon my mother's sister's three sons . . . in guiding and directing them by different paths to arrive in this state of California in that memorable year for pioneers, 1849 . . . . They settled in San Francisco and began its upbuilding in that year and continued its upbuilding until they died."

What really decided Peter to chuck it all as a miner was his accidental eavesdropping on a conversation between two strangers. He recognized James in their description of another fellow. He at once butted in, saying, "That is my brother! Where is he?"

According to Hawkins, Peter was staying in a miner's cabin when he learned that James had already established himself as the proprietor of a machine shop and boiler works in San Francisco. (More than likely, at this early stage, it was just a simple blacksmith's shop.) Hawkins said that "Peter's story of finding out that James was in California, as related by him—was graphic and intensely dramatic . . . ."

But according to another story, James was still prospecting like Peter, and the miners directed the latter to a certain mining camp to find him. Peter was too late; James had gone to San Francisco, possibly in search of him. In any case, Peter Donahue shouldered his bedroll of blankets and bearskin and went to San Francisco. When he could not find James there, he tried Benicia.

In Benicia, Peter met a man who, some accounts say, had been foreman of one of the Paterson shops in which he had worked. Other stories identified the man as W.W. Niles, an old friend who had been superintendent of the Novelty Iron Works while Peter was working on the *Rimac*. Whatever the case, the fellow was now part of a gold dredge company planning to work the Sacramento River bottom. Phoenix and Company was also building three sawmills on schooners to take upriver to cut timber, saw lumber, and ship the boards downriver for sale in the "City on the Plains," Sacramento.

Phoenix and Company hired Peter for ten dollars a day, plus board. He had worked only a week on one of the mill-schooners when the 755-ton sidewheeler *Senator* (built in New York by William H. Brown in 1848) reached Sacramento. Peter was curious about the schooner-rigged steamer, of course, and went aboard to look her over. On the *Senator*, he again heard a conversation in which his brother was mentioned. Peter quit his job and headed for San Francisco again, probably in November 1849. This time his hunt for James was successful.

The happy reunion was a strange one. James was so changed that at first Peter did not recognize him. "Don't you know me?," asked the "stranger." "Yes," Peter finally said, "You are my brother, James."

James had arrived in town on or about April 24, 1849. He introduced his older brother to his friends and had him join them at their lodgings, the Revere House. This was just a two hundred-foot long shed with a double table running down the middle. Here the guests ate, then spread their blankets to sleep on the floor. Plain as it was, the place was considered to be comfortable by lodging house standards of the time.

Shortly, the two Donahues apparently moved to the Isthmus House at 54 First Street near Jessie in Happy Valley. (Just across the street they were later to establish Donahue's Union Iron and Brass Works.) The structure was built in Boston in 1849, then taken apart and shipped around the Horn in sections, in the hold of the *Oregon.* J.B. Piper, a passenger on the sidewheeler, bought the pre-fabricated building after it was erected and made it into a popular residential "hotel" (or rather, dormitory) with bunks in tiers, three high. It was also run (perhaps managed for Piper) by a Mr. Haste, according to San Francisco chroniclers T.A. Barry and B.A. Patten. Later, it became the first hostelry ('twas said) to use gas and piped water. The Donahues were not the only illustrious pioneers to put up there; the Bonanza (or Silver) Kings, Flood, Fair, Mackay and O'Brien are said to have laid their Comstock Lode plans in the Isthmus House.

By late 1849, both James and Peter Donahue were completely recovered from gold fever. Together, they watched sailing ships arrive daily in the harbor—to be abandoned to rot on the mudflats. Most were operational, needing only minor repairs. They also saw three small steamers taking shape on the Embarcadero—the *Mink, Captain Sutter* and *Gamecock.*

* * *

It is often said that Peter Donahue founded the West's first machine shop and foundry in 1849. Others state that James and Peter combined to found it. Cousin Michael Hawkins, who should have known, always insisted that James was the sole founder, and that Peter came from the mines to join the firm several months after James opened it. This appears to have been the case. The *Industries of San Francisco* (1885) was certainly correct in describing the business as modest. One would have to stretch the "courteous phraseology of pioneer days" to call the place a foundry. It was really just a smithy. But the blacksmith shop on the west side of Montgomery Street, just north of Jackson Street and across the street from the site of the later Pioneers Building, was the city's best. And, as direct ancestor of the Union Iron Works and Bethlehem Shipyard, it marked the beginning of Western industry and the pioneering of large-scale California shipbuilding.

Kimball's San Francisco Directory (1850) reinforced Hawkins's view. It listed James as the proprietor of the shop, Peter as its blacksmith. It was not till 1884, after James had been dead for twenty-two years, that the *Industries of San Francisco* gave most of the credit to his brother—"Peter Donahue founded the works, starting with but a few men and doing much of the work of the shop himself. But so well and so promptly was the work done, that the natural result followed, and the business increased so fast that he soon enlarged the plant into a machine shop and then into a foundry."

The brothers' combined capital for the blacksmith shop at the end of 1849 was only $500. Luckily, James's old friend of the overland trail, J.Y. McDuffie, was willing to lend them enough money to pay their few workers their first wages.

(According to tradition, Peter repaid McDuffie's act of kindness and faith by becoming surety for him when he had to be bonded in 1856 as U.S. Marshal. Because of the hostility of the powerful Vigilance Committee to Irish Democrats, who were lumped with the corrupt Law and Order Party that the Vigilantes opposed, it was difficult to obtain bondsmen. More than likely, however, it was James who went bond for his old friend, not Peter. And it was certainly James, rather than Peter, who involved himself as a peacemaker in an attempt to resolve the Vigilante crisis.)

The shop, near the beach of Yerba Buena Cove (before it was filled), was described variously as an adobe, a tent, and a wooden workshop. (The latter description was that of both Benjamin Lloyd's *Lights and Shades in San Francisco* (1876) and H.H. Bancroft's unpublished notes for his *Chronicles of the Builders.*) Possibly, it was a bit of all three—an adobe shell roofed with old sails and extended by wooden siding. The blast for the charcoal forge was supplied by a pair of hand-operated leather blacksmith's bellows.

Blacksmithing flourished from the start, for the Donahues were diligent workers. The *Mining and Scientific Press* looked back on October 8, 1864 and noted, "The energy and enterprise of these gentlemen, both of whom were skilful mechanics, soon built up a large business. . . . Peter Donahue brought with him to this country an already ripe experience as a foundry man and machinist in the East."

So it was that, by the spring of 1850, the brothers found their Montgomery Street quarters to be too small for the volume of business directed their way. So they bought a lot on the northeast corner of First and Mission streets. This was in the open area across Market Street that was called sarcastically, Happy Valley. After the cable cars appeared on Market Street, it would be called "South of the Slot," that is to say, across the tracks. (The site was later occupied by Peter Donahue's great Union Foundry Block and, today, by the San Francisco-Oakland Bay Bridge bus terminal.)

The brothers were careful to locate themselves on the water so that they could continue doing the ship repairs in which both were now skilled. The *Mining and Scientific Press* story on the firm described their new quarters as "a tent on the beach." (A 1935 newspaper, with poetic license, had the boys moving their anvil to a spot under a buckeye tree at Montgomery and Market.) Shortly, they added a machine shop, boiler works and a general repair shop to their smithy. Just a year later, 1851, they added a foundry because of the growing demand for castings. Before long, as the *Industries of San Francisco* pointed out, "the unpretentious machine shop was the leading iron works on the Coast."

Old-time saloonkeeper-historians Theodore A. Barry and Benjamin A. Patten recalled in 1873 that Donahue buildings occupied both sides of First Street, with the tide rolling right under the workshop on the east side of their property. "It was here that James and Peter Donahue commenced laying the foundation of the fortune which has, ever since, so generously aided all enterprise and every scheme for the advancement of public good, aside from private deeds of kindness and more 'good by stealth' than can be here recorded."

By June 14, 1851, the brothers were running advertisements in such San Francisco papers as the *Evening Picayune*—"Steam engine and boiler iron for sale at Donahue's Union Iron and Brass Foundry, corner First and Mission, Happy Valley. Castings of iron or brass, smithing, boiler making, steamboat repairing, turning and finishing, executed with dispatch. Also quartz mining machinery made to order after the most advanced plans, and everything connected with the business promptly attended to."

Both James and Peter had been wondering—and worrying—about Michael. Cousin Michael Hawkins believed that they first heard of him "near San Diego." He, too, came to California by ship, the same old *Oregon.* When the sidewheeler put into San Blas, Michael helped coal her. The chief engineer learned that he was Peter's brother and arranged passage for him to San Francisco.

The youngest brother, little-known Thomas Donahue, arrived in San Francisco in 1852. He played no major role in family activities, though he worked for James and Peter, off and on.*

When Michael arrived in town, James and Peter generously welcomed him as a full partner in their foundry and machine shop. When the three were working together, they formed an unbeatable industrial team—an expert machinist (Peter), boiler maker (James), and molder or pattern-maker (Michael). Historian H.H. Bancroft called their firm "a union of three leading artists of their craft." David Sessions (like Alfred Bates a researcher and writer for Bancroft) added, "It was an industry of the greatest public utility and had a wide-reaching effect in promoting the development of San Francisco, directly, and of the Pacific Coast, indirectly." Kevin Starr in 1979 called the Donahues' efforts "a great chapter in the

---

*Thomas Donahue was, for a time, superintendent of Peter's Omnibus Railroad, an early San Francisco streetcar line. He was a machinist living with James, circa 1860-61, on the northwest corner of Beale and Harrison Streets. He acted as assistant superintendent of the Donahues' San Francisco Gas Company in 1861, and was listed as its foreman in 1862. In 1864, he was working for Peter as a machinist on the monitor, *Camanche.* Apparently, Tom Donahue was on the move quite a bit; several times during the 1860s and '70s he dropped out of the local city directory. He may have been the streetcar conductor of that name who dwelt on Fourth Street since that individual worked for Peter's North Beach and Mission Railroad. He was probably the Tom Donahue dwelling at 68 Minna in 1868-69. In 1874-75 he gave his occupation as machinist and his address as the third floor of 426 Montgomery Street, but in the city directory of 1876, a Thomas Donahue was listed as a "capitalist" at 420 Montgomery and another Thomas Donahue (confusingly) was listed as a common laborer for the gas company.

story of San Francisco industry." But the boys' cousin Michael Hawkins, said it best. "They prospered, for it was impossible, almost, to beat a combination of such skill, energy, force and industry, when united, as these three cousins of mine represented."

The first major contract for the foundry was the making of 200-pound castings for the drive shaft of the pillar blocks ("pillow blocks" in Bancrofts's words) for the drive shaft of the small screw steamer *John S. McKim,* the first "propellor" in the West. Universally known as just the *McKim,* she probably was very familiar to James and Michael. Built in Allowaystown, New Jersey, the 376-ton iron steamship was sold to the War Department for Quartermaster Corps use in the 1846 invasion of Mexico. After her wartime service as a troopship, she was returned to private ownership. The *McKim* arrived in San Francisco on October 3, 1849 to push aside the little *Mint* and *Pioneer* on the Sacramento River run. The newspaper *Alta California* on December 27, 1850 observed, "Other steamers soon followed in the lead of the *McKim,* and scarcely-ruffled waters of her wake soon were slashed into foam by the pattering buckets of the *Senator* and other water palaces."

By this time, there were already forty-eight steamers on the Bay and its rivers, or in the coastal trade. (Amazingly, the newspaper claimed that all but eleven had been put together on San Francisco Bay.) So there was plenty of maintenance work for the Donahues. The *Alta's* reporter gave the *McKim,* rather than the more famous *Senator,* credit for transforming Sacramento River travel, reducing the five for six days' passage of schooner travel to just seven hours by steam boat. "Previous to that time [the winter of '49]," the newspaper stated, "passengers depended on wind and time, and oars and human muscle, for transit, and generally had time to get over their hurry ere they reached their destination."

William Gaylor Corlett, later Captain Corlett, was a brawling third mate for the *McKim's* Captain Brenham. The vessel's propeller was still experimental, so she was not the fastest thing afloat, but she liked to race the crack *Senator* anyhow. In February 1850, when Corlett was second mate for Captain May, the two rivals collided with a great crash while racing for the Benicia wharf. There was no real damage except to some of the paddlewheeler's officers. For Corlett boarded the *Senator* like a Barbary pirate and "disposed" of the mates with his big fists, insuring that the poky *McKim* should make Benicia first.

(Besides her Sacramento River service, the *McKim* made one voyage to Panama, but was condemned at Acapulco on her way back to San Francisco. However, she was repaired by the end of July 1853 and on the Bay again. She was finally broken up in San Francisco in 1868.)

The *McKim's* owners were willing to pay any price for repairs in the dawn of the '50s, since she was worthless in her crippled condition. The Donahues charged them $1.00 a pound for the 200-pound pillar blocks. (By 1851, castings were only twenty-five cents a pound.) However, according to Oscar Shuck's book, *Representative and Leading Men of the Pacific,* this fee actually resulted in very little profit for the foundrymen because of the high cost of labor and materials. Some accounts, like that of Lloyd's *Lights and Shades* stated that the brothers charged 50 cents a pound, and that the casting was a steady bearing, or spring bearing, not a block. Apparently it *was* a bearing rather than a block that was later salvaged as the *McKim* was wrecked, to be placed on exhibit as a kind of monument to the Donahue's founding of heavy industry in San Francisco. The *Mining and Scientific Press* mentioned in 1864 that "In the building of the Mechanics Institute on California Street may be seen the steady bearing of an ocean propellor, the first iron casting ever made on the Pacific Coast."

All three brothers worked equally hard in the plant, but Peter, who lived so much longer than James, got most of the credit. (Michael pulled out of the partnership early, and only his new hometown, Davenport, Iowa, gave him the lion's share of credit for bringing industry to the Far West. "To Michael Donahue belongs the credit of melting the first cast iron on the Pacific Coast, with a blacksmith's bellows. It was a block for holding a propellor shaft.")

A San Francisco *Herald* reporter gave an up-to-date description of the Donahue works on June 9, 1853—"A small building containing a blacksmith's forge, a small lathe, driven by hand power, and a little cupola in which the iron for making the castings was melted with the aid of a common smith's bellows." He did not notice, or he forgot to mention, the crude furnace, made of an old smokestack from a dismantled steamer. The Donahues lined it with firebrick.

In 1877, the *Post* looked back and dubbed the Donahues alchemists of a kind, with their "engine shops and foundries on Montgomery Street and Happy Valley [which] proved better than the diggins; and the three brothers had good reason to believe in the transmutation of metals. . . . They proceeded to make gold by working iron."

There was no iron ore in California and what coal there was, in Mount Diablo, was of low grade. So both were high-priced until the series of dreadful fires that swept the city in the early 1850s, particularly the blazes of May and June of 1851. These disastrous acts of arson ironically proved to be a boon to the brothers. Suddenly, scrap iron was abundant and cheap—seared stoves, warped hinges, and sheet iron shutters and fire doors, ruined safes, twisted printing presses, entire walls of prefabricated metal houses. All was salvaged from the ashen ruins of the city—to find a market at First and Mission. Iron became a drug on the market. There was so much junk available that after 1,500 tons of it was shipped away, double that amount remained on hand because of the low price offered by speculating shipowners, only a cent, or three-quarters of a cent, a pound. This sum would not even cover the cost of collecting the scrap and hauling it to an Embarcadero wharf.

The brothers bought the rusty metal at $20 a ton to melt in their cupola and to sell, when transformed into fabricated products like quartz mining machinery, for $400 a ton. Soon they were making money hand over fist. Still, it could not be called "easy money," for the three Irishmen were among the hardest workers on the Coast.

The powerful Pacific Mail Steamship Company appreciated the quality of the work done on the *McKim.* Account books (investigated in the Huntington Library by historian James Delgado) reveal that the Donahue company did a lot of work on the S.S. *Tennessee,* for example, before she was wrecked at Tennessee Cove in Marin County on March 6, 1853. On May 25 and December 15, 1851, James Donahue (not Peter) was paid $33 and $171.40 for castings. In 1852, James was paid $18.30 and $183.85 on June 8 and September 21. In 1853, on February 26, three payments were made to him as head of the foundry—$252, $62.90 and $315.40. Some of the relic machinery found by divers at Tennessee Cove in recent years is, very likely, of Donahue Foundry fabrication. The brothers were not the main contractors for just the *Tennessee.* They worked on other ships of the PMSS Company fleet, like the trusty *Oregon* which required $10.60 of castings on March 21, 1853.

The foundry's business continued to increase since local merchants were eager to patronize home industry, especially when it was distinguished by excellent work at fair prices. As Oscar Shuck noted, plow shares, wagon parts and prefabricated house fronts by the Donahues were soon in great demand. They were shortly joined by kitchen ranges, though patterns were rare and cook stoves expensive to make. In the emergency, the Donahues' collective imagination was not found wanting. An English firm had a large consignment of boiler plate with little demand for it. The Irishmen bought it and made not only good stoves of it, but good money in the bargain. They simply cut holes, to take untensils, in sheets of boiler iron and then built what amounted to small furnaces under them. The simple models proved to be excellent cooking stoves and were sold to private homes and, especially, to hotels.

The growth of industry in the West, pioneered by the Donahues, was limited to San Francisco in the '50s. Before it could spread throughout the state, its momentum was slowed by an aftereffect of the Gold Rush. The boom of 1849-1852 turned into a bust by '53. Land speculation, high wages, and rents, and the inflated prices of goods all had raised costs so high that few would gamble money on manufacturing. Most speculators preferred to wheel and deal in real estate or mines. But the Donahues shrugged off the recession. They just rolled up their sleeves a bit higher and continued to turn San Francisco into a first-rate manufacturing center.

The Donahue plant was not yet the famous Union Iron Works. In advertisements in *Parker's San Francisco Directory* for 1851-1853 it was "Donahue's Union Iron and Brass Foundry" and, indeed, Peter's billheads of 1863 still carried that name. But, more and more, in the late 1850s and 1860s, public usage shortened it, for convenience, to "Union Iron Works." The brothers themselves described it as the first iron works established in the state. They advertised its services thus: "Quartz crushing and amalgamating machinery, mill irons, and castings of every description made to order. Steamboat repairing, boiler making, turning and finished executed with dispatch. Steam engines and boilers constantly on hand and for sale."

James, Peter and Michael were determined to make the prophecy of Dr. Victor Forgeaud in San Brannan's *California Star* (1848) come true. "Our now-flourishing little town is destined, ere long, to become the manufacturing metropolis and commercial emporium of Western America." But even such hardworking young fellows as the Donahues could not make San Francisco into a Pittsburgh overnight. It was still an overgrown country town on its way to becoming a metropolis. Its heart was Montgomery Street, with only a scatter of buildings reaching as far as Pacific Street on the north and California Street to the south. Washington, Clay, and Sacramento streets were but stubs running off of Kearny Street. Only a handful of buildings had toe-holds on the hillsides around Stockton and Dupont (now Grant Avenue) streets. Other business streets, were to the east of Montgomery, the mainstem—Sansome, Battery, Clay, Sacramento, and Commercial Street which ran down to Long Wharf, the only good landing on the Embarcadero in the earliest years.

Kearny and its side streets were mainly residential in the 1850s, at least beyond Sacramento Street; and south of California Street were saharan drifts of wind-blown sand. In Happy Valley there was a small population described by Alfred Bates as "simple folk of small means and little ambition." Mission Dolores and its satellite buildings formed a distant suburb. Less remote was St. Anne's Valley, Turk Street around Mason and Taylor streets, where cottages converged along a tiny stream.

Critics bemoaned the lack of factories in the 1850s, but many "firsts" were already being claimed for the Donahues: the first quartz mill, the first iron printing press, the first steam engine, and the first *heavy* locomotive.

Some heavy locomotives had been assembled in San Francisco, but none built till the Donahues; and others had built a few lightweight locomotives previously. When word of California's admission to the Union on September 9, 1850, was brought to the port city by the *Oregon* on October 18— her guns firing loudly to alert the town—news of it was printed on a Donahue-built press. The Donahue's "first" quartz mill was probably the third actually. A wheelwright in Yuba County had earlier knocked together an amateurish steam-powered mill. It was an improvement upon the pounding of ore in mortars with pestles attached to springy tree limbs, though not much of one. In Bates's words it was "a sorry affair." In the fall of 1851, Nathan Spalding of Mokelumne Hill in the Mother Lode built the second stamp mill of record. But the irons that he bought to shoe the stamps were a set made by the Donahues; in fact, only the second set made by them.

Alfred Bates recalled the inadequacy of pre-Donahue mining machinery. All kinds of rock crushing for gold and silver ore, dry or wet, with or without amalgamation, was done with the same old equipment. This usually consisted of a wooden-sided battery of mortars pounded by shoeless stamps on wooden stems. "All these defects were remedied at the Union Iron Works," recalled Bates.

The Donahues were responsible for innovative new technology for California (and later, Nevada) mines which made the transfer from placer mining to deep, hardrock (quartz) mining easy. They introduced new amalgamating pans, compressed air drills (replacing steam-powered drills) and, particularly, powerful pumps. One of the largest pumps in the world was eventually fabricated by the Donahue plant for the Comstock Lode's Union Consolidated Mine at a price of $500,000. Doubtless, the claim of some that the Union Iron Works delivered 90 percent of Nevada's mining machinery by the 1860s was an exaggeration. But mining and milling machinery loomed large in the firm's production, even though steam engines, saw mills, threshing machines, grist mills, malt rollers, stairs, columns, railings, balconies and whole building fronts were profitable lines, as well.

Thanks to the lead of James, Peter, and Michael Donahue, such rivals as the Vulcan, Eagle, Pacific, Alta, and Sutter Iron Works soon appeared. In 1866 came the important Pacific Rolling Mill of Major William Alvord, on Potrero Point, also the Risdon Iron and Locomotive Works, and the Selby Silver Smelting and Lead Works.

The Donahues found that the Far West was developing a ravenous appetite for industrial products, particularly mining machinery. When the output of established Eastern firms was found to be unsuitable to Western conditions at the same time that it was expensive, local industries began to boom. By 1860, there were thirteen foundries and machine shops besides the pioneering Union Iron Works. They turned out $1,200,000 of material so superior in design that they revolutionized mining methods. That year of 1860, San Francisco's general manufacturing was already worth $23,500,000. It jumped to $66,000,000 in 1870, to $116,000,000 a decade later and to $165,000,000 by 1890.

By creating the first true industry in the Far West—iron founding—the Donahues proved that San Francisco could industrialize to serve the West even with no iron, poor local coal, inconvenient-as-yet waterpower, high labor and transportation costs, and relatively scanty population and limited markets. What the

Donahues did for San Francisco was to initiate its ultimately successful declaration of industrial independence from the East. They pulled off something like a miracle.

* * *

Peter Donahue may be forgiven for exaggerating a bit when he said that he and James worked so hard at smithy, boiler works, machine shop and foundry that they scarcely noticed San Francisco's phenomenal physical growth during the Gold Rush. But in 1850, Peter took a break from work—a Sunday hike with a friend, Martin Bulger. They clambered to the top of a Bush Street sandhill to get some exercise and fresh air. When they reached the summit of the great dune (about where the H.S. Cocker stationery store would later be built) Peter confessed to being astounded by the sprawl of the young city. Slowly but surely, buildings were creeping southward into the wilderness of sand and chaparral.

With his customary foresight, Peter remarked to his friend, "Bulger, this is going to be a great city at no distant day. There will have to be a gas works and water works here, and whoever has faith enough to embark on either of these enterprises will make money from them."

Shortly afterward, Peter said to James and Michael, "Give me the privilege of supplying this city with gas and I care for no other fortune." This was not quite true, perhaps, but the idea of lighting the city's streets led to even more diversification by the industrial "iron men." O'Meara was probably thinking of the Donahues' gas company when he wrote in the June 16, 1877 *Argonaut,* "By their sagacity and energy, and toil, the brothers expanded their operations into other fields, by which they amassed immense wealth and made their name honored."

Profit and public service were always inextricably entwined in the Donahues' thinking. Such was certainly the case with their San Francisco Gas Company, the first of a combination of firms that became the Pacific Gas and Electric Company in 1905. As the 1877 *Post* said of the West's first public utility, Peter's tearing up of the streets to lay gas pipe was prompted not only by profit motives but also by the "spirit of improvement and enterprise taking strong hold on the young iron founder."

Peter knew no more about gas technology than did his brothers, which was nothing. It took great courage to gamble on a pig in a poke while blindfolded. Most captains of industry would have cautioned that San Francisco in 1850 was far from ready for illumination by modern gas lamps. An "expert," Alexander Stott, predicted that the city would not be lighted by gas for another twenty-five years. The Donahues scoffed at Stott's opinion, for the fellow was a manufacturer of camphene (oil of turpentine) used, like kerosene, in lamps.

But San Francisco *was* still a small city. Even little Benicia, on Carquinez Strait, hoped to eclipse the Golden Gate city as the West's great seaport and commercial center! And business was going down, everywhere. The dullness at the iron works may have been responsible for Peter's new interest in gas.

Peter calmly discussed gas for months with his less-impulsive brother, James; and James, too, became convinced of its future. As Sessions wrote, "He took a comprehensive view of the proposed enterprise and, after he had maturely deliberated upon it, he was not less pleased than his brother with the outlook for a splendid fortune." But where James was the prime mover in the iron works, the gas company was Peter's "baby." It was he, not James, who studied the subject of gas. And it was Peter who gave Joseph G. Eastland, their old comrade (now bookkeeper at the iron works) carte blanche to do the same. Eastland was to study coal gas manufacturing; to cram on the subject as if he were reading at law. (It was too early to contemplate natural gas.) He had been hired in March of 1851 as a clerk, but soon, according to Barry and Patten, he became James Donahue's confidential secretary as well as the keeper of the books for the industrial firm. Eastland proved to be an apt pupil; he quickly became the Far West's expert on the subject of illuminating and heating gas.

In the summer of 1852, Peter went East on a shopping trip. He was in Paterson by June 15 where, short on cash, he persuaded an old New Jersey friend, Peter Taggart, to lend him $2,000 to go with the $5,000 advanced him by brother James. With recommendations from Taggart and another friend named Smiley, he was able to sign a contract with R.D. Wood & Company of Philadelphia. He paid $5,000 down for gas pipe and was allowed time in which to come up with the balance.

In July of 1852, the Donahues secured a franchise to erect a gas works, lay pipes under the streets, install street lamps and light the city for fifteen years with "brilliant" gas at 32½ cents per lamp per night, once that the current whale oil lighting contract should expire. After fifteen years, the city would have the option of buying the system. Gas was to be supplied to householders at rates that would make it to their interest to use it in preference to other forms of lighting. The Donahue brothers and the City Council would each name a man to a rate board and these two nominees would round out the board by naming a third person.

James and Peter Donahue, with Beverly C. Sanders, J. Mora Moss, John Crane, John Saunders, and Giles H. DeVoe organized a corporation on August 31, 1852, with capital usually said to total $1,000,000. (However, the usually reliable *Annals of San Francisco* [1855] gave the corporation's worth as only $450,000.) Sanders served as the first president, 1852-55; Moss was vice president and Crane was secretary. James succeeded Sanders in 1856 and remained president until his untimely death in 1862.

Long before a single lamp was lit, the gas business became profitable for James, Peter, and Michael, because of all the metal work needed for the gas plant. Difficulties were great, however, since the foundry had but one cupola, holding enough iron for only a single retort; castings had to be made one at a time and put aside until all were ready. Worse, the brothers were unable to fabricate pipe in their iron works.

Company headquarters and the gas works were located on First Street from Howard to Fremont streets. Work on the gas system began in November of 1852. In August of the following year, the first 700 tons of "enriching" coal arrived from England, at $31.95 a ton.

The Donahues brought a new place name to Happy Valley—Tar Flat. It was so named because at first waste coal tar was allowed to run over an empty area adjacent to the gas works. Soon however, the by-product was put to good use as a roofing material; some people believe that San Francisco was the first city to use hot tar, gravel, and tar paper in roofing. There were other uses for the sticky stuff. Some streets were paved with upended redwood blocks set on a base of redwood boards, with hot tar poured between the blocks as a bond and a heavy coat of the stuff laid over the top, finished off with a layer of gravel spread over the tar. It was only an experiment in the city's quest for a pavement that would be quieter than cobblestones under carriage and wagon wheels. (When, years later, streetcar tracks were removed from Second Street, many tarry old redwood blocks were dug up around Minna and Natoma streets.

(*Chronicle* columnist Millie Robbins in 1970 turned up an alternative theory on the origin of the name, Tar Flat, but it has never been accepted. She suggested that the "slurring speech" of Irish workmen in Donahue's iron and brass workmen converted "Tower Flat," so named for the Shelby shot tower [cater-corner to the gas works on the north side of Howard, from First to Beale streets] to "Tar Flat.")

Once that the pipe arrived—1,500 feet of 6-inch, 5,000 of 4-inch, and 8,500 of 3-inch—progress was fast. Since there were as yet no cobbles on most streets, the laying of the pipes by the crews went quickly.

Montgomery, Clay, Commercial streets and portions of other streets had been lit by oil by James B.M. Crooks in October of 1850. In 1851, the Common Council (City Council) hired Perry and Dexter to light the streets, but these contractors were replaced, late in that year, by Crooks. He lit the area of Battery, Kearny, Jackson and California streets, but feebly. The unimpressed *Herald*, stated that the lamps barely rendered visible the darkness. The *Alta* described the contract as being carried out in typical San Francisco style—providing insufficient fixtures that burned for too short a time and gave off too few rays of light. (All but a few of Crooks's lamp posts were destroyed in the great fire of May 1851.)

In 1853, a few experimental gas lamps were tried on Montgomery Street by a firm charging 32 cents per lamp each night, plus $60 a thousand feet for gas. This experiment served to pave the way for the efficient San Francisco Gas Company of the Donahues.

The night of February 11, 1854 was a big one as San Francisco was properly illuminated for the first time. Oscar Shuck, writing in 1875, reported that the Donahues' efforts were "crowned with complete success." He added, "The illuminating fluid was coursing through the streets in its iron cells, lighting up the city with brilliant, useful light, to the great joy of its inhabitants." The downtown area was soon "alive," starting, of course, with the gas company's office on Front Street. Next was the Oriental Hotel at Battery and Bush streets.

On the 12th, the *Alta* reported that the city's thoroughfares were lighted, between 6 and 7 p.m. by eighty-four street lamps fed by three miles of pipe from Dupont Street to the Embarcadero, and from Jackson to California streets. Private service was more extensive, of course.

The *Alta* recorded that "Some of the lamps have been lighted within two or three nights past, but last night was the first general illumination." The paper gently chided the Donahues for choosing a moonlit night in which to unveil their new-fangled technology.

> It was not a very favorable evening for the exhibition of gaslight, as its brilliancy paled somewhat beneath the rays of Luna, who exhibited a full face last evening and seemed to be enjoying a good laugh at the gaslight. Nevertheless, a cheerfulness seemed to pervade the streets that has never been among us before. In traveling over the muddy sidewalks and in wading through the street crossing, there was a light ahead which showed the pedestrian how to pick his way and seemed as a sort of guiding star through the mud. The lights burned very brilliantly and it required only a large number of them to render our streets as light as day. The good results from the introduction into the city are almost incalculable. Beside the greater accommodation, the safety of the streets and property will be very much increased, and when the streets are more generally lighted, the frequent midnight robberies and burglaries will materially decrease in number.

While excited crowds gathered around the bright street lights, (none more fascinated than the Chinese) and bands blared outside, some three hundred citizens met that night in the Oriental Hotel, at Secretary Crane's invitation, as banquet guests of the company's trustees. The Oriental was a good choice, with gas lamps on its front and side exteriors as well as in the lobby and dining room. The lamps were deliberately kept dark until the guests were ready to sit down to dinner. When they were suddenly turned on, the gaslight was welcomed with a great cheer and much applause. Joseph Eastland solemnly told the assembly that the Donahue's gas company would follow the scriptural injunction "Let your light so shine before men that they will see your good works." He suggested that the phrase *Fiat Lux* (Let There be Light) be on the company's official seal.

J. Mora Moss spoke next. He pointed out that, despite San Francisco's scandalous inflation, with coal costing from $36 to $40 a ton, manual labor from $6.00 to $7.00 a day, and interest leaping to 36 percent per annum, San Francisco's gas would cost 20 percent less than New York's, and 50 percent less than that of New Orleans.

Some practical joker then dimmed the lights, just as Mayor Cornelius K. Garrison rose to toast the festive occasion. Mr. Campbell of the *Ledger* followed the mayor's blackout with a toast of his own—"To the Ladies of San Francisco, whose eyes only can eclipse the gas!"

The *Alta* reported that "the utmost good feeling and harmony prevailed. All seemed gratified at the success of the gas company in introducing into our city their brilliant light. All present seemed to enjoy themselves, from appearances when we left. There were a few in the large party who partook of the collation who seemed to be getting into a condition in which they would find gaslight 'mighty convenient' in illuminating their paths to their respective lodgings."

The Donahues dropped the price of gas from $15 per thousand cubic feet in 1854 and 1855 to $8.00 by 1857, to $5.75 in 1870, and to only $3.00 by 1880. A half-dozen firms, like the Citizens Gas Company (1864) tried to rival the San Francisco Gas Company, but all failed. They either went under or were bought up by the Donahues, who laid more pipe to satisfy increasing demands for service.

The company, called the "Derry Reservation" because so many workers were Irish, remained a folksy, family firm for years. In 1867 the payroll for all departments was but $13,601.99. The president's salary was only $300 a month, $50 less than the secretary's. The chief engineer received $200, the assistant engineer $100. At the time, A.H. Hawkins was bookkeeper; Tom Maguire and James W. O'Kane were clerks. All were "family."

Only a few weeks after the introduction of gas light, the Majestic became the first theater to convert to the modern lighting system. In 1855 the compilers of *Annals of San Francisco,* prophesied that the whole town would be similarly lit. "It [gas] will, of course, soon become general and prove a great benefit to the city . . . . San Francisco will present an appearance equally agreeable and striking to those who recollect the dangers and troubles of traversing its old swampy paths on dark nights . . . . San Francisco can now ask for nothing more on the score of domestic comforts. The streets and houses are well-lighted by a beautiful gas light."

When Joseph Eastland returned from a visit to Tennessee in 1855, James Donahue invited him to make a choice: he could remain with the iron works, or he could pursue a new career with the gas company. Eastland chose the latter and, according to Sessions, he soon was "largely entrusted with the executive management of the business."

In January of 1856, Eastland was elected secretary of the San Francisco Gas Company. He typified the talented and loyal men trained by James and Peter to continue their enterprise after they should be gone from the scene. When Barry and Patten tried to describe the caliber of Eastland, they wrote that "James Donahue was a man who selected none but good officers. . . . To anyone acquainted with the late Mr. Donahue, this fact is as good as many elaborated pages upon the character and qualifications of Mr. Eastland who is, indeed, a gentleman of refined and cultivated tastes, aside from his thorough business capacity."

Charles L. Barrett, who became secretary of the successor firm, the San Francisco Gas and Electric Company, described Eastland in a December 1917 article in *Pacific Service Magazine.* "He came of a fine Southern family, well-educated, and fitted into the gas projects of James and Peter Donahue perfectly. An excellent replica of Napoleon I in appearance, he was in his later years—as Napoleon was said to have been—a man of surpassing and unbending dignity."

The "honeymoon" of any new public utility is likely to be a short one. The "Napoleonic" Eastland soon had to deal with complaints from the public and the press about gas prices and service. As early as July 6, 1855, a crowd gathered at Commercial and Montgomery streets to devise means of reducing rates. In November, the company's attorney, J.C. Stebbins, had to file suit against the city to recover $40,000 on its street lighting contract.

In January of 1856, the *Chronicle* protested that "Some portions of the city, thickly peopled and much traveled at night, are not lighted at all." Extension of street lighting to the Donahues' old stomping ground, Happy Valley, calmed criticism somewhat in 1856, though the service was imperfect. Common complaints were that some street lamps were not turned on, others were dim and some were on if at all only for a part of the night. Since the service was a monopoly, accusations of "extortionate" rates were soon heard. In one ploy to force rates down in '56, the city council turned off all of the street fixtures except at intersections.

However, the family-run gas company enjoyed a lot of public goodwill, too. Mothers would even bring children who were sick with the whooping cough to the gas works. There they would get a whiff of the air in the purifying room, where coal gas was passed through water and slaked lime.

Even business meetings were pleasant, open, affairs. Charles L. Barrett used to go to Sunday morning meetings with his father, William G. Barrett, who joined the company in 1860 and became cashier seven years later, and secretary in 1879. "Uncle Pete," as Donahue was called by the youngsters, used to let Charles blot his signatures on dividend checks. "I remember how he disliked the signing, and how irksome it was for him. Having been brought up a foundryman, he favored heavy physical exertion." (The lad, who went to work for the company in 1879 himself, succeeded his father as secretary in 1902. He was a director of the successor company, Pacific Gas and Electric Company, till 1934, rounding out fifty-five years of service. He also attended the April stockholders' meetings. These were held in the large assembly room of the office building at First and Natoma until 1896. The atmosphere was always friendly because the Donahues provided elaborate lunches prepared by excellent cooks. The first cook was a lady named Mrs. Maume, a friend of Peter's who lived across the way on Natoma Street. She was the mother of the company's youngest collector. Later, as the task got to be too much for her, Peter switched to catering firms, starting with the famous Maison Doree restaurant.)

At Thanksgiving, the Donahues gave turkeys to all family men in their employ, and made collections for the hospital fees of employees who were sick and financially strapped. Another health care innovation, however, proved to be abortive. The San Francisco Gas Light Mutual Aid and Benevolent Society was formed in 1877. But it was speedily bankrupted by one man! An old, old lamplighter simply refused to die, year after year. He drew biweekly sick benefits until the society's treasury starved to death.

One year, the company promised to give firecrackers, candy, and tiny flags to the kids of Tar Flat on July 3, so that they could properly celebrate Independence Day. Word spread quickly and three hundred youngsters showed up before the company could close the gates to prevent the entry of more. The company ran out of "crackers" even though President Joseph B. Crockett sent John Yablonsky uptown with a buggy for more festive explosives.

Joseph G. Eastland used to say that his being hired by James Donahue as clerk-bookkeeper of the foundry was "the turning point in my life." It certainly marked the beginning of a great career. He became a stockholder in both the gas company and the foundry. He remained as an officer of the San Francisco Gas Company (and its successor) till 1878, when he resigned in grief at the accidental death of his daughter. (In the 1860s, Eastland was the projector and part-owner of the Oakland Gas Company, also its president; his brother Van Leer Eastland was superintendent. He also became president of the Stockton Gas Company, which he rescued. Eastland was not the only Donahue disciple to spread the good word of gas—Vallejo got its gas works in 1866 when M.P. Young moved there after having learned the business with James and Peter Donahue. In his later years, Joseph G. Eastland joined Lovell White to found the Mill Valley Land Company. They developed the town of Eastland, now Mill Valley, at the base of Mount Tamalpais, just north of San Francisco. Eastland was also president of St. Luke's Hospital in the city, a director of both the Donohoe-Kelly Bank and the San Francisco Savings Union. He died in Mill Valley on November 23, 1894.)

Almost as important to the success of gas in the city as the Donahues or Eastland was William W. Beggs—son of Hugh Beggs, the Donahue boys' old boss in Paterson. Peter ran into the younger Beggs in 1852 when he visited his old New Jersey haunts during his gaspipe-buying trip. He found him able in every way as an architect, designer, and engineer. Already, young Beggs had built a gas plant in Paterson. (Gas illumination came late to the Pacific Coast; New York had gas lamps by 1823, Chicago by 1850.) The final design of San Francisco's gas works was that of Beggs. More than any individual, he, as gas engineer, ran the plant for seventeen years. Layout, construction, and operations were all his responsibilities. He had to be on call at all times, like a surgeon, so Beggs had a sleeping room at the gas works, as did the secretary and one or two other men. (Johnny Yablonsky, janitor, doubled as "chamber maid," making up the beds.)

When William Beggs died, he was succeeded by his younger brother, James, who was highly skilled in coal gas engineering, but not as brilliant, technically, as his brother, who had been extremely well grounded in engineering theory as well as practice. James served until his own death in May 1876. He was succeeded by Joseph B. Crockett, who came from the City Gas Company, the Donahues' great rival. The two firms had a rate war, 1870-73 which dropped gas rates from $4.00 to an unprofitable, impossible, $1.60. Together with the weaker Metropolitan Gas Company, the two companies consolidated and became the San Francisco Gas Light Company in 1873. (In 1896, this became the San Franciso Gas and Electric Company, after a merger with the Edison Light and Power Company. The former, in 1905, became part of PG&E—today's Pacific Gas and Electric Company.)

David P. Marshall was a typical gas company employee. He was a "fighting Quaker," a Friend who served in the Mexican War like Michael Donahue. As inspector of house gas piping from 1861 until 1893, he was "the Nemesis of scheming pipe fitters" (Barrett). During his long career, he surveyed and passed on the piping and tubing in every building entered by gas lines in San Francisco. He also supervised the lamp lighting service with a military-like organization. Such discipline was definitely necessary because the gas lamps on seven thousand standards had to be attended to before the arrival of electric arc lamps in San Francisco.

Marshall was something of a character, but very different from Eastland. He could be distinguished at a great distance by his distinctive dress. He affected a long linen duster, and a heavy shepherd's crook always hung from one arm, which he used as a cane. He was also in charge of manipulating the holder valves, and he lived with his wife in a small brick residence, connected with the valve house, between the two big gas tanks at Fifth and Howard streets.

Marshall's head lighter was J.P. Claiborne, "a fine old Rebel" just like his superior and Eastland. He succeeded Marshall as superintendent of the lamp section, and was rigidly honest and a stickler for diligent work by his men. Superintendent Charles H. Hammond, who followed Claiborne was, in Barrett's opinion, too sensitive to command the lamp crew, yet he ran the service very well. "He had the remarkable gift of an intimate acquaintance with each individual lamp in San Francisco; could give its exact location, to the foot, together with its characteristics and history, instantly upon request."

Joseph Eastland liked to say the San Francisco Gas Company was really run by just four men—Beggs, Creigh, Norton Bush, and himself. But the Donahues, especially James, were always in the immediate background. The *North Pacific Review* in 1862 put it this way—"The success which has attended that company has been, in a great degree, attributable to his [James's] energy and that *uncommon* quality which he possessed largely, common sense. A phrase often used by him was an index to his character. 'I wish to understand, myself', he would say, 'before acting in any matter.' "

After James's death in 1862, J. Mora Moss became president. He was a member of the banking firm of Pioche and Bayerque and interested in ice, water, and the Alaska Fur Company; and a regent of the University of California, as well as a director of the asylum for the deaf, blind and dumb. (He died in November, 1880. Oakland's Mosswood Park is named in his honor.) Peter Donahue, who was a trustee (1856) of the Sacramento Gas Company, served briefly as president of the San Francisco Gas Company 1866-67; and then again from 1870 to 1883—only failing health and the distractions of his railroading ventures persuaded Peter to relinquish the executive post. He remained vitally interested in the gas company and was, like James before him, its largest stockholder until his death in 1885.

Joseph Donohoe, filled in as president of the San Francisco Gas Company (1868-69) as did Eugene P. Murphy in 1884. Colonel Hawkins said that his cousin liked these two men very much. "A close social intimacy always existed between James Donahue and these two men. James let them into the gas stock soon after it commenced operating, and they found it so profitable that they never sold out, but increased their holdings."

Donohoe had come to California around 1852 as a protege of the St. Louis and New York merchant-banker, Eugene Kelly, who founded a San Francisco branch of Eugene Kelly & Company. Like his better-known colleague (another friend of James Donahue's), William C. Ralston, Donohoe prospered because, in Hawkins's recall, "Mr. Kelly was very kind in giving his tried clerks an interest in his business." Donohoe was soon known on the Coast as "The Safe Banker."

Ralston, one of the giants of Western business history and commonly called "The Man Who Built San Francisco," was, like the Donahues, of Catholic Ulster-Irish stock. He had faults. He was extravagant; his speculations were not simply bold but downright hazardous. But his weaknesses were more than compensated for by his dazzling halo of virtues. Even his vices, it was said, had a dash of liberality—from farm boy, steamboat hand, and Panama Railroad flunky, he rose to a position of power as a San Francisco banker together with Donohoe and Kelly. At the very peak of his prominence, when president of the dominant Bank of California, "he fell to rise no more." He died by drowning in the Bay, very likely a suicide. It was just after his bank collapsed and dragged down much of the city's finances with it. His tough associate, William Sharon, had to pick up the pieces.

The Donahues met Ralston when he was purser of the *Yankee Blade,* a new wooden sidewheeler that arrived from New York on May 4, 1854 to operate between San Francisco and Panama for the Independent Opposition Line. Commodore Cornelius Vanderbilt was taking on the Pacific Mail Steamship Company's monopoly on "Panama steamers." Ralston became manager of the San Francisco offices of Garrison, Fritz & Company, affiliated with the Commodore, before he went into banking.

Since the *Yankee Blade* had boiler trouble, James probably repaired it. But, at the time of Ralston's death in 1875, Peter recalled that he had worked on the vessel, too. He also remembered that Ralston had tried to personally supervise everything. This might have been annoying, had not Ralston paid double wages for speed and accuracy in their overtime work. All of the Donahues' labors went for naught. The *Yankee Blade* was jinxed; and she had a very short life, being wrecked, when southbound, on Point Arguello on October 1, 1854. The crew behaved disgracefully in what amounted to a mutinous panic, and thirty lives were lost, along with $153,000 in specie. (Ralston remained a true friend of the foundrymen-gasmen. When, later, Peter needed money, he went to his fellow Ulsterman at the Donohoe, Ralston & Company banking house. For his own part, Ralston appreciated how Peter was able to secure or adapt new industrial techniques at the iron works while remaining involved with the gas company.)

By the mid-1850s, James and Peter had added a new specialty at their Mission and First Street complex—the Union Gas Fitting Shop. They advertised in such papers as the *Daily Herald* (July 21, 1855): "Gas fittings promptly attended to by experienced workmen at low rates. All work guaranteed to prove acceptable to the Engineer of the Gas Company. Gas chandeliers and fixtures furnished . . . . J. and P. Donahue have constantly on hand a large assortment of gas pipe and fittings for sale at reduced prices. Gas fitting attended to promptly. All work guaranteed."

* * *

As the decade of the 1860s opened, James and Peter Donahue were juggling careers in iron and gas with great aplomb. The San Francisco Gas Company and its successor, the San Francisco Gas Light Company, weathered the application of electricity to street lighting in pretty good shape, taking up the slack with increased gas service for cooking and heating.

In 1876, Reverend Joseph M. Neri, S.J., of St. Ignatius College (now the University of San Francisco) exhibited electric arc lights. By 1878, the city had a few private power plants and in 1879, the year in which Thomas Edison perfected his incandescent bulb, George H. Roe's California Electric Company introduced electric arc street lighting to San Francisco, to finally end the gas lamp era pioneered by James and Peter Donahue.

IV

WEDDINGS AND WANDERINGS

DURING HIS 1852 VISIT TO PATERSON, Peter Donahue had lived at the home of Michael Hawkins's parents, commuting to New York when necessary. Peter also spent considerable time in the home of his new friend, Peter Taggart. The Hawkins and Taggart families were close friends, but another reason for Peter's presence was the charming and comely governess of the Taggart children, Mary Jane Maguire of New York.

Peter wanted to combine business with pleasure on his first return trip East, so he attended many parties and Sunday school picnics. Hawkins wrote of his cousin—"All of his life, he was a jolly good fellow." (This opinion of Peter was not universal.)

One day, Michael picked up his cousin at the railroad station after a long business day, and took him to Paterson's picnic grounds. But they arrived just as the picnickers were packing up their hampers to leave. Peter was no orator, but he stopped them with a small speech. He said that he had been busy all day in New York while they had been enjoying themselves, and that he did not want the entire day to pass without some enjoyment of their company. He invited the entire party of over two hundred persons to be his guests at an impromptu dinner and spur-of-the-moment ball at the resort called the Cottage on the Cliff. The dancing did not end till 2 a.m.

The time for Peter's departure for California approached. He had New York steamer tickets for himself and his party, dated September 5, 1852. Suddenly, out of the blue, the 30-year-old

Peter asked Mary Jane Maguire if she would sail with him as his wife. Her mother objected to such a whirlwind courtship, but the girl told her, "I love him, and I want to go with him." At this, Mama gave her consent. The marriage was celebrated on the very morning of sailing day.

Hawkins said, fifty-four years later, "I have a vivid recollection of my Cousin Peter's wedding day. . . . My services as Puck immediately came into requisition, to hunt up her lady friends to assist her in getting ready and accompanying her on the train at 7 o'clock, as the marriage was to take place in New York. They got there and found the priest and were united."

According to Hawkins, the marriage was between a "splendid specimen of manhood in height, form and figure," and "a youthful, accomplished, good and beautiful bride." (The marriage was a very happy one while it lasted. "Alas," wrote Hawkins of Mary Jane Maguire Donahue, "she gave up her life in giving birth to a child." Of the four children born to the couple, two survived—James Mervyn and Mary Ellen, called Mamie, who became a German baroness when she married Baron Henry von Schroeder.)

While the wedding was going on, Mrs. Anne Donahue Fanning (Peter's widowed 31-year-old sister), together with a woman going to California with Peter's party to join her husband, were out buying the bride's trousseau! By a seeming miracle, everybody met on the wharf in time to board the steamer for its mid-day departure.

Also in the entourage was the patriarch of the family, Peter Donahue, Sr. He was then a large man, portly, but—according to Hawkins—"a helpless old man of 75 years." (He died only a couple of years later, in 1854 or '55.)

Mary Jane's brother, Thomas G. Maguire, was also in the group. He was, supposedly, just going to San Francisco for a visit. But Tom fell in love with the city and remained there for the rest of his life, working part of the time at the gas company.*

*In 1928, at age ninety-eight and still going strong, Maguire was living with his daughter Laura, and her husband Dr. Alexander S. Keenan, a very prominent California physician and surgeon, president of the San Francisco Medical Society and a member of the city's Board of Health. Another Maguire, Susan, Laura Maguire Keenan's aunt, married Martin Murphy III, son of Martin Murphy Jr., the Califormia pioneer and patron of the Sunnyvale area.

Peter was back in Paterson on business again just six weeks after his marriage. There, he not only "expatiated" to his cousin Michael Hawkins and his family on the beautifully-dressed bride with whom he had disembarked in San Francisco, he stressed how proud all his brothers, including Thomas who was newly arrived in the city, were of her.

But at the very time Peter was seeking to consolidate the family circle, ties between the brothers loosened, though their mutual friendship was never strained. Between 1852 and 1854, James, Michael, and Peter began to dissolve their partnership in the iron works. Some sources state that James and Michael sold out as early as 1852. Since Michael did not move away from San Francisco until 1854, some assume that he did not retire from the works before then, and maybe not even until 1857. As for James, others think that he retained his interest in the works only until 1856 when he took over the presidency of the gas company, while his descendents believe that he retained his interest until his death in 1862.

It is hard to believe that James, the boiler maker, was *not* involved in the plant's manufacture of the first boilers with horizontal tubes to be made in the West (reported by the *Alta California* on June 18, 1853). And it was James, not Peter, who signed his name to an advertisement in the San Francisco *Sun* of June 22, 1853 titled "Boiler Making By Steam." (This, and similar ads, also ran in the *Prices Current and Shipping List, Daily Herald,* and *Daily California Courier* in 1853 and even 1854.)

> The undersigned [James], having recently imported and erected an improved steam riveting machine and [in] other ways increased his facilities for making boilers, is consequently enabled to materially reduce the cost of same, and respectfully invites the attention of those interested. Gang, motley, sash and circular saws, iron mills and all other descriptions of machinery, together with casings of iron and brass of every kind, made to order. Steamboat repairing, blacksmithing, turning and finishing executed with dispatch. Steam engines constantly on hand for sale. Also circular saws and a full assortment of engineers' findings.

Probably the partnership was dissolved sometime later in 1853 when the name of firm finally became officially, "Union Iron Works, Peter Donahue, Proprietor." (Eastland claimed in 1886 that he persuaded Peter to make the name change, "as being more suggestive of the scope and character of the institution. I thought there was more style to it.")

In any case, the Donahues were able to shrug off the depression of 1853; though it curtailed the demand for metal products, it also reduced rents and wages.

While the brothers were still together in the plant (which consisted of a foundry, boiler shop and finishing shop of brick, and a frame office building), they worked superbly as a team. While his health was good, James seemed to take the lead. But as it worsened, he deferred to his dynamic older brother, Peter. It is not clear if Michael, oldest of all, chafed at working in Peter's shadow. Michael was also the most restless of the brothers; perhaps his desire to leave San Francisco was just a symptom of his continuing wanderlust.

Bancroft's amanuensis, Bates, could not single out any one Donahue as being "the brains of the outfit;" to him they were a team.

> With the exception of the great railroad quartet [the Central Pacific's Big Four], there has never existed on this coast a stronger combination of business ability than was found in the Donahue brothers. Though Mr. Peter Donahue was ever the guiding spirit of the firm, it was not by the efforts of any single member but by the harmonious cooperation of all members that success has so rapidly been achieved, success that, notwithstanding the keenest rivalry, was envied by none and by all admitted to be well-deserved. While men of strong individuality of character, they worked together in perfect unison and always with a single purpose.

Bates concluded that,

> If among them there was not what the world calls genius, neither was there any weakness, and there was that which is an excellent substitute, the faculty of observation, of quick and thorough dispatch of work, and of seizing promptly and firmly the opportunities within their grasp. Thus did they lay the foundation of their fortune and build on the foundation a noble superstructure.

James Donahue's role in the pioneering of Western industry has often been discounted because of the long shadow cast by Peter, who outlived him by twenty-three years. Hawkins and Quigley both stated that it was Peter who joined James at the smithy. Eastland also considered the iron works to be James's shop initially, not Peter's; he described the younger brother as "the head of the concern." On the other hand, the gas company was Peter's idea, though it was close to James heart and he served as its president from 1856 until his death in 1862. Hawkins, who obviously liked James better than Peter, was adamant that his favorite relative, the "good and gifted James," was the true founder of industry on the Coast. He wrote of James, "He seemed to have a genius for large undertakings. His older brothers freely conceded the leadership of the business affairs to him."

Quibbling over the leadership qualities of the brothers is unproductive. Actually, as Eastland explained many years later, the Donahues mastered the difficult art of effective division of labor and sharing of responsibility. Referring to the cupola melting of iron scrap and the casting of it into quartz stamp mills, for example, he remembered that "This part of the business was principally controlled by Michael Donahue and was a very profitable part of the shop. Peter Donahue managed the lathes and looked after the men who went aboard vessels to repair the engines. James Donahue was a boiler maker, and was the head of the concern, the financier. Peter managed the sales of machinery, Michael doing the profitable part of the works, turning old iron into castings. They made money rapidly . . . . The foundry did a very profitable business in repairing steamboats and building quartz mills."

David Sessions likewise stressed the fine teamwork that distinguished Donahue ventures from the start. "The reunion of the Donahue brothers was, in all respects, a happy one. They were not only fond of one another, but they formed a remarkably strong combination for business . . . . From this point, so long as they remained together, the history of any one of the three brothers, so far as the public at large are interested, is much the same as that of them all . . . . they worked always in harmony and toward the same great ends."

* * *

In 1854 Michael Donahue left San Francisco. According to Iowa sources, he went to New York, remaining there for almost a year.

Newspapers and books of that day were full of Iowa information, promoting settlement of the state whose name, in an Indian tongue, meant "Beautiful Land." Perhaps Michael stumbled on a promotional volume like the *A Glimpse of Iowa*, (1846) with its "picturesque" description of the Davenport area of Scott County, 330 miles above St. Louis and 90 miles below Dubuque. In the 1840s it was a fashionable resort for St. Louis families. It was easy to see why—

> Ever since the earliest settlement of Iowa, this portion has been justly esteemed among the most desirable and fascinating regions of the boundless West. Being entirely free from the low bottom lands (the usual causes of diseases), it was early selected by the sagacious pioneers among the favored spots of the upper Mississippi Valley.
>
> Perhaps no country in the world presents so happy a combination of picturesque beauties, blended with excellence of soil and salubrity of climate as the vicinity. . . . All who have ever visited this charming region concur in expressing their admiration of the surpassing beauties of nature's inimitable works. . . . The country has universally attracted the attention of all travelers and has often elicited the muse of both the poet and the painter. . . . Perhaps few spots in our country present a happier combination of rare and attractive beauty. . . Whether viewed from river or bluff, it is like a beauteous picture, varied in all its lights and shades.

The unknown author of *A Glimpse of Iowa* quoted the views of an 1841 New York newspaper correspondent named Newhall, a gentleman of "extensive observation and much taste" who wrote that "The country around Rock Island is, in our opinion, the most charming that the eye ever beheld. . . . Davenport, with its extended plains, its sloping lawns and wooded bluffs, completes one of the most perfect pictures that ever delighted the eyes of man."

If Michael saw this book, he must have been particularly intrigued by one paragraph about Davenport. "Its position near the foot of the [Mississippi River] rapids will cause it to become a place of commercial importance. Waterpower, building stone, and bituminous coal are convenient, and a sufficiency of timber is to be found upon the bluffs and neighboring streams."

The only Davenport "industry" in the 1840s was blacksmithing. But the population began to grow with a migration from the East and reached perhaps 4,500 by 1851. In 1854, the *Annals of Iowa* later (1863) reported, "The streets seemed thronged with strangers" as its population reached 6,000. (By 1857 it was somewhere between 14,000 and 15,000. Although a newspaper of

'57 still spoke of New Englanders and other substantial Easterners in the migration, "with enough of Western leaven to add go-ahead energy to backbone, "many of the newcomers were the ubiquitous Irish.)

The first Irishman supposedly did not arrive in Scott County until 1847. But there were fifteen Catholic families there as early as 1839 and fifty by 1843; surely they could not have all been old French, or immigrant "Dutchmen" (Germans). In any case, there were 400 Roman Catholics tallied in all of Iowa in 1839, and 125,000 by 1875.

(In 1856, Antoine LeClaire built St. Marguerite's Church, partly for the Irish of well-named Cork Hill, where fiddlers played reels for "shindigs" and where singing sprees and gab-fests alternated with wrestling matches. The W.P.A. *Guide to Iowa* in the 1930s paid tribute to these early Irish "who could mix their fun with hard work." An interesting 1882 tribute to the presence of the sons of Erin was the nickname given to the short-lived Davenport, Iowa and Dakota Railroad. The D.I.& D. was universally called the "Davenport, Irish and Dutch.")

According to the *Davenport Daily Democrat*'s obituary (October 3, 1884) for Michael, "His great desire [circa 1854] was to own a foundry and machine shop, and carry out his ideas with reference to steam engines and other mechanics." Somehow, he learned that the pioneer LeClaire Foundry, established in 1850 by the Indian interpreter, Antoine LeClaire, and George L. Davenport, was available. The *Iowa State Atlas*, of which Michael was a patron (sponsor), stated that he first visited Davenport in 1854. He probably came to look over the foundry, which had suffered a fire in 1851. Perhaps he looked into local coal deposits, too. These had been used, as early as 1835, to stoke Mississippi riverboats, and they promised to replace water power with steam as an energy source in the area's first industries—lumber, grist and flour mills. (There was even one wind-powered mill.)

The *Annals* recalled that year of 1854 as one of the busiest and most important in Davenport's history. The foundations of the city's prosperity were laid in those twelve months. The author was only paraphrasing Franc B. Wilkie's 1858 *Davenport, Past and Present*. "The year 1854 was distinguished as a busy one.... The Foundations of her prosperity were laid deep and permanent in the industry of her inhabitants . . . the settling of the back country, the establishment of manufacturing interests, and the development of other resources."

In February of '54 the railroad from Chicago reached Rock Island, across the river from Davenport, to tie the Mississippi to the East. Shortly, to the dismay of jealous St. Louis, a bridge was thrown across to Davenport. Although the Chicago, Rock Island and Pacific rails did not reach the capital, Des Moines, until 1867, as early as that year of 1854 daily stages were clattering westward from Davenport to Iowa City and Cedar Rapids and southwest to Tipton in central Missouri.

Michael Donahue was back in Davenport in 1855, this time to stay for good. The *Daily Democrat* exclaimed, twenty-nine years later, "And a lucky day it was for the city when he decided to settle here!" After LeClaire sold him the iron works, it took him a few months to get it back in shape. He personally ran the foundry, but leased the machine shop to Townsend, Hays & Company. Before long, the iron works was the most extensive business of its kind in all of Iowa. Donahue fabricated not only such agricultural implements as harrows, rakes, breaking plows, reapers, mowers, and horse-powered threshing machines, but also steam engines, corn mills, mill gearing and other mill machinery, even (grain) elevator works. Donahue was responding nicely to the booming grain trade. Stimulated by the railroad, Davenport was becoming *the* clearing house for wheat, corn, oats and barley, with the largest elevators in the state.

Michael ran his capital up to $50,000 in 1858, when he was employing forty hands on a yearly payroll of $30,000. He used about $30,000 worth of raw materials each year and manufactured products worth some $150,000. Small wonder that the compilers of the 1882 *History of Scott County* thought so highly of Donahue. "Everything he possesses has been accumulated by his own untiring energy and he is justly entitled to the appellation of a self-made man."

In 1862, Michael bought J.E. Burnside's mill in Blue Grass Township, west of the city. It was the first steam flouring mill of the area. He had William Neal run it for him for a few years. But since it operated at a loss, Michael moved it into Davenport and renamed it the Donahue and Sterling Mill. It later became very well known as

Johnston's Mill. It was enlarged as the Excelsior Mill, but burned in 1879.

Donahue had quickly sunk roots into the rich Iowa soil. He became a member of the Davenport fire department, working with an engine company just as he had done in Cincinnati before the Mexican War. He was proud to receive his veteran fireman's "diploma" in 1866, recognizing his ten years of service.

When his Liberty Engine Company proposed to buy a steam fire engine to replace its old hand pumper, Michael subscribed $300 to the purchase fund. The company named the engine the *Michael Donahue.* (It was still in the city's possession when he died, eighteen years later, and was still capable of excellent service. But, by then, it had been unused for a decade, put out of business by Donahue's remarkable city water system.)

In Iowa, Michael married Esther Ann Alexander (born 1834)—"a wise and lovable woman" in Michael Hawkins's view—and fathered two children, Mamie (not to be confused with Peter's daughter Mary Ellen who was also called Mamie) and James Peter.*

Michael served in the Civil War, and it is likely that the Michael Donahue who soldiered as a mere private in the second Veteran Infantry of Iowa Volunteers, was the forty-four-year-old brother of James, Peter, and Thomas.

At the Civil War's end in 1865, Michael ran a good-sized ad in the front matter of James T. Harris's *Iowa State Gazeteer* for his LeClair Foundry and Machine Shop at the corner of Front and Scott streets. He described the plant as a manufacturer of separators, corn shellers, sugar mills, steam engines, mill gearing, plow castings, kettles, road scrapers, sleigh shoes, tuyeres (furnace nozzles), and made-to-order brass and iron castings, plus all kinds of house work "of the latest styles," including caps, sills and columns. He also promised to repair all kinds of machinery on short notice.

Michael was an earnest enough Democrat but, like his brothers, rather apolitical. However, when a People's Party organized in the

---

*James was born in 1862, the same year his uncle and namesake died. He attended Georgetown College in Kentucky, and married a Miss Herman ("a Kentucky lady" according to Hawkins). By 1910 he was the last surviving son of any of the Donahue "boys." He died October 8, 1938. Mamie, who also attended Georgetown College, married William Thompson, and died circa 1931. Michael's wife, Esther, outlived him by three years, dying on September 17, 1887.

spring of 1867 and chose him as its unanimous candidate for mayor of Davenport, he accepted the nomination, and was elected on April 6, 1867 by a large majority. He was reelected to a second term on April 14, 1868, but declined when he was urged to run for a third term. He said that he could no longer afford to neglect his business interests. The *Daily Democratic Chronicle* said of him, "He was as good an executive as any city ever had."

During his second term in office, the Davenport and St. Paul Railroad project came up. Michael took tight hold of it with his customary determination and energy. He subscribed $10,000 of his own money to show his faith in the railway. He and John L. Davis worked together, day and night, to canvass the city for the tax that would be necessary in order to build the road. They organized and personally attended meetings in wards and neighborhoods. They made personal appeals and public speeches. Their efforts worked remarkably well, and they created a public sentiment that resulted in an overwhelming vote in support of the railroad, which was organized in 1868.

Once that the line was under construction, Michael enlarged his machine shop to prepare for increased business. He tore down the original frame structure and erected two brick buildings, a large shop, and an office.

When the Davenport and St. Paul passed through Allen's Grove Township in 1870 on its way northward from Davenport toward the county line, it established a station named Donahue, for Michael, "shortly after the advent of the cars," in the county historians' words. A small village grew up around the station, thanks largely to Phineas Curtis, and R.C. Ruller and H.A. Stokes opened the first store. Alas, the D.&.S.P. went into receivership in 1874, but the line survived as part of the Chicago, Milwaukee and St. Paul Railroad (1880). By 1882 there were two stores, two smithies and, of course, a saloon in the village named for the oldest of the Donahue brothers.

Michael took his family on a visit to San Francisco in 1872. He took in the eighth Mechanics' Institute Industrial Fair, where he had the pleasure of seeing the propeller shaft block (or bearing) cast for the *McKim* in '49. It was on exhibit at the fair as a historic relic—of "early California civilization"—as he jokingly put it. He probably conferred with Peter at this time on his idea for a water works for his adopted home of Davenport.

The compilers of the 1882 *History of Scott County* stated that in 1870s the city of Davenport found itself unable to do anything about constructing a much-needed water supply. Though talk of a water works had been cheap for a long time, the few efforts made by individuals were abandoned. The city itself was in debt to its constitutional limit and could not take on the project; it was up to the private sector. According to Donner's *History of Davenport and Scott County*, "Hon. Michael Donahue, a former mayor of the city, stepped to the front and offered to install a water system, provided the city would give him a reasonable franchise under which to work." With Peter's financial and technical help, Michael was sure that he could construct a water works without his foundry and machine shop suffering.

The city approved Michael's Davenport Water Company franchise on December 4, 1872. He accepted it on December 5 and, by January 13, 1873, had his company organized. He sold off his San Francisco Gas Company stock in order to capitalize (with some of Peter's money) the water project. The company's entire stock, worth $10,000,000, was paying 60 to 90 cents on the dollar.

As president, Michael took complete control of all financial and mechanical details of the enterprise. He broke ground for the pump house and the pipe system, a planned twenty miles of mains and two hundred fifty hydrants which would protect the bluffs and other residential areas as well as the downtown district. On the first day of 1874, Michael started up the engines, with their 22-inch pistons and 36-inch strokes, and the (17-inch diameter, 6-foot stroke) pumps to pull water through fifteen miles of pipes laid under the streets.

Coverage of so large an area taxed the pumps feeding the mains from the distant river, so Michael made some improvements. On Ripley Street between 14th and 15th streets, he built a pumping station. It, and its 5,000,000 gallon reservoir, bolstered the supply of ready water. He then divided his system into high and low pressure mains. The new pumping station and reservoir supplied the bluffs while the original river station continued to take care of downtown. "By this system," wrote historian Harry E. Donner in 1910, fire service is given under lower pressure, with better results, and the damage to the pumps and mains is minimized."

Michael found the increase in patronage less than he had expected. He blamed it (correctly) on the turbidity of the water. (The muddy Mississippi remained the only adequate water source for Davenport, but in 1910 his son, Colonel James P. Donahue, took steps to correct the situation. To provide cleaner and purer water, James P. studied filtration devices in various cities. He did not find even one that was operating adequately. But he went ahead and invested a large sum of money to install a filter plant, which proved to be very satisfactory.)

By 1880, the system had grown to twenty-two miles of pipe, as private consumers increased in number. The city was pleased with its utility. A.H. Sanders had already reported, in 1874, that "The water is better, for all ordinary purposes, than any other which has heretofore been used here." The *Davenport Daily Democrat* chimed in, "Mr. Donahue has given Davenport the best water works possessed in the West, if not in the entire land."

Michael took water from the channel of the Mississippi, 150 feet offshore, by a conduit cut into the solid rock of the river bed. The entire system cost half a million dollars. The expense of his cofferdam alone, to secure pure water far out and away from the city's contamination, was more than the whole cost of existing water works in some comparable cities. The main pipes were fourteen inches in diameter and the farthest point of the works from the river was three miles. There had been concern that Michael's water might not make it up to the bluffs behind the city. But it did so, easily. The highest point to which water was pumped was at 175 feet altitude. There was always enough pressure there to put out any fire, or to throw a flood of hosed water on the tallest house in the locality. Michael ran tests (secret, at first), then held an official, public demonstration in which two heavy streams of water were hosed 160 feet from the hydrants. By 1882, the writers of the county history could confidently claim that "Several fires, and the speedy subduing of them, have already demonstrated that no large fire can ever threaten Davenport under our present water arrangements." Only luck had spared Davenport from serious fires until Michael Donahue built his great water system.

Donahue placed fire hydrants all over the city. They were located at almost every major corner of downtown and also extended into the outskirts. By January 1, 1883, Davenport had 240 water hydrants, and the water works had "rendered the presence of any . . . steam engines entirely unnecessary." The city's insurance rates reflected, at last, the adequacy of water in Davenport, and they had dropped dramatically by 1882. Being privately owned, the water works threw no added tax burden on the city. Davenport paid for the use of Donahue's hydrants for fire fighting as individuals paid for household water taps. And Michael's rates were quite reasonable for "water that was as crystal-pure as the brightest spring water." The anonymous county historian crowed, "No city in the West—or the country—has a better supply of water for public use nor, through its water works, better protection against conflagration."

The water works established, Michael again became just a foundryman, and so the 1880 Census described the sixty-four-year-old former Californian. His wife Ester [*sic*] was listed as 40 years of age and "keeping house." His children Mamy [*sic*] and James, aged 18 and 19, were occupied with "work at home."

The city took over the volunteers and organized a paid city fire department. Long after Michael's death, the chief kept adding men and equipment until, in 1909, he had 45 firefighters and 24 horses—"the best for the purpose that money can buy"—in seven hose companies, with 14,000 feet of hose, two hook-and-ladder companies, a modern electric alarm system, and 669 public fire hydrants at street corners, supplied by 81 miles of water mains. The year, local historians described the water system, Michael's legacy, as "one of the public utilities of which the citizens of Davenport are justly proud."

* * *

While Michael had been forging a successful life in Iowa, back in California James and Peter's iron works was going great guns. As early as September 29, 1853, the San Francisco *Evening Journal* described the booming plant as employing one hundred workmen. An odd-looking metal structure towered over the surrounding buildings. Eastland briefed a reporter: the tall tower held hoisting apparatus. He showed the newsman machinery for a quartz mill under construction for an English company—"on a scale sufficient, we judge, to reduce whole ledges of rock in a few days' time." He showed off a steam sawmill bound for Downieville in the Sierra Nevada, retorts and other articles for the gas company, and iron brackets for the Halleck, Peachy and Billings Building on Montgomery Street. "The works are carried on by steam power," wrote the journalist, "supplied by a powerful engine. A huge riveting machine is well worth inspection; the apparatus for shearing and punching are of the most modern and improved description." The correspondent concluded, "We believe the day is not far distant when steamboats intended for this coast will cease to be transported around Cape Horn and freight will no longer be paid on machinery brought from the Atlantic states."

The journalist was a good prophet. As far back as 1850, some thirty-seven steamboats had been "built" on the Bay, but they were actually Eastern vessels, only reassembled in the West. However, in April of 1853, the *Alta California* was reporting on William Hammond, expecting to finish building his unnamed-as-yet sternwheeler at Rincon Point by June 10. Powered by two 60-horsepower engines, she was the first steamboat to have all of her construction done on the Coast. Naturally, all iron work was fabricated by the Donahues. Soon, they would bring San Francisco manufacturing to a point where, in the *Evening Journal* reporter's words, "freight will no longer be paid on machinery brought from the Atlantic states." Even before the 1860s opened, Peter would be sending 15-horsepower steam engines to quartz mines, and his iron works would be gobbling up a ton and a half of coal a day and three tons of pig iron a week.

Usually tolerant San Francisco was wracked in 1856 by a sociopolitical aberration, the rise of Vigilantism. It was abetted, to some degree, by an accompanying growth of bigotry and prejudice. Nativism, or xenophobia would result in an ugly wave of anti-Chinese sentiment in later years. But it was preceded by anti-Catholic and anti-Irish feeling in 1856. When the muckraking, reckless editor of the *Evening Bulletin*, James King of William, a so-called "anti-Romanist" newspaperman, and U.S. Marshal William Richardson were shot to death by James Casey and Charles Cora, both Catholic, the old Vigilante Committee of 1851 was revived. Josiah Royce called the movement a "businessman's revolution." It was a class war, the Establishment of middle and upper class merchants versus lower class workingmen, often Irish Democrats whose party ("machine" to the vigilantes) was in Tammany Hall-like control of local government. William T. Coleman was the leader of the Vigilance Committee, and most of their targets were "Micks"—like Billy Mulligan, Yankee Sullivan, Ned McGowan.

Opponents of the Vigilance Committee were lumped into a Law and Order Party. General William T. Sherman, commanding the State Militia, and Volney Howard, next in rank, were thrown in with the city's Irish politicos, honest or crooked. Many of the Irish Democrats were friends of the Donahues, but Coleman was also a friend and a business associate. James and Peter tried to remain neutral in the struggle but they "went bond" for their old friend, J.Y. McDuffie, the new (non-vigilante) U.S. Marshal for the Northern District of California. (Three years later, on March 30, 1859 he would be praised by the *Herald*, the sole anti-Vigilance Committee paper, as having had the confidence and respect of the community. "Occupying the office during a time of unparalleled difficulty and universal commotion, he fulfilled its arduous duties with a tact, delicacy and firmness which evoked the admiration of all, and evinced the possession of executive abilities of no common order.")

Truly, the brothers were caught in the middle. H.H. Bancroft described their situation perfectly in his *Popular Tribunals.* "There were yet in the city of St. Francis certain honored and esteemed men who held the people's interest above personal impulse or party spirit, who were neither of the Vigilance Committee nor yet of the Law and Order Party, but who enjoyed the respect and confidence of both factions."

Judge Joseph B. Crockett, of Crockett and Page, attorneys (and father of a later president of the Donahues' gas company), tried to bring peace to the embattled city as a mediator, a peacemaker. He formed up a Conciliation Commission of ten men, including James Donahue (but not Peter); Henry S. Foot, former governor of Mississippi; F.W. Macondray; Captain Archibald A. Ritchie and Bailie Peyton. They met first in front of the Oriental Hotel, and took a steamer to Benicia to see the governor after speaking to Coleman, who agreed to submit to writs of habeas corpus issued by regular courts, and to stop parading his Vigilante troops in the streets. General Sherman, who went up to Benicia on the same boat as Donahue and the peacemakers, later wrote that they had won greater concessions from Coleman. "They bore a proposition to the Governor to the effect that if he would not arm the militia, they would promise that the Vigilance Committee should adjourn and submit themselves to indictment and trial for past acts."

It appeared that Crockett's commission might be able to prevent the political collision from becoming a violent conflict. Sherman described the conciliators as men "professing not to belong to the Vigilance Committee, but simply citizens anxious to prevent strife." Sherman went to Benicia for a related purpose, a showdown with General John E. Wool, who had promised his (Sherman's) militiamen arms from Benicia Arsenal to take back the city from the Vigilantes, and then had reneged on the deal. Sherman refused to have any dealings with the Vigilantes; as a soldier, he saw them as mutineers or rebels. But he believed that the governor, as a civil officer, should give them a hearing.

General Sherman introduced the committeemen to Wool and to Governor J. Neely Johnson, a Nativist or Know-Nothing of the anti-Catholic American Party. Governor Johnson was accompanied by his advisors—the Southern firebrand, Judge Davis S. Terry; the noted orator, Edward Baker; Volney Howard; and Douglass and Jones, of Palmer, Cook and Company. The governor was furious, rattling on at a terrible rate at Wool's "baseness and falsehood," as Sherman advised him that he was helpless, thanks to Wool's refusal of arms, and that Johnson had better "secure the best terms he could through the mediation of the committee of citizens." Terry and Howard violently disagreed. They swore that they would issue a call for miners to rush from the gold camps in a crusade that would sweep "the damned pork-merchants [Vigilantes] into the Bay."

The governor demanded that all communications from Crockett and Donahue, *et al*, be in writing. Crockett even had to send a written note to ask for an interview. They were finally admitted, and some say that the governor was so impolite that he did not offer them seats, keeping them standing. But according to Sherman, they were seated and allowed to explain fully the state of affairs in San Francisco. However, the arrogant governor showed his boredom (or contempt) by smoking a cigar during the entire proceedings. An impertinent Terry pretended to doze, with his hat over his eyes.

Johnson said that he would reply to the committee in writing. He drafted an answer and read it aloud. But his advisors, Terry and Howard, altered it so much that, in Sherman's words, "it amounted to nothing." Before the committeemen withdrew, the governor told them that he hoped to avoid bloodshed—but would perform the duties of his office and execute the laws of the state. If a collision should occur, he said, it would be the responsibility of those disregarding the state's authority.

Sherman withdrew and went to Wool's quarters, where he found Donahue and the others explaining the Vigilance Committee situation. He asked Wool for the letter containing his refusal to the request for arms. Bailie Peyton spoke up. "General Wool, I think that General Sherman is entitled to the written answer." Reluctantly, Wool gave Sherman the letter. He found it inconclusive, not denying his promise to arm the militia, but referring to laws and Army regulations that forbade it without War Department orders. Sherman asked him to admit that he had simply changed his mind. Wool refused. Thereupon, Sherman sat down and wrote out his resignation as General of the California State Militia. Johnson immediately appointed Volney Howard to succeed him. In his *Memoirs,* Sherman recalled, "I never afterwards had anything to do with politics in California."

The Sacramento *Union* suggested James Donahue's feelings. "The members of the committee unite in saying that they were never before so formally and discourteously received on any occasion."

After the governor's disdainful treatment of James Donahue and his colleagues, Coleman withdrew his concessions and went on the offensive. He outbluffed the governor, the Army and the Navy, and particularly Johnson's stooge in Sherman's place, Volney Howard. When the latter shipped arms for the militia, some of Coleman's Vigilante "pirates" intercepted the vessel and confiscated the weapons.

Luckily, for San Francisco, Coleman allowed the vigilance movement to wind down of its own accord. The committee disbanded after a last great parade of its 6,000 paramilitary members. The vigilantes permitted the ballot box to take on the job of reforming sinful San Francisco.

The Donahues did not let the trauma of a vigilantized city deter them from new business activities. That summer of 1856, when Peter was elected to the Society of California Pioneers (July 8), he and James were ready for an entirely new venture—shipping. The *Daily California Chronicle* of June 6, for example, carried advertisements for their 800-ton steamer *Goliah,* skippered by Captain A. Clark. Described as a fast and favorite steamship that had been thoroughly overhauled and refitted by Union Iron Works for the coastal trade, she sailed from Long Wharf for Trinidad, Humboldt Bay, and Crescent City, touching at Mendocino City first to land passengers. She carried freight, but the Donahues were proudest of their passenger service and the *Goliah's* "excellent stateroom accommodation." Prospective travelers were asked to apply for tickets on board, or to James or Peter Donahue, personally at the "Union Foundry." Michael Hawkins, writing of this venture, stated that "James, in his lifetime, was more prominent than either of his brothers. He had his steamships, the *Goliah* and *Hermann,* sailing the Pacific Ocean between San Francisco and British Columbia."

On November 4, 1856, James Donahue took a big step. He was married to Mary Ann O'Kane by Father Gallagher in Peter's home. It was Election Day. James probably voted for the Democrat, James Buchanan, who won. The couple took a long tour of the United States and Europe, although not a full *wanderjahre* as is sometime said. The *Alta California* of November 7 asked New Orleans as well as New York papers to copy its brief wedding notice, because of James's friends there from pre-Mexican War days. The marriage was blessed with four children, but only two survived, Peter J. Donahue, called "Little Peter" to distinguish him from his uncle, and Margarete who married Richard Burke of Ireland.

From mid-1856 through 1857, as Morris Dobrzensky was making the first gas meters in the West for him, President James Donahue of the San Francisco Gas Company experienced a period of great anxiety despite the happiness of his marriage. He called it "The most desperate and trying time of my life." But it was an effort, a fight, he later insisted, not a depression, a time of "gloomy apprehension." In terms of pride as well as profits, it was of the utmost importance to the Donahue brothers that they retain control of the gas company that they had founded. Naturally, they expected obstacles, opposition, perhaps even attempts to dispossess them. (Over the years, a half-dozen firms tried to compete with them, but all succumbed or were absorbed.) But now James encountered a deeply laid plan in which "a heavy combination of capitalists," not otherwise identified, plotted to oust him and his brother from control of the gas company during the annual election, and to place its management in the hands of men hand-picked by the unnamed capitalists, for their own purposes.

It proved to be a *very* close thing. David Sessions observed that "the schemes were not lacking in boldness or cunning." What made the Donahues' situation critical was an embarrassment of funds at this worst of all times because they were extending their coastal freight and passenger service by running the *Goliah* on the Sacramento River.

The *Goliah* was a two-masted, decked, wooden sidewheeler, 148 feet long, of 333 tons burden. She was built in 1848 by the famed shipwright, William H. Webb of New York, as a tug, and she often acted in that capacity in California waters even when she was a passenger and freight vessel on the "Southern Run," from San Francisco to San Diego. She towed the S.S. *Lewis* into San Francisco on New Year's Day 1853 when the latter broke down twenty-five miles off the Golden Gate. She went to the rescue of Captain Knight's *Tennessee* when that sidewheeler piled up on the rocks of Indian Cove, now Tennessee Cove, just north of the Golden Gate on March 7, 1853. She was too late to save her, but joined with the *Confidence* in bringing the passengers to San Francisco, then tried to haul the Panama steamer off with the help of the *Thomas Hunt.* She failed, and the *Tennessee* was a total loss. When the *Lewis* was wrecked on Duxbury Reef, Bolinas Bay, on April 8, 1853, only a month after and eight miles north of the Tennessee, the *Goliah* and *Active* brought the rescued passengers to San Francisco. In January of 1854, *Goliah* pulled a Pacific Mail steamer off Point Loma and later rescued survivors of the *Yankee Blade,* wrecked on Point Arguello on October 1, 1854. The *Goliah's* Captain J.Healy had sailed from San Francisco for Monterey and San Diego with passengers and freight. She just happened upon the stricken *Yankee Blade* and took off some of her passengers.

The *Goliah* was powerful for her day. Her vertical beam engine by Theophilus Secor of New York, with its four- foot two-inch cylinder diameter and eight-foot stroke, delivered 250 horsepower. She had first arrived in San Francisco on January 21, 1851 to operate as a passenger steamer on the Sacramento River under her original name and also as the *Defender.* She was rebuilt in 1854 and enlarged to 185 feet and 613 tons to run in the coastwise trade, as the *Goliah,* for J.T. Wright and the Donahues. She later reverted to her original calling and was a towboat on both San Francisco Bay and Puget Sound. She was dismantled and burned in 1899.

The California Steam Navigation Company was a monopoly (controlled by the Central Pacific "Octopus" for many years) that stifled and squeezed out all competition on the Sacramento River. Now the company "declared war" on the Donahues at the same time that the gas schemers made their attack. James and Peter were fighting for their economic lives on two fronts, and with a great shortage of "ammunition" in the shape of liquid capital. They had to come up with bonds totalling $20,000 in gold coin as the CSNC filed a suit in the U.S. District Court over an alleged injury done by the *Goliah.* "A frivolous pretext," historian Bancroft called it. As for Joseph Eastland, he said, "They did not care about the right or wrong of the case—so long as they tied up Donahue's boat."

Fortunately, the rich friendships of the Donahues, as much as their rock-solid reputations in business, paid off in their hour of need. Banker Eugene Kelly, who considered the brothers to be men of perfect reliability, furnished them with the necessary funds. In James O'Meara's flowery prose, James Donahue's "sterling reputation for integrity and great business ability brought to him the generous hand which nobly saved him and enabled him to gain the double victory." In the simpler language of Bates, Kelly's opinion of James and his brother "was of the highest, not only as to their perfect integrity, but as to their ability to perform whatever they took in hand." Kelly was pleased to be able to help them with a loan.

The Donahues won their critical twin battles and, as O'Meara remarked, it was James, rather than Peter, who had "managed the whole business" of the counterattack. Had they lost in either or both of these business skirmishes, their future careers might have been crippled or even ruined. Hugh Quigley quoted the *Post* in applauding their riverboat victory. "It was a very practical protest against monopolizing the traffic between this [city] and our sleepy capital, in the shape of an opposition line of steamers." It cannot be said that the Donahues' modest rival line (probably consisting of only the *Goliah*) whipped the giant California Steam Navigation Company, which continued to dominate the river. But their example led the way for opposition boats on the Sacramento and one direct result of their battle was the forcing of a drop in the San Francisco-Sacramento fare from $5.00 to $1.00.

As for the gas war, James Donahue remained securely in his seat as president. In his unpublished sketch for Bancroft's *Chronicles of the Builders,* Alfred Bates commented, "Fortunately it was for the San Francisco Gas Company that during the most trying period of its history it had at the head a man of Mr. Donahue's executive ability. Many were the difficulties encountered, even after the company was firmly established, and in successful operation, but through his efforts, it was placed, ere long, beyond the ordinary vicissitudes of business."

James Donahue had one very strange habit; that of forgiving his enemies. O'Meara recalled in 1877, "It was, to his praise, that, before another year had passed, the various parties whose opposition had forced him to the verge of ruin, were numbered among his strongest supporters and warmest friends, so admirably had he, in the meantime, borne himself toward them. His candidacy for the control of the gasworks was never again opposed."

James began the building up of the gas works' capacity. It rose from 70,000 cubic feet a day in 1854 to 1,000,000 in 1881, by which time the firm employed four hundred workers. After buying out rivals, some at sheriff's sales after bankruptcies, the company finally met a tartar, circa 1870, in the City Gas Company of Mother Lode and Comstock mining magnate Alvinza Hayward and his cronies, James Ben Ali Haggin (mines, cattle, grain), Lloyd Tevis (later president of Wells Fargo), and Nicholas Luning (sugar refiner.) (A portion of the old City Gas Company's Potrero District gas works survived into the 1950s as part of the PG&E's manufactured-gas back-up plant, on stand-by after the conversion to natural gas.) A ruinous rate war led to consolidation in 1873 of the two rivals, plus a smaller competitor (Metropolitan Gas Company) as the San Francisco Gas Light Company. The new firm's authorized capital was ten million dollars. Gas rates were quickly restored to $4.00 a cubic foot. On December 11, 1896, the company merged with the Edison Light and Power Company to form the San Francisco Gas and Electric Company, the direct ancestor of the PG&E. James Donahue's son, Peter J. ("Little Peter") was one of the eleven directors of the SFG&E.

In 1873, Joseph B. Crockett went to work for the new company while still in his teens. At the age of twenty-three, he became president. In 1884 he got the company to buy three bayshore blocks of Webster, Laguna and Bay Streets and in 1893 he completed a complex of three buildings, a gasometer, two tanks (one of them the largest storage container west of Chicago) and an oiler dock in what came to be called Gas House Cove. The handsome brownstone Victorian office building still stands on Webster Street, beautifully renovated in recent years. It is now a Marina landmark.

With Michael gone to Iowa, and James largely restricting his activities to the gas company because of precarious health, Peter took over, entirely, the running of the iron works towards the end of the 1850s. James's name appeared in a January 30, 1857 *Herald* advertisement that read, "[We] manufacture steam engines, saw and grist mill machinery, boilers, quartz stampers, amalgamators, etc., etc., at reduced prices [and] have now the largest and best assortment of gear and machinery patterns in the state, a list of which will be forwarded to anyone desiring it, free of cost." The ad was initialed by both James (first) and Peter.

However, when the advertisement reappeared in the September 9 issue, the "J. Donahue" was missing and the text signed only by "Peter Donahue."

One of the most interesting pre-Civil War jobs for Peter was his part in the construction of Fort Point. This massive, star-shaped brick fortress guarded the Golden Gate. It squats beneath the Golden Gate Bridge today. It was a virtual twin of Charleston harbor's Fort Sumter, whose bombardment ignited the Civil War. The San Francisco bastion, meant to repel foreign invaders, was placed on the alert, 1861-1865, by threats of Rebel commerce raiders. (A plot to outfit one, the *J.M. Chapman*, was nipped in the bud, but Fort Point's cannon never had to fire in anger, only in salutes.)

A study of U.S. Army Corps of Engineers vouchers from October 7, 1858 to March 8, 1860 by Golden Gate National Recreation Area historian James Delgado revealed that much of the iron work that one sees today is that historic fort came from the Donahue plant. Deliveries included iron castings, pipes, water conductors, grates, plates, culverts, cisterns, manhole covers, sally port doors, a colonnade and a roof. Iron castings were 7 cents a pound. An hour of a Donahue blacksmith's time cost the Army $1.00, as of 1858, but labor for turning a shaft ran to $1.50 an hour.

Although James restricted himself largely to gas company affairs to cut back on demands on his limited strength, he took part in the 1859 founding of Richard Tobin's Hibernia Savings and Loan Society. It prospered and was soon the city's largest savings bank. As Michael Hawkins said, "As soon as the Hibernia Savings and Loan Society was incorporated, he [James] became an active and prominent director of what is now [1906] known as one of the greatest savings institutions west of the Rocky Mountains. With the great number of men in his employ, he directed many depositors to the new savings bank." (James died in 1862. Peter succeeded him as a Hibernia director and served in that capacity until his own death.)

In 1854 and 1855, the Mechanics' Institute was organized in San Francisco. James was never an officer, but Peter served as a director in 1858. The organization put on a series of industrial fairs or exhibitions, modest ancestors of San Francisco's Portola Festival, Midwinter Fair and the 1915 and 1939-40 international expositions. The first, 1857, was aided by the eccentric millionaire—the "generous miser"—James Lick. A second show was held in 1858, another in 1860 and a fourth in 1864.

The Honorable J.W. Cherry opened the 1860 exhibits with an address at the industrial pavilion on September 3. In his talk, he urged men in other pursuits to "come forward and assist in the support of the mechanic, to whose exertion all classes of our society are indebted." The *Mining and Scientific Press's* first story on a Mechanics' Institute Fair was on the front page of the September 6, 1860 issue.

Among the chief and most striking objects of curiousity, those that attract the eye immediately upon entering are: The large, vertical, condensing beam engine manufactured by Messrs. Donahue and Company of the Union Iron Works, which towers above all others, standing in the center of the building, and immediately rivets the attention of the eager visitor. This engine merits a more full description than we can today devote to it. It is, without doubt, for economy of space, beauty and approximate power, superior to any ever erected upon our coast. We should judge the capacity of this engine, from our limited knowledge of mechanics, to be about 350 horsepower, although we notice all the daily papers say it is of "a thousand."

Rave reviews of Donahue's iron works were not confined to trade papers. The 1860 *San Francisco City Directory* described the plant, employing 90-150 men, as the most extensive such works in the city, covering seven full-sized water lots. The factory, of brick, was 50 by 60 feet, a four-story machine shop 40 by 80 feet. Peter's brand-new combination machine shop, blacksmith shop and boiler works measured 46 by 160 feet. "These buildings hold the best tools to be found in the state," bragged the directory.

The publication was referring to the massive Wentworth drilling and slotting machines, the compound planers, the Z. Coffin lathe that swung eight feet and, together with a pit lathe, could turn a pully twenty-two feet in diameter. There was the Nasmyth steam hammer in the center of the smithy, and the recently added larger forge furnace to handle really heavy work. Besides other lathes, planes, drills and the great riveting machine, the directory writer was impressed by the Woodward's Patent Steam Pumps that Donahue manufactured.

The appropriately named editor of the *Mining and Scientific Press*, Julius Silversmith, gave front-page space to a story and a wood engraving of the Union Iron Works on July 27, 1861. The largest building depicted on the northeastern corner of First and Mission Streets bore on its side the words "P. Donahue Iron Works." The paper gave the owner as "Peter Donahue, Esq." (There was no mention of James.) After referring to its unexampled prosperity since 1849, Silversmith wrote, "To describe the machinery and the various departments as they deserve would fill our paper." But he tried to do so, in brief, anyway. "The works contain all the latest improvements in machinery and are capable of supplying all demands for boilers, machinery and castings, no matter how large or complicated." He then described Donahue's products—steam engines, quartz mills, threshing machines, sawmills, "horse powers," gearing, grist mills, malt rollers, mill work and every description of iron castings for buildings. Also steamboat and steam engine repair, and blacksmithing. Most impressive was Donahue's own Safety Steam Pump and Fire Engine, which the technical paper found admirable for quartz mining purposes, to raise water from flooded shafts.

In the same issue, the editor ran a story, "Mammoth Castings," on the production of the largest kettle, so far, in U.S. history. Governor John G. Downey, Peter's brother-in-law, and other gentlemen watched in fascination. The 9,114- pound container, holding 1,316 gallons of liquid, was cast for Phineas Banning, the so-called "Port Admiral" of San Pedro, and his partner, Mr. Hinchman. Banning planned to use the huge kettle for boiling tallow after it had first been "tried out" or reduced by steam boilers.

For all of the flattering attention paid to his pioneering iron works by the press, Peter began to realize that it was lagging behind some of its competitors. Once that he was in sole control, he seemed to lose interest in it. Actually, his attention was straying from iron castings to the iron horse. He wanted to get into railroading. But he did not just let the business slide.

The story is told that Peter was in Sacramento, lobbying for his San Francisco street railroad when his foundry foreman quit. He had a young draftsman, Irving Murray Scott, take over in the emergency. Scott performed so well that Peter let him stay in the post. Peter was still very proud of his iron works, "the first establishment in the state," and he was delighted when young Scott infused new life into the organization before it slipped very far.

Scott was a Quaker who came to California to make a career for himself as a civil engineer. He was born on Christmas Day in Hebron Mills. At the age of seventeen he went to work in the plant of Obed Hussey, inventor of the reaping machine. After three years, he continued his training at the Murray and Hazelton Iron Works, Baltimore, where he was put in charge of the production of fire engines and stationary boilers. Scott studied drafting in his spare time and it was as his chief draftsman that Peter Donahue hired him in 1859 on the recommendation of Murray and Hazelhurst.

While Peter was visiting the Baltimore iron works in 1859, a steam fire engine designed in part by Scott caught his eye. He bought it and shipped it to San Francisco, where it was more than a novelty—it was a public sensation. But it was used only briefly because it proved to be too heavy for San Francisco's sandy streets, still unpaved. It bogged down frequently and became immobilized far from the buildings that it was trying to reach. So it was sold to the city of Marysville. After it was superseded by more modern equipment, that Yuba County town presented it to the state's Sutter's Fort Museum in Sacramento.

Irving Scott did not have to stand at his drawing board very long. He was exactly what the Union Iron Works needed, for, as historian Ruth Teiser put it, Peter preferred to initiate enterprises rather than to run them. But Peter's promotion of Scott was not enough to hold him. Shortly after he came to work for Donahue, he left and went down the street to the rival Miners Foundry, where he was made superintendent of drafting department. Scott did not like the run-down condition of the Union Iron Works, as Peter's attention drifted away to railroad matters. (Another cause of Peter's distraction, of course, was his wife's illness and her death in 1861.) To Scott, the Union Iron Works seemed to be coasting on its reputation, though it was still producing a fourth of all West Coast iron products and fully half of the San Francisco manufacture.

The Miners Foundry was now ahead of Donahue's plant in technology and in labor relations. It was almost a cooperative. Scott found that its twenty skilled workmen were full partners with the firm's owners. The latter received their dividends at a fixed rate and the balance of the year's profits was divided up among the workingmen according to their salary levels.

Although Peter advertised (in the *Alta*, August 17, 1861) his fine steam engines, from 3-inch to 50 inch in cylinder, and was boasting, "We have the largest and best assortment of gear and machinery patterns in the state," the Miners Foundry and other rivals were taking quartz mining and milling machinery business away from Union. The latter's business was turning more to steamship repair, and pipes and other equipment for the gas works.

Not that Peter ignored the mining market. The October 12, 1861 *Mining and Scientific Press* ran a story on his shipping to Mexico some $11,000-worth of steam engines, quartz batteries, and amalgamators. And on January 11, 1862, the same paper reported that William T. Coleman's quartz mills were being rapidly finished, noting that "A great demand has been occassioned since his [Peter's] great improvements have been effected."

Nevertheless, Union Iron Works was losing business—and people. Scott was the greatest loss, of course, but William Brodie also left, to establish his own works, the California Foundry, in 1861.

Peter got to work. Early in 1863, he sold a two-thirds interest in the iron works to Henry J. Booth, ex-partner in the large Marysville Foundry, and Charles S. Higgins. Booth brought in his old Yuba County partner, George W. Prescott, and things got better. They really improved when Peter persuaded Scott to return to work for him as superintendent of the firm now called, briefly, Donahue, Booth & Company.

By 1865 Peter thought that it was safe to retire from the iron business. Leaving it in good hands, he devoted his time to railroad building. He sold his last third-interest and Higgins sold out his share, too. But wisely, Peter held onto the property and when the Union Iron Works moved to larger area at Potrero Point, he erected a huge business building, the Union Foundry Block, on the old site. It was destroyed by the April 1906 fire.

Booth and Prescott rewarded the brilliant Scott, not only promoting him to general manager in 1865, in which post he remained until his death in 1903, but also giving him a full partnership with himself and Prescott. (When Booth retired in 1875, Irving's brother, Henry T. Scott, became a partner.)

The new superintendent of H.J. Booth & Company, A.C. Austin, signed an advertisement in the *North Pacific Review* that suggested the revitalization of the old Union Iron Works.

> Having added to the several departments all the recent improved tools, the above establishment is now the most extensive and complete of any on the Pacific Coast. The undersigned is prepared to finish at short notice locomotive, marine [and] stationary engines and boilers of any size and description, quartz mills, sawmills, gearing for *arrastras* [quartz mills], flour mills, pumps, hoisting gear, German barrels, amalgamators. All kinds of machinery executed with dispatch. The pattern list embraces a great variety of pulleys, bevel and spur gear, boxes, gudgeons [pivots], hangers, ornamental house fronts, railings, balconies, &c. Having a blast furnace and one of Nasmyth's ten-ton hammers, forging of all kinds speedily furnished.

The old firm responded well to Scott's leadership. He had learned every detail of hardrock mining machinery at the Miners Foundry. He brought in new tools and men, and improved machinery. He increased the work force to three hundred. By the time that it was Prescott, Scott & Company in 1875, its capacity had doubled or tripled. (The public, stubbornly, continued to call the plant the Union Iron Works and the old name was eventually restored.) The Civil War, a disaster to most of the country, proved to be a boon to San Francisco, far from any fighting. Imports of heavy industrial manufactures from the East dried up. On its own, San Francisco industry expanded and declared its independence.

Scott gambled on the Comstock Lode having an insatiable appetite for modern machinery. He was right. Even before the Civil War cut off exports to California, Eastern manufacturers began to find that they could not compete with San Francisco foundries and machine shops like Union, Vulcan, Miners, Pacific and Sutter because in Bates's words, "nowhere else were so thoroughly understood the special appliances required to meet the emergencies of deep mining." Heavier and heavier equipment was needed. One great pump for the Comstock Lode's Union Consolidated Mine was clearing 400 feet deep shafts of water at the rate of 106,000 gallons an hour. Eastern machinery simply could not meet the test. San Francisco industry was revolutionizing world mining with its new technology.

So pressing was the workload that Scott's shifts labored night and day to turn out new-fangled equipment like the Excelsior Grinder and Amalgamator, advertised in the *Mining and Scientific Press* of July 8, 1864 as "far superior to any other pan in use." Other machinery touted by the iron works included Blake's Quartz Mills and Ore Crusher, and a circular sawmill capable (in 1866) of sawing 15,000 feet of one-inch boards in twelve hours.

The same journal observed, October 1, 1864, how necessity had been the mother of industrial invention in the city.

> The peculiar necessities of our leading industry [mining] drove us into this heavy branch of manufacture at an early day and compelled us to consign the hundreds and thousands of tons of worthless machinery shipped to this city in the early days of its history once more to the grasp of old Vulcan, to be re-forged and re-formed into those more suitable shapes which our experience early taught us were the only ones which could succeed when fairly applied to practice. It was under this extraordinary stimulus that the business was first started, and it was that which gave it such an impulse that we are now able to cope successfully with any part of the world in this specialty.

Senator John Conness, in opening the Mechanics' Institute's 1864 Industrial Fair at the pavilion set up in Union Square, reiterated these points and recast them in the perspective of the Civil War. "Wild speculation and sudden haste to be rich, [and] incompetent and fraudulent stock have depressed the mining interests of our states, yet the inventive, practiced mechanic and miner have been at work in the discovery of improved applications of motive power; new processes for the savings of labor in driving tunnels and sinking shafts, in new pumps for the draining of mines, in new modes for the reduction of ores, and new processes for separating the precious metals from the obdurate matrices."

Conness explained why the Civil War did not cause depression and stagnation of industry, as expected, but had rather the reverse effect. He quoted an anonymous writer—"Iron is in such demand the producers of it command their own prices . . . and the progress of invention during the war has been steadily increasing. The fact that so many men have been called from agriculture and industrial pursuits to the direct service of their country has compelled the invention and adoption of labor saving machinery." Conness singled out threshing machines and harvesters, particularly.

The senator was amazed by what fifteen years had produced since the first San Francisco industry, the Donahue works. He predicted that, in another fifteen years, "California will be known as a manufacturing as well as an agriculture and mining state . . . . The necessities of our position, the laws of trade, and the habits and education of our people all tend to make California a manufacturing state . . . . We shall have a steady, industrious people whose wants and necessities will keep busy our foundries, machine shops and factories. An ex-workingman himself, Conness concluded, "I know what is is to give my daily toil for years in the acquisition of a mechanic's trade . . . from apprentice to foreman."

Alfred Bates spoke of the revitalized Union Iron Works. "Here, in later years, were planned and constructed some of the most powerful and costly quartz mills and mining machinery in the world . . . . For the extraction or hoisting of ores, for their crushing or amalgamation, for the separation and melting of the bullion, here have been furnished the designs and models which have since been accepted as standards throughout the Pacific Coast."

Even with day-and night-shifts, Scott's great cranes, a giant steam hammer and planes capable of handling a column 10 feet square and 25 feet long, Union Iron Works could not keep up with its orders and was compelled to forward work to Vulcan Iron Works, the Miners Foundry, Goddard and Company's Pacific Foundry and Hanscom & Company's Aetna Iron Works. This was so, even though it was claimed that 90 percent of all Nevada mining machinery still came from Donahue's plant, including the new Varney's Amalgamating Pans, turned out, like clockwork, four a day.

Irving Scott was an efficiency expert long before his time. He introduced good management techniques. There were no time clocks as yet, but he gave each man a brass check with an assigned number on it. When the man came to work, he hung it on a peg marked with a corresponding number. A glance at the bare pegs told Scott who was absent or late for work. When the men returned from lunch, they retrieved their tags. Those checks still on the pegs when the whistle blew indicated those men who were tardy.

Scott set up an apprentice system. Boys of seventeen were bound to a four-year hitch at $4.00 a week for the first year. They were making $10 when they graduated. Scott proved to be an excellent manager. His men were not only content, they were proud to be part of Union Iron Works.

The historians who wrote the volume titled *Bay of San Francisco* praised Scott for his high order of talent, his superior executive ability, and his unconquerable energy. They also lauded his "lofty sense of honor, which gave him a reputation above question. Under excellent management, the business immediately exhibited new life in every department."

The 1864-65 *City Directory* had already said as much. "It [the Union Iron Works] has steadily improved in extent and importance and has remained the foremost work of its kind in the city. In this establishment is to be found all the recent improvements and extensive machinery and appliances used in similar foundries in Eastern cities. The engines manufactured at these works have been throroughly tested and bore away the palm of superiority. In addition to steam engines for navigation purposes, the Union has, during the past year, finished a large amount of mining machinery comprising twenty-five mills averaging fifteen horsepower each." The work force, 143 hands now, was also turning out a large amount of Varney's and Wheeler & Randall amalgamating pans. Daily, no less than three tons of pig iron and two and a half tons of coal was being used to produce iron products. Ten years later, when Booth retired, five hundred men were employed in eight different crafts, making up a $250,000 yearly payroll. Each year, 4,500 tons of pig iron was consumed to manufacture large hoisting and pumping machinery not only for Nevada's Comstock but also Alaska's Treadwell Mine.

At just about the time that Peter Donahue brought Irving Scott to San Francisco, the former's reputation won him a government contract. It was to supply engines, boilers, propulsion machinery and all iron work (except anchors and cables, to come from Boston Navy Yard) for the first steamer, warship and government vessel (all rolled in one) to be built on the West Coast. The 1860 *Translations* of the California State Agriculture Society stated that Peter won the contract because a congressional investigation committee was impressed by the $150,000 inventory of Union Iron Works equipment. The *Post* in 1877 simply said that Donahue's "aptitude and reliability again attracted government attention." The vessel was a 155-foot, 508-ton, two-masted sloop-of-war. She was lightly rigged but her maintopgallant mast towered a hundred feet above her deck. She carried a fifty-man crew, a hundred tons of coal, and armament consisting of a single 32-pound Parrott pivot gun and two boat guns.

On September 16, 1858, keel blocks were laid at Mare Island's naval shipyard for the steamer. (This place was familiar for years to Donahue. Until 1868 and the huge granite block Hunters Point Drydock, the only such facility for *Goliah* and *Hermann* was Mare Island's. The Neefus and Tickenor drydock in San Francisco was not large enough, taking only small coasting vessels.) In early November, the first frames were erected and framing was completed and planking begun by mid-December. All beams were installed by year's end. Labor trouble (Mare Island calkers got only $5.25 a day to San Francisco calkers' $7.00) and February rains slowed work, but the hull was ready by March 1 and given a coat of black paint.

On March 3, 1859, the warship was launched in the Napa River before many spectators, some jammed aboard the *Wilson G. Hunt*, *Carquinez* and *Active*. The daughter of Mare Island Commandant R.B. Cunningham launched and christened the *Toucey*, named (by her father) for the Secretary of the Navy because the Navy had forgotten to name the vessel. The *Herald* reported, "Miss Cunningham performed the ceremony of Naval Baptism by breaking a bottle of wine, the generous fluid being of California vintage." The sidewheeler was almost immediately renamed the *Saginaw*, for the Michigan town.

Supposedly, the *Saginaw* was to defend San Francisco from foreign invasion and, shortly, possible raids by Confederate cruisers like the *Alabama*. But she would also be used as a tender and dispatch boat for the Navy's Asiatic Squadron in the China Seas.

Her extremely light draft permitted her to close with the small islands and to enter the shallow river mouths of the Chinese coastline.

The *Saginaw* was doubly, or trebly, experimental. The Navy was taking a chance that both the Mare Island yard and Donahue's iron works were well-enough equipped to handle such a job on the far edge of a howling wilderness. She would be a test case to determine future policy on West Coast naval shipbuilding. The *Alta* (February 21, 1862) was optimistic about the *Saginaw* and, much later, Alonzo Phelps and Alfred Bates both described her as a staunch, serviceable and seaworthy craft, a model for modern naval architecture. But she was actually a disappointment. Not for ten years would another vessel be launched at the Mare Island ways, and then she was only a tug, the *Lively.*

The problem with the *Saginaw* was that she was just too experiperimental. The Navy decided to use local wood, live oak for her beams and California bay (laurel) for her hull. (General Mariano Vallejo had reported a laurel-built Mexican vessel still in service thirty years after launching.) Tales clustered around the *Saginaw* like barnacles. One report had her hull so rotten in just a couple of years that she had to be rebuilt; another that her Donahue engines were so well-made that they were salvaged from her wreck and placed in another vessel of the same name. (Her hull was no great shakes, but she survived until 1870 and died then only because of shipwreck, not decay. As for Donahue's $72,495 worth of engines and boilers, they were, indeed, a bright spot in the *Saginaw,* though left on lonely Ocean Island when the *Otsego* salvaged anchors, chain and some copper sheathing in 1873.)

The *Herald* (September 14, 1859), describing the molds and patterns of "the enterprizing pioneer," Donahue, reported that he expected to ship the engines and boilers to Mare Island in just a few days for a trial run by December 1. This was incorrect. She was towed to Donahue's yard for installation of engines. This proved to be slow work, because it was a "first" for San Francisco. She moved back to Mare Island to be rigged and fitted with sails and her ammunition, provisions and other stores put aboard. Since Navy anchors, cables and coal had not arrived, she borrowed some from Pacific Mail for her January 7, 1860 trial run, two days after her commissioning. Her captain, James F. Schenck, was quite pleased with her. On a second trial run to Pinole, her guns were tried out.

She made seven knots under 24 pounds of steam. Captain D.B. McDougal, who succeeded Cunningham in command of Mare Island, gave command of the *Saginaw* to his son, Lt. Commander J. McDougal, planning to summer her in San Francisco and winter her at Mare Island. A shakedown cruise gave her a taste of weather, a northwest gale testing her hull and engines. Yard Engineer George Sewall said that her boilers steamed in fine style "on pure sea water." After returning to Mare Island for minor repairs, she sailed (March 5, 1860) for China, apparently under Schenck's command, not young McDougal's, and made Shanghai in sixty days.

The *Herald's* story continued. "It will repay a visitor to examine the extensive machinery of the [Donahue] workshop . . . . The whole work has been done by Mr. Donahue under the inspection of Mr. George Sewall, Chief Engineer, United States Navy, specially detailed by the Department to supervise its construction . . . . This, the first marine engine constructed on the Pacific Coast, as a specimen of the skill of California mechanism, is well worthy of more than a passing notice, indicating the facilities afforded by our machine shops and foundries as well as the ability of our manufacturers to turn out work that will favorably compare with that of older establishments in the Eastern states."

The paper described the 11-foot shaft and the two inclined oscillating condensing engines with cylinders of 39½ inch diameter and a 4-foot stroke, opposing each other at an angle of 40 degrees and operating at 26 revolutions per minute. Also the pair of 10-by-12-foot boilers of the "Martin pattern" of three-eighths to one-fourth inch iron of the best quality, with perfectly turned flanges, standing steam pressure of 50 pounds per square inch to drive the pair of 20- foot paddlewheels. "The best impression upon the mind of the spectator is the great strength and compactness of the component parts, while the eye is captivated by the symmetry of the whole and the finish bestowed upon the heavier portions of the machine . . . . There is a superabundance of strength, both in boilers and machinery."

The 1862 *City Directory,* for its part, referred to Donahue's first marine engine as "one of the most complicated and perfect pieces of machine work ever finished in this state."

The *Saginaw* returned to San Francisco in 1862 from the Orient, for Civil War duty. After a plodding cruise on the west coast of Mexico in 1869, she was a tired ship. She had to return under sail, for

Donahue's engines were finally disabled after a decade of service. She was refitted for an expedition to Midway Island, to make it into a coaling station for Pacific Mail liners. En route home, Commander Montgomery Sicard called at Kure (Ocean) Island to look for castaways but ran on the reef and wrecked the sloop. He sent his gig to Hawaii for help. The only survivor, Coxswain William Halford, won the Congressional medal of Honor for the smallboat passage. On February 8, 1871, the shipwrecked officers and men from Ocean Island reached San Francisco, to write *finis* to the *Saginaw* story.

* * *

In the year of the *Saginaw* (1859), Peter's son, James Mervyn Donahue, was born, on April 30. Exactly a month earlier, the *Herald* predicted a successful incumbency for James' old pal J.Y. McDuffie, as Superintendent of Indian Affairs in California. The paper recalled his difficult days as U.S. Marshall in Vigilante San Francisco and commented, "A better or more judicious appointment could not have been made.... McDuffie will do as much honor to his new situation as he reflected upon his last."

That year of 1859 was also the one in which Peter Donahue's love affair with railroading began—in very modest fashion, via a San Francisco streetcar line. As early as 1852, there was a horse-drawn omnibus line in the city; by 1855 there were three.

The Market Street Railroad was organized in 1857, but actual grading and spiking of rails did not start till 1859. Service began on Independence Day 1860, the very day that the last spike was driven, with half-hour runs up Market Street from its foot to Mission Dolores via Hayes Valley (or Hayes Park) resorts, The Willows and Hayes Pavilion. The railroad's president was, naturally, real estate developer Thomas Hayes. Directors included Peter Donahue, H.A. Cobb (who would be Peter's State Militia C.O. during the Civil War) and Frank McCoppin, supervisor and future mayor (1867).

The company's charter provided for mule- or horse-powered vehicles, but the sandhills and morasses called streets only out of courtesy, or optimism, proved to be too much for the animals and the State Legislature was successfully petitioned to amend the charter to permit steam traction. The *San Francisco City Directory* extolled the speed of the steam cars, awkward-looking steam dummies towing one or two coaches from Fremont to Valencia Street, "a celerity exceeding even California experience." It also admired the cars' "Aladdin-like" effect on property; they transformed an area of scattered gardens into suburbs—"villages and embryo cities where rural loveliness is found combined with the luxuries and conveniences of a great commercial emporium."

All of the line's rolling stock and other equipment (save rails; there was, as yet, no rolling mill on the Coast) was made locally and some of it, probably, at Union Iron Works.

The *City Directory* crowed that the Market Street road was an enterprise of "considerable importance to the future growth and prosperity of San Francisco," but, at first, it did not pay. Despite a loan of $100,000 from Pioche, Bayerque & Company, it went into receivership and, after foreclosure, was sold for its debts to Peter Donahue's San Francisco and San Jose Railroad. When Donahue and his partners sold the railroad to the Central Pacific, they "threw in" the street railway for good measure.

In 1860, Peter Donahue began his own street railway, the first crosstown transportation in San Francisco. One line ran from Third and Townsend streets to Union and Powell streets, to connect South Park with the future "Little Italy"—North Beach. A second line ran South of Market, from Montgomery and Washington streets out Howard to Mission Dolores. Peter organized the Omnibus Railroad, with Michael Skelly as superintendent, as the successor to the Yellow Line of 1852. It was often called "the Skelly Line" for its energetic, omnipresent, supervisor.

The Omnibus Railroad Bill, which granted Peter a twenty-five-year franchise, with the city having the option to buy him out in fifteen years, was approved on April 17, 1861—and almost made labor history. John T. Doyle, an attorney later famous (1875-76) for securing the Pious Fund, got a clause inserted into the bill enfranchising Donahue's line. It would limit work to an eight-hour day. The bill passed, but Doyle's proviso was deleted. Skelly, with Peter's youngest brother, Thomas, and John Gardner, got down to work. They opened the line in October 1862.

Peter had to post a bond of $30,000 to guarantee fulfilment of the contract and he divided $1,000,000 of capital into one hundred shares. He was president, W.A. Piper his vice president, and John

A. McGlynn was secretary. Skelly served as both treasurer and superintendent. Directors were Peter (but not Thomas or James) Donahue, Piper, Gardner, A.H. Houston, and S.P. Bowman. The Omnibus Railroad's first office was on the northeast corner of Montgomery and Market streets.

Peter had persuaded the legislature to let him lay rails but, to overcome local opposition, he had to take in a large number of property owners and other prominent citizens and to accept modification of his plans. (For instance, his Montgomery Street route was moved to Sansome until he could, later, convince a majority of property owners on Montgomery to change their minds.)

The 1863-64 *City Directory* bragged that if the Omnibus Railroad's rails were reduced to a single track it would stretch for almost eleven miles. Some twenty-four horse-drawn cars were constantly running, with eight more in reserve. The company employed 90 men and 140 horses. Its office was now at 721 Howard Street near Third, and a large depot was located there, under Union Hall. Donahue in 1863 was busy building a great two-story brick stable, 157-by-160 feet, on Mission Street. The structure ran all the way back to Clementina Street. That year, Peter was still president, but Eugene Casserly, later a U.S. Senator, was his vice president, and powerful, cunning William Sharon his treasurer. James O'Neil was secretary.

Most workers were flattered when Peter Donahue paid attention to them. But one strong, dependable fellow was deaf to the boss's advice. His job was to inspect all rail connections and, during the rainy season of winter, to sand the tracks on steep Washington Street from Kearny to Stockton. He performed his tasks so well that Peter offered him a job in the car barn with higher pay. His answer was, "Just leave me alone, Mr. Donahue. I'm doing all right here, and this job suits me." He continued to patrol the tracks for years and when he died he left, besides a hefty bank account and some parcels of choice city property, a block of Omnibus stock.

After 1867, the "dummies" (or steam cars) were discarded and horse cars were substituted. There was considerable opposition to Peter Donahue now. Supposedly safety-conscious citizens feared that he would run cars of his San Francisco and San Jose Railroad right through the downtown portion of the city to North Beach, using his Omnibus right-of-way. Their apprehensions peaked in the

1870s when, on a few occasions, he ran his San Jose trains north from the terminal to Market Street and the new (1875) Palace Hotel site, each locomotive preceded by a man on horseback ringing a bell, waving a flag, and shouting "Look out for the train!"

President in 1860, Peter was still at the reins of his horse car line in 1880. It was a flourishing corporation and still going in 1885 when he died, but he sold out his interest by then, as his health declined and he concentrated his attention and energy on North Bay railroading. The Omnibus Railroad was later acquired by the Market Street Railway Company, the direct ancestor of today's "Muni"—the Municipal Railway.

V

CIVIL WAR DAYS

THE NEW DECADE of the 1860s brought many emotional setbacks to the would-be railroad magnate, Peter Donahue. First, his wife fell ill and then died in 1861. That same year, his brother James withdrew from all business affairs as his health began to fail. And, finally, there was the Civil War. Peter took his patriotism seriously; he involved himself both indirectly and directly in the war. He not only sustained the Union's far-flung frontier by plowing his profits back into increased industrialization of California, he took a prominent role in supporting the U.S. Sanitary Commission, the Civil War ancestor of the American Red Cross.

When Copperheads (Southern sympathizers) tried to subvert San Francisco, he helped organize a mass meeting of Unionists, appropriately on Washington's Birthday, February 22, 1861. Although he always refused political office, Peter consented to an appointment by Governor H.H. Haight as a lieutenant colonel on the staff of Major General H.A. Cobb, commanding the state's militia or National Guard. For the rest of his life, Peter was called "Colonel Donahue." During 1863-64 he was also involved in defense contract work. His successful powering of the *Saginaw* led to his being chosen by the Navy to assemble a monitor, the *Camanche,* for San Francisco defense.

During the war years, Peter also involved himself in the search for California coal, an ingredient as necessary for the future of California railroading as for its industrialization. The March 28, 1862 Marysville *Daily Appeal* copied an item, "Coal in San

Joaquin," from Stockton's *San Joaquin Republican.* Peter had purchased a large interest in the San Francisco Coal Mining Company in Corral Hollow, near the vein first opened by coal prospectors Carroll and Wright a few years before. The paper advised its readers that the company had struck "a solid vein of coal in the mountain, seven feet thick. During the coming summer, it is anticipated a large quantity of the mineral will be taken out." Alas, Mount Diablo coal proved to be of poor quality.

In the early 1860s, James Donahue devoted most of what was left of his flagging energy to the gas company. He did manage to continue his old interest in shipping also, becoming the proud half-owner of the big steamer *Hermann.* She was as large in size as his *Goliah* was modest—the *Hermann* was a 1,734-ton, three-decked sidewheeler some 234 feet long, with three masts. Built by Westervelt and Mackay in New York as a transatlantic liner, she was always a slow sailer but beautifully equipped and furnished. Her two side-lever engines by Peter Donahue's old Novelty Works delivered 434 horsepower. She cost $410,000. After a career on the New York-Bremen run, she came to San Francisco on November 27, 1857, supposedly as part of Commodore Cornelius Vanderbilt's new mail line (called both the Merchants and Miners Line and the Nicaragua Mail Line) to bring passengers up from Nicaragua to San Francisco. She was replaced by the *Pacific,* and in February or March of 1858, she was sold, for only $40,000, to J.T. Wright who, presumably with silent partners James and Peter Donahue, also operated the *Goliah.*

The *Hermann* made a trip up the coast to the Pacific Northwest, then was apparently bought from James Donahue, *et al,* by the powerful Pacific Mail Steamship Company and turned over to Vanderbilt as part of a truce. The commodore then began a joint, rather than a rival, San Francisco-to-Panama service, using the *Hermann,* 1860-65. On August 14, 1866, she was auctioned off by Vanderbilt to T.J.L. Smiley for $17,000 and he sold her back to the Pacific Mail for use as a back-up steamer in the Orient. She sailed from San Francisco to Yokohama on March 1, 1867. On February 13, 1869, en route from Yokohama to the Straits of Sangar, James Donahue's old treasure was wrecked on Point Kwatzu with a terrible (330) loss of lives.

James Donahue began in 1861 what would long remain his "monument" in San Francisco—the Occidental Hotel. When completed in 1864, it was the largest structure in the city, probably in the Far West. It was San Francisco's first truly *grand* hotel and remained *the* grandest for eleven years until the Palace Hotel opened in 1875.

By the summer of 1862, James found that his vitality was nearly gone although, as the *North Pacific Review* stated that fall, "He was in the very prime of his years and usefulness and many throughout the state who had sustained relations with him were not even aware that he had been taken ill."

O'Meara recalled in 1877, "His usually genial face sometimes bore traces of the acuteness of the agony he endured. But, generally, with his strong will and unflinching resolution not to succumb to it, he represssed all outward signs and would seem as cheerful in his sedate and subdued way as though he and pain were strangers."

Just as he had once forsaken the North for the Gulf in the 1840s, James now had to abandon foggy and cool San Francisco for a warmer clime, though not a distant one. He took up his residence in his country seat, Laurel Wood, a 607-acre "farm" (estate) on the left bank of the Guadalupe River just north of the town of Santa Clara. It lay west of the Alviso Road and north of Peter's San Francisco and San Jose railroad bed and today's Agnews State Hospital. It was an idyllic place, named for the spicy California laurel trees (also known as bay or pepperwood) which gave nearby Mission Santa Clara its nickname, the Laurelwood Mission. He was now completely broken in health, but he hoped to be able to gain a few extra years by means of doctor's care and total rest in the pleasant environment of the Peninsula.

It was not to be. On a bright Sunday, August 17, 1862, James Donahue, surrounded by family and friends, died at Laurel Wood. He was only thirty-eight years of age. According to the *North Pacific Review*, "He was perfectly cool under the most trying circumstances, his courage lasting to the latest moment of his life. When informed on the last day that his end was near, though he had, up to that time, been given constant hope of recovery, he bade his family farewell with perfect calmness and dictated a codicil to his will, then signed it with a steady hand. He was resigned to the will of his Father and gave up his life 'in the comfort of a reasonable, religious and holy hope' of a blessed hereafter. Praying with almost his last breath and then repeating the words 'Gently, gently, gently . . .', he passed away."

There was a curious, almost unique, explosion of grief at James Donahue's passing. Michael Hawkins recalled that James was "loved and mourned by the rich and poor of this city, as a public loss," and he wrote Michael Donahue's son, James Peter many years later that James "was loved, honored and respected by all classes in our own and surrounding cities and sincerely mourned in death."

In its very first issue (October 1862) the *North Pacific Review* ran his portrait and stated that "His death created a decided sensation throughout the city, when the painful intelligence was made known." The *Alta* stressed the city-wide sadness resulting from his death. "There is a mournful satisfaction in paying tribute of respect to the character and memory of James Donahue. The public sense of the loss sustained by San Francisco by this event is sufficiently attested by the manifestation of sorrow seen on every side . . . . His death is a public calamity."

O'Meara, fifteen years after his death, remembered that "The most tender and most solemn demonstration of the general grief were observed here and elsewhere in the state."

The coffin, richly ornamented with silver and covered with garlands and immortelles, arrived from Alviso at the Vallejo Street Wharf aboard the steamer *Sophie McLane* at 10.30 a.m. on August 18. The *McLane* was a half-hour late, delaying a funeral procession and the grand requiem mass at St. Mary's Cathedral.

Members of the Society of California Pioneers, of which James was an active and honored member (and former vice president), adopted resolutions of condolence at Pioneers Hall, across the street from James's original smithy on Montgomery Street. The Pioneers led the escort of the hearse on its way. They were followed by the pall bearers, walking on each side of the casket. These men formed a who's who of Californians—businessmen like H.F. Teschemacher and J. Mora Moss, Governor H.H. Haight, banker William C. Ralston, pioneer Martin Murphy; politicians like Phil Roach, and even the slippery Christopher Buckley, later famous (in-famous) as the Blind Boss of San Francisco.

Friends of the family followed the remains. Then came a line of 145 carriages extending for many blocks, besides a long procession of people on foot. Moving along Sansome to California, they climbed the steep hill of California to (Old) St. Mary's at Dupont Street. It was one of the largest and most imposing funeral "pageants" that San Francisco would ever see. And yet the *Alta* noted that it was perfectly unostentatious. (The quiet and unassuming James would have approved.) Just above the Montgomery Street junction, the Sisters of Charity and one hundred orphan girls, wearing black mourning bands on their straw hats, joined the procession. The presence of the girls, who filled the pews on the wall of the cathedral's last aisle, was symbolic of James's concern for the poor and the orphaned. He was the Catholic orphanage's great benefactor.

A mass of people filled California Street from Montgomery to Dupont. The crowd fronting the cathedral opened up briefly to let the casket, mourners and friends pass inside. They were met at the door by clergymen, who preceded them up the aisle to the altar. Galleries, pews and aisles were jammed with an audience whose faces, newspapermen noticed, "wore expressions of deep and sincere sorrow."

The Most Reverend Archbishop Joseph Sadoc Alemany officiated at a solemn Pontifical High Mass, assisted by many priests, acolytes, seminarians and "canonicals" (i.e. canons). The *Alta* thought that the pomp and ceremony were quite striking and that the vocalists of the grand requiem were most effective. The paper called the eulogy "a merited panygeric . . . . None who knew the man when living could say that the portraiture drawn by the pastor was not a truthful one."

After the conclusion of the services, thousands passed the bier for a last look at James Donahue. His countenance in death was greatly emaciated, but the *Alta* stated, morbidly if piously, that "a placid smile of apparent resignation to the Divine Will rested upon the expressive features."

The *Alta* concluded, "And thus another good man has gone from amongst us. The lines of the poet, applicable only to the good, may be appropriately quoted here. 'None but the ashes of the just smell sweet and blossom in the dust.' "

James was buried in the Donahue family vault at Lone Mountain. Because he knew that his brother wished to be remembered as a skilled mechanic, not as a capitalist, Peter placed a monument to James on the vault. It represented his useful life in the mechanical arts, commerce, and industries of California.

Eulogies of James Donahue were many and extended over years

of time. They varied from Bancroft's brief comments that James left a name respected by the entire community, to the fulsom praise of Barry and Patten. In their book, *Men and Memories of Early San Francisco,* they described their old friend from the vantage point of 1873 as one of the most practical, yet useful, citizens ever to live in the city. He was, they said, a man whose once-great energies were always devoted to some object that ultimately would result in public improvement or the bettering of the welfare of his fellow citizens. "His sagacity and foresight are proven by the eventuating of his undertakings," they wrote. "Having once conceived an enterprise, it was viewed on every side in the searching light of his strong, practical sense, and when determined upon, was persistently pursued to sure success. His worldly wisdom was equalled by his modesty and charity; and we may truly say that, among all the men whom we remember during the almost quarter of a century of our life in San Francisco, we recall not one more moral, useful and upright citizen than the late James Donahue."

The *Alta,* at the very hour of James's funeral, paid an equally sincere tribute to him.

Mr. Donahue was in many respects a remarkable man. For the fortune accumulated by him he was indebted to no successful speculation, but to his unaided energy, industry, sound judgment and integrity—qualities worthy of praise and imitation by all. He was a man of great force of character and strength of will. No difficulties or obstacles in his path deterred him from the execution of any plan deliberately formed and [to] the execution of which he had directed his energies.

His judgment was eminently sound and while his mind was fertile of great projects, and his conceptions were on a larger scale than those of ordinary men, they were always practical in high degree and in their executions nothing was left unfinished. His unassuming modesty and his natural frankness and artlessness of character and his kindly and generous impulses are best appreciated by those who knew him most intimately. Though unostentatious in his charities, his public spirit and liberality are known to all. The results of his energy and enterprise are indelibly stamped upon this city of his adoption and it seems a mysterious providence which removes a man in the very prime of early manhood, with some of his great plans and projects but half-finished, and others not even begun. In all the relations of life, he was an example, especially worthy of imitation by the young. His death is a public calamity. . . . Peace to his ashes, honor to his memory.

The *North Pacific Review* of October 1862 quoted others who saw James as a model for youth to emulate.

He was an example especially worthy of imitation by young men . . . . Mr. Donahue was noted for the politeness with which he was accustomed to treat those with whom he came into contact. The laborer looking for a job was not turned away coldly, but spoken to with kindness and sympathy. He was a firm believer in the Christian religion and followed its injunctions as to charity. The orphans were especially the objects of his care, and at his death he did not forget them. [James bequeathed to both Roman Catholic and Protestant orphan asylums in San Francisco, and also the asylum for boys, St. Vincent's of San Rafael, the usufruct of $5,000 of San Francisco Gas Company stock for a period of 20 years.] With only a limited education, and ill health to contend against, relying upon himself he succeeded in acquiring a very large fortune and, at the same time, the respect and confidence of his fellow-citizens.

Mr. Donahue was remarkable for his energy, industry and integrity, no less than for those traits which, springing from the most generous emotions of the heart, lead to those acts of charity and benevolence which redeem our common nature from the reproach under which it too often labors.

Than James Donahue none was more enterprising. He was a man of great force of character and strength of will and it was to these qualities, combined with a sound judgment and unimpeachable integrity, that he was indebted for the large fortune which he subsequently amassed. Obstacles served only as incentives to further exertion. Difficulties, instead of discouraging, were his stepping stones to success.

The conceptions of James Donahue were usually on a scale more extensive than is attempted by ordinary men, but they were always identified with the practical, and in their execution nothing was left unfinished.

A chief charm of his character was his unassuming modesty, a natural frankness, and the utter absence of all guile or deceit. His public spirit and liberality were the material offspring of these lofty and ennobling qualities."

A committee of the pioneer association, including President Phil Roach, drafted resolutions praising James Donahue for his blameless character, his life of unquestioned probity, his "simple and childlike honesty," and the patience and industry with which he advocated and inaugurated programs for the social and material advancement of his adopted city. "The record he leaves behind him is the most enduring guarantee of his remembrance in the future.

As a business man he was honest and above reproach; in social virtues pre-eminent; as a Christian, consistent; as an open-handed almoner to all true charities, without a superior. In losing him, we lose one of the noble illustrators of history and development of our new state."

After the adoption of the resolutions, Roach, an old personal friend, delivered an eloquent and touching testimonial of his own, dwelling again on James's noble traits of character.

At the San Francisco County Nomination Convention of the Union Democratic Party, beleaguered during the Civil War because to many "Democrat" was tantamount to Secessionist, another old friend, Senator Eugene Casserly eulogized James Donahue; the August 19, 1862 *Bulletin* carried some of of his words. Casserly moved the adjournment of the session in Donahue's memory,

> "that some small expression of feeling might be shown for one of our most useful, prominent, and respected citizens . . . . It is due to the man that his death pass not unnoticed, a man who had risen by all the steps of the ladder from the lowest to the highest ground . . . . Step by step he rose, a man to make his mark, wherever situated, unaided by accident, family or patron, by the aid only of his good right hand, honest purpose and unswerving manhood . . . . James Donahue was as fine a specimen of what the American workingman should be as could well be found . . . . Sorrow and sympathy, respect and grateful recollection have been evoked by his death such as the decease of no king, no prime minister, no noble, could have done.

Casserly's motion was seconded and endorsed by a Mr. Papy, who described James as not only a quiet, almost secret, philanthropist ("his death depriving a large portion of the poor of this country of their best benefactor"), but also a staunch party man—"a sincere and unswerving Democrat, always ready with his means and energy to assist the Democracy."

Although Bancroft had little to say of James in his history volumes, his amanuensis, David R. Sessions, became impressed by the man when called upon (circa 1886) to work up a biographical sketch, never published, for possible inclusion in Bancroft's *Chronicles of the Builders.* He made it clear that his subject was a brave man who suffered, without complaining, from "a powerful and painful disease [TB?]" since boyhood, as well as a restless man who was particularly happy when he was busy with big projects. With his constant pains, his slight frame, his frail system, it seemed to Sessions that "his vitality depended solely upon an inflexible will."

James's manner of living was moderate, half-way between asceticism and excess. On account of his delicate health, he had to deny himself some of the normal diversions of life, but he always enjoyed seeing others enjoying themselves. And though never free of pain, he repressed all symptoms of his physical distress and tried to appear at ease, so that he would not mar the pleasure of others. Because he did not hoard his funds, James was generous to charities. This philanthropy, just like his illness, he kept to himself. Few were ever aware of it.

Sessions continued, "His career was one not only of distinguished personal success in great undertakings, it was also one of general and particular usefulness. The forms in which his achievements appeared were not mere certificates of his own riches." Thus, while other wealthy men were sojourning in California to make their pile—counting their gold pieces prior to running away to "the States"—James was setting roots in the city whose dark streets he planned to light. Naturally, the get-rich-quick (and get out) gentry considered the gas works to be a harebrained project of a pair of mad Irishmen, on a par with James's "oversize" hotel, the Occidental. His bold gambles were "wild ventures" to them.

Sessions quoted the *Alta* obituary of fourteen years before. "The results of his energy and enterprise are indelibly stamped upon this city of his adoption." But then he added words of praise that were his own. "His wealth he had acquired by superior natural capabilities, rare industry and indefatigable labor. He had to make his way among men, alone, when most boys of this age lean upon father and mother. Each step he took upward was by mastering the way, himself. Labor, if not a native aptitude with him, became essential to his existence. . . . The character of his mind also was such that his energy was well-directed. . . . His works all point to the fact that he knew fairly well what San Francisco would be. . . . He demonstrated his ability to look years ahead, regardless of popular prejudice."

David Sessions considered the factors in Donahue's success, noting that, in just thirteen years, James accomplished for himself and for his city what few men could do in a normal lifetime. He decided that the essential key was James's scrupulous integrity. "His word was a perfect guarantee of good faith, and was accepted, by all who knew him, with absolute assurance."

Naturally, Michael Hawkins, who idolized his cousin, lamented James's untimely death. "Words cannot express the loving respect and reverence for the goodness, the greatness, the originality and progressiveness that I have always had for the achievements of my cousin." he wrote to Baroness von Schroeder in 1906. "He was a lovable character. He was a masterful man, but if he was masterful, he was endowed with the intellect, skill and force to back it. It was a rare thing to find two brothers, coming from the machine shop, so gifted for leadership in the founding of great undertakings that were so useful to the public in a young city . . . .

"He, too, was more than a millionaire. He was a high-minded, high-principled, broad-viewed, generous, thoughtful and helpful man, loved and respected by all classes of this community for his executive abilities, his foresight, his decency of life, added to his modest, unostentatious demeanor. In a word, Nature had created him a Gentleman."

Hawkins recalled the deceased's appearance. "My Cousin, James Donahue, was never the strong, robust, muscular or physically powerful man as were his brothers. He was of slight build, but well-proportioned, about my height, yet never weighed more than 137 pounds in his lifetime. His manners, likewise his features, bore no family resemblance to his robust brothers. In complection [*sic*], his widow thought mine so like his that she requested me to give sittings to [Charles C., or W.H.A.] Nahl, the artist who painted his portrait after his death."

Colonel Hawkins also described his favorite cousin to attorney Garrett McEnerny in another 1906 letter. He pictured him as the most beloved, respected and bereaved citizen of the city, for his age, at the time of his death. This was because of his many enterprises and progressive works, but likewise for his generosity, morality and decency of conduct. In 1910, in a letter to his fiancée, Flora A. Mills, Hawkins once again pictured James. "He was a good, honest, upright man and a charitable, benevolent and religious man." In contrast, he described Peter Donahue (on Thanksgiving Day, 1885) as "an enterprising, forceful, man."

James Donahue was remembered poetically, too, in the sentimental verse of Victorian times. An anonymous poet who signed himself only "Nobody" sent an impromptu eulogy in verse to one of the San Francisco papers. It was published under the heading "On Departed Worth," along with his note to the editors—"My abilities are few, my pretensions less. Many wish the following lines to be published. They are from the heart, and but a poor tribute to one so much regretted."

IMPROMPTU
"Hush, tread light," (the old man said,)
"James Donahue, the good, is dead!"
Mark the many thousands here,
In mournful silence o'er his bier,
Shed the honest, heart-felt tear.
"Stranger," he sighing said, "behold!
Those orphans, widows helpless old—
They were his care; man, Heaven can tell
The generous part he played full well.
Thus, through weary time we find
Death call the just, and leave behind
The cold and heartless, while the poor
The jibes of tyrants must endure."

EPITAPH
Good, honest men are few;
Beneath lies one—James Donahue.

On August 21, 1862, another amateur poet, James Linen, sent a page of maudlin verse to Peter. It was titled "Tribute to the Memory of James Donahue." In a covering note, Linen wrote, "It is a small tribute of my heartfelt appreciation of many virtues of your much lamented brother."

A warm friend and a brother now sleeps in the dust,
Tired of earth with its honors and burden of care;
If the author of being gives crowns to the just,
Then one of the brightest in Heaven he'll wear.

For orphans shall water his grave with their tears,
And bless the green turf that now wraps his cold clay,
And widows shall cherish his loved name for years,
A name which rude time will preserve from decay.

The chieftain may lead where the brave never yield,
And grand deeds trumpet-tongued may be sounded afar;
But *his* fame was not won on the red battle field,
Amid clashing of swords and loud thunder of war.

Where charity dwells in the sweet shades of peace,
As her favorite almoner there was he found,
Ever ready to aid with a smile of sweet grace,
Dispensing her gifts to the needy around.

Caring more for his soul than the riches he gained,
Like the wayworn and weary that seek gentle rest,
With a heart that was pure and with honor unstained,
He passed from our midst to the realm of the blest."

The most surprising tribute to James Donahue was a biographical sketch in the San Francisco *Argonaut.* Not because it was so belated, appearing thirteen years after his death, but because the periodical was anti-Catholic, anti-Irish, as well as anti-Chinese. Perhaps the bigot, Frank Pixley, had held a grudging respect for *one* "Paddy," James Donahue. In any case, he had a sympathetic writer, James O'Meara, do the honors. O'Meara was Irish himself, of course, and like Donahue, a non-Vigilante Democrat during the Vigilance Committee days of 1856.

On June 16, 1877, O'Meara's sketch, one of a series on "Early Californians," appeared. He boldly stated that

James Donahue was one of the very few pioneers and remarkable men who have left names built upon solid works which will be forever inseparably perpetuated with the existence, the destiny and the history of San Francisco. . . . His brief, yet singularly beneficent career earned his unchallenged worthiness to the praise and love of his fellow-men and his admitted title to stand among the foremost. . . . One who was trusted by all, admired by all, beloved by all, because he was the true friend of all—a stainless gentlemen and ever-sturdy in the virtues which most ennoble mankind and illuminate the soul."

The essayist, as was the custom, lumped James and Peter together.

Only a small number have left upon this community the impress of their genius or their enterprise, and among this most to be honored, brightest galaxy of our city's annals, the worth and works of these brothers—of the youngest [*sic*] of them, particularly, conspicuously shine. . . . By their sagacity and energy and toil, the brothers expanded their operations into fields by which they amassed immense wealth and made their names honored. . . .

It was in this city that James Donahue developed those extraordinary qualities which caused him to be regarded for several years before his death as one of the most sagacious, the most practical, the soundest and safest of business men of large enterprise and commanding abilities. He was rarely in error in his opinion or estimate of men, no matter in what capacity or under what circumstances he met or dealt with them, and with an almost infallible judgment in matters of business, he combined a faculty of foresight which was as unerring in its direction as it was grand in its comprehension.

In everything, whether bargaining for a trifle or embarking in colossal enterprises, he inflexibly adhered to the Golden Rule, and if his superior sagacity and unwavering integrity protected him from the over-reaching of others, he was no less exact in his determination to take no unjust advantage of any whom he mastered in the ways of trade, or in the diplomacy of stupendous operations. And it is to his everlasting praise that, of the vast fortune he died possessed [of], no one ever so much as insinuated that a dime of it had been gained in violation of the right, or saved against the observation of generous attention to the appeals of worthy charity.

But his charities were broader than the mere disposition of money or alms, it was of that true stamp which brightest shone in the forgiveness or merciful consideration with which he treated those who sought to do him harm, or had in any manner wronged him. In his composition, the ignoble alloy of vengeance had no part. . . . If they were worthy [of] his respect, he chose rather to aid and advance them; it was only the irrevocably unworthy that he left severely alone.

An example of Donahue's foresight, to O'Meara, was his choice of the ironically named Happy Valley for the site of the iron works. Its "dreary sands" were, naturally, viewed as an almost valueless desert, hardly likely to be of use for business or residence for many years. All traffic and construction was headed the other way, out of Montgomery. But, as O'Meara observed, "Time and events long since demonstrated the soundness of his judgment of the future in that selection. . . . To him, more than to any other, does that portion of San Francisco owe the prosperity it has enjoyed and the enhancement of property valuation which it has realized."

O'Meara admitted that the gas works was Peter's idea. But he reminded his readers that James grasped its great importance and directed his energies to accomplish it, "the most substantial and the most valuable corporation on this whole coast." To James O'Meara, the gas undertaking was colossal in terms of its day. It required not only money, and a lot of it, but judgment, tireless energy and, especially, "nerve." For to fail meant to be a victim of a loss of public confidence, which could be ruinous. As O'Meara said, it was "the chief capital stock of the world of finance." The tribute continued:

It would be difficult to parallel him in the even excellence of his disposition, but more difficult yet would it be to match the prodigious activity, the amazing force and the uncommon grasp of his mental nature. It worked like the ponderous Corliss Engine at the Centennial Exhibition, noiselessly, smoothly, perfectly, but with a power that could as easily crush a mass of iron as crack the shell of a nut.

Those who had the opportunity, through closest intimacy, to most attentively study and observe him, were always the most astonished and the most impressed with the latest great faculties he discovered and brought forth whenever the emergency called for extraordinary action. He was never known to be unequal, he was invariably superior, to the situation and, hence, he never failed in anything he determined to accomplish.

In the fervid glow of his manly heart, he loved his friends with a purity and constancy which nothing but dishonor could affect, and it was his joy to take by hand and lift up the worthy who were smitten by calamity, and help forward to success the toiling plodder. His charities were unceasing, always commensurate, never ostentatiously dispensed. They were poured like the dews of morning, silently . . . .

O'Meara was sure that Peter's elaborate funeral monument to his brother was unnecessary to have him remembered by the citizens of San Francisco. Something less solid, yet much more lasting, would serve to recall

the remarkable man who, in so brief a lifetime, accomplished so much of good and made his name famous by his sterling worth, his pure integrity, his unbounded spirit to benefit his race, and his aid in causing the city of his adoption to grow and flourish . . . . it is the unabated love and the steadfast devotion of most of intimate friends and companions, and the tenderness and affection with which he is enshrined in the hearts of thousands of humble and the poor to whom he always stood as a benefactor, that his name and memory will be most revered and kept forever green.

And San Francisco will perpetuate his fame in the lasting testimonies which he created and built by the power of his own energy and the grasp of his own genius, in his adherence to the simple and appropriate motto which he adopted as his own—*Labor Omni Vincit.*

O'Meara was a Victorian, so his tribute was verbose, sentimental, and purplish in its prose. He made the former boiler maker into a saint. But the tribute was from the heart, and there was more truth than poetry in his depiction of James Donahue—"None was more honored, none more worthy of honor. His word was a bond, neither to be questioned or refused; his friendship was more precious than gold. And from all classes and conditions he received the largest meed of respect and praise and love that it has ever been the happy lot of a citizen in private life among us to receive. . . . Had life been spared, it is impossible to conjecture what other works of grand proportions he might have projected and executed in this city and state."

James Donahue's will was filed on October 4, 1862. He left his wife, Mary Ann, and four children: Peter James ("Little Peter"), Margarete (Maggie), and the two youngest, Wallace (Willie) and Jennie, who did not even survive their mother, who died only six years after her husband.*

The widow was executrix and Peter was joined as executor by James's old friend, Joseph Donohoe. It was commonly said by city financiers that James had been the richest man of his age—thirty-eight—in San Francisco.

The will left one-third of James's estate to his wife and the other two-thirds, equally divided, to his children. James left many generous bequests, also. Among them were gifts of $25,000 to his younger brother, Thomas, and a "large amount" (according to Hawkins) to Michael Donahue. He apparently left no money to Peter's children, Mervyn and Mary Ellen.

Hawkins apparently acted as the children's guardian, held Mary Ann's power of attorney, and was her property agent. He was particularly proud of the way in which his favorite cousin took care of his family. "He left no poor relations among any of his mother's children or grandchildren."

*"Little Peter" never married; Margarete married Richard Burke—"an Irish gentleman of landed estate in [Tipperary] Ireland"—and bore four children, William, Alice, Edith, and Richard James.

Within two years of James's death, Mary Ann buried their two youngest children. Then her own health broke down. When Michael Hawkins's favorite sister married Dominic Gaven (a bachelor friend of James's who always took things easy), the couple kindly proposed to Mrs. Donahue that she accompany them on a tour of Europe. Mary Ann enjoyed the fifteen months of Continental touring; but after her return, her health broke down again. She died of tuberculosis ("consumption" then) at Laurel Wood on June 26, 1868.

A special train of Peter's San Francisco and San Jose Railroad brought the widow's body north on the 28th in a carriage draped with mourning black. It was said by the *Irish News* (July 11, 1868) that "profound respect" was paid the funeral train by people along the right-of-way. Several stops were made for persons to board the train to pay Mary Ann Donahue their last respects. In San Francisco, the coffin was met by a large number of citizens, including orphans, directors of charities, clergy, and Catholic sisters.

A solemn requiem high mass was held at 9 a.m. at St. Mary's Cathedral, draped in funeral black, with orphans again filling the side aisles. Officiating was the Very Reverend Father Prendergast. The Deacon was Father Griffin and the Sub-Deacon Father Hickey. The mass, Mozart's *Grand Requiem*, was sung by the cathedral choir augmented by other vocalists and instrumentalists. Prendergast's brief address stressed the departed's works of charity. He exhorted his listeners to emulate the example of the deceased.

Peter Donahue was a pallbearer, as was Senator Eugene Casserly. John Sullivan (not the world champion boxer, but an early, 1845, immigrant who made his fortune in real estate and in the Hibernia Savings and Loan Society) was there, as was another Hibernia director, Miles D. Sweeney, who had been city supervisor for the Second Ward in 1861-63. Also in attendence were the well-known Daniel J. Murphy, and D.J. Oliver, a real estate man whose chief claim to fame was that he had been knighted by Pope Pius IX in 1849 and had seen two of his children receive first communion from the Pontiff himself.

Other pallbearers included James's old friend, Joseph G. Eastland; Peter's fellow railroader, Henry M. Newhall; Thomas Breeze; George S. Wright; Philip McShane; Lawrence McNally; and J.C. Horan.

The crowd on foot outside the cathedral was a vast one, an "immense" concourse of persons according to the *Irish News,* and there were more than one hundred carriages in the mile-long funeral procession. Flags at half-mast were displayed on major buildings as the cortege passed through the streets. Mary Ann was buried by her husband's side in the family plot at Calvary Cemetery.

With his own wife dead, and his brother dead too, the early 1860s were sad and lonely years for Peter Donahue. In 1864 he married Annie Downey, the sister of the former governor of California, John Gately Downey. The ceremony was performed in Los Angeles on August 6, 1864, by Bishop Thaddeus Amat.

The second Mrs. Peter Donahue was born in 1836 in Castle Sampson, Roscommon, Ireland. She emigrated to Baltimore with her brother John and sister Eleanor. John pushed on to California, and the young ladies followed later, arriving in San Francisco on the day of James King of William's enormous funeral, May 22, 1856.

John G. Downey had arrived in California in 1849 with but $10 to his name. He settled in Los Angeles in 1850, going into cattle raising and real estate. In three years he made $30,000, so he bought 75,000 acres of San Pedro, Wilmington, and the town named for him, Downey. He served as governor from 1860 to 1862. Fears that he might be "soft" on his fellow Democrats in Secession were completely unfounded. Leland Stanford, his successor, is remembered as California's War Governor, but it was Downey who sent Colonel Patrick Edward Connor and California Volunteers to replace Federal troops withdrawn to the East from their patrols in the Indian country of the Overland Mail route. And it was Peter's new brother-in-law who dispatched Colonel James J. Carleton and his California Column to the Southwest, where it recovered Arizona and New Mexico for the Union, invaded and occupied westernmost Texas, part of the Confederacy, and kept the savage Apaches at bay in the desert country.

Bancroft thought highly of Downey. "His administration as Governor was universally commended and, as a private citizen, one to whose enterprise and liberality is largely due the prosperity of Southern California, he is no less widely esteemed."

Downey was unmarried, his sister Annie acted as his hostess in the governor's mansion. (She reportedly flirted with all of the handsome male guests.)

Annie Downey's beautiful and lively sister, Eleanor, in time became a San Francisco institution, a legend. She was educated at the Convent of Notre Dame, San Jose. Eventually she met a hero of the Mexican War, Major Walter Harvey, at her brother's Los Angeles home and soon married him. She lived in San Francisco with her husband, (who later became an invalid), until his death in 1861. (Major Harvey was a controversial figure. In 1852 he killed Jim Savage in a brawl after the latter accused him of attacking some peaceful Indians. Major Savage was commander of the Mariposa Battalion in the Mariposa War of 1851 against the Indians. He was also the so-called White King of the Tulare Indians and the rediscoverer [or effective discoverer] of Yosemite.)

Several years after Harvey's death, Eleanor married Edward Johnston Martin of Wexford, Ireland, who emigrated to California in '49 via Chile. He became one of the most successful Irishmen in California history. Quigley wrote, "We believe he is the largest landholder of our race [*sic*] in the United States, owning as he does over 600,000 acres in one body in Oregon and about 200,000 in this state." Martin became a founder of the Hibernia Savings and Loan Society (1859) with Richard and Robert Tobin, later the Hibernia Bank, and also the First National Bank. He won a first-class reputation for prudence and integrity. His face was the proverbial "map of Ireland." Quigley thought that his facial appearance indicated the true Irish gentleman. "He has in his physiognomy that mixture of dignity and wit which characterizes the genuine Irishman." When Martin died in the late 1870s, his estate was said to be one of the largest in the West.

Called "the Czarina," Mrs. Eleanor Martin ruled San Francisco society for, literally, decades, and with an iron hand. She hosted three presidents—Taft, Theodore Roosevelt, and McKinley—at her 2040 Broadway home. She was feared by those who did *not* know her and described by the ignorant as entering a salon with the dignity of a "serene battleship." She was actually a petite and gentle woman and those who knew her well, like Richard J. Burke, never saw anything of her purported ferocity. However, she exemplified Victorian "respectability" and had the strictest code of conduct. It was reported that she would not admit a divorced woman to her home and that ladies who drank more than one glass of champagne at her parties were not invited back. She was proud to be the sister of a governor, and a millionaire industrialist's wife.

With Ned Greenway, a champagne salesman(!), Eleanor Martin organized a "400" in San Francisco by inviting a social elite to the city's first (1887) Bachelor Cotillion. The chosen received beautifully engraved cards to five dances at—oddly enough—the declassé Odd Fellows Hall, after dinner at her home. The ladies, with elaborate coiffures, wore tight-fitting, decolleté, satin gowns and wore long gloves, fur muffs and feather boas: they glittered with jewelled earrings and chokers. The men were dressed to the nines. At 10 p.m. sharp, Eleanor and Ned, arm in arm, led the promenade around the ballroom to Strauss's *Blue Danube.* When they halted, Ned took a little gold whistle from his pocket and shrilly signalled for the dancing to begin. He later blew it again to announce that it was time to pitch into the banquet of duck, ham, turtle, tongue, scalloped oysters, and ice cream, washed down with Mumm's champagne. Then the Cotillion Master led his "troops" back onto the dance floor like a drill sergeant.

It was Annie Donahue who had first succeeded Mrs. Abby Parrott (widow of banker and Almadén quicksilver miner John Parrott) as San Francisco's social arbiter. Her sister soon took over the spotlight but, as one of "the Heavenly Twins," as the sisters were called, Annie continued to be socially prominent, and liked to be seen and admired. Perhaps Rudyard Kipling was thinking of the redoubtable Downey girls when he observed that women were in command of San Francisco, that ladies ruled their households like reigning monarchs.

(The Downey and Donahue clans remained close, even in death. On the main drive of Holy Cross Cemetery, Colma, where corteges stop, on the right side of the large upright stone over Governor Downey's grave is a white marble shaft marking the resting place of Peter and Annie Donahue.)

* * *

The Union Iron Works, along with the city's other industries, sailed through the Civil War years in good shape. The *Mining and Scientific Press,* in an October 1, 1864 article (on the rival Pacific Iron Works) reported:

> The most important branch of the manufacturing industry of this city at the present time is our iron foundries. No city in the Union has made such rapid strides in this branch of industry as San Francisco. Commencing

from the smallest beginnings only fourteen years ago, several of our foundries are now consuming fully a hundred tons of pig iron per month in addition to a proportional quantity of wrought iron, worked and forged into various descriptions of machinery.... It is mainly to such establishments as this that California is today indebted for the proud position she occupies in the great sisterhood of American states, and for her ability to erect in our midst the proud Temple of Industry [the Mechanics Institute Industrial Fair pavilion] which, for the past month, has been attracting thousands of pilgrims from all parts of the Pacific Coast, who came to pay a loftier tribute than any which the once-proud shrine of Mecca ever drew from her votaries, even during her palmiest days."

Exactly a week later, October 8, the same journal said of the Union Works, "It will now bear a favorable comparison with many of the leading establishments in the Atlantic states." The paper was impressed by the new wrought iron shaft of the steamer *Moses Tyler* at Donahue's works, which was "built from the original fagots—the only piece of work of the kind ever attempted on the Pacific Coast. No other foundry in the city would have attempted such a piece of work." Such appreciative comments were music to Peter Donahue's ears.

The enlarged Union Iron Works now hired between 200 and 250 workers at busy seasons. They used 1,500 tons of pig iron, 200 tons of boiler iron and 400 tons of bar iron each year, with the heaviest and most extensive machinery and tools on the Coast, save for the Navy Yard at Mare Island. Donahue was building a new 100-horsepower engine to drive the two monster (30-ton) planing machines, the 25-ton lathe, and other equipment. The engine was furnished with a new and improved cut-off, working directly from a governor, to save fuel over ordinary engines.

The new molding shop, occupying a 120-foot frontage on Mission Street, had doubled its capacity. The boiler department was the most complete in California , with all punching, riveting, shearing and rolling done by steam. It was making one hundred boilers a year.

The trade paper noted that the Union Iron Works was still supplying extensive castings and machinery for the Gas Company, and mammoth pumping machinery, engine and boiler for the Independent Coal Company of Mount Diablo, also a 135-horsepower engine and boilers for an Amos Phinney & Company sawmill, and a

60-horsepower engine and boiler for a Mexican mining company. It observed that Donahue's plant was also the agent for manufacturers of the celebrated Woodward steam pumps, the Wheeler and Randall Pan and Varney's Pan, among other amalgamating and ore crushing machinery. The paper lamented that Peter was temporarily absent from the city, so that it could not give more information about the current status of the pioneering San Francisco iron working establishment.

* * *

James Donahue had left several memorials behind him, but he did not live long enough to see the completion of his favorite—the Occidental Hotel. It was much more than the successor of the Oriental Hotel, where he and Peter had introduced the city to modern lighting in 1854. (Amelia Neville remembered the Oriental for its fine ballroom, which made it an early social center, but also because it lay across the street from the sandlots of James and Peter Donahue's establishment, where they manufactured boilers "with incessant din.")

James had not been a "sidewalk superintendent" during early construction of the Occidental. Though he was a partner with Joseph Donohoe in the project, it was James who personally supervised every detail of the building, from cornerstone to lightning rod.

James O'Meara noted that the building attested to Donahue's pride in his adopted city and his desire to improve and benefit it all that he could. "His purpose was to make it the completest structure of the kind on this coast, and, to that end, he gave it his constant personal supervision, from the laying of the foundation stone to the time he was called away to the eternal home."

Colonel Michael Hawkins was in on the very inception of the hotel. "I remember sitting with him [James] on a great slab of granite one afternoon on the southeast corner of Bush and Montgomery when the great foundation stones of the Occidental Hotel were being laid, [the hotel] that he had conceived, planned and built. He said to me, 'Michael, I want you to remember it, when I am dead, that I mean this hotel to be my monument.' "

Just two days before James's death, the *Alta* announced that the opening of the hotel was scheduled for early October 1862. The paper reported that the proprietorship of the "superb structure" would be entrusted by Donahue to S. Alstrom, John M. Lawlor, and G.S. Johnson. The first two men were former managers of the Oriental Hotel. "We are assured that the Occidental, in all of its appointments will exceed the anticipations of our citizens, who look forward to an establishment which will rival the far-famed hotels of the Atlantic states."

The Occidental was San Francisco's first first-class hotel in all respects, and it was run well by the initial trio and by those who followed them. James would have been proud of his staff. The Occidental immediately attracted and retained the patronage of well-bred, genteel visitors to San Francisco. Almost overnight, it became *the* place to stay for Army and Navy officers and their families. It dominated "Hotel Row" on Montgomery Street. The Lick House and Russ House were its neighbors. (The Baldwin was at Market and Powell; the Palace opened in 1875 at Market and New Montgomery.)

In his book "*A Backward Glance at Eighty* (1921), Charles A. Murdock pretended that he was showing off the city to an imaginary visitor of 1864. "We alight from the car when it reached Montgomery Street at the Occidental Hotel, new and attractive, well-managed by a New Yorker named [Warren] Leland, and especially patronized by Army People." (Barry and Patten remembered a manager named McShane, but that was in the 1870s and Theodore Hittell recalled Charles L. Wetherbee as the Occidental's host.) In 1866, Leland was still there, ssisted by his brother, for the *City Directory* noted that "Under the Messrs. Leland, who belong to a race of popular landlords—who 'are to the manner born'—the Occidental Hotel, with this important addition [a new wing], will rival in extent and accommodations any similar establishment on either side of the Atlantic."

The Occidental's rooms ranged in rates from $1.00 to $3.00 a day. The first section to rise was the eastern wing, on the site of the old Music Hall built by the absconding alderman, Henry ("Honest Harry") Meiggs. It faced Montgomery Street for 81 feet and Bush Street for 137½ feet. Another wing, created by additions of 1865 and 1869 to the "already gigantic proportions of this splendid hotel" (*City Directory* 1870) as leases on adjoining property expired, gave the hotel a final frontage of 208 feet, all the way to Sutter Street and the main entrance was now moved to Montgomery from Bush Street. There were 412 rooms exclusive of the dining room, bar, billiard parlor, offices and Ladies' Parlor. Fire hydrants and hoses were placed at convenient distances inside the building for safety and a great fire escape added. ("A special hall and staircase . . . to give free egress should a panic occur.") The added wing had a new fangled steam-powered elevator "for the accommodation of guests who do not wish to use the common stairs."

James had had to correct an embarrassing flaw in the hotel's initial construction in 1861—when part of the building fell down while it was still going up. But the 1870 directory was impressed not only by the sheer size of the hotel but by its suggestion of great strength. "The foundations of this substantial building are of stone, laid in the most secure manner and giving promise of the durability of time itself." The new wing featured iron-braced walls, anchored and secured by tie-rods in each story, "thereby securing the building against earthquake shocks."

Many wise men of the city believed that James's risking a hotel in *la grande manière* on the continent's edge in the middle of a civil war was a foolhardy gesture. (David Sessions later observed that public opinion was similar as Ralston planned his Palace Hotel a decade later.)

The reign of the Occidental was short. It was superior to the Oriental and Cosmopolitan, but was soon equalled by the ornate Lick House (as Julia Cooley Altrocchi remarked in her book, *The Spectacular San Franciscans*) and was totally eclipsed by the Palace Hotel of William Ralston and William Sharon in 1875. Even at that, the Palace's first manager, Warren Leland, was drawn from the Occidental, and he "stole" George Smith from the Occidental to be the Palace's first chief clerk. Besides his grand manner (which led to his being nicknamed "The Count"), Smith had a unique and uncanny ability *never* to forget a face or the name that went with it.

When Samuel Clemens, not yet famous as Mark Twain, arrived in San Francisco in 1864, he chose the Occidental for a fortnight of "butterfly idleness." He loved it. He described his new home as "opulent," leaving it only to take sightseeing drives or to attend plays and the opera. As a reporter on the *Call,* Clemens could not long afford the luxury of the Occidental and soon had to move to cheaper quarters. However, when he returned from the Mother Lode on February 26, 1865, he put up at his "heaven on the entire shell," the Occidental.

1. The Donahues learned their trades in Paterson, New Jersey. Paterson's growth as an industrial center was aided by the great power of the Passaic River and its 70-foot falls. SUTRO LIBRARY

2. Peter Donahue's interest in railroading began as an apprentice in Paterson's Rogers Locomotive Works. SUTRO LIBRARY

3. General Zachary Taylor (hatless) and staff at Walnut Springs, Mexico, where Michael Donahue was encamped with the First Ohio Volunteers during the Mexican War. NATIONAL PORTRAIT GALLERY

4. Michael Donahue. SUTRO LIBRARY

5. Davenport, Iowa, was so proud of Michael Donahue's waterworks (the most modern in the Midwest) that an engraving of the plant was included on a city map in Andreas's atlas of Iowa. Michael Donahue was also a popular two-term mayor of Davenport. SUTRO LIBRARY

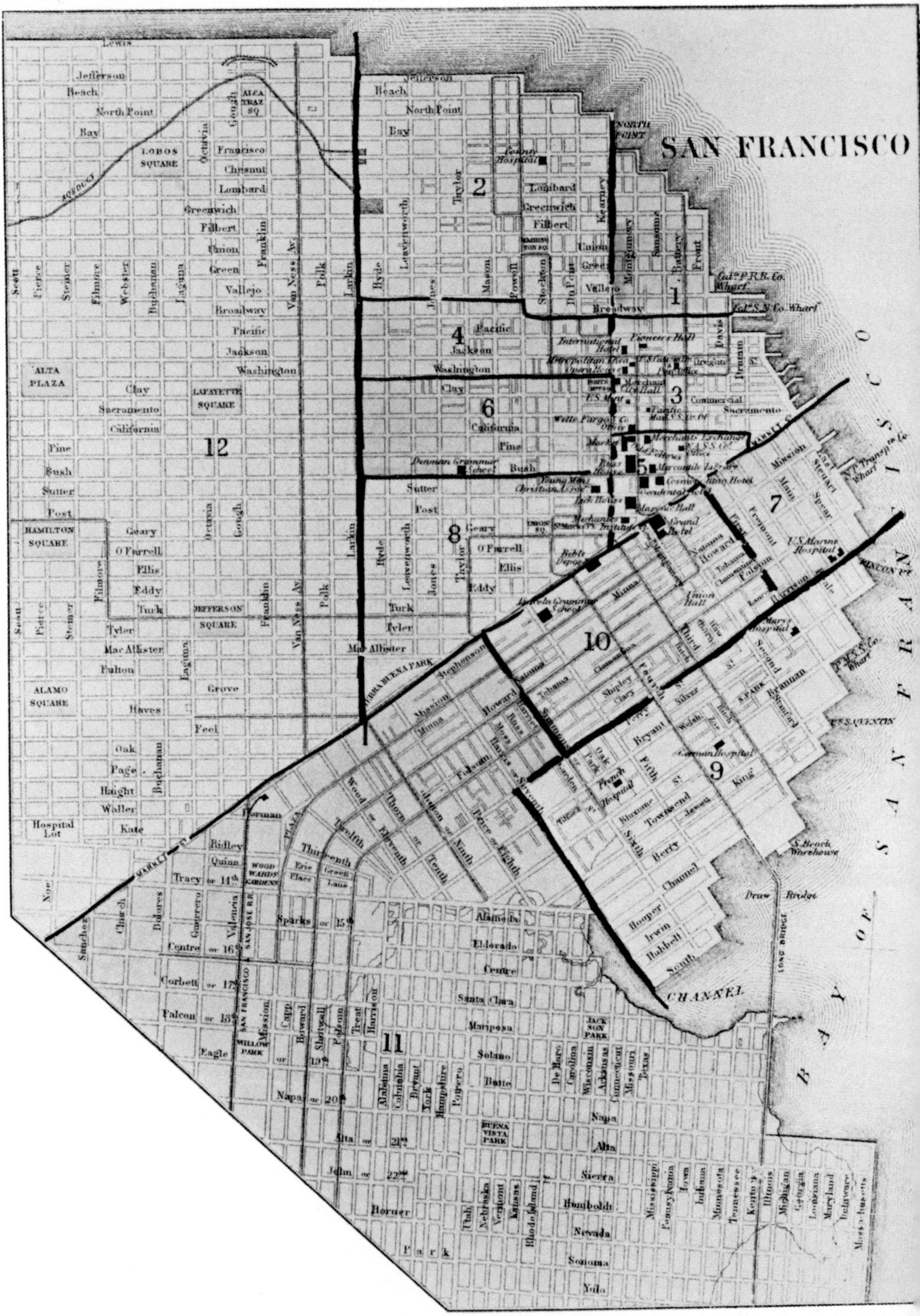

6. San Francisco during the heyday of the Union Iron Works, when [it] was broken up into electoral wards. The foundry was located at First a[nd] Mission streets, a block from the boundary of the Fifth and Seven[th] wards at Market Street. SUTRO LIBRARY

7. If any one structure can be said to have been the birthplace of the Industrial Revolution in the Far West, it would be the Donahue's Union Iron Works in San Francisco's Happy Valley. CLYDE ARBUCKLE

8. The Union Iron Works after its sale by Peter Donahue to his partners, Prescott and Scott. CALIFORNIA STATE LIBRARY

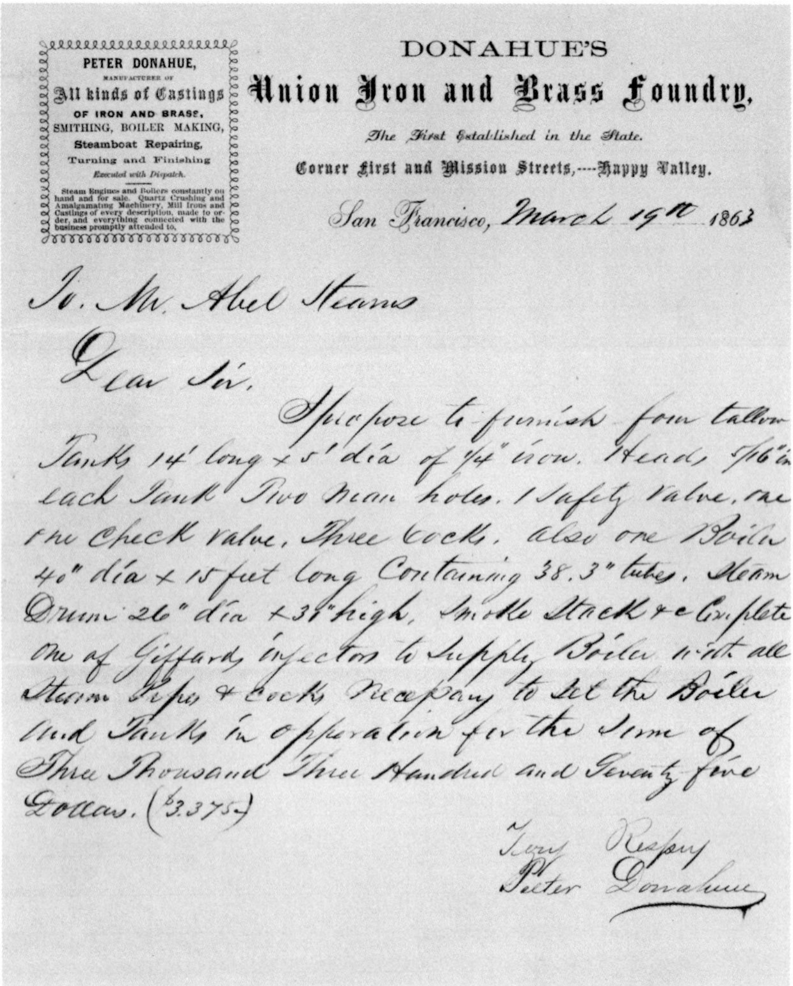

PETER DONAHUE,
MANUFACTURER OF
All kinds of Castings
OF IRON AND BRASS,
SMITHING, BOILER MAKING,
Steamboat Repairing,
Turning and Finishing
Executed with Dispatch.

Steam Engines and Boilers constantly on hand and for sale. Quartz Crushing and Amalgamating Machinery, Mill Irons and Castings of every description, made to order, and everything connected with the business promptly attended to.

DONAHUE'S
Union Iron and Brass Foundry,
The First Established in the State.
Corner First and Mission Streets,---Happy Valley.

San Francisco, March 19th 1863

To. Mr. Abel Stearns

Dear Sir,

I propose to furnish four tallow Tanks 14' long x 5' dia of 1/4" iron. Heads 5/16" in each Tank Two man holes. 1 Safety valve, one one Check valve, Three cocks. also one Boiler 40" dia x 15 feet long Containing 38. 3" tubes. Steam Drum 26" dia x 34" high, Smoke Stack &c Complete One of Giffards injectors to Supply Boiler with all Steam Pipes & cocks necessary to set the Boiler and Tanks in opperation for the sum of Three Thousand Three Hundred and Seventy-five Dollars. ($3.375-)

Yours Respy
Peter Donahue

9. A Union Iron Works proposal, signed by Peter Donahue, to Abel Stearns, an early settler in California (1829) who became a leading trader, landowner and cattleman. HENRY E. HUNTINGTON LIBRARY

10. Peter Donahue. BANCROFT LIBRARY

11. The Occidental Hotel was James Donahue's monument. A deluxe establishment (always the favorite of military and naval officers), it anticipated the opulence of William Ralston's Palace Hotel. CALIFORNIA HISTORICAL SOCIETY

12. James Donahue. PACIFIC GAS & ELECTRIC COMPANY

13. The *San Jose*—"*Little Josie*"—of Peter Donahue's San Francisco and San Jose, and San Francisco and North Pacific railroads. RAILWAY NEGATIVE EXCHANGE

14. The San Francisco and North Pacific Railroad's Engine #12, the *Peter Donahue.* ED MANION

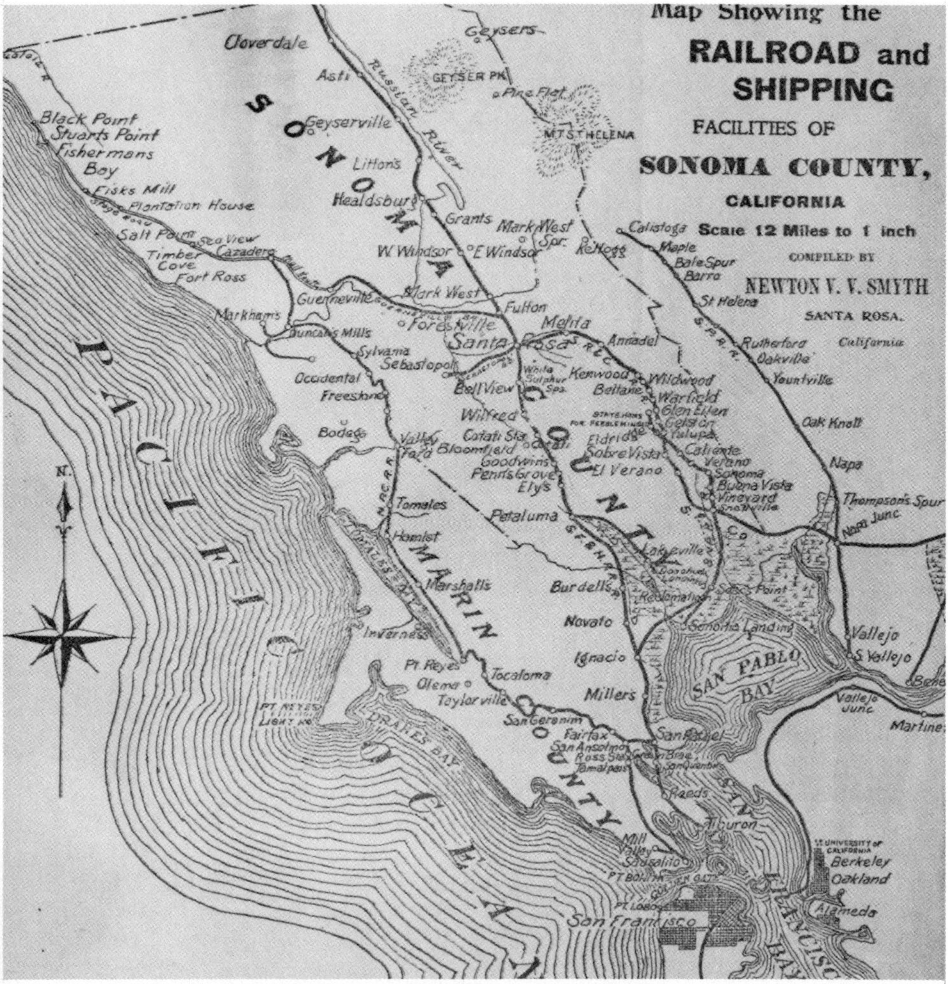

15. The San Francisco and North Pacific Railroad and rival routes. The little town of Donahue's Landing was in the marshes to the north and west of San Pablo Bay. ED MANION

16. The old *Antelope* at Donahue's Landing, the Sonoma House Hotel at right. She was called the "Wells, Fargo Gold Boat" because she had hauled so much bullion on the Sacramento River before Peter Donahue bought her. RAILWAY NEGATIVE EXCHANGE

17. The more modern sidewheeler, the *James M. Donahue,* built by Peter Donahue. (The endleaf photograph shows both steamers tied at Donahue's Landing.) RAILWAY NEGATIVE EXCHANGE

18. In 1884, Peter Donahue moved his terminal from Donahue's Landing to Point Tiburon on San Francisco Bay. CALIFORNIA STATE LIBRARY

19. The extension of Peter Donahue's SF & NP Railroad south from Petaluma to Point Tiburon entailed much tunneling and building of bridges, including extensive trestle work to cross Richardson's Bay. CALIFORNIA STATE LIBRARY

20. Engine #7 of the SF & NP, the *Petaluma*, was used on the Russian River freights and (as Northwestern Pacific's Engine #12) was seen in the 1923 film *Iron Horse*. RAILWAY NEGATIVE EXCHANGE

21. The *Santa Rosa,* Engine #5, was built for Peter Donahue's SF & NP by Booth. RAILWAY NEGATIVE EXCHANGE

22. All that remains of Donahue's Landing today are two old weather-beaten buildings, now a part of Petaluma Creek Ranch. ED MANION

23. "Men of Mark," a souvenir card of 1876. "A galaxy of persons of distinction on the Pacific Coast, also, embracing many persons of note who have visited California since 1849 . . . whose talent, culture, wealth, or birth give them right among the celebrated of the world, published by Bradley & Rulofson as a record of passing events." James Donahue (with mustache and short dark beard) is in the second row from the bottom, third from left. Peter Donahue, white-bearded and distinguished in his uniform, is third up from the right of the publisher's caption. RICHARD J. BURKE

A turning point in Clemens's life took place as he signed the register. The desk clerk handed him accumulated mail. One letter was from the humorist, Artemus Ward, soliciting a sketch. Twain dashed off his version of a hoary Mother Lode yarn that he had overheard at Tuttletown or Jackass Hill. When it was published as *The Celebrated Jumping Frog of Calaveras County,* he was on his way to fame and fortune.

Bret Harte, Twain's mentor and sometimes-deprecated rival, also liked to stay at the Occidental. So did theatrical people of some gentility or "class," like the actress, Adelaide Neilson, who put up there with her husband, Ralph Lee, when she was performing in *Romeo and Juliet.*

Another "actress" of sorts—the whole world was her stage—was fire buff and *femme fatale* Lillie Hitchcock. She made the Occidental her San Francisco home, starting in 1862 when she stayed there with her mother, Southern belle Martha Hunter, in a $250 a month suite. Lillie fell ill, perhaps because mama wanted her to stay away from fires and the firemen of Knickerbocker Engine Company #5. Hearing of her illness, the fire "bhoys" of Knickerbocker #5 spread tanbark over the cobbles of the street outside of her Occidental window, to muffle the noise of vehicles. Her mother gave in and Lillie attended all fires, wearing proudly her own uniform as an honorary member of the Knickerbockers. She wore a gold pin in the shape of the numeral "5" night and day. She even took to signing her name Lillie Hitchcock 5 and, after she married, Lillie Hitchcock Coit 5.

In 1869 Lillie was back at the Occidental as Mrs. Coit, wife of Howard Coit. Matron or not, Lillie rated a serenade by the men of #5 Company. The fire laddies offered their rendition of "Oh, We'll Hunt the Buffalo." After the band music stopped, Lillie appeared at her window, to receive a round of applause. A newspaperman described the Occidental's prettiest guest—"Lillie is a splendid specimen of the 'girl of the period,' and as she glides carelessly along Montgomery Street, she always reminds us of Byron's lines, 'She walks in beauty like the night, Of cloudless climes and starry skies . . . .' "

The Occidental was a favorite of writers as well as soldiers, at least till the Palace opened in 1875. Ralph Waldo Emerson stayed in the Occidental on his way to Yosemite in 1871. (Probably, cousin Colonel Michael Hawkins saw him there, as Hawkins resided at the

Occidental temporarily after his parents died within a year of each other.) In the 1870s, the grandfather of another famous California author, Kathleen Thompson Norris, became Occidental manager. London-born Paul Lansing Moroney was a former actor. The red headed Irishman turned into a feisty oldster with snow-white hair and fierce moustaches, glistening blue eyes and a complexion that Kathleen Norris remembered as "peach melba." When she was only a little girl, he used to take her, along with her brother Joe Thompson, to proudly show them off to his cronies in the lobby of the Occidental.

Much later (1888), Robert Louis Stevenson, "too ill to be lionized" as Amelia Neville recalled, chose to put up there because it was the best that a writer could afford. When he and his wife left, it was to charter the *Casco* and sail for Samoa in hopes of saving his health.

Gertrude Atherton (who instinctively knew such things) rated the Occidental, where she preferred to stay, as one of a handful of truly great hotels. She ranked it with the "Bonanza Inn" of Oscar Lewis—the Palace, and the Grand, Baldwin, Commercial, Lick, and Russ hostelries.

The Occidental was one of the first Western hotels to give up the prevailing Greek Revival architecture, and was the finest example of the new, severe, English-Roman style. It was five stories high, but its top floor had a lower ceiling than the others. On stone foundations, but built of brick, it was covered with a plaster or stucco painted in contrasting shades of reddish brown and cream.

The ground floor of the original wing was leased to six stores that were independent of the hotel. The west wing, completed in 1869, added six more shops. After the $190,000 addition of architects J.P. Johnson and William Mooser, the structure (grown from 156 to 412 rooms) covered two full 50-*vara* Mexican lots. (A *vara* is the short, or British, yard—thirty three inches.) It provided a lobby and offices, of course, but also a billiard parlor, a bar, a 300-seat dining room, where gourmand Sheriff David Scannell might spend five to six hours at a crack, a laundry, bathrooms, a telegraph, and a Ladies' Parlor. Its public rooms were lined with cabinets containing mineral specimens and other natural curiosities. According to Helen Holdredge, its rugs were ankle-deep in pile, and its cuspidors(!) on claws of Assyrian design, were constantly polished and of the most dazzling bright brass to be found in town. Another nice touch were the fresh flowers in every room for arriving guests, and the baskets for departing guests—fruits for sea voyagers, a light luncheon for rail trippers.

In 1875, Benjamin Lloyd also ranked the Occidental with the Baldwin, Lick and Cosmopolitan, even the brand-new Palace, terming it "the delight of the tourist . . . he can nowhere be better housed. The Occidental is really *the* popular first-class hotel." According to Lloyd, it was favored by California Street capitalists, lawyers of large income who were well up in their profession, wealthy retired merchants, favorite employees with good salaries, rich widows, and "true ladies and gentlemen who like its society *ton.*"

The new Palace notwithstanding, the Occidental was still what 1875's city directory claimed it to be, "One of the most celebrated hotels on the Pacific Coast—one of the most substantial in construction, convenient in arrangement, and complete in appointment." It was as genteel as the best Boston lodgings, and it remained a San Francisco landmark for nearly a half-century.

James's monument not only attracted the military, literary figures, world travelers, and wandering businessmen, it was a stylish place much frequented by "locals." Civic leaders on the federal, state, and local levels liked to meet there—including both White Hat McCarthy and the loony Emperor Norton. (In fact, it was a social center until the Palace began to overtake it in this respect in 1875.)

The Occidental became the residence of royalty in the fall of 1866 when a strange Union Jack-like flag was seen flying above the hotel. It was the royal standard of the Kingdom of Hawaii. The mayor and a load of civic "brass" met Queen Emma to drive her in a barouche, drawn by four matched white horses, from the Embarcadero, where her ship moored, to the Occidental. Mark Twain was staying there at the time and was about to give his very first public lecture—which, by coincidence, was about Hawaii. Her Majesty must have noticed Twain's eye-snagging placards for his talk, "The Sandwich Islands," at the Academy of Music in Baldwin's Hotel, only a block away. The handbills and broadsides were catchingly headed "The Trouble Will Begin at 8 O'clock."

In 1872, the Occidental became a diplomatic sanctuary. A great banquet was held at the Grand Hotel for the Japanese Ambassador and the Royal Princesses, who were being escorted by the

American Minister to Japan, the Honorable Charles De Long. But the *Nihonjin* preferred to actually reside in the Occidental, though they banqueted at the Grand.

At least once, James's sophisticated hostelry was hoaxed by an impostor. Sir George Bridges, a guest who awed other guests and staff alike with his upper crust manners—or, rather, his snooty *lack* of manners—turned out to be humble George Green, a music teacher from Hamilton, Ontario, who played the titled role because he enjoyed the extra attentions of an intimidated staff.

Naturally, the Eastern establishment roared with laughter at the news of the hoax, enjoying the discomfort of San Francisco's uppity *nouveau riche* society being taken in by a fraud. Amelia Neville, the social historian, never could understand how the Canadian pulled it off for, like a Cockney, he littered the hotel carpets with dropped "haitches" (h's). The *Chronicle*, which described Sir George's voice as being "as plaintive as a mud turtle dove's," also poked fun at "His Lordship's" delicate side whiskers and sewing-silk moustache, then punned about the acreage of aristocratic cheek that the charlatan displayed to the world.

Most prominent guests, however, were the real McCoy. *The* fashionable San Francisco social event of 1865, for example, was a grand ball for the wife of General Irvin McDowell, Commander of the Military Division of the Pacific. (In 1882, a gala farewell reception was held in the Occidental as the General retired from his command.)

The Industries of San Francisco (1884) paid James's hotel a nice compliment. "If there is one thing more than another for which San Francisco is justly famous, it is the number and excellence of its hotels. The Occidental, which has stood the test of time, is as popular now as it was in the earlier days of its existence and has never failed to maintain its hold upon the traveling public." Likewise, the *San Francisco Illustrated Review* (1887) called its readers's attention to the "host of obliging servants and competent cooks of the Occidental," as well as its writing rooms, and its large, airy and elegant sleeping rooms. "For genuine home-like comfort, combined with elegance, there is not on the Pacific Coast a more admirably arranged and managed hostelry than the Occidental Hotel. Major William B. Hooper is the manager and he is a genial, sociable gentleman and a businessman of integrity." A typical advertisement during the Major's reign described his hotel as "a quiet house of peculiar excellence. Headquarters of Army and Navy." Hooper would hire, and retain, only waiters possessed of proven elephantine memories. They were required to take dinner orders from a tableful of guests without making any notes and had to keep perhaps a hundred dishes straight in their heads.

The Occidental bar had a free lunch, of course, a San Francisco tradition. Evelyn Wells, in her *Champagne Days of San Francisco,* recalled that the hotel, from the 1880s to 1906, was an important station, as were the Hoffman Cafe and the Palace Hotel, on a sort of "underground railroad" of society, the zigzag trail of the 5 p.m. (weekdays) Cocktail Route, sometimes called the Ambrosial Path, when businessmen deserted their desks for the day. Judges, attorneys, bankers and, yes, even Mervyn Donahue, the handsome scion of "the Iron Works family," joined the promenade. On Saturdays, the Occidental lay athwart the route of ladies and gents stretching their legs after theater matinees.

During the last decades of the nineteenth century and the pre-Fire years of the twentieth, the star of greatest magnitude behind the celebrated Occidental bar was "Handsome Billy" Osborne, a dark, comely and smooth-shaven fellow in a hirsute age. Another well-thought-of gent in the distinctive white apron of his office was Mike Balf, son of the composer of *The Bohemian Girl.*

But an earlier Occidental barkeep was the greatest bartender in San Francisco history; better even than Duncan Nicol of the Bank Exchange, inventor of Pisco Punch. Jeremiah Thomas was such a master of mixology that he was called Professor Jerry Thomas. (He may have been the greatest bartender in the history of America. U.S. Grant once awarded him a cigar, and a flourish, for his bartending expertise.)

Thomas strayed far from the ministerial path that his parents selected for him. He came to San Francisco as a Forty-niner to become first assistant at the bar of the famed El Dorado saloon, but left for a go at mining. This was followed by more experience in his true profession, at the Planters House in New Orleans and the Metropolitan Hotel in New York.

The Professor was back in San Francisco in time to be named principal bartender in James's Donahue's new hotel. He drew upon his experience to write a classic book, *How to Mix Drinks, or The Bon Vivant's Companion,* in which he offered recipes for his most famous drinks—El Dorado Punch, the Blue Blazer, California Milk

Punch and, most important of all, the Martini. The Professor called it the Martinez Cocktail, for the small town on Carquinez Strait, but it soon became martini or dry martini. (Some say that it was really named the martini because of the popular brand of vermouth, Martini and Rossi.) Thomas made the martini popular in the Occidental. It spread through San Francisco, conquered the West and America and, in time, the world. But restless Professor Thomas spent only two years behind the Occidental's bar, then moved on again, to Virginia City and then back East, never to return.

The original—Occidental—martini was a far cry from today's slug of squarehead gin with a closed bottle of dry vermouth passed quickly over it. Thomas's recipe involved a dash of bitters, two dashes of maraschino, a pony of Old Tom Cordial "sweet" gin (perhaps named for the old tom cat that "fell in the vat"), a wineglassful of sweet vermouth, plus two lumps of ice. There were no neat ice cubes in his day. No olive, no pickled Gibsonian pearl of an onion. The sweetish mess was shaken and strained into a cocktail glass decorated with a quarter-slice of lemon and then, incredibly, it was drunk!

In a preface to an article on "The Old Occidental" by Stephen P. Jocelyn that appeared in the *California Historical Society Quarterly* of March 1953, Allen Chickering of the editorial advisory board remembered the hotel as "a feature of my younger life." The Chickering family, although living in Oakland, spent the winters of 1900-02 at the Occidental, young Allen having his own inside room, fronting on the court, for only $50 a month—American plan! He found that the hotel set an excellent table, and the courtesy and good service of all of the dining room's waiters, especially the legendary Victor, was superb. Because Chickering was engaged to a Fresno girl who later became his wife, he never forgot one standard menu item—"Roast Fresno Turkey *a la Farci.*"

Unfortunately, human guests were not the only ones who lived well in the Occidental. Great Norway rats roamed the attic and the box-like housings of a maze of lead pipes leading to lavatories. They grew so tame that boys staying in the hotel would sometimes feed them bits of bread in the corridors. Mostly, however, they stayed out of sight, if not out of hearing. Chickering remembered what seemed to be a rodent steeplechase above his ceiling. He would hear the distant rattle of running feet growing louder until, immediately over his bed, some sort of hurdle, probably a stud, forced the racing rats to jump and land with a thud.

Chickering found the hotel filled with very agreeable people indeed, most of them well-acquainted with each other and many of them permanent residents, practically "family." The delightfully friendly atmosphere was a tradition in James Donahue's house. It was different, far better than that of any hotel that Chickering ever stayed in during his entire lifetime. He thought that Major Hooper was largely responsible for continuing the tradition of hospitality.

The author of the article, Stephen Jocelyn was an "Army brat." He found the Occidental to be practically a posh barracks, or rather officers' quarters, during the Spanish American War. All officers made a beeline for it. For twenty years already, it had been a service tradition. It one wanted to know if a particular officer was a guest, or had recently been one, there was no need to consult the register. You simply buttonholed the gray-haired head waiter in his conservative and immaculate dress suit. Mr. Fay was always to be found at his post at the dining room door, opposite the toothpicks and the newsstand.

Jocelyn had a child's-eye view of the great hotel, since he was only seven at the time of his first stay in 1899. Like all resident kids, he liked to slide down the banisters, taking all floors in one swoop. Despite the watchmen, boys ran wild on the stairs and banisters of the front southwest corner of the hotel since adult guests rarely used them, preferring the elevator or other staircases. The boys, and tomboys, used all stairs spurned by adults, of course, but preferred the iron spiral staircase near the middle of the right (north) wing. They would run down it as fast as possible, always falling and tumbling out in a dizzied heap at the bottom.

Another favorite spot for exploring was the area of quarters for servants, domestics, nursemaids, and coachmen of guests. It was a supposedly off-limits region on the top floor, but children liked the narrow staircase zigzagging down from it to the kitchen, another forbidden area. There was also a staircase wrapped around the elevator shaft and Jocelyn used to race the ponderously moving car from street floor to top floor. He never lost a contest. The elevator, its passenger compartment two stories high, though slow, was elegant. Its dark, carved hardwood walls were mirrored and there was a comfortable seat for about fifteen passengers around the three walls, above a space for freight. The cage was moved into action by a passenger tugging on two ropes that ran through the lift's floor and ceiling. The elevator was never idle. Since it took about ten minutes for a roundtrip, which included leveling it carefully at each floor in order to unload people and luggage, one always had to ring and ring for it.

The Occidental had two service entrances and two "main" entries, the Lobby entrance and the Ladies' Entrance. The lobby was large, with plate glass windows and numerous armchairs and cuspidors. After breakfast, the chairs filled up with men reading the morning papers and puffing great dense clouds of cigar smoke. Kids like Steve Jocelyn scuttled around, retrieving discarded cigar bands for their collections. The left rear of the lobby held the long mahogany receiving desk and between it and the elevator on the right, behind swinging doors, were the billiard room and bar.

Social life centered on the second floor, in the big hall or parlor with plush seats along one wall in front of the corridor leading to the dining room and the debouche of the grand open staircase. (It was impossible for gamins to slide down its banister because a statuette of a maiden surmounted each newel post.) The ceiling of the parlor was sometimes accidentally decorated with toy balloons, escaped from their tethers. Army boys, of course, loved to prove their marksmanship by shooting them down with improvised slingshots. Many of the balloons, however, just shriveled up with old age and sank to the floor, or to the top of the piano that disturbed so many guests in nearby rooms.

In the center of the ceiling of the second and upper floors was a round light well used for toy balloon ascensions and "sponging"—an early version of water-bagging. The favorite target of the juvenile bombardiers, naturally, was the bald dome of the feared watchman.

The American Plan dining room delighted youngsters because the table d'hote meals of many courses were accompanied by water ices (sherbets). Breakfasts were Pantagruelian. On Sundays there were assorted bon bons for dessert. Carl, a rawboned Norwegian, was the dinner-coated captain of waiters in young Stephen's time. He would collect discarded bon bons for the boys. Dextrous waiters each carried a heavily-laden tray on their heads, on top of a doughnut-shaped cushion of red plush. They carried one hundred pounds at a time because they also held a tray balanced on each outstretched palm, sometimes scattering rats before them as they left the kitchen.

Since there was no central heating, nearly every room had its own open grate fireplace burning six-to-ten-inch chunks of soft coal. Jocelyn was always surprised that the hundred or more chimneys did not burn the place down (as happened to Baldwin's Hotel), even though they were regularly cleaned by chimney sweeps.

* * *

In 1861, just before the Occidental opened, both citizens and military officers in San Francisco petitioned the Navy Department for a floating battery to bolster San Francisco's defenses (consisting chiefly of Peter's U.S.S. *Saginaw)* against Confederate privateers roaming the seas. The Navy more than had its hands full in patrolling the Pacific from Panama and San Francisco to China with just few sloops-of-war. The artillery batteries at Fort Point and Fort Alcatraz were inadequate to repel a determined assault on the metropolis of the West.

California's State Senator James T. Ryan of Humboldt County successfully lobbied in Washington in 1862, via California congressmen, for a monitor or ironclad, like the U.S.S. *Monitor* (the so-called "Cheesebox on a Raft") that had turned back the Confederate's armored ram *Merrimac* in March of that year. Ryan formed a partnership with Peter Donahue and New Jersey shipbuilder Francis Secor. The new firm, not surprisingly, won the half-million dollar contract; they made the only bid. The actual cost of the war vessel would be $589,165.31.

Plans and specifications were by John Ericsson, designer of the *Monitor*, but the San Francisco-bound warship was larger and more powerfully armed than the prototype. She was manned by fifty seamen and eight officers. She displaced 1,875 tons, was 200-feet long, and her turret mounted not one but two 15-inch guns. The *Camanche* (a variant of the name of the Comanche Indian tribe) had twin steam boilers driving nine engines—two for propulsion at nine knots, two for pumping, two to rotate the turret, two to power ventilator fans, and one for vacuum. Her coal bunkers carried enough fuel for a week's steaming. The deck of the low-lying vessel and her sides above the water line were armored with wrought iron plates ranging from an inch to six inches in thickness. The turret's plates were eleven inches thick.

It took Secor nine months to build the monitor and then disassemble it at his Jersey City yard. The *Camanche* left New York in pieces, tucked in the hold of the sailing ship *Aquila* as cargo. The *Aquila* arrived in San Francisco on November 10, 1863, but while she lay alongside of Hathaway's Wharf at the tip of Rincon Point, a November 16 southeaster sank her with the *Camanche* still in her bowels. Ryan was sure that the warship could be saved. In fact, he swore that he would not shave again until the *Camanche* was launched.

The *Alta* had fun with the Navy's shipwrecked vessel. It pointed out that the homely *Aquila* was the greatest of America's warships since "she was the first to sink one of our monitors." A wag reversed the joke by quipping that the *Camanche* had already proved its worth by sinking a vessel even before being launched.

Everyone in San Francisco seemed to have a plan for raising the *Aquila* and her jigsaw puzzle cargo. E.L. Fall wanted the sunken vessel circled with pilings and raised by hydraulic jacks. W.H. Irwin recommended a cofferdam. One proposal in the *Alta* would lift the whole shebang with hot air balloons. Admiral A. Popoff of the Russian Navy, paying a courtesy call on San Francisco, offered to lend men and four diving suits. The insurance underwriters accepted Horace Cole's bid to raise the ship for $100,000. He calked the leaks and pumped her out. But he could not raise her.

San Franciscans were annoyed to learn that the underwriters, via a Prescott Fletcher (as Peter Donahue recalled) had hired a crew of professional salvage divers in New York. The editor of the *Alta*, bursting with (wounded) local pride, protested that there were men in San Francisco who were just as competent to do the salvage diving.

After quarrels over the ownership and liability of the pair of sunken vessels, the Navy and the underwriters agreed to work together in salvaging operations. At the end of January 1864, Captain Israel E. Merritt's crew of ten wreckers and four divers (later increased to eight) began work after surveying the wrecks. They found that it would be impossible to raise the *Aquila* after pumping her dry because her decks would collapse from the 2,600 tons of water pressure on them, even at low tide. So the divers cut away sections of the hull to get at *Camanche* parts in her hold. The pieces of the monitor were hoisted out to be identified, cleaned of rust, and painted; some thirty tons came up the very first day. On May 27 the

Aquila herself was finally raised; the last of her bellicose freight did not come ashore till June 15, 1864.

On May 2, the *Alta*, in describing the new terminus for Peter Donahue's Omnibus Line, referred to the *Camanche* as the "stricken monster." The terminal lay southeast of Townsend Street, at the end of Third Street near Farr's Hotel on Steamboat Point. (This was the point where shipwright Patrick Henry Truman reconverted the Donahues' *Goliah* to a tug.) The paper noted how, only four years before, the area had been an uninhabited wasteland. Now the city was marching southward with a vengeance, just as Peter had predicted to Bulger so long before. The area was now covered with dwellings, shops, saloons and factories. "The 'resurrected' *Camanche* lies in an adjoining yard and hundreds of loyal citizens visit the spot daily to see her—to be sure, only in pieces—[but] soon to be put together again in her proper element."

The contractors—meaning Peter Donahue—received all parts for assembly except the guns and ammunition. They were sent to Mare Island for safekeeping. But Donahue protested that the sinking had nullified the contract, since increased labor costs for the renovation of salt-water-damaged parts, and the 30% decrease in the value of currency since he and his partner made their bid, meant that they would be out-of-pocket if they did the work. They firmly refused to put the *Camanche* together again unless they were guaranteed a bonus of $60,000 in gold coin, not depreciated paper money. Peter expected the underwriters, not the government to pay; however fourteen insurance companies were involved.

Finally, San Francisco's Board of Supervisors and Chamber of Commerce, to prevent a long litigation—and a possible sacking of San Francisco by Rebels—paid Donahue, Ryan and Secor with city funds. (The contractors endorsed the insurance policies over to the city but, after sixteen years of fruitless lawsuits, San Francisco gave up and swallowed the loss.)

Peter Donahue began work on the monitor the moment that money was available, choosing to reassemble her at the water's edge at Third and King streets. In just three months from the time that he laid her keel, he launched the *Camanche*. It was November 14, 1864, almost a year since the foundering of the *Aquila*. At last, the monitor was "ready to repel the invasions of the Rebel cruisers," as the press put it.

Captain John Leale, the "Tule Sailor" of the Sacramento Delta, used to hire out his vessel to bring spectators to view the reincarnation of the *Camanche.* He was there on November 14 when a crowd overflowed the bleachers erected near the marine ways on Steamboat Point. It seemed to him that the whole city was *en fete.* About 25,000 persons came to watch the launching, among them the sixty-one-year-old Captain John Sutter, California's eminent pioneer. The launch was the greatest public event ever held "South of the Slot" and, appropriately, the man who presided over it was one of the two original South of Market Boys, Peter Donahue.

The crowd was just too big for one celebrity, Bret Harte. In a comic ode to the monitor, titled "A Lay of the Launch," he lamented his inability to see the actual launching. The doggerel, in the November 19, 1864 *Californian*, read, in part:

My heart is wasted with my woe, *Camanche;*
In vain I strove to see the show, *Camanche;*
I did not see thee launched at all, *Camanche;*
The crowd was large—the gate was small, *Camanche;*
I stood without and cursed my fate,
The time, the tide that did not wait,
With others who had come too late, *Camanche;*
Why did they send thee off so soon? *Camanche;*
They should have waited until noon, *Camanche;*

It was not a lucky launch. Two special sightseeing boats with very important people aboard missed it entirely, like Harte, because they arrived too late, though at the appointed time of 11.30 a.m. For some reason, Peter floated her seven minutes early. Next, the champagne bottle (at first) refused to break for the christening. Then, as the *Camanche* slid into the Bay, she dug in her stern and a wave of water swept her deck, scaring the daylights out of the prominent men taking a joy ride aboard her. Finally came tragedy. One of the party aboard her, State Senator John P. Buckley, got his foot caught in ropes coiled on deck and suffered injuries that led to his death within a matter of days.

The mood of the crowd (unaware of the accident) was as good as the speeches, naval gun salutes, patriotic cheers, and the airs of an Army band concert were accompanied by tours of the *Camanche* and refreshments for six hundred invited guests in a building on the wharf. More cheers followed, this time for Peter Donahue, his workers, and the "spread" prepared by him to assuage his guests' hunger and thirst. After a member of a San Francisco opera company sang "The Fall of Our Union" and everyone sang the "Star Spangled Banner," Ryan ceremoniously shaved off his whiskers.

Peter's workmen installed engines, turret and pilot house during the next two months. Her great 15-inch guns were readied for the turret in December, and in mid-January of 1865 the *Camanche* had her trial run to Mare Island, to be fitted with her armament. She was escorted by two tugs, a revenue cutter, and a civilian steamer. Her maiden voyage was a great success, again thanks to a wardroom repast that Peter Donahue prepared for two hundred guests aboard. The Commandant of the Mare Island Navy Yard accepted the monitor with reluctance since he had no orders or authorization to take custody of her; however, he took her in and posted a Marine guard on her deck.

The official trial of engines and rudder, turret and guns, took place in February 1865. The tests were very satisfactory and the *Camanche* was commissioned on August 22, four months after the Civil War had ended at Appomattox on April 9.

Briefly, San Francisco had its ironclad—and something of an Irish Navy. Irishmen dominated Lt. Commander Charles J. McDougal's crew—Flynn, Berry, Regan, Flanagan, Donovan, Brennan, Lynch, Farley, O'Brien, Muldoon, Brophy, and so on. The *Camanche* made a few cruises around the Bay, but spent most of her time at a Mare Island pier. Post-war "demob" budget cuts virtually retired her. She was decommissioned on September 3, 1866 without ever having even growled at an enemy. Her Celtic crewmen were transferred to other war vessels and, to use a modern term, she was "mothballed." A newspaper bragged in 1880 that "She is at present lying at the Mare Island Navy Yard and, with three days notice, can be put in perfect fighting order." But no notice ever came over the next thirty years. A wooden superstructure, with an incongruous and un-Navy shingle roof, was built on her deck to serve, first, as a warehouse and later as a Marine barracks.

In 1896 the *Camanche* finally got back to San Francisco, to serve as a training vessel for the state's naval militia. She was still in good shape (except for her wooden deck, now covered with a mixture of tar and sawdust) but she had to be ignominiously towed down-Bay.

The antiquated *Camanche* was placed on active duty in 1898 during the emergency of the Spanish American War, as San

Francisco's old fear of Confederate privateers was recalled by rumors of raiding Spanish cruisers. The rumors proved groundless.

Since the state had acquired, in the meantime, a bark-rigged steamer for training the marine militiamen, the *Camanche* was not needed. In March of 1899, the Oakland firm of Pantesky, Bircovich and Livingston bought her, ostensibly to convert her into a freight ferry boat. But she actually did duty as a collier—really a lowly coal hulk—on the Bay. The *Camanche* was finally junked for her metal in the 1920s.

Captain Leale bought two officer's bunks before she was scrapped, one for the den of his home, and the other for Al Gerberding, then president of the Bohemian Club, who had just bought a country home in Belvedere.

Alfred Bates tried to defend the pathetic brute of an ironclad as a war vessel of national importance. "Though she never saw actual service, her presence on this coast largely aided to check the tendency to Secession, while her construction marked an era in California shipbuilding." Bates was probably right in stating that her (re)construction was "not without value in its tendency to strengthen and support the patriotic sentiment in the state." But the monitor did not really scare away any piratical Rebels.

Peter must have known that both his vessels—the *Saginaw* and the *Camanche*—were somewhat jinxed ships. However, they made him known to Washington and the Navy, and paved the way for later construction by the Union Iron Works of such powerful warships as the U.S.S. *Charleston*, *Olympic* and *Oregon*.

Honors came to Peter—the Colonel—Donahue after the war. He was chosen to serve as vice-president of the Society of California Pioneers during 1867-68 and as president, the youngest in the society's history, in 1872-73. The *City Directory* of 1867-68 gave his residence as San Mateo, but from 1867 until his death in 1885 he lived in his home on the corner of Second and Bryant streets, near South Park, even though the Second Street Cut (1869) began the ruination of the area as a posh residential district. Earlier he had lived at 66 Minna Street.

Even before the critical years of the Civil War, Peter's main interest had shifted from gas, iron and even shipbuilding to a new love—railroading. He was determined now to spend the rest of his years in this field of endeavor.

VI

THE WAY TO SAN JOSE

DURING THE CIVIL WAR, Peter Donahue transformed his early interest in railroads from streetcar lines to the real thing. He held considerable capital to work with now, for he had prospered along with the miners of the Comstock Lode whom he had equipped. The Nevada mines poured millions into San Francisco, driving down interest rates and feeding investments in industry and the new "glamor" field of business, railroading.

As early as 1849, San Franciscans planned a railway south for fifty miles along El Camino Real to the old Mexican *pueblo* of San Jose, chosen as the state's first capital. Engineer William J. Lewis got up a cost estimate for a road along the very shoreline of the Bay, though he did not actually examine the route. But interest in a railroad declined after May 1850 when a through-stage line went into service. The nine-hour ride cost a jolting $32 at first, on a road that was passable about half of the year. But rates and times shrank and some one thousand passengers took advantage of the service each month.

Citizens of both communities tired of costly and time-consuming stage travel, however, even though there was now a choice—either a through-stage taking eight hours or a boat to the Alviso stage, taking six hours. The people revived the idea of a San Jose railroad. And, imaginatively, they began to think of it as the last link of the long-promised Pacific (i.e, transcontinental) Railroad connecting the Atlantic states with San Francisco.

San Jose's Judge Davis Divine called for public meetings on the proposal on January 26, 1851, to start a drive. Subscription books were opened. To attract subscribers, estimates of public travel between the two points were published. For the seven months prior to February 1851, 10,500 had traveled to San Jose at an average fare of $15 a head. In addition, 2,000 board feet of lumber had been shipped to Alviso, making up a transportation total of almost $200,000.

Some accounts state that, in only a month, $100,000 was raised, but others insist that, as late as July, the railroad had only $50,000 of the sum that it needed, although Ralston, representing Vanderbilt, and agents of the Rothschilds were approached. Whatever "deal" was put together, the state's corporations code found it illegal and Divine had to lobby the so-called "Legislature of a Thousand Drinks" to rush through a new railroad law before adjourning to move the wandering capital on its merry way to Vallejo, en route (via Benicia) to a permanent location in Sacramento.

The Pacific and Atlantic Railroad, as it was grandiosely called, was organized as a company on September 6, 1851, with Judge Divine as president and Lewis as engineer. Lewis, dissatisfied with his earlier cost figures, saddled up his horse and finally rode over the terrain of his shoreline (Bayshore) route. By year's end, he gave the road's leaders a new cost estimate of $1,539,126.17 for all construction, including buildings and rolling stock. He reported that the grades of the alternate route through the San Bruno Hills were prohibitive.

After two years of effort, the would-be railroad had only $100,000, even on paper; all efforts to sell additional stock were in vain. Vanderbilt and the Rothschilds were not interested. The distraction of easier money in mining was blamed. Nor could British, or other foreign capital be attracted since not one tie had been laid as proof that the visionary Californians really meant business. The project died with bills in Congress for bonds and land grants. The Senate bill passed, but the other failed of passage in the House.

The railroad plan lay dormant, almost comatose, until October 23, 1853 when the company was reorganized with private money, and no franchise, by San Francisco's mayor, Commodore C.K. Garrison, already the vice president of the Sacramento Valley Railroad (the only railroad in California), and three associates. They took the huge block of unsold capital stock—$1,945,000 out of $2,000,000. They secured it, but apparently paid no cash.

A new route was planned by Lewis through a pass (really just a gap) in the San Bruno Hills in order to tap Mission Dolores traffic before descending the valley of Islais Creek. The Dolores district was busy not because of mission masses but the racetrack and bull-and-bear fight arena in the area. Garrison and his friends claimed title to tracts nearby which would increase rapidly in value if on a railroad.

Lewis estimated that stage and boat passenger traffic to San Jose averaged 150 passengers a day. He also expected considerable freight traffic to develop, including New Almadén quicksilver and San Francisquito redwood lumber as well as farm products, although most of the fifteen small sawmills were shut down because of the depressed price of lumber, and the equal number of lumber sloops on the "inside" (Bay) coast were tied up. Lewis predicted that the railway would change all of that. He estimated a future production of 30,000,000 board feet of lumber a year. His new figures showed the cost of the railroad to be $1,744,680.30, with annual expenses of $297,000 against receipts of $895,000, yielding a neat yearly profit of $598,000.

Assuming that Peter Donahue saw prophet Lewis's figures (it is almost certain that he did) and believed them, he must have drooled, figuratively speaking, at the latter's predictions of bonanza returns of 34 percent annually on one's investment.

The restrictions of railroad laws again impeded construction, so Judge Divine, with the help of Colonel C.L. Wilson of the Sacramento Valley Railroad, got an amendment through the legislature in 1854. But, before the railroad company could get up steam, the whole country was plunged into an economic depression by the Panic of 1855.

A February 1859 mass meeting resparked the project, but this time with a more realistic goal and name—the San Francisco and San Jose Railroad. (At first, in fact, it was planned to run from San Francisco only to San Jose's steamer landing at Alviso.) The state legislature was asked to pass a bill permitting a vote in San Francisco, San Mateo and Santa Clara counties on a proposition to subscribe $900,000 to the company's capitalization. When the suspicious San Francisco press opposed the plan, labelling it a fraud, a scheme of unscrupulous speculators to fleece an unwary and sheepish public, the promoters dissolved the company in June of 1860 by mutual consent. It was not to abandon the enterprise, but to "avoid several objections" and then to reorganize.

Was this the (unbuilt) railway to which Peter Donahue referred later in March 1874 when he told the Senate Committee on Corporations of his difficulty in raising money for his line, or did he mean the Sacramento Valley Railroad? "The first road built in San Francisco [*sic*] was on credit for the iron, and neither principal or interest was met, and when I built the San Jose Road, I had a lively time, by reason of it."

The *Alta* and other papers did not give up. They urged the public to organize a new company, and now Peter Donahue stepped in. he became treasurer of a reincarnated San Francisco and San Jose Railroad whose figurehead president was Judge Timothy Dame, Peter's friend. The vice president was another of Peter's friends, Henry M. Newhall, San Francisco's leading auctioneer. He became involved when he took a chance and cosigned a friend's note for $90,000 in 1857. When the note came due, his friend could not handle it, so Newhall paid it off in return for a one-third interest in the rail line. It was a total loss, thanks to the company's collapse. But Newhall was now as badly bitten by the railroad bug as was Donahue. He invested $2,000 in stock in the latter's railroad and was chosen for the vice presidency and membership on the board of directors. Charles W. Sanger was secretary. Other directors were M.D. Sweeney, C.H. Bodfish, B.F. Mann, T.C. Phelps, C.T. Ryland, and John Cater. Charles B. Polhemus and Charles Mayne later joined the board and, indeed, played major roles in the success of this second railroad to be built in the Far West.

Donahue, Newhall, *et al*, organized the railroad company in July, 1860 and got it incorporated on August 18. Peter let a construction contract to Charles McLaughlin and Alexander H. Houston in October. As usual, Lewis served as chief engineer. The line would be cheap to build, he assured Peter, except through the hills.

Houston and McLaughlin (the latter named general superintendent of the line) were natural choices since they held stock in the company. There was no advertising for bids. They were to complete the work in three years for $2,000,000. Houston was one of Donahue's Omnibus street car line associates. (But in 1864, Donahue and his colleagues, for their own protection, had to buy the contractors out and take over the entire enterprise. They found

McLaughlin's work unsatisfactory, and Houston was involving himself in too many losing speculations.)

Of the expected two millions in capitalization, individual subscriptions totalled somewhere around $238,000, $255,300 or $258,300, according to various sources. And some said that only $100,000 of these pledges was actually paid in. Donahue and friends had to, figuratively, dig into their own socks and mattresses and the balance would have to be raised by assessments as the road progressed. For almost a year, not a clod of earth was turned, but the directors were busy lobbying county boards of supervisors. Just in the nick of time, in April 1861, by a vote of the electorates, San Francisco County kicked in $300,000; followed by $200,000 from Santa Clara County, and $100,000 from San Mateo County. (The constituents had no say in the running of the railroad.) By July, $1,500,000 was already paid in. Until a permanent headquarters could be built, temporary offices for the San Francisco and San Jose Railroad were found at 415 and 302 Montgomery Street.

Donahue and Newhall's railroad should have been the first one completed in California. It was the oldest in conception. But delays caused it to be second to the short Sacramento Valley Railroad, from the capital to Folsom. However, the SF & SJ was the first important railroad in the Far West and one that was totally unlike most roads that followed it, such as the Central Pacific. They were the products of governmental largesse. Donahue's road received no federal subsidy or grants of alternating sections of land along the right-of-way. Alonzo Phelps later bragged that Donahue was "the man who had the skill to release the San Jose Railroad from its enthrallment . . . the only man in California who ever ventured to build a railroad without the aid of a land grant." Oscar Shuck, looking back, put the case in just about the same terms. To him, Donahue was "the man to lift the San Jose Railroad out of the quagmire in which that concern was engulphed." Perhaps Alfred Bates said it best. "The many perplexities and financial difficulties by which, at first, the directors were confronted, soon vanished before his [Peter's] iron will."

Of course, Newhall was a strong presence, too. In 1862 he and Peter each purchased one-third of the stock. But Donahue was anything but a figurehead treasurer. A perusal, for example, of the Minute Book for October 1864, now in the keeping of the California History Section of the State Library, records Donahue's many motions on nuts-and-bolts matters, from rewriting both passenger and freight timetables to canceling special Sunday trains.

Ground was broken in May of 1861 at San Francisquito in the middle of the line. But work really began at the San Francisco end and, that summer, pushed southward. The contractors set up five work camps, three in the one difficult stretch, the San Bruno Hills just south of the city where the land rose to 259 feet of elevation in the gap to be traversed. Another crew worked at San Jose and one at San Mateo, then just a hamlet that had been built around a hotel shipped around the Horn from Boston in pieces for reassembly in California.

The typical laborer was a green immigrant Irishman from the East who was given a hearty board of fresh beef, fresh-baked bread and, of course, potatoes. He probably saved his pay for a stake to take him to the gold mines in the Sierra foothills or the new Nevada silver mines.

As Civil War inflation increased, Donahue upped the pay of his gandy dancers. The San Jose *Daily Mercury,* for example, advertised on April 19, 1862 for would-be SF & SJ laborers to report to the Stockton Ranch near Santa Clara if they were interested in working for $30 a month and found. The track workers were fed "royally," said the press, because Donahue wanted them strong and content. He hoped to complete the line by January 1863. He was overly optimistic, not fully appreciating the delays in delivery of rails, engines, and other equipment from the East because of the Civil War. San Francisco was not quite ready to build locomotives when Peter began his railway, and there was no rolling mill on the Coast for rails.

The *Alta* wrote waggishly of the symbiotic relationship between the trackmen's progress and Donahue's walking commissary of beef cattle. The latter were "chewing their cuds under the great bay laurels and doomed to die for the route's sake. Converted from tender beef into stout Hibernian muscle, they do their best work after their death, and soon are promoted to the privilege of voting."

It would cost Donahue and his associates $40,000 a mile to finally spike rails of American iron, weighing fifty pounds a yard, into the durable redwood ties. But, by October 30, 1862, ties were distributed from San Jose to a point within fourteen miles of San Francisco on a roadbed already graded, bridged and trestled. Donahue imported his first locomotives from the East, the *A.H.*

Houston and *Charles McLaughlin,* followed by the *San Jose,* and began to build up a fleet of thirty-six passenger and freight cars.

On September 14, 1863, Donahue held a preliminary inspection trip over the completed portion of the line for San Francisco's supervisors, The *Call* on the 15th reported that the City Hall group took omnibuses to the San Francisco end-of-track, examined the last stub of the route, where rails were not yet laid, then boarded a platform car. Donahue had fitted up a new flatcar with temporary seats. The aldermen traveled at "a leisurely gait" behind the splendid engine *San Jose* to 17 Mile House, or Belmont, then the end-of-track. En route, they stopped to examine and admire culverts—"superior specimens of masonry"—and other works. From Belmont, the dignitaries and reporters were "whisked . . . at lightning speed" to the Club House at Easton's Race Track for a fine feast. Many toasts were made—to the railroad, its officers, builders, engineer, to the city of San Francisco, its representatives, the mayor, the press, and so on.

The *Alta* agreed with the *Call,* calling the trial run a perfect success. "The engine succeeded in passing all the native mustangs and wild, untamed, cattle that, with emulative folly, attempted a race. . . . The locomotive's whistle shooed cows off the track and persuaded an 'Open sesame!' to tollgates established along the road to protect private interests."

From the Club House to San Francisco, Donahue had his engineer run the *San Jose* at top speed. The *Call* reporter wrote, "And well she acquitted herself, making the remarkable speed of fifteen miles in fifteen minutes. Hats had to be held on with a tightened grip, while cigars fell from mouths because the speed was so great that smokers could not compress their lips about their Havanas." Small wonder that the thrilled travelers were in unanimous agreement that San Francisco's stock subscription was, far and away, the best investment that the city had ever made.

The first semi-public excursion to the end-of-track, then Mayfield (Palo Alto area), thirty-five miles from San Francisco, ran on Saturday morning, October 17, 1863. The *San Jose* (and perhaps another engine) hauled four hundred guests, half of them ladies, invited by Donahue. Governor Leland Stanford and Governor Gibbs of Oregon were among the passengers in six shiny new coaches costing $3,500 apiece, coupled to three baggage cars and a few freight cars, representing most of Peter's existing rolling stock.

The excursionists were crowded and uncomfortable, but remained in good spirits during the otherwise pleasant journey.

Backing up a mile and a half from end-of-track to the twin redwoods of San Francisquito Creek that gave Palo Alto its name, the travelers enjoyed a picnic feast of cold fowl, topped by chilled champagne and ice cream as President Dame circulated, chatting, through the crowd. He and Donahue promised to have more of the very latest and best passenger cars when the road should be extended to "the States," that is, all the way back East. Both men were really thinking big. They spoke of a "Lightning Train" running ahead of the sun on its return trips to San Francisco from a St. Louis terminal, with coaches fitted with seats having high adjustable backs, or convertible into beds.

From the 18th and Valencia Street terminal across from the Willows Resort near the Pioneer Race Course, or Mission Dolores Racetrack, regular passenger service was begun to Mayfield on Sunday, October 18, 1863 by General Superintendent Houston. The first train left at 8:30 a.m. and passed through Adolph Sutro's San Miguel Rancho, San Bruno, San Mateo, 17 Mile House, Belmont, Redwood City, and Menlo Park to arrive at Mayfield at 10:30. There the train connected with stages for San Jose. At San Mateo, stagecoaches for Crystal Springs connected with the "cars;" at Redwood City coaches departed for (now-vanished) Searsville. Donahue promised a daily round-trip to end-of-track, and hoped to add an additional train when his crews reached Menlo Park. San Jose stages connected with the return train at 10:45 to whisk people to San Francisco by 12:45.

McLaughlin hurried the work along and the rails were completed from Big Tree Station (Palo Alto) to San Jose in January of 1864. On the 16th, Donahue celebrated the formal opening of the entire line to passenger service only three and a half years after he started the company. Freight service began a month later and, by June, he had an all-freight train on schedule. Peter's San Jose station, at Fourth and Market and San Pedro streets, was described as an "imposing" brick building, at first. But, subsequently, the depot was dubbed "The Dog Kennel" because it was so small in comparison to the roundhouse and an adjacent wine warehouse. It was eventually turned into an S.P. freight depot.

January 16, 1864 dawned drizzly and chilly, but the cold and wet did not deter the two thousand people who crowded muddy Folsom and Napa streets in San Francisco from getting a ride to San Jose. Invited guests had to fight for seats with cash customers. In a great scramble, the red plush seats of the five passenger coaches were soon filled, mostly by ladies. A few dignitaries, San Francisco supervisors and such-like, refused to be "bumped" into the cattle cars, box cars, and flatcars fitted with railings and seats in Donahue's back-up second train which carried an overflow of more than seven hundred persons. One of the last to board the train was Donahue himself, reputedly distracted by some monitor *Camanche* business.

When the sun broke through the overcast by departure time, 11:30 a.m., spirits rose and the excursionists cheered as the Judge gave Engineer Keith the "high sign" or "highball" to urge the *San Jose* into a crawl up the stinking grade near the slaughter houses of Butchertown. The train passed St. Mary's College after crossing Precita Creek, then chugged up through the Deep Cut, or San Bruno Pass, dug through half a mile of solid rock, before crossing the high bridge leading to Summit Station, altitude 279 feet above sea level. Donahue's guests were now seven miles from San Francisco at a depot near the Abbey Hotel. This fancy roadhouse was far-famed for its $100 champagne dinners which got gents and their ladies in the mood for moonlight buggy rides back to town. It was downgrade to Twelve Mile Farm and Darius Ogden Mill's country retreat, to Twin Trees and Big Tree Station, historic Santa Clara Mission and, finally, the San Pedro Street station in San Jose.

Details of the trip are a bit fuzzy now. A San Jose *Mercury* reporter described the journey as a non-stop trip with would-be excursionists waving in vain attempts to halt the train at Redwood City and Mountain View as it flew past them at forty miles an hour. The conductor of the first train, Hugh McCormick, remembered (in 1925) that there were three stops—San Mateo, Redwood City, and Mayfield—where a few more celebrants were sardined aboard. (The conductor was a cousin of E.O. McCormick, general traffic manager and, eventually, president of the Southern Pacific, who started his own career by hauling buckets of water to thirsty track layers.) Perhaps both recollections were correct. Maybe the first section of the train declined to halt en route while the second section made a few stops to pick up passengers.

The shrill whistle of the train approaching the end of the line alerted Captain Isaac Bluxome's crack artillery battery of the militia, or California National Guard, on the lawn behind the depot. Some who were there recall a thirty-six gun salute, some only thirteen guns. (Memories are tricky.) The artillerymen had come down by stage the night before to lie in wait for the first iron horse.

Buildings were decked with flags of many countries and festooned with evergreen wreaths. Arrival of the first train had been set for noon, but the two trains, which puffed in together from a rendezvous at Santa Clara, did not heave into the sight of the mob at the station until 1:30. The *Mercury* reported electric excitement in the crowd of several thousand.

> Men, women and children cheered, hats and handkerchiefs were waved as the two trains came rolling up. . . . All through the morning hours squads of men dressed in military uniform were hurried through the streets. Stages loaded with military companies from adjoining towns came rattling over the pavements. Civilians were gathering in from the rural districts. . . . It was a glorious sight, such as was never witnessed in San Jose before. . . . The grand celebration, so much thought of, a day long to be remembered by the people of our city.

Certainly, conductor McCormick never forgot that day. Sixty-one years later, he recalled how "People crowded into the town from the San Joaquin Valley, from Gilroy, and Santa Cruz, on horseback and mules, and in rigs of every description."

Keynote speaker Mayor John A. Quimby of San Jose thanked the men of the San Francisco and San Jose Railroad who had completed their work in just three years' time. He then told his audience, "Today you will be convinced of the fidelity to the trust you have reposed in them. . . . Behold the substantially-built road! Its ponderous cars and buildings thronged with living freight of the eminent, the great, the gifted and beautiful. . . ."

Quimby introduced President Dame. Peter Donahue, no public speaker, maintained his usual low profile, but both he and Newhall spoke a few words. Dame, in contrast, had much to say. After all, he was a judge and, *ipso facto,* an orator. He recapitulated the long fourteen years of striving to tie San Francisco and San Jose together with iron rails, and the three years of actual building, vigorously prosecuted though the railroad was put to the test by Civil War inflation. He blamed the war for "disturbing our once-healthy commercial relations and the currency of the country . . . and the prices of material greatly enhanced until, finally, nothing short of cash, or its equivalent, would bring railroad equipment to this coast."

Dame optimistically called the road "the first link in the grand chain of railroads which is to bind the golden shores of the Pacific with the cornfields of the Mississippi Valley . . . . It is the equal," he said, "if not the superior, of any railroad in the United States." He praised his associates for their perseverence in overcoming all difficulties—he called them "impossibilities"—and added, "What the American is to the rest of the world, the Californian is to the American." He paid particular tribute to the financial ability of the railroad's directors. "Fortunately for the Company and the public, such gentlemen as Peter Donahue, Henry M. Newhall, and Charles B. Polhemus of San Francisco formed a part of the board of directors and, for them, to conceive is to execute. They declared that the road must and should be built and their money, their names, their influence, and their personal exertions were immediately devoted to the accomplishment of that object. To them, all praise!"

Dame then waxed poetic. "The time is not far distant when the 'Iron Horse' will be shouting his cry of joy on the hills and through the valleys of the great plain that separates us from the homes of our childhood."

Judge Dame ended his remarks with some lame railroadiana punning. Since he was "on time," he said that he would now "shut down the brakes" on his speech and "tender" his thanks to his audience.

Director T.J. Phelps followed Dame, to express his gratification at the changes that the railroad had already wrought and for those it would make in the future. "Well may we be proud and happy, this day," he concluded.

Phelps was succeeded by gentlemen offering resolutions of thanks—to the company, its stockholders, the community, Dame, the contractors—for the efficient, highly creditable, manner in which they had discharged their duties in building the road.

Music and drilling by military and firefighting companies followed the speeches, then a cold "collation" or buffet, plus a beef barbecue, wound up the festivities. The *Mercury* reporter, like everyone else, was torn between a desire to march (or to watch the marchers) and an urge to eat, as a savory aroma rose from the barbecue pits. He dutifully listened to the music and observed the drilling of the San Joaquin Zouaves in their baggy Algerian trousers; the Alviso Rifles; the Santa Clara Guards; Almadén Guards; San Francisco's Washington Guards; and Captain Bluxome's artillerymen. Firemen and even civilians drilled right along with the militiamen; after all, the Civil War was raging.

"At last," reported the *Mercury,* "having marched and counter-marched to the entire satisfaction of all, [they] arrived at the starting place, the depot buildings, where a free, bounteous repast awaited the multitude." According to the San Francisco *Bulletin* of January 17 and 18, 1864 (the *Mercury* of the 15th was silent on the point), the crowd's raving thirst was "moistened by no end of claret and champagne."

Conductor McCormick remembered that "six or seven cattle were roasted and three men were busy carving for four hours. Whiskey flowed freely and the merry-making continued through the town, for days."

The *Mercury* newsman whimsically recorded that order finally broke down in the chow line as thousands battled for position. "A captain from an adjoining township with his entire command were unable, without a single exception, to throw themselves around a particle of food, and fell back to the rear in disorder. We sympathized deeply with the captain, knowing that he handled his men with skill and dignity."

The excursionists returned to San Francisco in the cars during the cool of the evening. It had been a great day for San Jose. McCormick stated, "There hadn't been anything in this Peninsula region that had caused so much excitement since the discovery of gold."

Only a few weeks after the opening, Superintendent Houston added a second, afternoon, train. Passengers averaged seven hundred a day in February. The two passenger trains, plus a mixed train daily (a freight with one passenger car added on) served San Francisco's commuter public. Trains were well patronized, but Donahue and his associates soon discontinued the initial two-class system of travel. Many people bought cheaper second-class section tickets, to save a dollar, then sat in first. The conductor recalled, "Often, they would be loaded down with liquor as well as with firearms, so we didn't think it healthy to dispute with them."

In June of 1864, Mayor H.P. Coon of San Francisco and members of the boards of supervisors of San Francisco, San Mateo, and

Santa Clara counties made a formal final tour of inspection in behalf of the counties' stockholders. They reported their complete satisfaction with the SF & SJ.

The first regular train, October 18, 1863, hit a horse, but most runs were uneventful except for an occasional grass or crop fire started by sparks from the locomotive smokestacks. These blazes naturally angered the farmers. Stations, at first, were just sheds, and Menlo Park and Palo Alto had no shelters at all. The run initially took three and a half hours, then three hours, although there were, in the beginning only three stops. (The June 1864 Special train set a record. The *A.H. Houston* made it, non-stop, from San Jose to San Francisco in only one hour and twelve minutes.)

The trip to San Jose cost $3.00, making the railroad a big saving in money as well as time for the traveler. The days of $32, even $16, uncomfortable through-stage rides were long gone. Competition now was the Alviso boat, with a fare of only $3.00, but followed by a stage ride into San Jose costing an additional $5.00. These combination boat-and-coach travelers, according to biased McCormick, really got "Full value for the bumps they experienced in the two and a half hours on the road to San Jose, that was very dusty when dry and like a bog when wet." To make his point about swampy roads, the conductor told a San Jose *News* reporter who was interviewing him at age eighty-three (1925 that he had once gazed out of the window of San Jose's Auzerais Hotel in the 1860s to see a six-horse team mired in the middle of San Fernando Street.

McCormick remembered only one exciting event in subsequent SF & SJ history—the flood of 1867. Nine houses were washed up against the roadbed near the Guadalupe River. Using a raft, he helped rescue people. children, goats and chickens marooned on roof tops.

The railroad ran smoothly, though disgruntled San Mateo and Santa Clara county supervisors by the end of 1864 were claiming that too much profit was being plowed back into salaries and the purchase of new equipment, rather than into dividends. They demanded to be represented on the board of directors, but Peter and his colleagues simply ignored them.

Naturally, Peter Donahue worked hand-in-glove with his successors at the Union Iron Works to improve his railroad. When Nevada's silver boom began to imitate California's gold slowdown,

H.J. Booth and, especially, Irving M. Scott, were ready. Scott shifted to increased work in shipbuilding and repair and continued the beginnings of locomotive production, both begun by Donahue. Scott knew next-to-nil about railway engines, but he was a master of fire engines and stationary steam engines and had, doubtless, poked about the Baltimore and Ohio shops while working for Murray and Hazelton in the Maryland city. Donahue had great faith in him.

In any case, the SF & SJ needed the Union Iron Works. Peter was having problems with his Mason and two Norris engines on the steep San Bruno Hills pull, even though the record time of his *A.H. Houston* compares well with that of the crack Daylight Limited (fifty-eight minutes) using the S.P.'s later straightaway, the Bayshore Cut-off. He had begun the construction of the first two local engines, the *California* and *Atlantic*, for his San Jose Road; and the Sacramento Valley Railroad gave him orders for two more, but he had sold out his interest in the iron works by the time that they were ready for action.

Scott designed and built a superior locomotive. The compilers of the *Bay of San Francisco* described the *California* as "an elegant machine embodying several improved features originated by the builders." Many Westerners still believe, as did H.H. Bancroft in his "Iron Industries" article, San Francisco *Bulletin*, July 18 and August 7, 1865, that "The first railway locomotive was made in 1865 at United Iron Works for the San Jose Road, and so well that a dozen have been ordered there." Earlier, several small "tea kettles," small engines, had been shipped from the East in parts and reassembled for a San Francisco and Oakland Railroad. The May 18, 1862 (and October 13, 1871) *Alta* and the May 22, 1862 Sacramento *Union* described an engine built by Vulcan Iron Works for a proposed Oregon shortline. In 1864 a light engine, the *B. Mastick*, was built by a rival foundry for the Alameda Valley Railroad, though her trucks and wheels were shipped from the East. (Earliest of all was a toy locomotive! It was made by a Chinese and exhibited in San Francisco in 1856.)

But the *California* was, indeed, the first heavy locomotive built in the West. She was a 29-ton, 4-4-0, standard gauge engine with 60-inch drivers. When fully wooded and watered, she weighed in at 46 tons. Of excellent workmanship and graceful lines, she stood 16 feet tall from the rails to the top of her balloon stack. She was 42 feet long from the tip of her pilot, or cow catcher, to the tender's draw bar. Best of all, Donahue found that she cost less than inferior Eastern engines, when freight was figured in.

A big crowd gathered to see the *California* make her shortest, but most difficult, run at the end of July 1865. One account related that "The trial trip of the pioneer loco . . . was made the occasion of a festivity. When it made its appearance on the streets, drawn by eight horses over a temporary track to the railroad, much interest was manifested by the people of the city." In the telling, the number of dray horses in some accounts grew to twenty, as the locomotive was dragged bodily for the eight to ten blocks from the iron works to the terminal. The sweating and cursing teamsters had to employ hydraulic jacks many times to lift the maiden engine as her wheels sank to their axles in the soft, sandy streets.

Only a few days later, Scott was ready to give his pride and joy a trial. He invited some one hundred and fifty or more special guests, including Governor Stanford. The *California* set forth from the depot, tugging four coaches built in the SF & SJ's own shops near Mission Dolores. She not only ran well on Brannan Street and through the Mission district, she took in stride the steep grade of the San Bruno Hills (now called San Bruno Mountain) to Summit Station.

The *California* halted at San Mateo Station where little Josephine Polhemus waited. Her father, Charles B. Polhemus, was the road's new director and superintendent and owned the property on which the San Mateo track and depot stood. He took a wreath of flowers from his daughter and hung it between the flags above the locomotive's cow catcher, indicating a "Special" train. At Twin Trees in Palo Alto, the excursionists enjoyed a picnic buffet on the banks of San Francisquito Creek, dancing to the music of Walcott's Brass Band, and listening to speeches complimenting the engine's performance. H.J. Booth responded in behalf of Union Iron Works—and when Stanford just had to brag about his Central Pacific, Newhall, who had succeeded Dame as president, spoke spiritedly of the SF & SJ. The former auctioneer said that the line was no bagatelle, but a strong link of the Pacific (i.e., transcontinental) Railroad.

On the return trip, departing at 3:30, the engineer opened the throttle in Bernal Heights and Donahue's shiny new "loco" promptly equalled the west-of-the-Rockies speed record of the

Houston made a year earlier—sixty-seven miles per hour between Twin Trees and San Mateo. "This trial," recorded the *Bay of San Francisco,* "was an event in the mechanical history of California."

The *California* was soon joined by her UIW sister, the *Atlantic,* the SF & SJ's #7. (Engine #5 was a non-Union Iron Works machine, the *San Mateo.*) Donahue's friend, William Ralston, did not get two Scott engines for his Sacramento Valley Railroad, however. The Central Pacific, having taken over the short line, decided not to build the planned Placerville–Virginia City extension. It cancelled the order for one engine, but accepted Union Iron Works' #3, naming it the *A.A. Sargent* for the California Congressman who had introduced the Pacific Railroad Bill. These first Western engines were all called "Booth locomotives" but the greater share of the glory belongs to Scott, not H. J. Booth.

In the years 1866-67, Scott had to design a class of locomotives very different from his first 4-4-0 passenger engines. Five were for the steep grades of the Pittsburg, Antioch, and Black Diamond roads—three short lines getting coal out of Mt. Diablo. He also built a third locomotive of his own design for Donahue, the *Union.* It was an 0-4-0 "shunting" engine. The pioneer switch engine was remarkable for its short wheel base, only six feet, four inches, allowing her to take very sharp curves. Her cylinders were 16-by-18 inches; she had 48-inch drivers, and operated at 120 pounds of steam pressure.

By 1873, Donahue's old plant was a pretty fair replica of the Rogers plant in Paterson. Scott had built seventeen locomotives and had more work than he could handle. As early as 1866, he had $180,000 worth of unfilled orders on hand, for four locomotives and eight railroad cars, as well as for three large hoisting engines, six quartz mills aggregating seventy five stamps, two hundred tons of extra stamp shoes, dies, and many other smaller jobs.

Donahue's SF & SJ was, from the first, a paying proposition. Thanks to good management, it met its heavy obligations satisfactorily and enjoyed good will, though the *Mercury,* fearful of boosted fares once a ridership was established, suggested completion of a horse car line to passenger boats at Alviso to give the SF & SJ a taste of real competition to guarantee low fares. The railroad *was* remunerative. The average daily income in October 1863 was $298; in March 1864 it was $860.

Both Peter and Newhall worked to improve service. One of the latter's innovations was a special hunting car added to some trains on weekends. Under each of the fifty seats reserved for nimrods was a strong iron post for leashing a bird dog. Each mutt's fare was 20 cents.

Donahue gave his hometown a Valentine's Day present in 1864. On February 14, he moved the city terminal from the Pioneer Race Course to closer-in Fourth and Brannan streets after completing a spur from the main line at 20th and Valencia. He erected an improved station. Both passenger and freight depots remained on the north side of Brannan until 1866, when the passenger station was again relocated, this time to Market and Valencia. There it remained until the Southern Pacific moved it to Third and Townsend and placed the freight depot at Fifth and Townsend.

During the Civil War the so-called San Jose Road was used by militiamen to modernize training maneuvers and reviews. On a Washington's Birthday, for example, the 2d Brigade of the State Militia, (California National Guard) formed up, 1,300 strong, in San Francisco's Union Square. The militiamen than marched to the Fourth and Brannan depot, accompanied by a large flock of spectators. Once again, the capacity of the rolling stock was strained to the breaking point. When the *San Jose* finally pulled away with a long train of nineteen coaches, boxcars, and "flats" (flatcars), it was 11:15 rather than the announced departure time of 10:30. The *San Francisco* had already left with the early birds, largely the committee in charge of the affair. The *T. Dame* was busy hauling San Jose visitors to the parade grounds at Rocky Canyon near Summit Station. The regular morning train was cancelled.

The overload proved to be too much for the *San Jose,* the little engine that couldn't. It crawled up the heavy grade beyond Mission Dolores, but Houston had to send the *T. Dame* to her rescue. Both engines then stalled further up the grade and the *San Francisco* had to be sent to their aid. It almost took Donahue's whole fleet of "locos" just to get the soldier boys to their maneuvers. (Later, the railroad was rerouted to engineer Lewis's original Bayshore terrain of flat marshes, mudflats and water lots along Mission Bay, the latter filled for a roadbed and also to attract industry to the area beyond Donahue's Tar Flat. One of the first newcomers was Thomas Selby, who transferred his smelter and shot tower there from North Beach. Hills Brothers coffee led the way for food processors to the outer South of Market area, followed by Pacific Sugar Refining Company. Even the Pacific Mail Steamship Company, after a flyer at Benicia, moved to docks in the district.)

At 1 p.m., the Napa Artillery Battery fired the Governor's Salute. Governor F.F. Low sat his horse in review as cavalry, infantry and artillery—San Francisco's City Guards, the Ellsworth Zouaves in Franco-African garb, and the Franklin Guards—marched and countermarched in a display worthy of London's Earl's Court.

There was a big rush for the train after the ceremony and many people were left behind. Nobly, the 2d Regiment gave up its seats and marched all the way back to San Francisco. There were a lot of sore and blistered feet at that night's Grand Military Ball.

The railroad played a role in public service after the Civil War, as well. For example, in December of 1869 a new superintendent, Major Richard P. Hammond, provided free transportation when the California State Normal School, the first teachers' college in the Far West, uprooted itself from sinful San Francisco and moved to sunny San Jose.

In 1867 Polhemus sold his shares to Charles Mayne, who joined Peter and Newhall in promoting a thirty-nine mile extension of the SF & SJ to be called the Santa Clara and Pajaro Valley Railroad. Because of his San Jose Road's bonded indebtedness, $968,000, Peter had to scurry around to find money to finance the line to Gilroy, the next link in his dreamed-of transcontinental railway. He called on Billy Ralston, who was agreeable. Ralston liked Donahue, and he liked to race his trains on El Camino Real with his coach and four. Ralston also had a harebrained scheme to turn Gilroy into the tobacco capital of the West, a new Havana.

Ralston was now cashier of the powerful Bank of California. At the end of 1860, he and Ralph S. Fretz had merged their Fretz and Ralston Bank with Joseph A. Donohoe and Eugene Kelly's firm to form Donohoe, Ralston and Company. But Peter's old friend, Joseph Donohoe, was as conservative as he was honest. (In a time of wild speculation, he was called "The Safe Banker.") Donohoe became dissatisfied with some of Ralston's loans so, in mid-June 1864, the latter got the Bank of California incorporated. Donohoe, Ralston & Co. was dissolved, to be followed by Donohoe, Kelly and

Company. Briefly, Fretz and Ralston was revived until the Bank of California could open on July 5, 1864.

Cashier Ralston spoke to D.O. Mills, president of the Bank of California. Donahue soon had his money, and a treasurer for the SC & PV—William Ralston. Peter incorporated the new railroad and broke ground for it at San Jose's Fourth Street Station on April 21, 1868. Peter Donahue hoped to use his transcontinental link to tap new agricultural markets and the movement south of population toward Gilroy and its popular spa, Gilroy Hot Springs.

Peter Donahue, by now called Colonel Donahue, ran his first passenger train partway down the line on January 11,1869. He had the line completed and in running order by March 13. The opening was celebrated with a feast of chicken, turkey, ham, mutton, and pies and cakes, all sluiced down with champagne and claret. The food was followed by speeches. Newhall spoke of the early difficulties, when friends said that he had a "wild elephant", not a *pájaro* (bird) on his hands. The *Alta* paraphrased his remarks. "He begged to call the attention of those croakers to the fact that he had got the 'wild elephant' perfectly tame and in very good order. In fact, he proposed continuing the road to Kansas and St. Louis and New York; to much applause."

In January of 1870, the California Southern Railroad Company was incorporated to extend Peter's line from Gilroy to Salinas. Ralston was an officer of the company. But it did no building, probably because of Central Pacific—"Big Four"—machinations. Five years earlier, Peter had tried to merge his SF & SJ with a "paper" railroad, the Southern Pacific, that he and Newhall and other San Francisco financiers had incorporated on December 2, 1865. By combining several lines, Colonel Donahue had hoped to build over Pacheco Pass in the Coast Range from Gilroy, to run down the San Joaquin Valley to Los Angeles or San Diego; then hook eastward to the Colorado River to connect with a second transcontinental line rivaling the Union Pacific—Central Pacific's Central Route. This rival Pacific Railroad was being built by Cyrus K. Holliday from St. Louis down the Santa Fe Trail. Congress had allotted to the Southern Pacific alternate sections of public land on either side of the right-of-way, providing that it should join up with Holliday's Atlantic and Pacific Railroad. No other money or land subsidy was offered. Work had to start in two years, with a minimum of fifty miles of rails laid annually after the second year.

Originally, the Central Pacific's Collis P. Huntington and engineer Theodore Judah had sought Donahue's cooperation in building a transcontinental road. Donahue, Polhemus, and Newhall had bought up most of the SF & SJ stock to keep it out of the hands of politicians. On December 4, 1862, to quiet opposition to C.P. lobbying and monopoly, Huntington and Judah made public an agreement with an SF & SJ director, T.G. Phelps, to assign certain parties representing Donahue's railroad (apparently Dame, McLaughlin, and Houston) the rights, grants and franchises, and a subsidy of $16,000-a- mile, of the Central Pacific for that portion of the road between Sacramento and San Francisco. The C.P. would connect with the SF & SJ by a third "paper" road to be incorporated, the Western Pacific.

But Judah died unexpectedly and tragically, of typhoid fever, in 1863, and the Big Four had already suffered a (typical) change of heart as they reconsidered handing over $16,000-a-mile to Peter Donahue. The land grant sops to be thrown to him were eliminated from railroad bills in Congress and when President Lincoln signed the Pacific Railroad Act on July 1, 1862, Donahue found himself left out in the cold. The Big Four were determined to build, from tidewater to Promontory, without him.

The Colonel's old partner, Dame, had left the San Jose Road in 1861 to head the Western Pacific, incorporated by the so-called "Donahue Group." The first assignees of the SF & SJ had waived the rights to the Sacramento-San Francisco rail link and these were assigned to the Western Pacific. Dame got the ubiquitous McLaughlin and Houston to start construction in January of 1865. Rails were laid to Niles Canyon by October and the final link-up planned for just a year later.

But the cunning Big Four outflanked the Western Pacific by December of 1866, building a line from the C.P. terminus in Sacramento to deep water (and ferries) at Vallejo. When McLaughlin then got into a financial problem as a result of litigation over contracts and asked that all arrangements with the W.P. be cancelled, work on his railroad was halted. The C.P. made a deal with McLaughlin to repossess the franchise, letting him keep the land grants in exchange for the work that he had completed. With the Western Pacific now their creature, the C.P.'s Big Four blocked Donahue from a share—the last link—of the transcontinental railroad by running a line from Sacramento to Niles, buying up the local Oakland and Alameda Railroad and extending it to their track at Niles. In this manner, they were able to bring the first overland train to San Francisco Bay on September 6, 1869 entirely on Central Pacific iron, without touching one of Donahue's rails.

Meanwhile, Lloyd Tevis secured control of the Southern Pacific in the financial jockeying and, supposedly, squared off against Peter. But the public, suspicious of railroad barons, cried "Collusion!" and "Monopoly!" A bill of March 1868 in the state legislature made grants (outright donations) of thirty-acre parcels of land on Mission Bay, and the belief grew that the Central Pacific "Octopus" really controlled both lines. Leland Stanford, spokesman for the Big Four, repeatedly denied it, possibly on a technicality, because negotiations were not completed. If Tevis was independent of the Big Four, he may never have intended to build the Southern Pacific as a rival to their Central Pacific. Perhaps it was all a bluff, a device to block the C.P. from taking over the San Francisco waterfront.

Still, C.P. Huntington told Charles Crocker and Mark Hopkins that he did not want to take over the Southern Pacific. "As for the San Jose line," he said, "I would not do it." In fact, the C.P. was given the option of buying the SF & SJ, but chose not to exercise it. As historian David Lavender put it, the Big Four let Colonel Donahue's line slip through their fingers. But somehow Tevis then led the S.P. to acquire control of the SF & SJ, on February 2, 1868, though they remained separate entities.

The complicated behind-the-scenes maneuvering continued. On March 14, 1868, the *Bulletin* published Stanford's statement labelling as false the rumors that the C.P. or its lackey, the Western Pacific, was negotiating for the purchase of either the S.P. or the SF & SJ. The former governor said that the tale was entirely without foundation. (However on September 25, 1868, Stanford's crony, Huntington, signed the letter transmitting the required annual report of the Southern Pacific to the Secretary of the Interior. Small wonder that press and public scoffed at C.P. denials.)

When Congress, on July 25, 1868, extended the Southern Pacific's time allowance and lowered trackage requirements to thirty miles of rails by July 11, 1870, and only twenty miles per year after that date, the Big Four became nervous. They moved and shook the financial scene and took over the S.P., planning to run it to San Diego and from there to the Mississippi River.

Then the Big Four played the last cards of their hand. They remedied their earlier blunder in not exercising the option to buy Donahue's line and bought up the S.P.'s controlling share of SF & SJ stock. Then they pressured Colonel Donahue, Newhall and Mayne until they sold it and its extension, the SC & PV, to the Central Pacific. It was now October 12, 1870. Peter and his partners were made directors of the "new" S.P., into which the Central Pacific would eventually merge. Some say that William Ralston, "brokered" the sale. Lavender sugggests that it was Tevis, still nominally the president of the S.P. and a part-owner of the SF & SJ, who engineered the deal. He got a one-twentieth interest in the S.P.'s land grants, over Huntington's violent objections. The latter called it an exorbitant commission.

The sale of San Francisco's first railroad, and its Gilroy extension, resulted in "a very large advance on cost," in the masterful understatement of the day. The price of $3,250,000 meant a profit of almost $2,000,000 for Colonel Donahue, Newhall, and Mayne to share. They had invested about $500,000 in the two roads.

So quietly did the Big Four work in their machinations and, alas, so mum was the Colonel, that when trains reached Gilroy in 1869, the town was blissfully unaware of the deal in progress, or at least of its goal. Hopeful still of being on a rival transcontinental route, citizens erected a welcoming arch to put down the Central Pacific's High Sierra route. On the arch was lettered "No Snow Blockade."

Acquisition of Donahue's lines was part of the grand strategy of the Central Pacific to "build a fence" around San Francisco to keep competition away. It already had a beachhead on the Oakland shore and had designs on Goat Island (Yerba Buena) even if it could acquire the waterfront of San Francisco, south of Market Street. San Franciscans were suspicious of the bullying Big Four and opposed to their strangling all opposition. The wharves of the Embarcadero north of Market Street belonged to the state, not the city, but the C.P. got the legislature in '68 to introduce a bill to turn over to it (and its future subsidiary, the SF & SJ) title to a 6,000-acre strip of southern bay front, eight miles of it, to prevent any competing line from ever entering San Francisco.

Mass meetings denounced the C.P. plot and the bill was withdrawn. Next, the Big Four tried to "annex" Goat Island as its transcontinental railroad-ferry terminal. Again, the Big Four tasted (rare) defeat. They had to settle for the Oakland Mole built far out into the Bay on trestles.

In October of 1870 the Big Four merged Colonel Donahue's two lines—the Southern Pacific, and the "paper" line, the California Southern—to form a new corporation, the Southern Pacific Railroad of California. Even though Donahue, Newhall, Mayne, and Tevis all served on the board, they were no match for the financial wizardry of the Big Four who, of course, were also board members. (An 1884-85 reorganization of the system transformed the company into the Southern Pacific of today.)

The Big Four did not make Colonel Donahue's road the last leg of a transcontinental route. They were content with their mole off the Oakland shore. The SF & SJ grew into the Coast Division of the Southern Pacific, however. It was extended to Watsonville in January of 1871, to Salinas in 1872, and to Soledad the following year. It was not extended into Los Angeles for years, since the S.P. reached that city via the San Joaquin Valley and Tehachapi Mountains in 1876. However, the buying up of Donahue effectively sealed off any competition from entering San Francisco from the south.

Although outfoxed by the Big Four, Peter was not quite ready to surrender. He tried again, with Newhall and Ralston (who may have been the driving force in this particular project) to create a truly independent line to serve San Francisco. The San Francisco and Colorado River Railroad was organized on July 12, 1872, to be chartered for fifty years. The 900-mile-long road would reach the Colorado River between the 32d and 35th parallels of latitude, either in San Bernardino or San Diego County. At the California line of the river, it would connect with whichever road made it that far, the Texas Pacific or the Atlantic and Pacific.

Donahue *et al* estimated that $50,000,000 in capital stock, in 500,000 shares, would do the trick. This sum was the actual estimated cost of the right-of-way, motive power and rolling stock, and other equipment. The project received $3,900,000 in subscriptions and several millions more in promises. The company asked San Francisco for a subsidy of $10,000,000, expecting other counties—especially those of Southern California—to chip in their quotas. But the voters in the November election rejected the proposal, afraid that the money would go to the Southern Pacific. Naturally, the public did not want to buy, all over again, a road which their money in taxes and gifts of land had already subsidized. So, by happenstance, the Big Four again won out over a rival, even though Colonal Donahue had such allies as Newhall; Ralston; J. Mora Moss of the Sacramento Valley Railroad; bankers F.L.A. Pioche, Jules Bayerque and John Parrott; wholesale merchant William T. Coleman; Michael Reese, a shrewd merchant and real estate developer; A. Gansl, the Rothschilds' representative in the West; George E. Howard and John O. Earl, trustees and incorporators of the Bank of California; pioneer Josiah Belden; and Henry D. Bacon, the banker who helped Ralston and the Pacific Insurance Company out of the financial trouble caused by the great Chicago fire.

The public, suspicious as ever, would not buy it. When the press, ("scurrilous newspapers," charged H.H. Bancroft) turned against Donahue and his associates, it was all over. The Committee of One Hundred dissolved itself in late August of 1873 and Peter's last try for a transcontinental line to rival the Southern Pacific's Central Route—"a good and feasible plan," opined Bancroft—fell through.

VII

RAILROAD MAN

ALFRED BATES, in summing up Colonel Peter Donahue's life for Bancroft, wrote that "It is in connection with railroads that Mr. Donahue's influence had made itself most indelibly felt. . . . His enterprise and ability accomplished more for the common good than any one man or any combination of men, with the exception of the syndicate which controlled the Central Pacific system." For, although his two roads south of the city had disappeared into the monopolistic maw of the Central Pacific, the Colonel was now looking north of the Bay for new railroad worlds to conquer.

Peter became interested in the sunny hills and shady redwood groves of Sonoma County. He decided to tap the trade in grain, fruit, and sandstone, the latter supplying the city's cobblestones and building blocks. Nor did he fail to notice the dairy products of adjoining Marin County, where 2,000 to 3,000-head herds fattened in the meadows. But he had his eye particularly on the redwood lumbering of the Russian River Valley. Like Henry ("Honest Harry") Meiggs before him, Donahue saw the Redwood Coast as a perennial provider of lumber for the growing metropolis of San Francisco. He was also visionary enough to see the recreational potential of the two counties' beauty spots, especially their wooded valleys.

Of course, the Colonel was not single minded in business. He did not cut himself off from non-railroad affairs during his "boomer" days, the 1870s and early 1880s. He kept in touch with the Union Iron Works as Irving Scott toured the world's shipyards (1873) to prepare for expansion of shipbuilding in new quarters in the Potrero district. When H.J. Booth retired in 1875, the works became Prescott, Scott & Co. under George Prescott and Irving and Henry Scott, the biggest business of its kind west of the Rockies. Some five hundred or more men were at work, many on marine engines, but others on mining machinery. (In 1881-82 there was a burst of railroad activity; the UIW turned out eleven locomotives, mostly narrow gauge engines for mining or logging operations.)

B.E. Lloyd in his *Lights and Shades in San Francisco* (1876) praised Irving Scott, along with Risdon's Moore and Pacific's Fogg, as men "having no superior anywhere in the knowledge of the details of mining machinery." They had learned well from the example of the pioneering brothers. What Lloyd wrote in 1876 had been even more true back in the heyday of the Donahues, twenty years earlier. Lloyd, describing Prescott, Scott & Co. (still called the Union Iron Works by everyone) as the most extensive foundry and shops on the Coast, added,

> The foundrymen of San Francisco labor under some peculiar disadvantages. Everything that is ordered is wanted in the greatest hurry possible! The mining companies, in particular, never make up their minds what they want until they want it, and then it is needed immediately. Plenty of jobs have been undertaken and finished by our local workers in a space of time which would look preposterous to persons in older communities. Another thing is that people on this coast expect more out of machinery than they do anywhere else. An engine is generally made to do twice as much work as it is expected to do by other people.

On February 23, 1878, the *Argonaut* paid a call on the iron works and came away impressed by the sight of several hundred able-bodied men, "swart-visaged and broad shouldered," under the leadership of one guiding mind (Irving Scott's), manufacturing 1,200 tons—$300,000 dollars worth—of pumping machinery requiring specially-built (stronger) railroad cars to freight it to Nevada's Yellow Jacket Mine. "It is composed of innumerable screws, cranks, pulleys, pistons, rods, belts, bars and all sorts of, to us, mysterious machinery."

Editor Frank Pixley thought that the monstrous hunk of machinery taught a good lesson in economics. "Here there is no conflict between labor and capital." Built by capital, and for capitalists, it provided labor for many of the shops' 550 men.

Moreover, such labor-saving devices in the mines kept American workers independent citizens, rather than peons. The *Argonaut* then lambasted San Francisco's whining idlers—"mainly foreigners," the anti-Irish Pixley reassured his readers—who complained that they could find no work, while mouthing platitudes about labor versus capital.

In 1879, the talk of the (industrial) town was the Union Iron Works' $500,000 pump for the Union Consolidated Mine, capable of removing 106,000 gallons of water an hour.

In 1875, the Colonel's mind was taken off of plans for North Bay railroading when the Bank of California collapsed after accusations that his friend Ralston had misused four or five million dollars of its capital. Ralston drowned in the Bay, quite possibly a suicide. A nine-man syndicate, headed by William Sharon, resuscitated the bank. Sharon subscribed a million dollars and bullied a reluctant D.O. Mills to contribute an equal amount. E.J. (Lucky) Baldwin threw in a like sum. Donahue became one of the nine and made strong "verbal guarantees" that helped restore the bank's credibility and made it easier for Sharon to raise $7,000,000 in all. But Peter actually contributed only $100,000 of his own money. Possibly this was because he had to respond to a cry for help from Los Angeles, and from his own brother-in-law, former governor John G. Downey.

The enforced closing of the Bank of California in San Francisco sent almost seismic shocks statewide through the economy. Donohoe, Kelly & Company was one of only two banks that remained unscathed. Isaiah W. Hellman, cashier of the Farmers and Merchants Bank of Los Angeles, was on vacation in Europe when banking crashed in Southern California in an 1875 domino effect. Hellman's partner, President John. G. Downey, Mrs. Donahue's brother, took charge. Downey and Hellman made a good team, but Hellman was the more astute banker.

Donahue's brother-in-law first made a special report to the public that the bank had never been in better shape. "We have now in our vaults as much coin as is needed for the transaction of our business." However, lines began to form; none of the customers in the queues were depositors. Downey decided to close the bank.

Downey was a Forty-Niner who, as a San Francisco druggist, took ship to San Pedro and walked from there to Los Angeles to save the stage fare. As an apothecary who dabbled in cattle, sheep, and real estate he gathered in a modest fortune. In 1868, with Alvinza Hayward's help, he founded Los Angeles's first major bank, in the Downey block. In 1871 he merged with Hellman & Company to form the Farmers and Merchants Bank.

At the age of forty-eight in 1875, the former governor was a pleasant and accessible man, ruddy of face, active in his movements and a little below medium height.

When the crisis came, Downey got his only major rival, the Temple and Workman Bank, to agree to close its doors also, as a precautionary measure. Since the two firms dominated Southern California banking, their suspension of business panicked the whole area.

Downey hurried to San Francisco for financial help. Unable to get assistance through normal banking channels, he appealed to Colonel Donahue and, possibly, to Edward Martin. According to legend, he borrowed about $200,000 from Donahue at an excessive, "ruinous," rate of interest. (The interest norm in 1875 was 1¼ to 1¾ percent a month). Actually, he borrowed $20,000 from Peter on September 3 at 1 percent a month and, on September 9, another $20,000 at 1½ percent. He also obtained a credit of $100,000, *personally* guaranteed by Colonel Donahue at the National Gold Bank. Downey pledged as collateral fifteen notes totalling more than $175,000, most bearing interest of 1½ percent a month, though some bore only 1 percent.

When Hellman returned from Europe, he got his friends and business associates, the Haas brothers of San Francisco, to guarantee to pay every cent of Farmers and Merchants deposits, should it become necessary. He then hurried to San Francisco, supposedly to quickly pay off the debt to a usurious Donahue. Actually, he did nothing of the sort. He did not pay off the debt from his own resources, though a loyal associate told historian Dr. Ira Cross that had necessity arisen Hellman was ready to use every dollar that he possessed to save his bank from disaster. Dr. Robert Glass Cleland examined Farmers and Merchants records and found that the Donahue loan was paid off gradually by the bank over the next year. Hellman actually borrowed $15,000 from the Haas brothers at the same 1½ percent and also $4,000 from Lazard Freres. It is said that he also got a cash committment of $55,000.

Hellman returned to Los Angeles on September 29 and announced the bank's reopening for business, which took place on

October 1. Although Downey had closed its doors, he had not suspended payments. Every check presented at Hellman, Haas & Company was paid. The result was that, when the doors opened again, there were more deposits than withdrawals.

F.P.F. Temple of the rival Los Angeles bank also rushed to San Francisco for help, but he had no Donahue brother-in-law. The short Temple, five foot four, was called *Templito*—"Little Temple"—by his *Californio* friends, and was married to the daughter of pioneer William Workman. He went to Lucky Baldwin, who advanced him $210,000 in exchange for a blanket mortgage on his landholdings and those of Workmen and a friend, Juan M. Sánchez. Sánchez was very worried about dealing with the tricky Baldwin. He told Harris Newmark, "*No quiero morir de hambre.*" ("I don't want to starve to death.") He nearly did.

The Temple and Workman Bank had the reputation of being a place where you could get a loan without adequate security, so it suffered from some bad-risk loans and might have collapsed of its own weight even without the shove given it by Ralston's failure up north.

Temple personally escorted a total loan of $240,000 in gold onto the 7 a.m. Southern Pacific train of December 4, 1875. Under Wells, Fargo guard, it was transferred at the S.P.'s end-of-track, Caliente, to a stagecoach for the twenty-three-hour ride over the Tehachapi Mountains to Los Angeles. The Wells Fargo guards were disguised as passengers. They were alert because of a rumor (true) that bandit Dick Fellows had "smelled out" the bullion shipment and was after it. Each guard had his own revolver, and shared two double-barreled shotguns and a Henry repeating rifle.

The gold got through safely and Temple reopened his bank on December 6, 1875. He was, briefly, a local hero, the "Ralston of Los Angeles" to that city's *Daily Star.* But the *Star* completely underestimated the gravity of the situation, stating that the panic was but a passing surface ripple that would soon be forgotten as trade returned to its usual channels. The bank soon exhausted its transfusion of funds and closed again, forever, on January 13, 1876.

Lucky Baldwin took over the lands around Santa Anita and when he died in 1909 he left a $20,000,000 estate. Sánchez died penniless, like so many *Californios;* Workman committed suicide on May 17, 1876; and Temple died, broken-hearted, in April of 1877.

Thanks to Colonel Peter Donahue, the Farmers and Merchants

Bank averted such tragedy. It weathered the financial storm and remained solvent. Hellman and the directors were displeased with Downey's closing the bank, so he was replaced as president at the next meeting of the stockholders, July 19, 1877. Hellman took over as president and held the office for decades. Downey was continued as a director. He was involved in some small litigation with the bank after he retired, but he and Hellman retained their relationship in business interests.

* * *

Peter Donahue continued his strong interest in the gas company. He was pleased to run twenty miles of gas pipes within the new Palace Hotel in 1875; its courtyard alone had 516 gas jets. He was a guest on October 14, 1875 at the hotel's first formal banquet, for General Philip Sheridan. The *Alta* noted that "Hon. Peter Donahue proposed a toast to the memory of Admiral Farragut."

In 1874, the Colonel had reduced gas rates from $4.00 to $3.15, perhaps seeing the handwriting on the wall. In November of 1878 he dropped them to $3.00, as a new state law set maximum rates. But this did not satisfy all gas company critics, especially the editor-publisher of the *Argonaut*, Frank Pixley.

Ostensibly a muckraking reformer, Pixley was a supporter of Stanford and the Central Pacific and anti just about everything else. He was as careless with fact as was the discounted "martyr" of Vigilante days, James King of William. Ambrose Bierce ("Bitter Bierce") once proposed an epitaph for him—"Here lies Frank Pixley—as usual."

The *Argonaut* ran social notes on Irish families, such as the "news" that the Colonel's daughter Mary Ellen (Mamie), who gave a dance for friends in December 1878, spoke French; that Mrs. Annie Donahue (on August 16, 1879) wore a blue and white silk dress; and that former governor Downey's wife, visiting Edward and Eleanor Martin with her husband, was of Spanish descent, had married at fourteen and now, twenty-seven years later, still looked "like a school girl." Pixley also maintained a running battle with Donahue and his business activities, missing no opportunity to denounce them.

In December of 1877, the *Argonaut* supported Jennings Cox and his associates when they asked the city for permission to lay gas pipes in competition with Donahue's monopoly. Cox offered to give bonds for honest performance of the work and to forfeit the plant if he should fail to carry out the work. "To bring relief to San Francisco house-holders . . . ," editorialized Pixley, "We say to the Board of Supervisors that it cannot honestly withhold the concession asked for by the new concern." Piously, Pixley added, "It is not our mode of argument to attack the personnel of the existing gas company. Its stockholders have a good thing. It is natural that they should desire to retain it. But the people have rights that ought to be respected." The Colonel's gas works weathered the storm, as usual.

Pixley was soon back, March 9, 1878, with a new attack. He now (absurdly) lumped Donahue's Gas Light Company with the "Octopus," the Central Pacific (and the Spring Valley Water Company and the Butchers' Association—"wealthy killers") as "monopolies above the law, independent of the courts . . . . Their history has been an uninterrupted conflict with authority." And, warned Pixley, "Great financial powers never compete, they always combine."

"The Gas Company," he wrote, "is the growth of an early enterprise that has seized and enjoyed the exclusive right to light our streets and houses and, by force of its purchasable power over legislatures and rival companies, has now, for a quarter of a century, held our people in its iron vise and retailed to us its light, deficient in quantity and defective in quality, at its own price and its own measurements. There has never been found a legislature or a board of supervisors, or a Gas Inspector, resolute and unpurchasable enough to withstand the blandishments of its persuasions, the influence of its bribes, or the terror of its threats."

According to Pixley, the San Francisco Board of Supervisors had long demonstrated its weakness, ignorance, and dishonesty. While the press took both sides of the gas issue, public men violated their word, said Pixley. Every supervisor, "a defiant and fearless enemy of monopoly," eventually crawfished and sold himself out of ambitious desire for office or a lust for "cold, clinking coin."

To Pixley, Donahue's gas company was "the most vexatious of all our monopolies." The remedy was not legislation, or regulation of the price and quality of gas, but simply the granting of other gas franchises. "It is said that a concession being given, the Company will buy it up. Let them do so; then grant another one every Monday till the Company tires of being blackmailed, and until an honest man is found who will do as he agrees and [will] introduce honest competition in gas. The city should make no contract with the Company for a period longer than a year." Pixley actually realized that the solution lay only a few years off, for he added, "We believe the time is not too far distant when the electric light will relieve us."

On May 24, 1879, Pixley got in a new dig at the San Francisco Gas Light Company, by noting that gas lights were not allowed to be substituted for candles on church altars. He was unsure whether it was a matter of religious scruple or simple economics. "At the present rates for gas, few churches, either Catholic or Protestant, can really afford that precious fluid.... It has been suggested that, by an arrangement with the directors of the Company, the surprising bills might be paid in salvation; but as corporations have no souls, and the equivalent of even the most remarkable gas bill would not go very far toward saving the individual mortal parts of the directors, the proposition has not met with much favor."

On December 6, 1879, Pixley—never averse to spreading rumors, even those he seemingly repudiated—reported on a tale that was being laughed at in the streets as a good joke. The story was that Donahue's gas company, desirous of a five-year contract renewal, needed four board votes, so it bribed four supervisors, paying the whole bribe to one of them. However, the recipient failed to divvy up the $80,000 of loot with his fellow supervisors and, instead, bolted for the East. Neither the gas company or the three close-mouthed supervisors had a right to complain, even if they had dared to do so.

Pixley, with tongue presumably in cheek, concluded. "We do not believe a word of this story. The history of the Gas Company forbids the idea that any member of its directory would use money to corrupt a legislature, court or supervisors, while there is no member of the retiring Board against whom there is the remotest suspicion of bribery or other dishonest practice."

In the July 30, 1880 issue of the *Argonaut* Pixley devoted almost an entire page to an attack on Colonel Donahue as a split personality, a Jekyll and Hyde. He titled the long profile "The Dual Peter:"

There are two Peter Donahues in San Francisco—Peter Donahue the Individual, and Peter Donahue the Institution. Peter the Individual is an exceedingly generous, warm-hearted, amiable person who delights in doing kind and clever things. Peter Donahue the Institution is a grasping, heartless, soulless, crusty old curmudgeon, mercenary, mean and illiberal. Peter the Individual is an enterprising man; Peter the Institution is an obstructionist. Peter the Institution is a black, greedy spider that weaves its web of monopoly in every dirty corner where he can fix it, and murders by starvation every unhappy fly caught in its meshes.

Peter the Individual conceived the generous idea of building a railroad through the fertile and beautiful counties of Marin and Sonoma; as soon as he had accomplished this work, Peter the Institution comes in and runs it in the crankiest, meanest way. Peter the Individual was popular all through both counties; Peter the Institution is hated and despised for its narrow and illiberal administration of a property that is enriching it.

Peter the Individual was one of the first to aid in building street railways, and the city gave to him generous charters and special privileges; but so soon as completed, and as soon as Peter the Individual had become the Institution, it became Peter the Monopolist and undertook to squat down in Montgomery Avenue and steal its use from the people who opened and paid for it. Peter the Institution began to play the dog in the manger, and while it did not use the avenue for its own road, it went to law with the company that did want to use it. Peter the Individual would scorn to do a mean, or dishonest, or dishonorable act; but Peter the Institution would blackmail and rob, and take its neighbors by the throat, and choke them till they gave it money.

Peter the Individual, away back in the early days of San Francisco, conceived and carried out the enterprise of lighting the streets and houses of San Francisco with gas. It was a bold and daring experiment, costly and venturesome, demanding nerve and business capacity. He imported pipe, machinery and skilled scientists; gave us a gas system quite creditable to our city; and, considering those early times and our remote position, and the fact that the gas business was then in its infancy, our friend Peter (we mean Peter the Individual) did exceedingly well. Then he was very popular, and very justly popular, and if he had not permitted the business to get away from him, and let it fall under the control of Peter the Institution, he would have prospered. But, unfortunately, he turned it over to the Institution; and of all the fraudulent practices ever indulged in by a most exacting, illiberal, unjust Institution, this double of our friend Peter played us the worst. From the very day that, as Individual, he yielded its control, it was blackmailed right and left; blackmailed by individuals, by supervisors, and by legislators. It was pounced upon by lawyers; it was mulcted, and robbed, and plundered, and sweated. Then its stock was increased and watered till a property that ought not to have cost four millions, and can be duplicated for three millions, cost—or was said to have cost—ten millions. The result—a set of dilapidated, shaky, old-fashioned, tumble-down works with leaky pipes and thieving meters, that produce and distribute bad gas at an exorbitant rate.

Peter the Individual is an exceedingly courteous person, and entirely without airs, approachable by anybody; but Peter the Institution, when it resolves itself into a "board", becomes obstinate, pig-headed, and uncommunicative, thinking everybody has a price, and concluding that the best way to settle any difference of opinion is to purchase the man holding that adverse opinion. Hence, when Peter the Institution has a controversy in any business matter, it is apt to consider that it is dealing with institutions instead of with gentlemen.

Peter the Individual is a popular person, and in friendly relations with the community in which he resides, and which has enriched and honored him; Peter the Institution is a quarrelsome, irascible, swaggering brute, quarreling with everybody with whom it comes in contact. It is in bad odor in Sonoma County; it is quarreling with thirty thousand people in the north end of the city because it is depreciating the value of their property, and subjecting them to annoying personal inconvenience; and it is quarreling with all the people of the city of San Francisco by the conduct of its business.

Peter the Individual never goes to law and is in no sense litigious, but Peter the Institution is an unceasing litigant. It has a suit now pending against the Potrero Railroad Company, and it has provoked the biggest sort of a fight concerning gas. The court will defeat the institution "It"and allow the thirty thousand people along Montgomery Avenue and Union Street to enjoy the right-of-way over those avenues without paying tribute to "It"; and the new Pacific Gaslight Company will either compel Peter Donahue—the old gas institution—to reform its ways, improve the quality of its gas, and reduce its price, or go into bankruptcy or into annihilation, where it belongs.

We are not sorry for our friend Peter the Individual, because he has more money than he knows what to do with, more than is good for him; and we would rejoice to see our enemy, Peter the Institution, go to the devil just as fast as possible.

It is a curious thing, this dual character, and one that we often philosophize upon and which, so far, we have not satisfactorily solved. We do not quite understand how it is that clever, honorable, honest and most kind-hearted gentlemen do such infernally nasty, mean and contemptible things when, as directors or trustees, they become institutions. Men that, as individuals, would scorn to do any dishonorable act, and who are full of generous and kindly sentiments, will, as directors of a mining company (using this as an illustration) lie and cheat and steal, and commit perjury and subornation of perjury, bribe judges and lawyers and supervisors and legislators, and would burglariously break into a church in the night-time to steal the last crumb from a blind and aged mouse in the final agony of starvation.

There are a great many of these dual characters in California—in San Francisco—and they are a curse to the community. It is a privilege and a duty to help to destroy them in their institutional capacity, just as we are now endeavoring to defeat the institutions known as Peter Donahue the Omnibus Railroad Company and Peter Donahue the old San Francisco Gaslight Company. In doing this we are working to give a comfortable cable-road through Montgomery Avenue and Union Street, instead of the nasty old bad-smelling cars, drawn by over-strained horses; and instead of bad-smelling high-priced, inferior gas, to give the community clear, brilliant, pure gas, in sufficient quantity and at the lowest possible cost of production. In this last business, every man or woman who consumes gas can assist—that is, assist themselves—by encouraging the new gas project; not by advancing money, but by simply agreeing to take the new product at two dollars per one thousand cubic feet, provided it is of an illuminating power equal to twenty sperm candles.

And when Peter Donahue the Individual dies—at some far distant day—we shall hope the golden gates may swing wide for his entrance, and that the good Saint Peter will hand him the easiest of golden stools and the sweetest of golden harps, and usher him into the brightest place and nearest to the throne, where in the enjoyment of a celestial light ever so many millions bright in candle-power, he may go singing down the groves of eternal time.

But when the "Institution" dies—and may the devil give it speedy shrift—we hope to see it kicked past the dogs and through the iron gates to the darkest and deepest hell, where it may suffer in torment the pangs of hottest tar and chokiest ammonia and best of burning anthracite, through the unending cycles of eternal time, in company with all the other monopolies of this city and state—except the Spring Valley Water Company; and the reason we would except this company is because its mains would be liable to burst and put out the fire.

Few, if any writers, had Pixley's gift of gab—and diatribe. But most of them offered a different picture of Colonel Donahue. Oscar Shuck, for example, in his *Sketches of Leading and Representative Men of the Pacific* (1870) had lavished praise on the Colonel.

The leading incidents in the life of Mr. Donahue serve to show, better than any labored eulogium, the manner of man he is. These facts tell their own story; each of them is eloquent of his characteristics—of duties fulfilled and difficulties overcome. . . . He rose with every occasion until, from being the instrument in carrying out other men's ideas he became himself, a projector of great enterprises and the controller of enormous wealth . . . . Firm and self-reliant, with the will to dare and judgement and business experience joined to the command of capital, he is able to carry out to a successful termination any project upon which he may enter. To such men the progress of our country is due . . . .

Being yet in the prime of life, it is reserved for him, no doubt, to add other monuments of enterprise to those we have already named, and to share in the future glories of the city he has watched and so ably assisted from its inception . . . .

While Mr. Donahue has become a millionaire in the course of his business he, at the same time, has kept his heart free from what some writer calls "metallic corrosion." His charities are everywhere spoken of, and those that reach the public ear are but a tithe of the generous deeds he is constantly performing . . . . Struggling merit has no stronger supporting hand, and suffering poverty no more prompt alleviation. No worthy object appeals to him in vain . . . . We honor him as a man and feel pride in him as a Californian. This shows to what a position a poor boy, by industry and honesty, may attain.

Shuck considered Colonel Donahue eminently qualified to bear the title of *Founder* of San Francisco. "His was not the task to apply his capital in carrying out the schemes of others, but he inaugurated the schemes, and his energy brought them to a successful conclusion . . . ."

Shuck ended with a pretty and poetic note, "The evidence of his active usefulness is diffused throughout the community, [so] that it is as difficult to enumerate or catalogue his many works as to segregate the atoms of the sunbeam that fills a room with light."

The April 7, 1877 "Pen Portraits" in the *Post* was more descriptive than eulogistic in treating the local business hero, Peter Donahue: "A fine-looking man with a finely-set head and a free bearing . . . . Particularly: strong, thick hair, brushed well back from a low, broad forehead; eyes deep-set and clear; cheeks smooth, full and clean-shorn; the mouth covered by a heavy, straight moustache and the chin also hidden by a tuft of grizzled beard; nose short but firm; ears set close to the head with more above them than behind them; neck massive but not stubby; shoulders broad; chest full. To these are added neatness of attire, geniality of manner, a clear voice, the love of a joke, even though it play at boomerang, a swinging walk, a fresh laugh, and the knowledge of how to fit himself anywhere . . . ."

So much for Peter's looks. As for his character, the paper added a *Post*script: "A splendid example of honest 'push,' he has ever a compassionate ear for those who have not so successfully striven;

for whilst his one hand is a stranger to the good the other does, there is no man [who] can say he has unavailing presented a worthy cause to Mr. Donahue."

Even muckraker Pixley had something nice to say about Colonel Donahue when, on October 27, 1877, he scotched false rumors about the failure of Milton Latham's North Pacific Coast Railroad. He attributed the tales to the city's ubiquitous mining stock speculators, who were hoping to depress the stock market by spreading malicious slanders against certain leading businessmen of San Francisco. In lecturing his readers, Pixley tossed a bone of praise to Donahue as well as to Latham and even the hated head of the "Octopus," Stanford. "The prosperity of our country and the progress of our city depend upon such legitimate undertakings as have been accomplished by Governor Stanford and his associates, Mr. Peter Donahue's North Pacific, and Mr. Latham's North Coast. Railroad men, merchants who own shops, manufacturers who create, miners who develop, farmers who produce, are an infinitely more desirable class of rich men than bankers, brokers, speculators and usurers."

But Frank Pixley was soon back to his old tricks. In an April 24, 1879 editorial in the *Argonaut*, he noted that Peter was on the board of the Hibernia Bank. Sure that the firm was all-Irish in ownership, he wrote of the directors—"they are suspect."

Hibernophobe Pixley's polar opposite was Dr. Hugh Quigley, author of the 1878 book, *The Irish Race in California.* He, unfortunately, tangled the Donahues up with the Donohoes in discussing railroad barons. (Banker Joe Donohoe was a subscriber, or sponsor, of Quigley's volume). He also confused Latham's North Pacific Coast and the Colonel's SF & NP but, nevertheless, managed to praise Peter at the same time that he blasted the Central Pacific clique. Quigley accused the Big Four of avarice and a kind of reverse racism. He claimed that the C.P. directors coveted money, but found their covetousness natural in such an upstart aristocracy as theirs. Worse, wrote Quigley, the Big Four testified that their "China heathens" (his words) were "far better men, and cleaner and more truthful than any white poor trash." Quigley continued, "The statements we are compelled to make in the interests of truth do not apply [to]. . . roads under the direction of Peter Donahue. . . . He could never rival the others in meanness, nor approve of their insulting distinctions in favor of Chinese in preference to other nationalities."

Peter Donahue can deservedly be called "The Father of California Industry," but North Bay railroading occupied the Colonel's attention almost exclusively in his last years. His anonymous memorialist of 1888 (perhaps Bates) wrote, "His health had become impaired by too constant application to business, and he was thus led to confine himself to a single enterprise."

Peter realized that the counties north of San Francisco Bay had little ready access to the city even after the Civil War. The only railroads were on paper, unbuilt. Sonoma County's first banker, Isaac G. Wickersham, and other promoters, like John McNear, put together an undercapitalized Petaluma and Healdsburg Railroad in 1865. But it really never got off the drawing boards, though a few clods were turned north of town. There was plenty of railroading "big talk," but nothing solid, and the March 5, 1870 Petaluma *Journal and Argus* wrote skeptically, "We want to hear the locomotive screech; get down and bite the rail to see if it is made of iron; have a man or two run over."

San Francisco steamboats called at Petaluma, San Quentin, and Sausalito; and San Rafael stages tied Olema, Nicasio, and Tomales to the Marin county seat. From Petaluma, stagecoaches ran to Bloomfield and Bodega; from Santa Rosa they reached Duncan's Mills and other Russian River logging sites. Supplementing the stage lines and freight wagons were coasting vessels called "doghole" schooners that hauled lumber and a few passengers by calling at dangerous little coves (so small that a dog could barely turn around in them before settling down) on the rugged Redwood Coast. But what was needed was a trunk line railroad through Sonoma County, with branches to outlying settlements.

Alonzo Phelps (who called Donahue's railroad "The Healdsburg Line," though Peter eventually ran it to Cloverdale, and his son to Ukiah) commended him for constructing the Sonoma Valley road and "reviving a railroad project which has been sleeping for years."

The *National Cyclopedia* called Peter's franchise the "Petaluma and Cloverdale Line;" it was actually the San Francisco and North Pacific and in Bates's apt words, "the crowning enterprise of his career." Donahue now had plenty of money for dabbling in railroads. As of July 1877, when his nephew Patrick E. Dougherty was SF & NP General Passenger and Ticket Agent, with an office at 426 Montgomery Street in San Francisco, Peter's worth (according to the San Francisco *Bulletin* and Petaluma *Weekly Argus*) was $5,000,000 in capital and an annual income of $400,000.

Sonoma County's first bona fide railway was the shortest of shortlines, the Petaluma and Haystack Railroad of Charles Minturn, San Francisco Bay's early "Ferryboat King." It connected the Petaluma embarcadero, usable only at high tide, with Haystack Landing, the point two and a half miles down stream to which steamers were banished by low water. Petaluma Creek, or Petaluma River, is actually a tidal slough that shoals to mud banks and tule patches in its sinuous, slow descent to San Pablo Bay.

Minturn got the legislature's approval on April 18, 1862 and opened his line in July 1864 to connect Petaluma with his ferries *Clinton* and *Contra Costa*. He extended the road to Rudesill's Landing in 1866, but never got anywhere near the southern limit of his franchise, Black Point, at the mouth of Petaluma Creek. San Francisco's Atlas Foundry, rather than Union Iron Works, built his lone 26-horsepower locomotive, for $5,000. Her boiler blew up on August 27,1866, killing the engineer and several passengers, and she was replaced with horses as the motive power for the coaches. Minturn, who had prospered at first, had to sell out to the syndicate that was building the North Pacific Coast Railroad. His two ferries were shifted to Point San Quentin, to serve the cars of the San Rafael and San Quentin Railroad.

The second railroad line was largely on paper. The Sonoma County Railroad, incorporated January 10, 1868, and voted in by the electorate on May 12, took advantage of an 1863 bill that enfranchised a railroad from any point on San Francisco Bay to Humboldt Bay. There was the proviso that electors of the involved counties must vote bonds of $5,000 per mile, subsidies payable as each twenty-five mile stretch of road should be completed. This sum would, at least, pay for the rails actually laid down.

The Sonoma County Railroad Company had great expectations of building northward from Petaluma to Santa Rosa and Healdsburg, with a branch westward to Bloomfield. But hardly had a shovelful of earth been turned before a deed of sale of July 28, 1868 transferred its rights to a standard gauge line backed by Donahue, the San Francisco and Humboldt Bay Railroad Company. However, about all that the underpowered new outfit could do was to grade around Petaluma that fall and scatter a few ties, as an indication of intent—like "showing the flag"—on a roadbed inching from there toward Santa Rosa. It looked as if the SF & HB would go under, like the rest, for all rights would revert should the company fail to build ten miles of track by a date in 1869.

Rescue came from several directions. Milton S. Latham's California Pacific Railroad offered to build a line from Adelante (Napa Junction) through Petaluma and Santa Rosa to Cloverdale and Bloomfield—*if* Sonoma County would vote the subsidy. At a June 14, 1869 election, the electors did just that: $5,000 a mile was available, this time with a three-year completion deadline. Now Colonel Donahue also rode into Sonoma County, although in somewhat roundabout fashion and clinging to Bill Ralston's coattails. Still, the minor magnate (minor compared to any fourth of the Big Four, at least) was welcomed as Sonoma County's savior.

The San Francisco and Humboldt Bay Railroad announced that it would build a narrow gauge line up the Redwood Coast to the lumber port of Eureka. The franchise was held by Fred McCrellish of the *Alta*, General Patrick Edward Connor of the Army, and H. T. Templeton and John F. McCauley. The ambitious, aggressive Asbury Harpending, friend and sometimes partner of Ralston (and "Copperhead"—Confederate plotter—who outfitted a commerce raider on the Embarcadero during the Civil War) described McCauley as "a well-known business rustler." He suggested that none of them had any capital to speak of. Their design, Harpending said, was simply to peddle the franchise to someone who did have the wherewithal. The surveyor of the route was another former Civil War general, William S. Rosecrans.

With virtually no construction accomplished and the franchise about to lapse, McCrellish asked Harpending to make an offer for the company. The latter admitted to being quite "railroad mad," like so many Californians of that day. "I was personally infatuated with the railroad business and determined to devote my life and energies to the work. The way things were going, it would have been no trouble at all to introduce a bill in Congress asking for a land grant through a country to be traversed by a railroad—and get half a million acres, just for the asking."

Harpending got the opinion of Rosecrans and other engineers before he went over the projected route himself. He thought that the Eel River redwood forests, still government land, would be a "bigger game" than the gold mines of the Sierra, or other speculations that he dreamed of. He decided to buy out the partners.

Harpending and Ralston had invested heavily in San Francisco real estate, especially South of Market, where New Montgomery Street had been driven and the Second Street Cut opened the way to the Pacific Mail docks. With earth from these excavations, the two men filled water lots. Now Harpending suggested to Ralston that they sell their lots at auction. He, Ralston, and Maurice Doré met in an office of Ralston's Bank of California one night to figure out the average price per foot for the lots. Harpending based his figure on a profit of $2,500,000. Doré's figure was a bit more, but Ralston's was double that of Harpending's. The latter commented, "He had supreme confidence."

Doré's spieler or auctioneer was H. A. Cobb, Peter Donahue's C.O. in the state militia during the Civil War. He had cappers, shills, in the audience to make fake bids, keeping interest high—and bids still higher. The sale was a smashing success. Harpending's share allowed him to buy up 90 percent of the railroad franchise, the cautious McCauley hanging on to 10 percent. Harpending later tried to get his old partner to throw in with him. "I tried to interest Ralston, but he said I was a visionary, and made some remarks about 'back lands' and 'coyote ranges.' "

Harpending ordered fifty miles of ties and rails. (Some sources state that he ordered rails from Union Iron Works, but it had no rolling mill.) He got McCauley and Frederick Bee to start work on a right-of-way. By March of 1869, they had the road graded to within three miles of Santa Rosa, and the bridge over Petaluma Creek was begun. Ties were arriving and fifteen miles of "iron" (i.e. rails) were due from England. Just three days short of the reversion deadline, Harpending organized a new railroad, the San Francisco and North Pacific, using some of the directors of his SF & HB, and got a new contract from the county. He then persuaded San Francisco Assemblyman John L. Romer to write a bill giving grants of 3,625 acres of "tidelands and salt marshes"—including all of Marin County's Richardson's Bay and even 200 acres of San Francisco's North Beach—plus a $300,000 subsidy by Marin County. A Marin rancher typified the general denunciation of the land-grabbing scheme. He renamed Harpending's SF & NP the "San Francisco and North Pacific, North Pole and Open Sea Railroad." The bill died.

Now, Harpending changed his mind—and his route. The wary "Pacific Quartet," as he called the Big Four, pricked up their ears in alarm as he got engineering reports from Rosecrans and Arthur W. Keddie on a planned transcontinental route across the Sierra via Beckwourth Pass, which the Central Pacific had, unaccountably, overlooked. Harpending recalled, "I guess this gave the Big Four the largest scare they received in years."

According to Ralston's biographers, the Big Four now leaned on Harpending, who was already running short of funds. Supposedly, they used Ralston and Peter Donahue. According to Harpending, the Union Iron Works "conveniently" defaulted on an order for ten miles of rails. (But he was mistaken as Union did not manufacture rails, and furthermore Peter was no longer active in the concern.) As for the fifteen to twenty miles of iron from England, it went to the bottom of Valparaíso harbor in the hold of a ship. Harpending's attorney, Alfred A. Cohen, claimed that the vessel was deliberately scuttled to put his client out of business.

Stanford next asked Ralston to "subdue" his friend Harpending. Otherwise, the Big Four hinted, there might be a war with him and the first casualty just might be Ralston. They mentioned cancelling a promised concession, a contract for him to build C.P. railroad cars.

Harpending remembered those times all too well. "Ralston laid the matter before me as a friend. He admitted that he had no right to influence my action, but said he was facing an enormous loss; that I could sell out at a large profit, and frankly asked me to strain a point. I yielded, with great reluctance. After some negotiations, I sold my railroad rights to Peter Donahue. These rights, only partially developed, contributed the bulk of his great fortune . . . . Left to myself, I would now be the owner of the Northwestern Pacific Railroad." (The NWP was the successor of Peter's SF & NP.)

Poor Ralston! Harpending recorded that the slippery Central Pacific quartet reneged on its promise. He never did receive the contract for the coaches. The building that he erected for his Kimball Manufacturing Company, turning from wagon making to the production of railroad cars, he finally had to convert into the Coast Furniture Factory. It operated at a loss during the few remaining years of his life. Nor was Ralston's sleeping car able to compete with George Pullman's model in the East. Ralston did not get a single order for it, though he sold a few of his regular passenger coaches to Donahue's San Francisco and San Jose road, and took some for his own Virginia and Truckee Railroad in Nevada.

Alfred Bates wrote that a deputation of Sonoma County citizens called on Peter in San Francisco to urge him to undertake construction of the stalled Sonoma railroad. "To this he consented, after a thorough examination of the country through which the line was to pass, not only in Sonoma [County] but in the adjacent county of Marin, through which, he foresaw, it would in time be extended."

Probably, Bates was merely echoing Donahue's sentiments when he wrote, "Nowhere, perhaps, throughout the broad surface of California is there any more favored section than the counties of Sonoma and Marin. In the former are the finest grain- and fruit-growing lands in the state; in the latter the finest grazing lands; and in both are some of the fairest vales in all the fair Western lands, such as to the jaded denizens of the metropolis appear as the very gardens of the gods. . . . Not least among its advantages to the general public is that the road passes through some of the finest hunting, fishing and camping grounds in the state, and through some of the finest scenery, along high bluffs, steep mountain sides, through fertile valleys and dense forests of redwoods."

Donahue bought some of the SF & HB's franchise rights on August 2, 1869, right out from under the nose of Latham's California Pacific, and completed negotiations for the "Sonoma County Railroad" on November 17. He paid either $45,000 or $50,000 (accounts differ) for the work already done and for company goodwill. Peter wanted that $5,000-a-mile subsidy for the first road to build through Sonoma County, border to border, and he wanted first crack at the Russian River redwood groves.

Necessary rights-of-way were donated by property owners and Peter's superintendent, Robert Harris, really got the dirt flying. Peter used one hundred men on the grading, all whites. (He hired no Chinese at this time.) He interested the Hibernia Bank in the railroad project and hired away Sonoma County's District Attorney Overton to act as the road's counsel. In the space of only a few days, he rush-ordered 20,000 railroad ties, also locomotives and cars from Union Iron Works, and sent ties and iron up Petaluma Creek in the propellor *Twin Sister*. The Colonel had his first spike driven on August 30, 1869 and, just twelve days later, organized a hasty and informal excursion to open the line. Peter used a construction locomotive landed from the *Twin Sister*, probably old

Engine #2 of his SF & SJ. This was the *San Jose*, better known as the *Josie* or *Little Josie*. She became Engine #1 on his San Francisco and North Pacific. (When the Northwestern Pacific scrapped her in 1920, she was the oldest active steam engine in the United States.) Donahue had to cram himself, Harris, Conductor George W. Craig and a 10-gallon keg of Edwards Cream Ale into the engineer's cab for the ride over two miles of track and the Cinnabar Knoll bridge. He had no coaches as yet.

Shortly, the first of his distinctively bright yellow fifty-passenger coaches, the *Lakeville*, with lengthwise, plush-upholstered, seats arrived aboard the *Twin Sister*. it was soon joined by two coaches from Ralston's Kimball plant, the *Petaluma* and the *Santa Rosa*.

There were minor problems, like the "blockade" of Mrs. White, the wife of a doctor of Petaluma's eastern suburb, Newton. She piled hay or straw on Peter's right-of-way and sat down there with a shotgun to block it and convince him that he was trespassing on private property. But Peter's Irish blarney eventually cajoled her off of his roadbed. The one major problem was the location of the SF & NP's terminal. Petaluma was the obvious site, but the Colonel and the city began wrangling immediately over depot rights and the use of busy Main Street for his right-of-way through town. Fed up, Peter decided to build a sort of company town of his own in the tules some eight miles down Petaluma Creek from the city, instead of using Petaluma. Naturally, Petaluma's city fathers considered this action to be perfidy on the part of their erstwhile savior.

In early November 1869, Peter had finished five miles of track toward the lonely landing which he now, immodestly, named Donahue for himself. As he completed the spur, he finished another five miles of track north of Petaluma and began refitting the steamers *Sacramento* and *Wilson G. Hunt* for the Petaluma Creek run. On New Year's Day 1870, his rails reached Santa Rosa, but passenger trains did not clatter up to its depot behind the *San Jose* till October 31.

The *San Jose* left East Petaluma with its cars at 8 a.m. and 1:30 each day, returning from the county seat at noon and 4 p.m. Santa Rosa enjoyed a modest boom as a result of Peter's road. Ash Wilkinson, its Beau Brummel, met all trains with his omnibus. The California and Fashion stage lines for up-country towns moved their terminals from Petaluma to Santa Rosa, and the Philadelphia Brewery opened the Willows, a public garden (resort) that featured dancing, skating, shuffleboard, and billiards as well as much quaffing of beer.

Petaluma's *Argus*, later very critical of the Colonel, was in a congratulatory mood at this time. "The energy that has been displayed in this enterprise is highly commendable and deserves unqualified praise. Peter Donahue has demonstrated in a practical way what can be accomplished when there is capital at command and a determination to go ahead. To him the people of Sonoma [County] are largely indebted for the inauguration of the most important enterprise ever undertaken in the country."

Although some townsfolk feared that the railroad might hurt Petaluma as a port, the newspaper argued to the contrary, stating that the city would ultimately benefit from the new and cheaper means of communication with both the metropolis, San Francisco, and with the interior. To the *Argus*, completion of the Donahue line to Santa Rosa was the dawning of a new era for the region. The editor hoped to announce the extension of the railroad to Healdsburg and Cloverdale within a year's time.

The January 7, 1870 *Argus* carried a story on Peter's special inaugural run on Saturday, December 31, to Santa Rosa, as well as an SF & NP advertisement and time table. (Regular service started on New Year's Day.) The paper described the event as a "first-class blowout." The 1,200 excursionists invited by the Colonel included several Petalumans who wanted to make the entire trip, so they showed up aboard the *Sacramento* when she left San Francisco's Jackson Street Wharf at 8:30 a.m. The steamer was loaded to the gunwales with prominent men like McCrellish, McCauley, Romer, and William T. Coleman. (Harpending was in London at the time). There were two bands, the musicians of the Industrial School and Kidd's Brass Band. Company A of the California Guards, Captain Isaac Bluxome's celebrated militia artillery battery, fired salutes at different points on the bay from two cannon. The long train of three coaches and a dozen "flats", one holding the pair of cannon, that departed from the little terminal of Donahue, or Donahue's Landing (Donahue's Embarcadero), was an hour late in reaching the station at East Petaluma.

The mayor—backed by a brass band and the local militia, the Hueston Guard—greeted the visitors. As the train chugged into sight, cannon in Petaluma's plaza belched a salute that Bluxome returned with his fieldpieces on the flatcar. After a three-quarters of an hour halt to pick up excited Petalumans, the excursionists continued their ride for fifty minutes to Santa Rosa on a particularly pleasant day for January. The ride was smooth, for the tracks had had plenty of time to settle. The Petaluma paper wrote that "The passengers were all so highly elated at the beautiful appearance of our valley that in passing farmhouses, residences, or even single individuals, their enthusiasm would find vent in prolonged cheers, while ladies' handkerchiefs waved in wild profusion."

According to tradition, Donahue had failed to alert Santa Rosa to the celebration. But, if true, he was nevertheless met with another brass band (perhaps hurried into the breach), plus many citizens in carriages and wagons. The old tradition of firing salutes with powder-stuffed anvils, as impromptu cannon, was also carried out. The trippers spent an hour wandering around the county seat. Admiring San Franciscans went into raptures over the mild climate, such an agreeable surprise after the bitter-cold winds and fogs of the big city.

The return trip from Santa Rosa to Petaluma took scarcely thirty-seven minutes. But when the train pulled up to the wharf at Donahue it was dark because the halt at Petaluma had to be extended. The National Guard battery had insisted on marching in escort as the local militiamen moved off to disband and return to their homes.

Aboard the *Sacramento* the travelers, some of whom had not eaten since leaving home that morning, found that the Colonel had spread an ample smorgasbord-like supper in the spacious saloon. There were toasts and speeches by the passengers after their ravenous appetites were quieted by the feast prepared for them by J.D. Hendricks. Coleman praised Donahue for fast work, white labor, and locally-built cars and locomotives. Donahue and his old friend, Newhall, made some remarks in response. The Colonel stressed the fact that the bills were all paid. The railroad owed no man, not even a dollar. The guests formed a committee to draft resolutions of gratitude which thanked Hendricks; Captain Galloway of the *Sacramento*; Mr. Gerdes; Captain Robert Hayley, the railroads's chief engineer; Bob Harris, its superintendent; Captain I. Wright; Mr. Wilson, who had seen to the actual building of the road; and Chief Engineer of Navigation W.M. Kilduff.

The main resolution, however, was directed to the driving force behind the entire North Bay transportation network idea. "Resolved that the people of California are greatly indebted to our worthy fellow citizen, Colonel Peter Donahue, for the energy displayed by him in the completion of a first-class railroad from the town of Donahue to Santa Rosa, the said road now being in perfect order and having been completed in four months, traversing a portion of the most fertile and beautiful section of our state. And we are specially gratified in stating that this important work has been completed with white labor and upon cash principles."

Already, the Colonel had put together a network of travel and communication. The 8:30 a.m. *Sacramento* arrived at Donahue each day at 11 a.m., where it met not only the "cars" (train) for Petaluma and Santa Rosa, but the horse-drawn stages for Sonoma, Bodega, Bloomfield, Duncan's Mills, Tomales, Windsor, Healdsburg, Geyserville, Skaggs Springs, Anderson Valley, Navarro, Big River (Mendocino), Noyo, Fort Bragg, Ukiah, Long Valley, Clear Lake, and Lakeport. By now, the roundhouse, machine shops, foundry, car sheds, and hotel were complete at Donahue. Santa Rosa Creek was bridged and a thousand-dollar Santa Rosa station was built on seven acres between Third and Fourth streets as Donahue prepared to drive the work toward Healdsburg.

Professor Hugh Quigley quoted a San Francisco *Examiner* story of the day that described the SF & NP as "a stupendous project for one man," since it required not only capital but brains and pluck a'plenty. The newspaper observed that Colonel Donahue possessed these virtues "in an advanced degree." An *Alta* story also paid the new railroad baron a nice compliment.

The name of Peter Donahue is intimately associated with prominent enterprises and acts of benevolence on this coast. He has done as much, perhaps, toward building up the great commercial mart of the Pacific Coast as any man residing in San Francisco, while the records of the various benevolent institutions will bear evidence of his generous contributions. He is now considered one of the most enterprising residents of the Bay city and his interests are varied and diversified, ranging from blocks of massive buildings, railroads and steamboats, mining, insurance, banks, stock, tracts of the finest land, together with cattle on a thousand hills. The present happy condition of Mr. Donahue may be attributed to his energy, honor and industry, aided by firmness an good morals.

On February 11, 1871, the Petaluma *Journal and Argus* ran a story on the first Sunday excursion trip from San Francisco all the way to Santa Rosa. Quite a crowd made the journey, though, in the paper's opinion, the announcement was made awfully late. (The expansive but often close-mouthed Donahue had made no public announcement when, earlier, he had run his first through-train. He had just stood his guests to champagne and havanas.) Many Sonoma county folk returned home on the special train with the day trippers from San Francisco who, said the *Journal and Argus*, were visiting the country on the only day that they could really call their own. The journalist was of the opinion that the 8:30 Sunday boat would attract lots of city workingmen who needed outdoor recreation and exercise after enjoying one of Mr. Hendricks's breakfasts—"superb and unequalled"—aboard the steamer. They would visit the wineries and the county seat. The paper ended with a good plug for the Colonel and his aides, "The officers and attachés of the line are accommodating gentlemen, and everything is done that is possible for the comfort of the passengers."

By April of 1871, the Colonel had rammed his line past Fulton to Healdsburg, only ten miles short of his temporary goal of Cloverdale. Ultimately, he hoped to build to Ukiah and on up to Eureka. The press cried out that he had "brought within a few hours of San Francisco the most populous and important trade points of Sonoma County, famous as it is for its wealth of farming lands."

Suddenly, one of the "paper" railways turned into a tiger. In March of 1871, Milton S. Latham's apparently well-heeled California Pacific, hopeful of gaining the subsidy, had used one hundred Chinese to grade a right-of-way parallel to the Donahue Road being built by the Colonel's fellow Hibernians between Santa Rosa and Healdsburg. Peter sent in more men. Latham countered with two hundred Chinese, then one thousand more. When his Irish workers struck for higher pay, Donahue gave in to them. Latham bought in still more Chinese and some Irish of his own. The Colonel fought back, temporarily almost abandoning the lower part of his line. Kids hitched horses to his idle flat cars, and towed them back and forth for fun.

Sonoma county folk had been startled by these developments but they were completely flabbergasted when the tough old Colonel capitulated to Latham! Donahue sold his SF & NP to the California

Pacific on April 13, 1871 and for only $750,000, apparently on the advice of his banker-friend, Ralston.

Latham paid off his Chinese gandy dancers. There is a story that the See Yup Tong paymaster and foreman had to be rescued from a lynch mob of his countrymen. Donahue's contract of sale provided for his "Harps" to keep working to complete the line to the Russian River at Healdsburg, which was reached on July 1, 1871.

The grateful Irishmen presented their old boss, Donahue, with a gold-headed cane, thinking that they had seen the last of him. But he was only lying low for the moment.

Petalumans had hardly been ecstatic about the pushy Colonel, but they soon began to miss him as the bullying Central Pacific (S.P.) on August 1 took over the California Pacific, which had itself increased passenger fares and freight rates over Donahue's charges. To qualify for the county subsidy of $300,000 by the March 1872 deadline, the Big Four pushed construction to Cloverdale. Rails were laid on the Howe truss bridge across the Russian River by Christmas, as Engineer Charles Black worked two hundred men on the roadbed.

Superintendent A.A. Bean invited the editor of the *Argus* to inspect the completed portion of the Cloverdale extension. They rode to Healdsburg in the cab of a regular train's locomotive. There they shifted to a construction train to see five miles of new track built by a force of Chinese and Americans now grown to six hundred men. The gandy dancers were spiking down half a mile of track a day in their race with the deadline. Bean was using every exertion to advance the work. The reporter noted, . . . "If anyone thinks that railroad building is very rapid work, he should 'go to the front' . . . and see the obstacles that on every side beset the work. Men are compelled to work whether it rains or not, and in grading the bed it will readily dawn upon the minds of the most obtuse that the foundation they made [i.e., in the rain] is not a very solid one. But the road must be built, and down the ties go and the rails are laid on them immediately." The road would settle, of course, under the weight of passing gravel cars and the busy construction trains. But, as the *Argus* admitted, "The five miles just laid down could hardly be praised at the moment for its regularity or smoothness of ride."

By the time of the journalist's visit, the workers had laid fourteen miles of track beyond Healdsburg. The foreman of the crew promised that rails would be in Geyserville by the time the story saw print, and in Cloverdale in a fortnight. Rough weather delayed the work, but the men *had* to get to Cloverdale by mid-March, unless Governor Newton Booth should extend the deadline.

They made it. The March 16, 1872 *Journal and Argus* reported the line complete and the first special train coming up over it from Petaluma on the 15th, bearing the Central Pacific's Richard P. Hammond, Superintendent Bean, and others including pioneer J.G. Dow, who claimed to have laid out the route, as a trail, back in the spring of 1849.

The newsman was delighted. "We regard the completion of this work as a great achievement, as the heavy rains have rendered railroad work this winter anything but rapid or pleasant work. Men have been compelled to work in all kinds of weather, in slush and mud, and all the inconveniences and impediments that could well be imagined have been contended against. Superintendent Bean, however, has proved equal to the emergency, and the completion of the road within the prescribed time is, in a good measure, attributable to his excellent management." However, Bean advised the public that regular passenger trains would not make the run till mid-April, since the roadbed still had to be properly ballasted and otherwise put into good condition.

The paper predicted that Bean would soon start on the Bloomfield branch, but it was never built, probably because Marin County voters subsidized Latham's North Pacific Coast Railroad, running north from Sausalito to that region. (It would have been built by Bean, in any case, only if the State senate concurred with the assembly in passing a bill to extend the SF & NP's deadline.) Still assuming that the extension would be built, the paper prophesied prettily that "another section of our country will throb in unison with the great commercial center. And thus, Sonoma County shall spring forward by the aid of railroads, and will stand pre-eminently great among other counties of the state in point of wealth, population and resources."

The Big Four, fearful that Latham might get too big for his breeches, now lowered the boom on him. They built a line to Sacramento, shorter than his California Pacific, crossing the "impossible" (seemingly bottomless) marshes beyond Benicia, got the franchise for the critical Sacramento River bridge, and left

Latham's California Pacific out in the cold. Latham caved in on September 1, 1871. The Central Pacific/Southern Pacific had now defeated all independent railroaders. The "Octopus" was King of California.

Sonoma County historian C.A. Menefee wrote in the 1880s that Donahue's road was of inestimable value and benefit to the Redwood Coast counties. He indicated how the population increase, in both towns and rural areas, was due to the new, direct and convenient communication with "the City"—the metropolis of San Francisco. "People in the metropolis come up along the road to select pleasant residences. The value of land has increased very much, and business has more than doubled."

Had Donahue turned his back on the SF & NP? Not at all. In another *volte-face* that jolted the citizens of the North Bay area, the Big Four, after talking grandly about making Sausalito the new terminus of their transcontinental road, and after incorporating the SF & NP with a capitalization of $12,350,000 inexplicably sold the railway back to Donahue in January of 1873 for a cool million, but with the Cloverdale extension (seventeen miles) thrown in. It was another bargain for the Colonel. Apparently, only Stanford of the foursome disagreed with Ralston in evaluating the North Bay area as just "coyote ranges."

William T. Coleman, amazed that Austin Moore's North Pacific Coast would bypass his town of San Rafael, urged Donahue in 1873 to extend his reacquired SF & NP to that city. At a meeting of citizens, Peter said that he would start work in just forty-eight hours—*if* they would bore a tunnel for him north of San Rafael and help him bridge Petaluma Creek. All that Coleman and his cohorts could come up with was an option to buy Minturn's San Francisco-San Quentin Ferry. Negotiations collapsed. Nevertheless, the North Pacific Coast blocked Donahue from San Rafael by taking out a long-term lease on the San Rafael-San Quentin Railroad. But the Colonel kept the idea of an extension to San Rafael in the back of his mind.

The *Argus-Courier*, as confused and suspicious as the general public, tried to straighten things out in a March 21, 1873 story.

Since the reported sale and informal transfer of the S.F. & North Pacific Railroad to Peter Donahue, some weeks since, there has been considerable discussion as to whether the transfer is one of trust or a genuine

> sale . . . . All attachés of the road report to, and are under the dominion of Mr. Donahue. We are satisfied, and hope that the order of things may be to all a source of profit. We trust that Mr. Donahue and the people on the line of the route may work in unison together. That right and justice may be the aim of the company and the desire of the people. That prejudices and misunderstandings may be carefully avoided . . . [and] the desire and the aim won. Be first to build up the country and, this done, success of the other is assured.

Petaluma's civic leaders still viewed Peter with jaundiced eyes. To spite the bumptious Irishman and his upstart town of Donahue, they pooled enough capital (they hoped) after public meetings in San Rafael and Petaluma to support Coleman's idea of a narrow gauge Sonoma and Marin Railroad from Petaluma to San Rafael. The line would compete with the SF & NP, going down the west side of Petaluma Creek to the Marin county seat, to connect there with the short San Rafael-San Quentin Railroad to Minturn's old ferry landing at Point San Quentin.

The Contra Costa Navigation Company, which owned the right-of-way, conveyed it to Milton Latham, who was bloodied but unbowed by the Big Four, on September 30, 1874.

Latham held the land only as a trustee and deeded it, and the dilapidated Petaluma and Haystack road, to the new company on March 23, 1875 for $6,000. Wickersham was president; Coleman, vice president; E. S. Lippincott, secretary; and H.T. Fairbanks, treasurer, of the S & M. They acquired a locomotive and some cars after discarding the idea of a "prismoidal," or monorail, system. They graded a bed along the survey stakes of Chief Engineer Stangroom in the spring of '75, but ran out of money in the middle of the Novato salt marshes. Critics called it the railroad that began nowhere and ended in a swamp.

Assistant Engineer Frank Zook was not ready to quit. He marked the north approach of the key tunnel, just north of San Rafael, under Puerto Suello Hill, and J.A. Martin made the opening furrow of the bore with what was described as a "monster plow." The bore was expected to be 1,100 feet long, plus a 600-foot approach from the north side and a 700-foot approach on the south. Gangs of Chinese worked on both ends and the *Marin County Journal* expected completion of the hole within a year. However, the contractor, discouraged, gave up after only a few weeks of digging, with only 275 feet of tunnel opened.

Now Colonel Donahue swooped down like an Irish falcon on the helpless road, carrying $85,000 in his claws. He bought the line, "as is," on October 27, 1876. It was another bargain, a steal. He replaced the narrow gauge roadbed with one capable of handling his broad gauge track and finished the line into San Rafael on June 2, 1879.

All the while, Peter kept an eye cocked on his friendly rival, Latham, now building the North Pacific Coast towards the lucrative Russian River redwood lumber business. Donahue decided to head him off. He did not have to be persuaded in September 1874 when George Guerne and the Bohemian (Czech) brothers, Anton, Franc and Joseph Korbel, asked him to build a branch from Fulton, on his main line four miles north of Santa Rosa, to the river in order to replace the inefficient hauling of timber and lumber by ox teams to Santa Rosa and Petaluma. The Colonel told the mill owners, "Gentlemen, I will build the railroad if you will supply the right-of-way, give me free bridge timbers, and let me buy ties wholesale."

The Korbels had, earlier, been near-neighbors of Donahue in San Francisco, employing one hundred-fifty Chinese to fashion cigar boxes of Mazatlán cedar at First and Brannan streets. When their building burned, they relocated and got into multiple-color printing (chromolithography) of labels, and even illustrations for San Francisco's critical and literary magazine, the *Wasp*. Then they acquired Russian river land for dairying—cheese making, particularly—but had to turn to logging and lumbering to survive. (At the advice of University of California professors, they later converted their logged-off land into vineyards, and soon began producing California's premium champagne.)

Anton Korbel was chosen to secure the right-of-way for Donahue's projected Fulton and Guerneville Railroad. A dubious Donahue bet him that he could not secure all of them. In just nine months, the Czech had them all, with the necessary legal documents filed. Peter paid up—$5.00.

In the summer of 1875, the Colonel sent surveyors and chainmen under John Frederick Burgin to stake the route. Construction began at Fulton in September and, by mid-month, two hundred graders were at work, half of them Chinese, and a few hundred token yards of iron were laid at Fulton. At month's end, the workmen numbered four hundred and construction trains were rolling back and forth over two and a half miles of track in a mad dash to beat the winter rains. The going was good until the workers ran into the "bottomless pit" of Laguna Swamp. The bog swallowed carload after carload of rock and earth fill before it would float a solid foundation for the trestles. By Christmas, however, the six-mile stretch from Fulton to Laguna (Trenton) was ballasted, and Peter leapfrogged his work by beginning construction of the piers for his Russian River bridge at Hacienda, or Cosmo, while he framed his Howe truss span in his shops at Donahue. He hoped to see all grading done in three weeks, but, beyond Hilton, his workers had to dig and blast through the side of a mountain. The mountain not only slowed progress, it raised construction costs to $75,000 a mile.

A January 1876 rainstorm slowed work even more but, according to the *Argus-Courier*, there was only one washout on the line. At the cattle guard above a bridge at George Campbell's ranch, a stream was diverted from its normal channel. Only one train was delayed and only for an hour, but repairs cost $2,000—and some bad publicity. Campbell wrote the *Argus-Courier* (February 4) to complain; to blame the railroad; and to state that he had hired a civil engineer to estimate his damages.

With his bridge for Green Valley Creek already framed, painted, and readied to be put together on the site in just ten days, Peter thought that he could get to Guerneville by May 1, 1876. Ten days of steady rain in March, resulting in the loss of the little ferryboat at the Russian River bridgehead, again slowed progress. By April's end, however, Donahue had the river span in place and two miles of roadbed on the far side ready for his rails.

Now the mill owners waffled on their promise to supply free timbers for the Russian River bridge and several trestles. They offered Peter a lump sum of $10,000 instead. If this offer was meant to mollify the feisty Celt, it failed. A stubborn Donahue said that he would stop building at Korbel's unless the agreement were carried out. It was not, and he stopped. He was 13 miles from Fulton, still 3.27 miles short of his destination of Guerneville. "That's as far as I am going," he grumped.

The first of many excursions to the redwood groves took place on Saturday, May 28, with 1,200 German Social Club guests, jammed into seven cars, junketing to Korbel's. Peter started regular service the next day. The Fulton and Guerneville had no rolling stock of its own, but used SF & NP equipment. Peter built a large lumber and cordwood storage shed at Fulton that for years supplied his Russian River woodburners. Korbel's, his terminal, was composed of two sawmills, a shingle mill, a hotel (reputedly a good country inn) kept by John Baelser, Jacob Snelling's store, and a boarding house and cabins for fifty-two mill hands.

The Colonel ran mixed trains daily from Fulton at 10:20 and 6:20, except Sundays, and from Korbel's at 7:30 and 3:00. Each Sunday, except in soppy weather, an excursion train connected with the SF & NP #7 at Fulton at 11:15 and arrived at the Korbel groves at 12;07. Leaving at 3:00, it reached Fulton in time for vacationers to catch the last train (the #8) back to Donahue. Peter had to reduce the schedule in September of 1876 to just one round-trip mixed train daily. He dropped the Sunday excursion on January 7, 1877, but he reinstated it on March 25.

Anton Korbel reminded Peter that his rights-of-way were good only if construction started on them within a year; otherwise, the land would revert to its owners. Since his rival, Latham, had already staked a route from Tomales to Duncan's Mills, downstream from him, Peter, grudgingly, came around. He knew that if he did not run his broad gauge westward down Russian River, Latham would certainly send his narrow gauge up the stream. Peter was not about to lose all of the potential logging business around Guerneville just because of a snit with mill owners. He called his directors and got their agreement to surrender, and built the road to Guerneville. Work was finished in March of 1877.

The San Francisco *Argonaut* of May 21, 1877 reported on a "select group" of gentlemen and ladies who took the steamboat *James M. Donahue* to the cars which carried them to the redwoods as the Colonel's guests in a preview of the line. The official opening was on the 24th. The first train made a Sunday excursion trip as far as Guerneville's station, although the end-of-track was actually at Fife Creek, dammed into a logging pond for the Heald and Guerneville Lumber Company's mill. Its arrival was celebrated by the traditional firing off of anvils in Guerneville.

Guerneville (which remained the river's broad-gauge terminal for fifteen years, before the line was extended to the Bohemian Grove and Monte Rio area) was founded as Stumptown in 1860 by R.B.

Lunsford, and renamed for George Guerne of the Heald and Guerne mill (Heald was Guerne's son-in-law). Winter floods of 1867 washed the mill away, but a new one was soon up and employing fifty loggers and lumbermen. They produced 20,000 board feet of lumber a day during eight months of the year. By 1874, S.W. Faudre had begun his rustic furniture factory there. When he passed it on to Florence Bremer in 1877, it was turning out seventy chairs a day.

Peter's Fulton and Guerneville almost ran an extension for tourists from Guerneville to Armstrong Grove, set aside as a Sonoma County park. (It is now a California State Park.) But the owner of a small tract close to Guerneville refused to sell for a right-of-way, and stalled the Company until it gave up the idea, though it threatened to force a sale by court action.

George Guerne was an odd duck. His little old logging engine, *Polly Ann*, of his Heald and Guerne days was too feeble for his later Guerne and Murphy Lumber Company of the '80s. He replaced her first with a brute of a loco, an 0-4-0 called *Bully Boy*. Finally, on New Year's Eve of 1888, Guerne decided to kill two birds—the Old Year and useless *Polly Ann*—with one stone. He placed dynamite sticks in *Polly Ann's* tender and blew her to scrap. Unfortunately, the fireworks blasted out every window in Guerneville, too, and George had to pay quite a tab to reglaze the town.

Donahue reorganized his railroad companies, consolidating his separately-named units—the SF & NP, Sonoma and Marin, Fulton and Guerneville, and Sonoma Valley Railroad—into the one San Francisco and North Pacific Railway. He now had seven locomotives, thirteen passenger cars, two baggage and mail cars, and one hundred and eleven freight cars. The railroad was becoming a favorite of vacationers, day trippers, and picnickers. Hugh Quigley rightly stated that the line provided travelers with "some of the rarest scenes on the Coast. It is a route particularly worthy [of] the attention of tourists: there the noted redwood groves of California are to be seen in grandest proportions. The detour from the main road to visit old 'Stumptown' will be enjoyed by all who make it."

An SF & NP timetable of May 29, 1876 outlined the road—Donahue to Lakeville and Petaluma, to Ely's, Penn's Grove (now Penngrove) and Cotate Ranch (now Cotati), Oak Grove, Santa Rosa, Fulton, Mark West, Windsor, Grant's, Healdsburg, Litton's Springs, Geyserville, Truett's, and Cloverdale. At Fulton, the Russian River branch peeled off to Meacham's, Laguna, Forestville, Green Valley, Korbel's, and Guerneville.

The same timetable, printed "for the government and information of employees only," suggested how safety-conscious was the Colonel, although it was signed by his superintendent, A.A. Bean. It warned trainmen, for example, that trains that were stopped at stations were under the immediate direction of the agent, whose orders they were to respect and obey as long as they were there. Engineers of passenger trains were ordered not to exceed speeds of six miles per hour when crossing the Russian River, Mark West, Santa Rosa, and Petaluma Creek bridges and when within the city limits of Petaluma, Santa Rosa, and Healdsburg. Bean spoke the Colonel's mind—"Carefulness is enjoined upon all employees. Always take the safer side in case of any uncertainty. No free travel will be allowed. The use of intoxicating drinks while on duty is strictly forbidden."

Even with such precautions, the SF & NP was not free of mishaps. An early accident involved the killing of five cattle in December of 1871 by a locomotive that was knocked off the track by the collision with them. The *Argus*, January 27, 1872, reported that the track was being fenced—"sheep high, pig tight, and bull strong."

In the spring of 1872, on the new Healdsburg-to-Cloverdale link, two hand cars collided in the dark. Two little girls had their legs broken and one of the children died.

In October of 1876, Sebastian Romero sued the railroad company for $50,000 for a non train-related accident. During an Independence celebration held on July 5, an unskilled laborer named Holland was put in charge of a 24-pound mountain howitzer, to fire a salute. Plaintiff Romero protested the man's mismanagement of the cannon, which discharged prematurely and blew off his (Romero's) arm.

One accident occurred right in Donahue itself. On the first Thursday of August 1874, an engine that had been sent to Petaluma to pick up a Dr. Stewart, "flew the track" as it entered the company town. The locomotive's tender was driven up the bank, throwing a Mr. Wier to the ground; no one was seriously injured. (According to Keenan family tradition, Dr. Stewart assisted on the 5th at the birth of Harriet Keenan (Toner), who died in 1969 at the age of ninety-five. The use of a locomotive, even to fetch a doctor in an emergency, was unauthorized. Stern Peter Donahue fired W.M. Kilduff, the engineer; but Alexander Keenan, the baby's proud father, persuaded him to give the man's job back to him.)

The last accident of note involved the passenger and mail train en route to Donahue from Santa Rosa on the last Saturday in August, 1877, two miles south of the county seat. Some boys, out hunting, tied their horse to a fence. The animal broke loose and, in attempting to jump the track, became stuck in a cattle guard. Engineer A.W. Frary could not stop the *Santa Rosa* in time. The horse was literally torn to pieces (its heart was found twenty feet from the track). Frary and Fireman James Hunapple stuck to the cab as the engine fell five feet down the embankment and was badly damaged. Luckily, both men suffered only from shock. Conductor William Corbaly got a hand car and went to Santa Rosa to telegraph Superintendent Bean at his Petaluma headquarters, who hurried to the scene on the express train to inspect the damages. The Petaluma paper reported that "None of the passengers were injured, and no blame is attached to the employees of the road. This is the first accident of importance that has happened on the road since its inauguration."

Colonel Bean was interviewed about safety by the *Argus* for its May 4, 1877 edition. He stressed that the utmost care was taken on the railroad to avoid accidents. In six years of operation, he said, mostly under him, there had been only two fatal accidents on the road and neither was the fault of railway employees. One reason for the fine, and expensive, safety record was the fact that Donahue had each section hand patrolling only two miles of track.

Latham was right on the Colonel's heels. He entered Sonoma County near Valley Ford with his NPC in 1876 and extended it to the Russian River at Duncan's Mills, then onward to its dead-end at Cazadero in 1877. The line was more scenic than Donahue's and attracted more hikers and picnickers, and was possibly more instrumental in the creation of the world-famous Bohemian Grove, of which railroad historian, and "Bohemian," David Myrick has written in his *Rails Around the Bohemian Grove.* (In 1906 the S.P. and the Santa Fe combined to buy up both SF & NP and NPC as part of their new Northwestern Pacific Railroad.)

The relationship between Donahue and Latham was complicated. Supposedly "deadly" rivals, they were actually friends. Peter's old colleague, Joseph Eastland, advanced a large sum of money to Latham and accepted a trusteeship of the North Pacific Coast line. He was next elected its president. Eastland planned to retire after Latham returned home from a bond-selling trip to Europe. However, on an inspection trip in 1878, Eastland's car overturned and tumbled down an embankment; he was severely hurt, though he did not at first realize the severity of his injuries. His wife was less badly injured, but their seven-year old daughter survived only a few days. The shocked Eastland resigned from the North Pacific Coast and as secretary of Peter's San Francisco Gas Light Company and went to Europe for more than a year to try to recover from the trauma of his loss.

Peter Donahue was often ahead of his time in technology. In psychology or sociology, and in politics, however, he was very much a man of his time. Thus he did not protest the compliments showered on him by anti-Chinese propagandists for not hiring "coolies." His policy of preferment for "white" (usually Irish) track layers was at odds with that of the Big Four. The Central Pacific/Southern Pacific's numerous Asian gandy dancers were called "Charlie Crocker's Pets." Bigoted writers often praised Peter for his supposed all-white hiring policy. Thus the San Francisco *Post*, August 10, 1872, commending the Joint State Central Committee of the Democratic and Liberal Republican Parties for choosing Peter (a so-called Horace Greeley Democrat) as a committeeman, harped on the kind of racist "reform" that was so popular in the economically depressed '70s.

> Peter Donahue is one of the richest and yet one of the most popular men in the state, a man of the people who has won his wealth by his industry and far-sighted enterprise . . . . Mr. Donahue has been connected with nearly every great enterprise that has ever been carried out here . . . . What is most to his credit, he is the only man on this coast who ever built a railroad by white labor, the Donahue and Healdsburg line through Sonoma County . . . . Colonel Donahue not only showed that a railroad should be built by white labor but, at the same time, proved what California mechanics could do by building all his rolling stock and engines in San Francisco.

Oscar Shuck added in 1875,

> The most astonishing feature of all this history is that the entire road, with all its branches, has been built by exclusively white labor; and that

> the rolling stock and engines have been built in San Francisco, in Mr. Donahue's own foundry and machine shop. This has been done by Mr. Donahue in adherence to the principle to which he has conformed through life, of spending his money where he has accumulated it, and refusing to avail himself of the benefits and advantages of cheap coolie labor. Of course, Mr. Donahue has no one's opinion to please in all this matter, he being the sole owner.

The *Pioneer Record* (1880) of the Society of California Pioneers also commended Peter for what it saw as timely bigotry. "This labor was accomplished by white men, and it may in this connection be remarked that Mr. Donahue is steadfastly opposed to the employment of Mongolians on any service which will be antagonistic to that of the white race."

Actually, many of the men on the California Pacific extension of the SF & NP were Asians, as were many of Donahue's own trackmen on the Fulton and Guerneville and the Sonoma and Marin lines. In fact, so many of his Chinese workers stayed on in Sonoma County after all rail work was finished, going into vineyards, lumber camps and orchards, that their presence led to an anti-Chinese movement in rural areas during the 1880s.

The other repeated myth is that Peter's locomotives and rolling stock came from "his" Union Iron Works. The *John G. Downey, W. J. Ralston, Geyser, Santa Rosa* and *Ukiah*, were all Union Iron Works products, but built after he had sold out in 1865. He also contracted for engines and coaches from the East. Locomotives #12 and #13, the *Peter Donahue* and *Tom Rogers*, for example, were from Rogers's Paterson plant; and some cars came from Ralston's Kimball works. Possibly some cars were old SF & SJ cars made at Donahue's Mission District shops, and other cars came from the shops at Donahue. The most beautiful of all his passenger coaches, his palace car *Donahue*, was built at the little landing on Petaluma Creek.

Union Iron Works turned out the *Downey, Ralston* and *Geyser* in 1870, the *Santa Rosa* in 1873. Then, with seventeen well-received locomotives delivered to various lines, Donahue's protegé, Scott, did not build another engine for almost a decade, the *Ukiah* of 1882. This was because he was distracted by his new main interest—shipbuilding. But with its 1873 Circular and Pattern List, the Union

Iron Works in a modest sales pitch documented the most impressive and dramatic of its products (at least, until it began to build armored cruisers!)—the iron horse.

It may well be doubted if there is any branch of the manufacturing of machinery which imposes greater responsibility upon the builder and, at the same time, taxes his mechanical skill to a greater degree than the construction of locomotives. Strength, durability, speed, perfect proportions, and beauty are demanded at his hands. Upon a single beam, bolt, tie or spring may hang the lives of a multitude. This branch of business on the Pacific Coast has, thus far, been entrusted almost or quite entirely to ourselves, and it is with considerable pride that we point to the results of our labors, confident that no country produces better. With the desire to produce a first-class engine, we have corrected every defect as fast as circumstances would allow, and added all the improvements that have stood the test of usage.

Because of the confusion of the SF and North Pacific with the North Pacific Coast, the former was often called the "Donahue Broad Gauge Route," but the completed SF & NP was a *gem* of a railway. Peter's cousin Michael Hawkins (though resentful of him for dying while still owing him $18,000) wrote after the Colonel's death that "it was a splendid, paying, piece of property." The "Pen Portraits" article in the *Post* of 1877, almost confusing the name of Peter's line with that of its rival, correctly described his road. "Starting from a town which bears his name, it passes through a long, pleasant, fruitful valley, crosses the Russian River and climbs into the mountains beyond, and places the passengers amongst some of the grandest scenery in the state. Costly and bold in construction, the North Pacific is now worth a fortune, a well-deserved fortune."

VIII

DONAHUE'S LANDING

PETALUMA'S ADAMANT OPPOSITION to Peter's using Main Street for his railroad right-of-way so exasperated the capitalist colonel that he decided not to use the old (established in 1850) inland port, but to build his own. It is said that, because of his running battle with Petaluma's councilmen, he told them that he would see grass growing in their streets.

Peter crossed San Francisco Bay to Black Point, still called Black John's Slough then (circa 1869) in spite of local efforts to give it a more elegant and genteel name, like Grandview, even The Valley of No Regrets. It was a port on Petaluma Creek's right bank, at its mouth, for scow schooners and occasional steamboats hauling hay, grain, cattle, hogs, eggs, and milk to the city from both Marin and Sonoma county ranches. From the live oak-dotted high ground, Donahue looked northeastward across the creek to spy out the Petaluma Valley. He saw that dry land almost reached the tule marshes edging Petaluma Creek south of Lakeville. So he decided to buy property there for his new town, to be called Donahue. The site had once been part of General Mariano Vallejo's Mexican land grant, the *Rancho Petaluma.* His great adobe, the *Casa Grande*, still stands a few miles beyond; and today is a California State Historical Monument.

Mexican land grants were informal and vague, laid out in crude drawings called *diseños* instead of being surveyed and mapped properly. The grants were often contested by land-greedy *Anglos*, especially by squatters who made a cult of the belief that possession is nine points of the law. Such was the case with the Lakeville-Donahue area.

Lakeville's first settler (1852-53) had been a squatter, A.M. Bradley. He had sold out to Joshua Chadborne, George Carter, and Josiah Bacon. These men, in turn, sold their possessary rights, or squatters' rights, to Niles Mills and Peter Donahue around 1869. James Fair, one of the Nevada silver Bonanza Kings, also held a stretch of the creekside property, as did owners Sears, Peoples, J.R. Rose, and William Bihler. (The latter owned 8,900 acres, running across the dry and largely treeless hills from Petaluma Creek almost to Sonoma. He raised grapes, potatoes, and livestock, and stored his spuds in a brick warehouse on the creek at Lakeville until it was time to sell them.)

In 1860, Charles Minturn began running a San Francisco steamboat to Lakeville, to connect with stages to Petaluma, Sonoma, Santa Rosa, and Ukiah, even San Rafael before he opened his Point San Quentin route. In February 1865, the city fathers of Petaluma were, temporarily, scared out of their wits by a rumor that a through-railroad's terminal would be situated in Lakeville, rather than in their city. (Usually, Vallejo was Petaluma's main worry as a potential rail rival.) But nothing came of the transcontinental idea.

Peter chose a knoll about eight-tenths of a mile south of Lakeville and about half-way between Cloudy Bend, on the north, and False Bay, with its Hog Island, to the south. He found Petaluma Creek to be narrow and shallow, muddy and rushy, but with enough room at the knoll to swing his single-ended steamboats around, and with enough depth of water to moor them safely at a wharf. The townsite lay directly across the marshy valley from the huge bulk of Marin County's Burdell Mountain, and about eight miles by road from Petaluma and seven from Sonoma. Donahue lay about thirty-seven miles "by sea" from San Francisco.

The first sod was turned over at Donahue by September 1870. Work was rapid and in seven months cars were running on the line from the tiny port. Donahue was more than just a new Sonoma County village. It was more than a company town and a railhead. It was one of the very last ports established on greater San Francisco Bay and a pretty busy one, even though it was on a meandering slough with fifty changes of course and the hazard of thirteen-foot spring tides. (Minturn's pioneering *Petaluma* had sometimes been stranded in the tules by mudbanks till he had dredged a channel up to his rail terminus at Haystack Landing.)

Lakeville did not fade away when Donahue came along, less than a mile away. The settlement, 5.65 miles southeast of Petaluma, was not named for its wide spot in the creek below Cloudy Bend, but for little Laguna Tolay on the ridge to the east. This lagoon, which drained into Tolay Creek and the marshes of San Pablo Bay, was named by Father Jose Altimira for an Indian chief who lived on its shores. The lake ranged in width from 150 to 200 *varas* (a *vara* was a short yard, about thirty-three inches) and was almost a quarter-league in length (the Spanish league was about three miles). Eventually, the lakelet was drained for a potato patch. Tolay Creek still flows, intermittently, past Sear's Point and under Highway 37, the Black Point Cutoff.

Stagecoach passengers from the town of Sonoma used to transfer to Petaluma stages or San Francisco-bound steamers at Lakeville before Peter built Donahue. George T. Bromley, who had sold the Patent Sunlight Gas Burner in San Francisco in 1859, and surely knew the Gas Company Donahues, took a vacation trip that was typical of North Bay excursions of that day. He went by carriage from Sacramento to Sonoma. At 6 a.m. he started over the seven miles of the Lakeville-Sonoma Road (today called Stage Gulch Road) to catch the S.F. boat at Lakeville. It deposited him on San Francisco's East Street (the Embarcadero), at 11 a.m.

Coaches continued to run to Lakeville from the Sonoma plaza after Peter's railroad reached that old landing beyond Donahue, but now they connected with his morning and afternoon trains. Bradley's original Lakeville landing (1857) was replaced by a new one, built by C.A. Bodwell in February 1879. A post office of 1857 was joined by a blacksmith shop run by E.J. Holley and, later, George Branch. The ruins of the forge's furnace, parts of a brick chimney, are still to be seen across Lakeville Highway from Gilardi's fishing resort at Lakeville's landing. The post office and Peter's SF & NP Lakeville Station were located near the smithy.

On New Year's Day 1871, Peter put his two rebuilt steamers into service on the San Francisco-to-Donahue run, the *Sacramento* and the *Wilson G. Hunt*. (He may have used the *Milton S. Latham*, too, named for his rival, ironically. He later used it as a dormitory for his track gangs.)

The most famous vessel to call regularly at Donahue was not the historic *Sacramento* but the crack *Antelope* of captains W. Warner and David Van Pelt, although she was well beyond her prime when on the Petaluma Creek run. The best-known photo of Donahue's Landing shows the *Antelope* moored, bow in, in front of the Sonoma House hotel, while the more modern *James M. Donahue* is moored alongside the train shed on the wharf. Perhaps a streak of nostalgia lurked deep within no-nonsense Peter. He seemed to like to rescue aging steamers, like the *Sacramento* and *Antelope.*

The *Antelope* was a graceful sidewheeler of 425 tons, a wooden two-decker 178 feet long, with two masts and a rounded stern. Built by Bishop and Simonson with a Secor engine, she was launched on June 17, 1847, just two months after Peter's Peruvian *Rimac.* (She was twice rebuilt; enlarged in 1850 to 650 tons, but reduced in 1865 to 581 tons.) She came West by steaming from New York in May 1850 to San Juan del Sur on Nicaragua's Pacific coast, then plied between San Francisco and Panama for George Low's opposition line, from October 1850 until March 1851. She was sold that spring to the dominant Pacific Mail Steamship Company for $92,000. That company later sold her into Sacramento River service. Here she carried the first *mochilas* (leather mail pouches) of the Pony Express from Sacramento to San Francisco on April 15, 1860. On the Sacramento River, the *Antelope* won fame and the nickname of "Wells, Fargo's Gold Boat" because of her many cargoes of gold dust and bullion.

The tiring *Antelope* was superseded on the Donahue run by the magnificent new *James M. Donahue*, built in San Francisco in 1875 by William E. Collyer and named by Peter for his brother, James. She could accommodate five hundred passengers. The wooden, single-end, 227-foot sidewheeler had a jet condensing, walking beam engine by Quintard Iron Works to drive her large, 28-foot paddle wheels at eighteen knots. Her boilers were by the Fulton Iron Works. The *Examiner* reported that "Her engine is a model of the perfection of machinery." She was of such light draft, to negotiate shallow and tidal Petaluma Creek, that she had a peculiar paddle shaft lumped four feet above the main deck. (Small boys liked to take dangerous rides on the shaft, to the Colonel's alarm.) The *James M. Donahue's* cabin and grand staircase were gorgeous, and a great golden eagle crowned her tall pilot house.

Even as a back-up to the *James M. Donahue*, the old *Antelope* had her problems. She was laid up for months, under repair, at the beginning of 1876. Then, on a downward trip in early April, the members joining her walking beam with the engine's connecting rod broke off while she was passing Red Rock in San Pablo Bay. Disabled, she had to lay to for two hours till the *Sonoma* came alongside to take off passengers, mail and express for San Francisco. The steamer *Parthenius* then towed her ignominiously to the city before taking her place on the up run. The accident caused much delay, and the cars from Donahue did not reach Petaluma till eight at night.

In April of 1881, the *Antelope* had another accident and "the imperious Colonel Donahue" (the *Courier*) had to change his timetable and run all passenger and mail trains via San Rafael. This suited Petalumans beautifully, since they hated the roundabout Donahue run, anyway. They could now go straight down to the city on business on the 6:22 a.m. Santa Rosa train, arriving at 7:55, and return on the 4:45 to reach home again at a reasonable hour, 7:30 in the evening. The *Courier* chided Peter, "Not having a controlling interest in the road, we dislike to dictate to the Colonel, but can't he see that it would be a very great accommodation to continue it?" Sarcastically, the paper added, "Surely the beautiful view one obtains at Donahue and Sonoma landing does not recompense him for the hour's stoppage he has to endure at these two places. Think over the suggestion, P."

By 1884, the old "Gold Boat" was arthritic and nigh exhausted. The *Courier* ran a story on her on April 30. "The old steamer *Antelope* (ye gods and little fishes, what a misnomer!) commenced running on the creek route last Monday in place of the *James M. Donahue*, which has been transferred to the ferry route between Point Tiburon and San Francisco. The cars on that day arrived here via Donahue at 12 o'clock noon; usual time 10:30 a.m. She would probably not have reached Donahue until late in the afternoon, but the tide being favorable, the Captain turned her full side to it so as to catch all of its assistant force and, by crowding on all the steam she could bear, came up from Frisco at the rattling speed of eight miles an hour. O, but isn't she a daisy!"

Dr. Alexander S. Keenan knew the *Antelope* well, and he recalled that when the landing was moved to Tiburon the bow of the *James*

M. Donahue was curved to suit the new ferry slip there, but not so the *Antelope*. She remained at Donahue for many years after that landing became inactive. According to Dr. Keenan, she was finally towed to Benicia to be wrecked. (Some sources state that she was broken up in 1888, but in San Francisco rather than in Benicia.)

Captain Warner's *James M. Donahue* left San Francisco's Washington Street Wharf daily, except Sundays, at 3:00 with mail and express to connect with the cars for Cloverdale at Donahue and, at Fulton, for the Russian River's "Great Redwood Forests." (There was also a 7:15 a.m. daily boat to Donahue.) The Cloverdale train left for Donahue at 6 a.m. daily except Sunday, to connect with the city-bound steamer and the stages to the interior. The "*Donahue*" also made Sunday excursions, leaving the wharf at San Francisco at 8 a.m. and returning at 7:20 p.m.

Newspapers of the 1870s described the *James M. Donahue* as the finest, fleetest steamboat in California waters. By the 1880s, however, the *Examiner* was calling her a slow boat. (The noble steamer ended up as a hulk on the beach at Point San Quentin near the Marin Rod and Gun Club pier in 1920. She was used as a bait and tackle shop and shrimp drying plant until she burned in 1940. This writer used to see her bones in the mud at low tide while waiting for the Richmond Ferry. They were given decent burial by the fill for the anchorage of the Richmond-San Rafael Bridge.)

A Donahue's Landing craft that was as dissimilar as possible from the sleek *Antelope* and the *James M. Donahue* was the *Hattie Fickett*, a big and cumbersome old sternwheeler that would waddle up to the east bank of Petaluma Creek and tie up inside the Donahue wharf. Workers then laid timbers from the shore to her bow. The *Hattie Fickett* had rails running down her middle, and a light switch engine from the yards at Donahue, the old *San Jose*, would shunt flatcars loaded with logs, sand, or rock aboard her. Extra-long redwood logs would be placed in a pile straddling two flats. No passengers were carried.

The skipper of the *Hattie Fickett*, and also of the *Milton S. Latham*, at times, was Captain Stephen W. Burdick. He had been mate of the "*Donahue*". When age and infirmity caused him to finally "swallow the anchor" and retire, he chose Donahue for his home. He died on May Day 1884, the day that Peter opened his new line south from San Rafael to the port that replaced Donahue,

Tiburon. On the first Sunday of May, flags at Donahue and on vessels in San Francisco Bay were lowered to half-staff in honor of the Colonel's old steamboat captain.

In its heyday, Donahue boasted a large wharf, a depot, fire house, a long wooden machine shop and carpenter shop with railroad tracks down the middle of each one, a telegraph office, warehouses, two blacksmith shops, a railroad car repair shop, a paintshop at the rear of the carpenters' shop, and a roundhouse with stalls for five locomotives, with a turnstile in front. There were two laundries (one of them Chinese), and quarters for workmen back up the knoll in six two-story buildings that held flats of four and five rooms each, with large yards in the rear. There was a saloon run by a man named Burdick (probably the retired steamboat captain) and a combined dance hall and stable.

In 1955, Mrs. Julia Gregory looked back over the years and remembered attending a one-room school for thirty to forty children "in" Donahue. However, the school might have been the Lakeville School where, in March 1873, many of the thirty-two pupils were actually *from* Donahue. In 1877, there was also a Lake School as well as a Lakeville School, located two and a half miles south of Donahue.

According to Mrs. Gregory, there were often too many students in the Donahue school for the number of desks, (even though each desk accommodated two), so the overflow sat in chairs where they could find room. The teacher had a desk, a world atlas, a large blackboard with erasers, maps on a stand as well as on the walls, and a small reference library. Firewood was stored in a shed with a sink where the kids washed up. Teachers whom Mr. Gregory remembered were Ann McCarthy and W.D. Kelly. Mr. Kelly used a strap and a buggy whip to keep order among his more unruly male students.

The Petaluma *Argus*, after a visit, criticized (May 11, 1877) Donahue for having one of the poorest schools—if not *the* poorest—in the county. The school population of the Donahue district was then thirty-nine students, but the teacher, Miss Singley of Petaluma, had only nine pupils in attendance. The paper did concede, however, that "The few scholars that were present seemed to be much interested in their work," But it added, "So poor a school building and so small an attendance of children show how little interest the people of the district feel in the education of their children." In contrast, Lakeville School was a good building, though in a badly maintained yard. It was kept open eight months of the year by the teacher, Miss Shover of Petaluma. She had currently enrolled on her attendance roster twenty-eight of the thirty-six children in her district. The *Argus* reported that her school received $478.26 of aid from the state and county in 1876.

Petaluma, like Lakeville, was always jealous of Peter's upstart village. The editor of the *Journal-Argus* accepted an invitation from SF & NP Superintendent Bean to visit the 100-acre landing, to pick up items of railroad interest. He used his material on February 17, 1872 to do something of a "hatchet job" on the little port and railway terminal. "Donahue, as a town, may be properly called a failure. It consists of one hotel, the Company's machine shops, car houses, a long wharf where the steamboat lands." The editor admitted that Donahue figured as a town on maps and schedules because it was a steamer landing and railroad terminus, but he insisted, "Donahue is not a town and can never be made one, which is all contrary to him whose name it bears . . . . A great deal of money was uselessly expended here to perpetuate a name by building up a town. But we can imagine, a few years hence, when the traveler flying past the point at thirty miles an hour will say, 'This place used to be called . . . . What the devil's the name? Anyhow, where the steamboat used to land.' " The writer, unable to resist punning on Donahue's name, concluded, "And so its greatness will Peter out."

The newspaperman was very hospitably received at Donahue and he expressed his gratitude to all hands there, but especially to Bean, Thomas P. Carter, foreman in the car department, and C.C. Garslip, foreman of the machine shop, for their kindness—"and for the insight into the practical workings of a railroad, of which we have, heretofore, been in darkness." He even added a social footnote by mentioning that the landlord of the Sonoma House had just been married, that the wedding had created "a profound sensation," and that it was still the main topic of conversation in Donahue's social circles. Because of the nuptials, he even allowed himself to praise the town that he had just doomed—"Donahue is looking up."

The visitor's main object was a train ride, and Bean gave him a good one in the cab of a locomotive. He also examined two nicely-upholstered first-class passenger coaches, "as comfortable as any traveler could wish," and equipped with the new-fangled Westinghouse air brakes. He learned that two more cars were in the shops being fitted with the new safety brakes. These saved money by sharply reducing the number of brakemen needed on the line while they saved "precious necks" by preventing accidents. Now the engineer could apply all of the train's brakes at the same time, and with equal force on each wheel. These were demonstrated for the newspaperman. Had he visited a few years later, he would have seen another of the Colonel's modernizations—Hobbs automatic couplers replacing the old Lincoln Pins. The former were more efficient, and the latter had a nasty habit of removing brakemen's fingers.

The Donahue wharf was piled with railroad "iron," ties and lumber, with vessels arriving each day with more, indicating to the *Argus* editor that the company was confident of completing the Cloverdale line on time. He could not help being impressed by the fleet of rolling stock in the yards—five locomotives, a steam dummy, seven passenger coaches, two baggage cars, twenty freight cars, thirty-six platform or flatcars, ten hand cars, three large sleeping and dining cars for the track layers, and five push cars. Three boxcars were being built in the shops, and an Eastern engine and twenty-five cars were expected soon from Sacramento. The firemen, he noticed, not only kept the engines "wooded up," but also kept the locomotives shining until they gleamed, with a mixture of oil and graphite.

Doomed or not, Donahue grew from a shaky start in 1870 into quite a railroad town and port by 1873. Even the *Argus-Courier* had to admit, in its heading of February 21, 1872 "Donahue All Right." The story read, "Ever since the day that Peter Donahue sold the San Francisco and North Pacific Railroad until the time that he purchased it again, the town that bears his name went backwards. Immediately, however, upon his resumption of authority there, it takes on new life and renewed vigor. The population is rapidly increasing and, yesterday, the wife of one of its citizens presented her husband with twin daughters which are now the pride and boast of the town. If they were boys, we would say name one Peter and the other Donahue. But as their sex will not permit of this, we leave the matter of their names to the mamma of Donahue."

Apparently, Peter spent a good deal of time working in Donahue rather than in San Francisco, although he was still listed as a "Capitalist" in city directories, with an office at the northeast corner of Montgomery and Market streets in 1871 and, after that date, in Rooms 3 and 4 of 426 Montgomery. For example, he wrote from his SF & NP office in Donahue on November 24, 1873 to Petaluma's City Clerk, D.D. Carder. It was to remind him that the contract to supply gas to that city expired that very day. "For the information of the Board of Trustees of the City of Petaluma, I beg to say that I am prepared to continue the supply of gas on the same terms [as] heretofore, hoping this will be satisfactory to your Board."

Earlier, Peter had run an advertisement in the *Argus-Courier* (August 17, 1873) for threshing machinery for sale—cheap—by agents of his SF & NP at Donahue, Petaluma, Santa Rosa and Healdsburg. And not just any old threshers, but the "celebrated" Western Donahue Threshing Machines. Perhaps Peter "kept his hand in" at the Union Iron Works long after supposedly parting company with that firm. Or was he turning out agricultural machinery in his railroad shops at Donahue?

The hub of activity at Donahue was always the dock, or wharf, built on hundreds of piles barged there by Peter, circa 1870. Some twenty-odd lumber schooners had also been "stacked up" in the stream at one time, waiting to unload, as Donahue first began to take shape. The rails came right down the left bank of Petaluma Creek to mount a trestle at the water's edge, curved slightly eastward, then ran straight to the end of the pier. The end of the wharf was covered so that a full train—an engine and eight coaches—could be protected from inclement weather. The *James M. Donahue* was moored to the outside of the wharf, only a step or two away for disembarking train passengers. Scow schooners tied up to the inner side of the wharf. When they became frequent callers Peter added a projection to his wharf and extended his track to it so that flatcars could accommodate the scows. Once again, he confined them to the inner side of the wharf, where they would not interfere with the navigation of busy Petaluma Creek.

Donahue suffered a temporary setback in late February 1874 because of a costly conflagration. In its February 20 story, "The Fire Fiend At Donahue," the *Argus-Courier* reported that the 2:30

a.m. blaze in the car shop spread so rapidly that, in spite of an alarm being given immediately, and great efforts by the sleepy population, the car shop and adjacent machine shop were both destroyed. Two elegant passenger coaches that were being put in readiness were burned up, along with three flatcars and several dump cars. Also burned were a stationary engine and a great quantity of blacksmiths' and carpenters' tools. Workers who had sleeping apartments in the car shop lost clothing and other valuables. Locomotive #2, the *J.G. Downey*, in the machine shop for repairs, was saved, with the exception of its pilot.

The paper estimated the company's loss to be between $65,000 and $75,000, but later estimates ran to $100,000. The fire burned so rapidly that, in barely a half-hour after the alarm was first sounded, both buildings were in ruins. The SF & NP expressed no opinion as to the origin of the blaze, but told the newspaper that its property was insured by the State Investment Insurance Company.

Donahue's Landing had little to fear, Peter sat on the insurance company's board of directors. In fact, during 1873-74 he was its president; and it was a sound insurance company. (In 1881, John S. Hittell's *Commerce and Industries of the Pacific Coast* gave its income as $53,000 annually, of which about half went into dividends, the balance into net assets. As Hittell observed, "This record ought to satisfy policy holders as well as stockholders.")

After the rebuilding of the burned shops, Donahue was as good as new. Better. In February 1875, a new forty-room, up-to-date hotel, the Sonoma House, opened, boasting of piped water and gas in each room. It was described locally as a resort for pleasure-seeking San Franciscans.

The *Argus* paid another visit to Donahue and reported on it January 28, 1876. The writer found the machine shop very busy working on the *Antelope*. The old steamer had been undergoing repairs for several months, but would be ready for the painters in a fortnight and for regular service by mid-March. A splendid new train of passenger coaches, all built right there in Donahue, would be complete in just two more weeks. Two new coaches had already gone ahead to Cloverdale. Peter was also beginning construction of one hundred flatcars. All iron work—wheels, castings, and so on—was on order, but from the East curiously, not from Union Iron Works. They were due at the landing by February 1. The newspaper also noted a combination express-baggage car, bigger than the existing one by a third, under construction in the yards, plus a new smoking car for the passenger trains.

The paper had both good and bad railroad news for its readers that day. The excursion trains would resume their schedule, weather permitting, about March 1. But Peter's master mechanic at Donahue, W.M. Kilduff, had suffered a partial paralytic stroke in January and had to be taken to San Francisco for medical treatment. He was replaced by H.C. Whiting. The most interesting news of all at Donahue was a railway coach still on paper, still on the drawing boards. It was Peter's private car, the *Donahue.*

The Santa Rosa *Press-Democrat* also paid a call on Donahue, reporting on June 27, 1876 that it was "quite a village," with shops that could apparently build anything from a flatcar to a steamboat or a palace car. He saw the one hundred flats noted by his fellow-journalist, also the *Antelope*, being rebuilt, and an anonymous steamer, under construction, carrying two sets of rails to haul freight cars to San Francisco. This must have been one of the West's pioneer car ferries. (Could it have been the *Hattie Fickett*?)

Naturally, the *Argonaut*, hostile to Peter, was cool to the Irish seaport of Donahue. It noted in March of 1878 that it was less impressed with Peter's route than that of the NPC. The *Argonaut* described the latter as leaving Sausalito and "skirting bay and ocean shores, through shaded glens . . . and a thousand beautiful spots for picnics and camping grounds." Garbling the name of the NPC a little, as did so many, the *Argonaut's* Pixley went on, "We are not informed whether the North Coast Railroad will run excursions this summer or not. We presume not until Mr. Donahue shall bring his road to San Rafael, when it will be less tedious than by the present long ferry to that very uninteresting spot called Donahue."

Dr. Alexander S. Keenan was the first Donahue descendent to be born in the little port of Donahue. Born November 14, 1872, he was the son of Alexander Keenan of Ballycastle, Ireland, and Peter's Glasgow-born niece Mary Dougherty, the daughter of Ellen Donahue Dougherty. In a memoir for the 1955 Centennial Edition of the Petaluma *Argus-Courier*, Dr. Keenan wrote that Peter had needed a man of his father's outstanding character as superintendent of the new rail yards and shipping point of Donahue, so invited his brother-in-law and his family to come to the United States.

Mr. and Mrs. Keenan and their children, Ellen and James, passed through Chicago just after its great fire of 1871. They became Peter's guests at his Second and Bryant Street mansion in October or November. Then one day, Peter took Keenan on the boat to Donahue to meet his master mechanic and others. He made him Superintendent of Shipping, both passenger and freight, on the spot, and gave him an office on the covered end of the wharf. The Keenans moved to a well-built ranch house of many rooms up on the hill behind the town, given them, free of rent, by a generous Peter Donahue. (However, Peter's generosity—or perhaps his memory—slipped a bit in his later years. Before his grandnephew, Peter Keenan, was born, the Colonel had told the mother, "If you name the boy after me, you'll never regret it." According to family tradition, the railway magnate did not quite forget the lad. But he nearly did. On his ninth birthday, Peter gave him a dollar. Period.)

Alexander Keenan found himself to be much more than a glorified shipping clerk. Besides being manager, chief accountant and general factotum of Donahue, he was soon named Clerk of the Board of Trustees of the local school, then the Vallejo Township School, whose sole teacher was paid by the county. He was next made Justice of the Peace, and held court in half of his wharf office, dividing its space with his desk and keeping visitors on one side while dispensing justice on the other. The county appointed a constable for Donahue and this law officer brought prisoners before the J.P. Most of the offenses were petty—drunkeness, fighting, occasional thefts—but Keenan's case load was pretty high because his jurisdiction extended far beyond the landing. His penalties were usually fines of $10 to $20. In serious cases, felonies, Keenan would set bail and refer the accused to the Superior Court in Santa Rosa.

The judge-harbor master's son, Dr. Alexander S. Keenan, remembered the stylish Union Iron Works-built fire engine in the Donahue firehouse. It was so handsome that it was often shipped by boat to take part in San Francisco parades. Shop workers formed up a volunteer fire department. The men would sometimes draw the engine out of the firehouse, attach a hose to a hydrant and pretend that they were putting out a blaze, to the amusement of all the small boys of the town.*

Peter Donahue, the stern—almost brusque—elder statesman of San Francisco's business community, displayed a seldom-seen side of his nature, one that was kindly, even sentimental, at the Keenan ranch house at Donahue. He used its fields as a kind of rest home for horses of his Omnibus street railway in the city. Peter's great-grandnephew, attorney Alexander (Alex) S. Keenan, Jr., reminisced to Richard J. Burke in a letter of May 23, 1967. "My grandfather [Alexander Keenan, the elder]. . . continued to recondition Peter's tired horses. Peter made frequent visits to inspect the terminal, and always stayed at the Keenan farm. Where he slept, I do not know, but it must have been with two or three of the Keenan children. My grandfather did not touch strong liquor, but had to keep a supply of 'the best' on hand for Peter's visits." Young James Keenan (Keenan the elder's oldest son) was often given the honor of driving Peter to Petaluma.

* * *

In the Donahue shops, master mechanic Whiting built a magnificent private car for Peter, a ten-foot wide, fifty-one foot long, six-wheeled "Silver Palace" of a Pullman-like model, built to hold fifteen guests, with a drawing room, dining room, sleeping compartment, kitchen and observatory. The *Argus-Courier* predicted on January 28, 1876 that the car would surpass any on wheels in convenience and luxurious appointment. The Santa Rosa *Press-Democrat* chimed in on April 28, 1876. "It is to be the most com-

*Dr. Keenan, who spent his childhood in his home village of Donahue, went on to Santa Clara University and was graduated from the University of California Medical School with the Class of 1898. He was a surgeon-physician on the staff of Mary's Help Hospital, president of both the San Francisco Medical Society and the San Francisco City and County Board of Health, and one of the three founders of the San Francisco City Employees Health Service in 1937-38. The San Francisco Medical Society honored him with an award dinner, giving him a gold medal on his fiftieth anniversary as a doctor. Dr. Keenan was married to Laura Maguire, a niece of Peter Donahue's first wife. He died on October 19, 1958, survived by his children Alexander S. Keenan, Jr., an attorney; Peter D. Keenan, M.D.; Mary Jane (Mrs. Wallace) Sheehan; and Olive (Mrs. William) Carroll. Dr. Keenan's niece, Patricia, the daughter of his older brother James, is today's family historian.

plete in regard to elegance, comfort and adaptability to pleasant traveling ever constructed in this state. It will doubtless attract much attention, [and] as a Sonoma County enterprise, we have reason to be proud of it."

Peter's posh private railway car was given a trial run toward the end of July 1876. It was pulled from Donahue to Cloverdale by his powerful new Paterson-built Rogers locomotive. Peter planned a family trip in the private car to Cloverdale in September. The *Argus-Courier* reported (July 26), "We are informed by those who ought to know that it is not only the best on the road, but one of the best on any road in the state. The car is of a most elegant structure, built at Donahue under the superintendency of H.C. Whiting."

The grand palace car was for Peter's exclusive use. But he loaned it to a friend, James Flood of the Bonanza Kings, for a trip to the nation's Centennial (1776-1876) Exposition in Philadelphia. The *Argus* reported, August 18, 1876, that "The drawing room car built at Donahue . . . will be used by James C. Flood of bonanza fame in a trip to the Centennial. The car passed down the road yesterday morning." The luxurious car actually departed for the East Coast at the end of August. Flood took his wife and daughter, Peter's son, Mervyn, former governor Downey, Edward Martin, and a gentleman named Wilkes.

Peter also took the car to the Centennial Exposition. He had had it built partly to be able to show it off there. Perhaps he remembered the old *Saginaw*. In any case, he ordered Whiting to build the car with only local woods—redwood, laurel (bay), white pine, oak.

Peter often called on his cousin, Michael Hawkins, to help entertain when he gave parties for his daughter, Mary Ellen (Mamie). Hawkins remembered that season of 1876 very well. "Thomas Donahue, Mamie's bachelor uncle, [Peter's youngest brother] was stopping at the house at the time. We would take the young ladies for a morning drive to the beach, and breakfast at the Cliff House. In the evening, we would take in the theater. On their day at home, I would fill the house with young men and there would be dancing."

When Peter decided to go the Exposition in Philadelphia, he showed his gratitude to Hawkins by inviting him to come along. He asked him in an offhand way, Hawkins remembered. "I replied, carelessly, laughing while firing at a billiard ball, 'That will be fine,

I'll go!' The time was indefinite and I did not treat the invitation seriously." Because of his partner's weakness for strong drink, Hawkins did not want to commit himself to leaving his office. To his surprise, on a Saturday night just two weeks later, Peter and Ed Martin called on him in his room at the Occidental Hotel.

The Colonel came right to the point. "Michael, my car is at the Oakland Mole, all provisioned for the trip, and we start at half-past seven o'clock, Monday morning." Hawkins protested, "But, Cousin, I can't go. I can't leave my business." Donahue snorted, "Oh, Daly can take care of the business, and it won't cost you a cent, from the time you leave here until you return, except for what you wish to spend, yourself." Hawkins was still reluctant. "Cousin, I know Mr. Daly's habits better than you do. I appreciate your invitation, but for the reason stated, I cannot go."

Peter turned back to Martin. "Ned, I am sick, and this was to be the first real pleasure trip of my life. And Michael is the only one of my people I can depend on. He has promised, and now he says he can't go. And my trip is spoiled." Apparently quite an actor when he had to be, Peter lowered his head to the table top, rested it on his arms, and seemed to weep. He did not have to sob very long. Hawkins, of course, gave in. The latter recalled, "This was very touching. I thought of his great personal achievement in the upbuilding of this city and state. Like a flash, I called out, "Cousin, stop it! I'll go.' "

Hawkins continued his reminiscence. "Peter Donahue raised his head instantly, saying to his brother-in-law, 'Ned, did you hear that? He says he'll go. Now I'll cinch it.' " The Colonel took a wallet from his breast pocket and put it in his cousin's hands, saying, "It contains $1,500 in bills, and passes over all the railroads between here and New York. Now put that book in your pocket. If there are any disbursements required on the trip, you pay them out of this money." After Hawkins pocketed the billfold, Peter said, "Ned, now I'm content. Now for a bottle of wine."

When Peter asked him to buy some good cigars for him, to give to a friend, Hawkins went to a tobacconist near the Occidental and bought the most expensive havanas that he could find, using money from the Philadelphia-trip wallet. They cost $25 a box. Both Peter and Martin were open-mouthed with astonishment at the price. Finally, the Colonel commented, "Michael, isn't that a high-priced cigar?" "Yes, of course," was the answer. "It is the highest-priced in the city. But it is a first-class one, and you told me your friend was a first-class man." Donahue turned to Edward Martin and said, "By George, Ned, he is right."

Boarding the palace car, besides Peter, Annie, Mamie, and Hawkins, were Miss Mamie Rafferty, visiting the Donahues, and 16-year old Jennie Martin, on her way back to a convent school in Baltimore. Also along was the Honorable Patrick Murphy of Santa Clara, owner of historic Rancho Santa Margarita in San Luis Obispo County, whose family had crossed the plains in 1844 with the Murphy-Stevens party of emigrants, and whose older brother had married one of Mrs. Donahue's sisters in 1860. Actually, Patrick Murphy had only come across the bay to see the party off. But Peter said, "Pat, you had better come along with us." Murphy promptly plunked himself down in a seat, saying, "All right, Colonel."

The first stop en route to Philadelphia was Davenport, Iowa, where Peter persuaded his brother Michael to join the group since his wife was already East, visiting her mother in New York. According to Hawkins, Peter found after reaching Chicago, that the *Donahue* was not of the proper gauge to run on the rails east of the Windy City. But the railroad showed him every consideration and he was able to put the party up in a hotel for the night while Rock Island line workmen labored around the clock to jack the private car up and replace the trucks and wheels with those of the proper gauge.

Three days later, the *Donahue* reached Pittsburgh, where a Pennsylvania Railroad man measured the car to see if it would pass through the tunnels ahead. His measuring rod showed the eaves to be slightly beyond the standard width dictated by Eastern bores. But, to Peter's great relief, he did not have to leave the *Donahue* in Pittsburgh, *or* tear off its eaves. The railway official detained the train for only ten minutes before telegraphing Tom Scott, president of the Pennsylvania Railroad, that he thought that he could "squeeze the *Donahue* through." Scott wired back, "All right. Push the Colonel through."

Arriving in Philadelphia, the members of the Donahue party were joined by Mamie Rafferty's mother at the Continental Hotel, where they put up for a fortnight. Apparently, Peter parked the

Donahue on a siding at the edge of the fairgrounds where the public could inspect it, although it was not listed in the exhibit guides to the Exposition.

Peter (who today would be called a workaholic) was often absent from the group, mixing business with pleasure, as usual. Hawkins explained, "My cousin was very well acquainted with the iron merchants of Philadelphia and not particular about the ladies' dinner hour; so, in his absence, I would take the head of the table. Peter would come in, bring two—sometimes three—friends, and, one night, my wine bill was $40. I was his guest on the car, but I saw to it that myself and Mr. Murphy paid our own hotel bills."

Not that cousin Michael had to depend on the Continental Hotel for decent meals. "The chef that we had on the car was unsurpassed as a cook, and in catering for the meals. I have eaten at Delmonico's in New York and the principal cafes in Paris and London, but no meals were better-cooked than on the private car, *Donahue.*"

Peter described his visit and his palace car to a New York *Sun* reporter. "It was made at my own establishment for exhibition at the Centennial. Its peculiar feature is that it is made of wood indigenous to the Sonoma Valley. About a fortnight ago, I started with my wife and children from San Francisco. We came over the Central and Southern Pacific, Rock Island, and Pennsylvania roads. Our trip was delightful, and we rode on easy springs and without annoyance from dust, the car having double windows and closely-fitting doors."

Alfred Bates in 1890 also recalled the sumptuous *Donahue.* "It was, in truth, a marvel of architecture, though with its walls and paneling unadorned except by the rich hues of native California wood, the beautiful California coloring of the white pine and the mammoth redwood. The furniture, hangings and upholstery were in excellent taste; the ladies' apartment fitted for the accommodation of a princess, and all the apartments supplied with every convenience that human ingenuity could devise."

In Baltimore, Hawkins had to leave his friends and kinsmen to their leisurely return trip in order to hurry back to rescue his business from the fumbling hands of his bibulous partner. While in the East, he learned that Daly had not been in the office for even a week since his departure.

* * *

The life span of the town of Donahue was less than twenty years. It dwarfed Lakeville and stole its post office, but only from January to July of 1875. The new port never really boomed. In the fall election of 1877, for example, the October 28 *Argus* recorded only eighteen votes cast there. Peter's "convenient" Petaluma Creek service was a joke, a bad one, to Petalumans desirous of doing business in "The City." A long, sarcastic *Courier* article of April 20, 1881 was headlined "A Real Undertaking. Being A Truthful Account Of A Trip To San Francisco And Return In One Day." It was actually a letter submitted to the editor under the *nom de plume* of Shady. The latter confessed that he had oft postponed the trip from Donahue—"the undertaking was one that I shrank from."

One day, Shady rose at 6 a.m., "alarmed the house" for his breakfast, bought his ticket at the East Petaluma depot at 6:45, boarded the train at 7, and was at Donahue only a few minutes later. So far, so good.

At Donahue, however, things changed. "On taking a casual glance at the surroundings at this stopping place, I was greatly discomfited by two things. One was that I noticed the steamer [*James M.*] *Donahue* laid up for repairs and the old *Antelope* pulled up at the wharf. . . . Another, the more terrible because the more permanent, was the fact that great improvements were being made to the wharf there, which is conclusive evidence that Colonel Donahue has no idea of running his road to a larger place than Donahue, and no nearer to San Francisco than the end of his wharf."

Shady then followed two "smoked Italians," (apparently a derogatory term for blacks) who were trundling a truckload of dead calves down the gangplank to the *Antelope's* deck. He bumped against a pig pen, setting its 150 inhabitants into a chorus of squeals. He next carommed off a tier of chicken coops. The ancient *Antelope* was a Noah's Ark. The chickens cackled, the ducks quacked, the geese babbled, the pigs squealed, the cattle bellowed, the horses neighed. All the while, the air was freighted with such a variety of smells that it was hard for Shady to tell whether he was in a pig pen, a hen house, a horse stable or a slaughter pen. "Oh, my unhappy country," he cried.

When Shady climbed up to the darkened cabin on the upper deck, he sat down—on top of a sick Chinese, stretched out on the seats.

"He groaned and cursed, and I at last found anchor on a chair on the rear deck, and soon began to compose my fears and still my nerves." There were only about thirty passengers. The bigoted Shady counted only whites; the others were "cussed, heathen Chinese." And the *Antelope* was in no hurry. Manager Hughes wore an expression which as much as said aloud, "We have got all day."

At 8 a.m., Captain Warner started the engine, cast off the lines, and headed the *Antelope* downstream, the vessel trembling like an aspen leaf in a stiff breeze. Shady remarked to a lady passenger, "I fear the steamer will shake in two before we get to the city." She retorted, "You ought to be ashamed to speak that way." Shakily, the *Antelope* reached Sonoma Landing in three-quarters of an hour. There at the mouth of Petaluma Creek, she halted to load wine casks that filled the large wharf. During the half-hour layover, a Sonoma vintner had sharp words with supercargo Hughes about his wine lying in the hot sun, day after day. Then pilot Van Pelt lost his best Sunday hat overboard. But, finally, the *Antelope* got vibratingly under way again, after 9 a.m. The weather was pleasant and clear, and a friend said to Shady, "Whatever else may happen, there is no danger of a collision."

The rival *Pilot*, from Petaluma, had by now almost caught up with the Donahue craft, but two more hours of slow and tedious travel finally brought her past the lightship, then Angel Island, and the frowning cannon of Fort Alcatraz. Warner's long warning whistle signaled his approach to the Embarcadero. The lady came up and said, "You see that we are here, and no accident has happened." "But," protested Shady, "we are not yet landed." He took a shortcut through the cabin just as—"Crash! Bang! Whang!—everything keeled over, women fainted, pigs squealed and fowl fluttered in protest. "Terror and dismay were in the air," he wrote.

An officer shouted, "There has been a collision! Our boat is filling with water! The passengers must go aft!" The *Antelope* had run her muzzle into the bow of the tug *Monarch.* The latter took the blow well, but, in Shady's words, "the crumbling nose of our ancient craft suffered severely." Luckily, the sidewheeler was quite close to her wharf, and she tied up safely. But it was nearly noon when the Petaluman finally took his seat in a street car, five hours after leaving the railroad depot. "What splendid facilities!," he exclaimed sourly, "What magnificent accommodations! What a stupendous enterprise! Is it any wonder that so many people are crowding into Sonoma County?"

He had just two hours to transact his business, at a cost (he figured) of a dollar an hour, before starting back for the wharf at 2:30. But the *Antelope* was so damaged that she was taken out of service. Shady had to leave the city at 4:45 on the San Rafael train-ferry. But he was "only too glad to escape the torture of a return by the old way." He was home at 7:15, having been traveling all day in order to conduct two hours of business. "Is it any wonder that our people are agitating the building of a Creek boat?," he asked rhetorically.

Have we not, as a community, reason to complain to Colonel Donahue on the management of his railroad? Is it to be wondered at that nearly every pound of freight that comes to, or goes from, Petaluma comes or goes by the steamer *Pilot,* or by schooners? The astonishment is that people will even travel by the Donahue route.

As a community, we respectively petitioned Colonel Donahue to give us a morning and night train by San Rafael. The prayer was denied and the question sneeringly asked if we 'wanted to run his business.' In the light of past events and present inconveniences, would it be rude to reply that *any* change of management would be for the better? As, in no contingency, could it possibly prove worse. Excuse me, Mr. Editor, for taking up so much space in writing up such a short trip.

Donahue's only real rival on Petaluma Creek was the Petaluma Transportation Company's *Pilot,* which left San Francisco's Jackson Street Wharf daily at 3 p.m. for Haystack Landing, with special ("excursion") fares, probably to make her competitive, of only $1.00, round-trip. She touched at Point San Pedro, Black Point, and Lakeville en route to Haystack Landing. But the *Pilot* was removed, dramatically, from competition in May of 1883 when her boiler blew up between Haystack and Lakeville. SF & NP people in Donahue heard the explosion and felt the earthquake-like shock. They sent rescue boats up the creek and hurried a train to Petaluma for doctors. The May 3 *Courier* praised Donahue's firm—"This same company continued its good works throughout the day."

A *Courier* reporter who paid a call on Donahue in the spring of 1882 enjoyed a nice hot lunch at H. Leslie's Sonoma House. He next saw laborers busy as bees turning out new railroad cars and repairing old ones. John Martin, the boss, had thirty men working for him and planned to add more as the season advanced. He had received lumber to build a new type of flatcar, one with only four wheels. Martin was particularly pleased with the handsome, new-design excursion car that was a'building. It was open on all sides above the seats and was very roomy. "As things are now at Donahue," wrote the newsman, "there is work enough ahead to take the present force of workmen a year to clean up."

On March 21, 1883, the *Courier* reported a steam yacht, the *Mamie Donahue,* being built in the SF & NP shops at Donahue. She would run in connection with Peter's new railroad extension, between San Rafael and "Kershaw's" (i.e., Kashow's) Island—Belvedere—on Raccoon Straits. She was forty feet long; seven feet, ten inches in breadth of beam; with a three-and-a-half-foot depth of hold. The *Mamie Donahue* was powered by double engines turning a 32-inch propeller. The locomotive *J.G. Downey* was back in the shop at the same time, undergoing thorough repairs. She was being given new innards—replacement cylinders and new tubes in her boiler. At the same time, forty freight cars and two passenger cars for the Sonoma road were under construction in the shops, bringing them to full capacity in new work and repairs, with a large number of mechanics employed. Small wonder that the Santa Rosan concluded, "Business looks lively and prosperous about Donahue."

The *Marin County Journal* begged to differ on October 9, 1884. "The Donahue Railroad will, in a few days, have their [*sic*] arrangements completed to transfer all their freight business to the Tiburon route and desert the Donahue [route] altogether. . . ." Donahue's days did seem numbered, yet a correspondent at the landing (who signed herself Nellie) reported on October 13, 1884 that engineers #12 and #13, the *Peter Donahue* and the *Tom Rogers,* just received at Tiburon, were being assembled in the Donahue shops. And she noted that there were enough voters still in Donahue to make it worthwhile for Republican senatorial nominee Colonel H.W. Byington to give a speech there on October 8. Indeed, it was not till November 5, 1885 that the *Journal* reported, "The shops of the SF & NP will be removed to Tiburon the first of the new year."

To the very last, Petalumans hoped to persuade Peter to move his rail shops to their city. The *Courier* on May 21, 1884 stated that Petaluma was more favorably situated for the main depot and machine shops than the county seat of Santa Rosa or any other point on the route. The paper understood that $20,000, or possibly less, would induce Donahue to relocate the SF & NP shops to Petaluma. The paper suggested an additional inducement—the city trustees could exempt the railway property from taxes for a while. The move would mean an increase in population of 200 to 300 people. This would benefit local merchants since the Donahue's Landing payroll was about $10,000 a month. Former residents of Donahue would also buy homes and lots. "We understand," said the editor, "the employees would rather live at Petaluma than any other point on the road." This was so because of its unsurpassed schools and churches, and the best markets outside of San Francisco. It was a healthy city with a pleasant climate, and a cost of living much less than that of San Francisco. The paper pointed out that Petaluma was out of debt and that taxes were reasonable. The editor reminded readers that the city had voted, almost unanimously, for the railroad subsidy, though knowing it would be injurious for a time by cutting off the up-country trade. He added that the city gave the plaza where the SF & NP depot now stood "with the express understanding at the time that the machine shops would be located there."

The *Courier* called for a citizens' meeting to discuss means to persuade the Colonel to move the shops from Donahue to Petaluma. Such a meeting was held in the Petaluma Theater in June. Seven speakers were in favor of the move and all of them, even the *Courier* man among them, said, oddly enough, "some very complimentary things" about the Colonel. A committee was appointed to see Peter and to ascertain his terms. "On motion, the meeting adjourned with three rousing cheers for Colonel Donahue." Whether or not any huzzahs stuck in throats, the committee's optimism showed in a July 11 *Courier* story on the meeting. "The first step has been taken towards having Colonel Donahue move his machine shops to this city. . . . May it be but a short time. . . . It would give Petaluma a boost that would call to mind the awakening of Rip Van Winkle after his sleep of a hundred years. We would not recognize our native place. Who said we wanted the courthouse?"

Petaluma was too late. Peter had decided to move the Donahue shops, all right, but not to Santa Rosa *or* Petaluma. He planned to, literally, haul the whole town away, barging the buildings down to

Tiburon. He began the task and, after his death in 1885, his son, Mervyn, finished it.

Dr. Keenan recalled that Peter hired house movers to shift his settlement, and a wrecking crew from Tiburon to dismantle the covered wharf. The piles had to be left behind, of course. (The Harbor Commission later ordered their removal as hazards to navigation, but a handful of rotting stumps remain in the mud at creekside to mark the side today.) According to Keenan, the shops went first, then the Sonoma House, and the dwellings.

The *Marin County Journal* surveyed the marshy scene and reported on September 29, 1887 that the one-time creek port was dormant and dying, almost a ghost town. "The old railroad village of Donahue is desolate and lonesome. The hotel and shops have gone downward on the flood to Tiburon, where they are still en route to permanent quarters." The only structure that Peter and Mervyn could not move was the earth-floored roundhouse. It was left behind, empty and abandoned, to burn only a few years later.

Once the buildings were removed, the site of Donahue changed. The creek shoaled and the deep swimming hole at the landing filled with mud, tules, and sedges. But some things did not change. You could always dig a bucket of clams there, or find good fishing for smelt, even a run of salmon. Day and night, Keenan hunted ducks. There was a season, but there was no law against night shooting. He remembered that Petaluma sportsmen used to come down to a club house at Lakeville on weekends and hunt ducks, often right across the creek from the wharf in the marshy ponds.

In 1898 the SF & NP became the California Northwestern Railroad and in 1907 the Northwestern Pacific. The Lakeville branch of the NWP was taken up in the early 1930s. Only the faint line of the old roadbed still curves into the site of Donahue, and much of it has been obliterated by filling for a straightened-out Lakeville Highway.

Only two unpainted, decrepit buildings, with the gray-green mossy-lichenous patina of old age, remain on the site of "downtown" Donahue. (On the far side of the knoll, alongside the highway, a few abandoned frame structures remain, probably the southern outskirts of once-thriving Donahue.) A dilapidated barn, the old stable, hugs one building in slightly better shape, as if for comfort. (The latter was occupied, after Donahue died, by the Conboy family. An elderly lady told historian Ed Manion that she used to dance in the building years before.

The great eucalyptus trees that once shaded the wharf now tower over unimproved ranchland where a few sheep and cattle, over the years, have grazed among the pesky thistles. Since 1933, Donahue has been the Marcucci place. (According to Petaluma historian Ed Fratini, the giant gum trees were probably planted by James Fair, when, as an owner of a strip of the creek bank, he improved the property by planting trees and reclaiming the mucky marsh with ditches and dikes. Ed Phelps managed the Lake Ranch portion of Fair's property, while Henry Sinclair took care of his winery and vineyards. After Fair died in 1894, his property was sold to A.W. Foster of the Northwestern Pacific Railroad. When Foster died, the tract was broken up and sold as smaller ranches.)

The migrant railroad shops that once dominated Tiburon are now gone, too, victims of redevelopment. The wide area of the old railroad yards now holds a parking lot and plans for future condominiums or other housing. Nothing remains from the olden days but the passenger station, now the Donahue Building.

At one point in Peter's career, it appeared that he might chuck railroading entirely, much as he loved it, out of disgust with what he saw as ever-increasing government meddling, mostly in the shape of regulation of tariffs. On March 6, 1874, the *Argus-Courier* ran a story based on his testimony before the State Senate's Committee on Corporations, as it considered the Freeman Fare and Freight Bill. Under oath, Peter stated that the SF & NP's capital stock was $19,350,000, that cash paid in totalled $1,830,000, and that first mortgage bonds were never issued. He gave 1873's gross earnings as $275,153, gross expenses as $158,263, leaving a net profit of $116,500, all of which was expended on the road, its buildings, side tracks, and so forth. No dividends were declared, and no interest was charged as an expense since no bonds were sold.

The Colonel also stated that he was a practical engineer who had built the SF & SJ and the SF & NP. The latter was built more cheaply than any other road in the state, he claimed. But according to him, freight shipped to or from San Francisco had to be handled three times. Competition on the water routes of his network forced fares and freights there lower than on other parts of his line. It *had* to be. "It is to the interest of California," he said, "to make business, as the trains have to run, anyway."

The paper paid Donahue a compliment. "Northern Sonoma [County] was a new country when he commenced the construction of the road. It has since doubled in wealth and population, is very prosperous and the finest region in the state." Without using the word, the paper also praised the Colonel for virtually inventing the San Francisco commuter. "The passenger trains run faster than on any road in the state—thirty miles an hour—so that people may go to the city to do business and get back on the same day."

According to the *Argus-Courier*, the Colonel had plenty of "iron" and locomotives to build from Donahue around to Sausalito (as had long been expected before he chose Tiburon), but that he was not going to do it because there had been such a hue and cry against railroads by both press and public. "I will not build any more roads," said Peter. Another reason for his decision was the fact that railroad credit had been greatly injured in Europe. In fact, railroad bonds could not be sold there at all any longer.

But Donahue saved most of his displeasure for the Freeman Bill, which he saw as very unfair, a law that might well drive him from the railroad business. He warned the senators that "If this Freeman Bill passes, this [SF & NP] road will not pay expenses, and will have to suspend business. If the sheriff has to take the road, let him do it. I could not pay expenses under the bill; and would fight it through the Supreme Court. Look at my road. No mortgages, no bonds. A free, prosperous road; but I can't get a dollar on the road to extend it. The first road built [i.e., the Sacramento Valley Railroad] in San Francisco was on credit for the iron, and neither principal nor interest was met; and when I built the San Jose road, I had a lively time of it.

"Stanford and Company established railroad credit in Europe and that credit was shaken by the so called Popular [Populist] movement here. The failure of the Oregon road was the first blow, however. Up to two years ago, there was no trouble in negotiating bonds for a good road. There are no complaints in Sonoma County against railroads. I never knew of any discrimination against individuals on any road in the state."

State Senator Benjamin F. Tuttle, a Democrat from Sonoma County, stated that he believed Colonel Donahue, and was convinced that if the tariff regulations of the Freeman Bill were passed into law the SF & NP could not make expenses. By it, the cheap passenger fares and freight rates on the lower end of the route would have to be raised to make up for losses inflicted by forced reductions of rates at the northern end. Grain and wood were already being carried at low rates. (The only rate complaint had been made by a single furniture dealer.) The senator said that his section of Sonoma County was not ambitious to pay the operating expenses of the other end of the road, as it would have to do should the bill pass the Legislature.

Peter was not forced out of railroading. Indeed, he expanded his SF & NP. He made his Donahue-to-Cloverdale track the trunk line of a real rail system of both broad and narrow gauges. The most prosperous section of his network remained the Russian River route, with the longest trains of all, sometimes numbering twenty-six cars.

Peter took over the foundering Sonoma Valley Railroad in 1879. This short line had superceded the bizarre "Prismoidal" line, the West's first monorail system. It was variously called a stock swindle and the most economical transport scheme of the age.

Joseph H. Kohn had arranged a meeting of citizens of Sonoma in February 1875 and had sold them on the idea of a wooden monorail, the Crew Prismoidal System, as being safe and cheap. It was invented by a Mr. Crew of Opelika, Alabama. (Only one line was actually in operation, near Chicago, before the Sonoma experiment.) The Sonoma Valley Railroad was organized in June 1876 and the road begun at Norfolk, near later Wingo, where a steamer landing and warehouses were built on Sonoma Creek at the old mission and pueblo embarcadero. The road's destination was the old "plaza" (town) of Sonoma.

Fill was dumped in the tule marsh and work on the road proper began in August 1876 with 68,000 feet of lumber being used per mile. By Thanksgiving Day of 1876, the first three and a half miles of track had been laid, "coincidentally" right up to Joe Kohn's fields. There he was laying out a farm. Guests from San Francisco came on the steamer *Sonoma* to Norfolk. An odd-looking engine towed a few flatcars fitted with benches. George Fox, who built the contraption at San Francisco's Pacific Foundry, was its engineer. The *Alta* reporter claimed that the ride was as smooth as that on England's Great Western Railway. But neither Kohn or Fox, or anyone else, had a solution for the problem of grade crossings and the experimental line just withered away.

The primitive wooden monorail was replaced in 1878 by a regular narrow gauge Sonoma Valley Railroad. Kohn laid a few miles of three-foot-gauge track before funds ran out, along with his dreams of connecting tidewater Norfolk with Sonoma and, via Los Guilucos, Santa Rosa.

Peter finished the line, running it through the Schell Ranch, now Schellville, to a point a little more than a mile east of Sonoma. He then drove it west to Spain Street and down that thoroughfare to enter the Plaza, or main square, on its north side in front of Mission San Francisco de Solano. Donahue erected a station, turntable, freight house, car barns, and other structures. His flower-bedecked locomotive, *General Vallejo,* tooted its way into the Plaza in December of 1879. But he soon abandoned Norfolk and shallow Sonoma Creek entirely as his terminal. He ran a seven-mile spur to the left (east) bank of Petaluma Creek's mouth, opposite Black Point, creating the small port of Sonoma Landing there on deep water. With fourteen feet of water, the *James M. Donahue* could call there. (The site is now a yacht harbor.) Peter's son Mervyn later abandoned Sonoma Landing, and ran a connecting line instead from Schellville to Ignacio, north of San Rafael, to tie in there to his main line, heading for Tiburon and San Francisco. Later, broad-gauged throughout, these feeders became the Sonoma Valley Branch of Mervyn Donahue's San Francisco and North Pacific. Mervyn also extended the line north from Sonoma to the village that would become Jack London's base, Glen Ellen.

The townsfolk of Sonoma held a different view of Donahue than did the Petaluma populace. Alonzo Phelps in 1882 wrote that Peter had "gladdened the hearts of the people of that ancient, Rip Van Winkle pueblo, by transforming it into a modern railroad town."

As early as February 23, 1873, Petaluma became very excited—prematurely—at the prospect of Colonel Donahue running a railway from that city to San Rafael on the west side of Petaluma Creek, and thence to a ferry port in lower Marin County. The *Argus-Courier* headed an item "Railroad Talk" with reports of a construction car at Donahue and large quantities of ties to be landed opposite the wharf, along with some iron. The newspaper was all for the project and sure that it would engender popular feelings of support for the SF & NP since it would tap "a more lucrative, large, valuable trade, which the present route can never command." But, not for the first time, the paper cautioned its readers about the Colonel. "He who puts up collateral to build, has the privilege, and will probably exercise it, of building the road just where he likes it, whether outsiders like it or not." Donahue was, indeed, interested in building the line, presumably to protect the flank of his Sonoma roads; but local supporters had no money, so he put the project on the back burner.

A branch which Donahue never did build, although he toyed with the idea, was the Geyser Narrow Gauge from Cloverdale to the thermal springs, the Geysers. (However, he did plant a station at Geyserville on his main line, and he named one of his locomotives *Geyser.*) The *Argus-Courier* of February 21, 1873 referred to a report that Peter contemplated building it, adding that "the San Francisco *Post* correctly says that one thing may be relied [upon] as a fixed fact, which is that if he decides to build this or any other piece of road, he will build it without the fuss and feathers usually attendant upon such an undertaking. It is probably that he has not given the subject of this particular piece of road a great deal of thought; but if the interests of that part of the country demand its construction, we do not know of a gentleman in the state more likely to see and meet the want than Colonel Peter Donahue. The rumor that he contemplates building the narrow gauge to the Geysers is much more likely to be true than that other rumor that he proposes to take up the Cloverdale track." In fact, Peter did neither.

As for the expected extension northward of his trunk line, two years of talk about connecting Cloverdale with Ukiah produced exactly nil. So a January 12, 1876 public meeting was held in that seat of government for Mendocino County. It featured speakers advocating construction of such a railroad. A committee of concerned citizens was appointed to approach Peter, with John S. Reed being chosen to personally interview the great man in San Francisco. The *Argus* observed it all approvingly (January 21), saying, "They have only to look southward to Sonoma County to see what large advantages are derivable from the construction of railroads."

On February 4, the *Argus-Courier* reported on a proposal by the committee to empower Mendocino County to aid the SF & NP in building north from Cloverdale, four miles south of the county line, to Ukiah, twenty-eight miles north of that line. The Board of Supervisors would call an election in June to submit to the voters the proposition of issuing $1,000 SF & NP bonds to subsidize construction at $5,000 a mile. The 8 percent bonds would be payable on January 1 and June 1, and the principal would be paid in twenty years from the date of issue. There were very few restrictions: The line must be broad gauge; the Ukiah depot must be within a quarter-mile of the courthouse; the road would have to be completed within two years of passage of the bonds.

The bonds would be delivered to the company in sums of $25,000 upon the completion of each five-mile segment. The Board of Supervisors was to levy a tax, not exceeding 10 cents on each $100 of taxable property, to create a sinking fund to redeem the bonds. The *Ukiah Democrat* urged passage of the proposition.

But the time was not yet ripe for the Ukiah line, although in the 1880s the *Examiner* expected Peter to extend his line there to reach rich lands that were beginning to fill up with people, though served only by inadequate stage transportation. The paper noted that it would be "singular" if the Colonel, with his much-remarked spirit of enterprise, and his ability to push ahead on works of great magnitude, should not carry it out. But Peter's energy was declining by the '80s. It would be up to his son, Mervyn, to carry out the extension to Ukiah in 1889.

While Peter was figuratively peering across the line into Mendocino County, things were hardly happy in his own backyard, Sonoma County. In 1874 he was faced with another rival line, and closer to his SF & NP than the North Pacific Coast. It was the Sonoma and Marin Railroad of his old friends, William T. Coleman and Isaac G. Wickersham. A public meeting in the Petaluma Theater (now the Opera House) at 145 Kentucky Street whipped up enthusiasm. Many people subscribed once the McNears promised to donate an acre of land to anyone who would buy five shares.

On March 24, 1875, the new company took over the old Petaluma and Haystack Railroad and its decrepit rolling stock, and in April secured the rights to the twenty-two miles separating the latter's end-of-track at Rudesill's Landing from the North Pacific Coast depot in San Rafael. (From there, San Rafael and San Quentin Railroad cars took passengers to San Francisco via the Point San

Quentin ferries.) In mid-1875, grading and tunnel construction contracts were awarded, and grading was begun at Rudesill's on July 2.

In only a few months, the narrow gauge Sonoma and Marin had graded its way to Novato, but stockholders were slow in paying their assessments and both contractors failed. The *Argus,* in chagrin, compared the fifty-four miles of track built by the NPC from Sausalito to Tomales (population 500), while the S & M could not finish twenty-one miles to connect the 5,000 people of Petaluma with the metropolis of the entire Pacific Coast. "Oh, for a Napoleon to lead us to victory!" the paper wailed. Coleman and Wickersham were only part-time railroaders; they accepted no salary for work which they saw as their civic duty. A Napoleon *was* in the wings; but Peter Donahue was not yet ready to make his entrance.

Black powder blasts gnawed at the rock of Puerto Suello Hill north of San Rafael but, a year later, there was only a ten-mile stretch of roadbed in the Petaluma Creek marshes, a mile of roadbed north of San Rafael, leading to the (would-be) tunnel portal, and not a foot of iron laid. The bore itself was cut in only eighty feet, leaving an estimated 1,120 to go. The line was to be built with local (Petaluma) capital, without subsidy. But only $60,000 had been collected, so far, and all of that had now been spent on construction.

The *Argus-Courier* continued to ooze confidence, stating (April 14, 1876) "Our reply to all is that the railroad will certainly be completed during the Centennial Year. We get our information from those who should know whereof they speak, and who can have no possible motive in deceiving us." By now, all grading was complete and 150 feet of the barrier tunneled on its north face. The paper reported the approach on the south side to be "under a good heading," too, with burrowing from that side expected to begin soon. The tunnel, the key to the line, would be finished by mid-July; by August 1 at the latest. Cars would be running in time for the Petaluma fair in the fall. The paper, reporting that the company's board had met recently in Petaluma, stated that the outlook for early completion never looked more promising.

The Petaluma press called the S & M "Our Railroad," a term of endearment never previously associated with the Donahue Road. On June 9, the paper reported on that month's satisfactory annual meeting. The large number of shares showed the public's interest and the perfect satisfaction of the stockholders in the administration of the company. It considered the engineer's report to be wonderful. With little money in the kitty, the company had surveyed, located and graded the road for eleven miles. The (expensive) San Rafael tunnel was well advanced and $7,000 of real estate and other property had been bought, plus the usual horses, carts, instruments, and materials necessary to lay out a railway. Yet the total expenses were only $49,373.52, leaving the treasurer a nice nest egg of $9,425.49.

The *Argus-Courier* stressed the importance—the necessity—of a competitive road to Donahue's. The protection from monopoly and the advancement of Petaluma's interests should be apparent to everyone. The city had just two alternatives: to go to work on the enterprise and become an independent community, or "sit supinely [*sic!*] down at the risk of becoming the toy of a corporation, to be squeezed, oppressed, snubbed; aye, and mayhap ruined. . . ." The newspaper was careful not to burn all of its trestles behind it, however, adding, "This does not imply that any unnecessary war should be waged against Mr. Donahue or his railroad, but simply putting ourselves upon the defensive and out of the reach of any man or corporation to do us harm, or inflict upon us unjust discrimination. The surest relief from such tyranny is a healthy competition. Petaluma will never have another opportunity like the present to avail herself of immunity from railroad despotism. . . . We congratulate the people of Petaluma on the prospect of an immediate and competitive railroad."

Congratulations were not in order. They were premature. The October 20, 1876 issue of the *Argus-Courier* might well have been edged in funereal black. Its main article was sadly titled "Sold Out." The paper reported that most citizens, despite a flurry of dire rumors, were genuinely astonished to learn that the S & M directors had transferred the property to Colonel Donahue. The people felt not only disappointed but duped. Ostensibly, the reason that Petaluma wanted the line was that it would run west of the creek and bring the city closer, in travel time, to San Francisco. But the paper admitted to the long-standing vendetta. "It is also a fact that a bad feeling has existed between the people of Petaluma and Colonel Donahue. It now remains to be seen whether, by fulfilling the terms of the recent sale, Colonel Donahue will heal all wounds and make Petaluma his friend, or whether there is still to be 'splitting of hairs' and taking advantage of technicalities that will widen the breach and perpetuate ill feeling." The paper said that it welcomed concessions on both sides in the long quarrel. "We hope for the best."

When the Sonoma and Marin first threatened to collapse, Coleman and President Wickersham tried to dicker with Peter to take over. But his best offer to them was to accept the line as a gift and finish it when he could. Since his rival, Latham, was not interested, the two men kept hammering at him and he finally agreed to buy. Wickersham outlined the terms of sale to the public. The Colonel would pay $85,000 in coin, the amount actually spent on the line already, upon the surrender of the stock by its holders. The latter could choose to receive SF & NP stock, in the proper amounts, in exchange, if they preferred. As purchaser, Peter agreed to assume and carry out in good faith all existing contracts and to complete the road to San Rafael by May 1, 1877, "or as near thereto as can be accomplished." He was to use the existing line of survey, but was free to vary and modify it in minor ways if advised to do so by his own engineer. The Colonel also agreed to run an early train, no later than 7 a.m., to Petaluma and one from San Francisco to that city as late as 4 p.m. Two members of the S & M board opposed the sale, A.P. Whitney and H.T. Fairbanks. But Wickersham, Coleman, J.N. McCune, J.M. Bowles, and William Zartman all voted for the transfer.

On the last Saturday of October, Wickersham and Donahue drove to San Rafael, where the latter formally accepted the S & M and gave the banker his check. The night before, the *Argus-Courier* had interviewed the Colonel. The "irrepressible magnate," as friendlier papers called him, gave the strongest assurances that he would keep faith with Petaluma and have his road aid the city's interests. He planned to cross Petaluma Creek within the city limits, not at Donahue (as many feared) and thereby would not bypass the city. He would place a depot in Petaluma, where the old Minturn warehouse was located. He promised to reduce fares and "freights," and he was sure that he could finish the work by May of 1877 since he had already arranged for the purchase of necessary rails in New York.

Petaluma was still suspicious of its unaccommodating railway magnate, but San Rafael was delirious with joy. Its *bête noire* of monopoly was Latham. The *Herald* said, "Had the managers of the narrow gauge [NPC] secured the road, our thriving town would continue to be the abused slave of a tyrant monopoly." Now the editor even dreamed grandiose dreams of San Rafael becoming the entrepot of trunk lines to Chicago and New York.

Petaluma's *Argus-Courier* observed that, should the Colonel follow the course that he had mapped, he would win the heartiest good will of Sonoma County and would "heal all past asperities and ill feelings.... It seems to us...that the interests of the city and the railroad are identical.... We have Mr. Donahue's word that he will bend every energy toward the upbuilding of Petaluma."

On January 5, 1877, in reporting the shipment of 2,500 tons of railroad iron from New York and Philadelphia, the *Argus- Courier* apparently warmed to Peter and applied the possessive to what was now his company, in a headline—"Iron For Our Railroad." It also quoted a Washington, D.C. dispatch of December 29. Peter was traveling in the East in his "Sonoma County Palace Car" and trying, in the Capital, to settle an account with the government for carrying the U.S. Mail over his SF & NP, without pay, for three years.

On February 9, the *Argus-Courier* reported on the final meeting of the Sonoma and Marin Railroad's original board in the Phoenix block. Present were Wickersham, Coleman, McCune, Whitney, Zartman, Bowles and J.B. Sweetser; Fairbanks and Dr. Galen Burdell were absent. The resignations of Whitney, Zartman, Bowles, Sweetser and Fairbanks were handed in and accepted. Elected in their stead were Peter, as president; Michael Reese, vice president; Edward Martin, treasurer; T.I. Bergin; and Arthur Hughes. The offices were moved to San Francisco.

The newspaper reported that the Colonel had spent $250,000 on iron and other materials for the "San Rafael Extension." Some rails were already en route and all were expected in two months. Donahue hoped to commence operations in February, when he expected his tunnel (given as 1,400 feet) should be finished.

Rumors were rife that the exact route across Petaluma Creek was still "a matter of speculation"—that is, up in the air—despite the Colonel's assurances to the city. Certainly, the *Argus-Courier* was still worried. "There are already rumors that Colonel Donahue will disregard the agreement...and will cross the creek at Donahue. But this we are not prepared to believe, as it is certainly in violation of a contract. In any case, the cost of constructing a drawbridge at

Donahue would be more trouble than any obstacle or inconvenience of the west-side route." The paper tried to reassure its readers. "The relations of Colonel Donahue with the citizens of Petaluma are now most pleasant and we do not believe that he is prepared to make a rupture just at this moment."

On March 2, the paper reported that the steamer *Hattie Fickett* and a large barge were moored at Burdell's landing at Olompoli, north of Novato, about eight miles south of Petaluma and thus in the middle of the projected railroad. "It is expected that operations will be commenced on the road at that point. What route the road will take from this city is yet a matter of speculation. That it would be for the interest of Colonel Donahue and the welfare of Petaluma to have the road run on the west side of the creek but few can doubt. The right-of-way can be obtained at a trifling cost; there would be no expensive drawbridge for the Company to maintain; and all interested would be better served and accommodated. We have full confidence that Colonel Donahue will decide upon that route."

Fifty Chinese trackmen were camped on Burdell's ranch while rails and ties were landed at Burdell's Embarcadero. A construction train of a locomotive and flats was expected in a few days, to push work southward toward San Rafael. But the manager and officers of the company remained reticent about the exact route as the nervous *Argus* again expressed its "confidence" that the Colonel would "keep faith with Petaluma. . . . We have no reason to doubt the sincerity of his motives when he made the contract with the former managers of the Sonoma and Marin Company." However, the editor stated that it behooved Petaluma to grant the Colonel the right-of-way through town (denied to him, long before) so that no technicality could be claimed by him to break his solemn word.

At a March 6 meeting, the new directors of the S & M voted an assessment of $10 per share of the company's stock. The *Argus* explained, "As Colonel Donahue owns the stock, with the exception of a few shares, we presume this is an assessment meant to quiet title."

In the same issue, it was noted that the ambling *Antelope* would again have to spell the *James M. Donahue,* which would soon be dry-docked, overhauled, repainted and her boilers repaired to put her in tip-top condition to compete with Latham's fast new boats, currently on their way to the Coast. Finally, the editor quashed San Francisco rumors that Peter was ill.

The April 13, 1877 issue reported that two hundred Chinese were at work with the *San Jose* and its train of construction flats. Two miles of iron had been laid and water piped to the track from Petaluma Creek. Ironically, the steamboat that Peter moored at Burdell's Embarcadero as a boarding house for his "Celestials" was the *Milton S. Latham,* named for his rival. The editor was gloomy, despite rapid progress on the road. "We are informed that it is the intention to cross the creek at Donahue, if the route can be made at all practicable."

But a mellowed magnate was mending fences. On April 20, Peter announced that he was providing a train for an excursion to the Russian River redwoods for the benefit of the Petaluma Library. It was quite a blast. The committee on arrangements hired the Petaluma Brass Band and the Apollo Orchestra and built a 50-by-60-foot dance platform. "Every necessary arrangement for a day of pleasure will be made," the committee promised in the *Weekly Argus* of April 20, adding "The point chosen for the picnic is among the grandest of the many rare attractions of the state, being in the heart of one of California's Forest Wonders." The returning picnickers, who paid $2.00 for coach seats or $1.50 for bench space on flatcars, said that it was a very pleasant affair.

The newspaper reported the town to be almost deserted during the absence of the 800 participants. Some of those who stayed at home surfaced at the station for the return of the train. This "home guard" did yeoman duty leading tired little boys and girls by the hand, or carrying emptied lunch boxes and sleeping babies. When they got home they had to listen to "interminable recitals about the grandeur of the redwoods and the pleasure of the trip."

In the opinion of the *Argus,* the trip was a victory for the Colonel, a grand affair, certainly creditable to the management of the railroad, that yielded a nice profit for the library and was an event that would not soon be forgotten.

On May 11, the paper reported on another SF & NP excursion coming up. It would be for the pupils of St. Vincent's Sunday School. The railroad promised a splendid train of cars. There would be music and the children would be carefully looked after. Round-trips were only $1.50, 75 cents for children under twelve. (St.

Vincent's orphanage, north of San Rafael, was a favorite Donahue family charity.) "Let all the children go and have a good time," exhorted the editor.

These redwoods excursions turned into love feasts for Peter and Petaluma. They figuratively kissed and made up, especially since he was true to his word and did not run his bridge across the "crick" at Donahue but (almost) looped through town.

Not all excursions were so jolly as the library and orphanage affairs. Some were disastrous. Superintendent Whiting once sampled a "holiday special" in which, right off the bat, two decent young men had their arms broken by toughs who thought that they were too snooty. On the return trip, a riot almost ensued. Roughnecks made a target of four young women, one of whom sassed them back with a practiced tongue. The men held her down and removed her drawers, then paraded through the coaches waving the underwear and asking embarrassed women if the undergarments belonged to them. The conductor was asked to restore order. He replied, "Interfere? I'm only one man and there were fully six hundred toughs on board. But I would have taken the chance of a beating and interfered when I saw the way they handled the girl, only the language she used convinced me that her modesty was not particularly outraged, and I did not see the use of killing a hoodlum, or being killed, myself, to spare the blushes of a girl whose language made *me* blush." The anonymous conductor disapproved of group excursions anyway, even when the crowd was not a rough one. The oganization chartering the train was given a 25 percent discount, or rebate. A committee that previewed the route had to be wined and dined and fussed over like delegates being met by candidates. And finally, he said, "People who would pay full fare, anyhow, go on the cheap rides. . . . It hurts the regular business of the road. And after a picnic, our cars have to go to the shops to be repaired."

In a compromise, Donahue built his swing bridge just south of town. (It was replaced in 1903 by the present drawbridge after decades of complaints by shippers that, even when "swung," it jutted out into the stream enough to be a menace to navigation.) It was acceptable to Petaluma, and the *Argus* quickly spread the word, on July 27, 1877. "After months of contemplation, Colonel Donahue has concluded to cross the creek with his road at May's Landing, about two miles below this city. An additional force of laborers will be put to work immediately, and the road completed in as short a time as possible. The grading on the lower portion of the road is nearly completed to the tunnel at San Rafael and the loco will pass through the hole in a short time. Colonel Donahue has also made arrangements with M.S. Latham to carry the passengers on the extra trains from Petaluma to Santa Rosa on the steamers of the North Pacific Coast Railroad. This will be a great convenience to the traveling public. A branch railroad to Sonoma is also talked of, and we are informed that some officers of the road, with Colonel Rogers of Sonoma Valley, viewed the proposed locations of the road last Monday."

Rumors in March of 1878 in both San Francisco and Petaluma had Donahue planning to buy Latham's NPC in order to standard-gauge it from San Rafael to Sausalito. The *Argus* tried to verify the tale, but could not do so. Still, it was cautiously—and erroneously—convinced of its authenticity. "Should the report be founded upon fact, the new combination will certainly be fraught with immense benefit to all that territory lying west of San Pablo Bay. The comparative failure of the narrow gauge, its impracticability, and the great cost of its operation, tend to give a semblance of truth to the rumor." The paper then prophesied that when Donahue restructured the San Rafael-to-Sausalito road, he would run a connection to the NPC's "Coast Road" at Valley Ford, via Bloomfield, from Petaluma. "The traffic of that rich country will be brought through the channel that the laws of commerce plainly dictate. And if ever a railroad is built to Humboldt [Bay], this undoubtedly must be the trunk."

The *Weekly Argus* passed on some more bona fide good news on September 7, 1877. On the first of the month, the first construction locomotive passed through "the big hole in the hill" at Puerto Suello. The Colonel invited a small party from Petaluma to join him in an impromptu opening exercise. It included SF & NP General Manager Hughes, Superintendent Bean, Master Mechanic Whiting, Wickersham, Zartman and R. Jewell, plus a man from the *Argus.* They drove to Burdell's to meet Engine #1, the veteran *San Jose,* for the fourteen-mile run to the tunnel's mouth. The *Argus* reporter was much taken with the "*Josie*" when the Colonel told him that the locomotive had done all construction work on his San Jose line and all between Donahue and Cloverdale on the SF & NP, and then was used as a passenger and freight engine till she could be replaced by larger and faster models. The "*Josie*" was again put to work to complete the San Rafael extension. The reporter, a romantic, wrote, "Surely, if an inanimate servant can appeal to the finer feelings of the human heart, Colonel Donahue should love the *Josie* for the good and faithful service it has done him."

At 4:10 the *San Jose* signaled its departure. The reporter noted, "It's got one of the most outrageous whistles that ever startled a cow." The party, on benches mounted on flatcars, enjoyed a rough ride, jolting over the unballasted roadbed. "Yet the ride was most delightful, and all hands were in the best of humor. The Colonel halted first at the drawbridge over Novato Creek. "The bridge is a most substantial piece of work and reflects credit upon the builder, Mr. Whiting. Notwithstanding its great weight, one man can open and close the bridge with ease." There were two other bridges on the extension, one over Petaluma Creek, of course, the other over smaller Gallinas Creek north of the brickyard. At St. Vincent's orphan asylum, the travelers waved to the children in the playfields.

The tunnel, 1,300 feet long by eighteen feet high and fourteen feet wide, in the clear, was heavily timbered, with slabs between the timbers to prevent rocks or earth from cascading down on the track. The *San Jose* halted till it received an "All clear!" signal. The Colonel and Wickersham then took seats on the pilot of the locomotive. The "*Josie*"screamed and made a dash for the black hole in the high hill. "With the darkness, the shower of cinders, the peculiar earthy dampness and the fearful scream of the echoing whistle, the sensations were both weird and terrible. On and on we sped, now a total darkness, then a dawn; and, at last, in the broad day, the party stood beneath the shadow of [Mount] Tamalpais, beside the rippling waters of the bay within sight of the great metropolis and in the incorporate limits of our sister town, San Rafael."

After the obligatory "Hip! Hip! Hip! Hooray!"-ing of the cheering, congratulating and handshaking travelers came a meeting with a reception committee bearing a basket of wine for a social half-hour. The Colonel spoke, followed by Wickersham and Coleman. "The whole business was a success and everyone [was] pleased and happy at the prospect of a speedy completion of so important an enterprise."

The *Argus* predicted that the San Rafael extension would be followed with connections to Sonoma and Napa that would put Petaluma on "the great railroad system of the state [i.e., the S.P.]

and make it an important place." But the rumors of a flurry of Donahue Road expansion were premature. The completion of the San Rafael line was delayed by winter rains. The *Weekly Argus* of April 12, 1878 noted that eighty men would soon resume work with a gravel and construction train to repair storm damage, raise the roadbed and ballast it. "It is understood that the work will be prosecuted with the utmost vigor, and it will be but a few months, at least, before passenger trains will be running directly to San Rafael."

Even at this late date, with the line virtually completed, there was still some uneasiness over Donahue's "secret" route. "Where the southern terminus of the road will be, or where the road will cross Petaluma Creek, has not yet been made public, but we are convinced that all these details have been agreed upon by the managers of the company . . ." (Donahue would stick to his plan to cross the creek at May's Landing, but he kept mum about his ultimate southern terminal.) "It may be that we give too much importance to the completion of this enterprise, but we honestly believe that when the road is completed and in running order, Petaluma will experience a season of prosperity heretofore unequalled in its history as a city."

Not till September 19, 1878, a year after "*Josie's*" penetration of Puerto Suello Hill, did Peter open the new route for business. He brought 2,000 picnickers down the line to San Rafael's Magnolia Park, where the ladies spread so much food that leftovers were taken to St. Vincent's. San Rafael's equivalent of San Francisco's Emperor Norton, the Indian "chief," Fagundo, was there in his military regalia, complete with shako and plume. He got so drunk that he had to be put in jail to sober up. Donahue's friend, Coleman, gave the address of welcome.

Oddly, Peter was absent. Was he ill? Or was he having second thoughts about his new route? Did he fear that it would put Donahue's Landing out of business? Apparently so, for he abruptly stopped the daily San Rafael round-trips. His new rails rusted and the *Courier* chortled, "The gophers have taken possession of the . . . railroad and are rooting out the ties and rails. Go-pher them!, little fellows, as they are of no practical use. The sooner they are thrown out of the way, the better."

The San Rafael *Herald* picked up on the theme, exaggerating, "Yes, but the gophers are out of a job, for the recent rains swept the entire road away, leaving only the hole in the tunnel." When the storms of the winter of '78 continued, even the tunnel caved in.

During the summer of '79, Peter repaired the tunnel and ran one train a day. Even so, the line was becoming too popular. Few rode the *James M. Donahue* to his creek landing any more. So he abolished passenger service on the Sonoma and Marin, after yielding to entreaties to continue it till after the Sonoma and Marin Fair of 1879 in Petaluma.

Coleman and Wickersham were irate, fuming. They forced their old friend's hand now by getting a bill into the legislature making a six-month failure to operate a railroad grounds for confiscation and reversion of rights-of-way. This threw a real scare into Peter. He scrambled to restore the daily Petaluma-to-San Rafael passenger service and seemed to be shifting his interest from the marshes of Sonoma to the sunny hills of Marin. He left only one ferry connection with his Cloverdale trains at Donahue.

But, stubbornly, Peter built no Sonoma and Marin offices or depots, hired no agents, nor did he publish a time table. The Colonel's deliberately sloppy operation of the S & M was in high contrast to his efficient running of the balance of the SF & NP system, to which he now added two Grant locomotives, the *Cloverdale* and *Petaluma*, to join the *San Jose* and four Union Iron Works engines.

Peter had taken care of the Petaluma Creek crossing to the public's satisfaction, but he still had a problem at San Rafael. There was a half-mile gap between the end of his track and the NPC station. It was covered by a short stage ride. When he found the shuttle unsatisfactory, he tried to suspend Marin passenger service again, directing all of it back to Donahue. But the tedious, thirty-four mile, two-and-a-half-hour ferry trip to the city from his namesake-village was becoming too much for even the Colonel. He reinstated passenger service to the Marin County seat on June 21, 1880 and shortly, April 3, 1882, upgraded it to running a spur track to cover the annoying gap to the NPC tracks at Lindaro and B streets. In fact, he added a long building and loading platform and created a station at Second and Tamalpais streets. From there, San Francisco-bound travelers had a choice. They could either take the San Quentin short line and ferry, the narrow gauge NPC to Sausalito's ferry, or Peter's round-about route through Donahue.

The NPC charged 15 cents a head for SF & NP transfers. After several years, Peter suggested that the fare be reduced to a dime. The directors of the "cooperating" road refused. This was probably the last straw for Peter. Since the NPC had locked up Sausalito, he began to look for another possible ferry terminal in southern Marin County.

But Donahue also looked northward. He still dreamed of running his road from tidewater to tidewater, to connect San Francisco Bay with Humboldt Bay. The Ukiah press published a letter of invitation (March 12, 1878) to him which the *Weekly Argus* picked up and republished on March 29. It was signed by F.O. Townsend and others. "It has currently been reported here that you have promised to stand ready to build and equip a first-class railroad from Cloverdale to Ukiah whenever the cities of the county would pay you a subsidy of $60,000. Believing your offer a generous one, we arranged in a short time a subscription of $60,000 for you, to be paid upon your executing a contract to construct such a road. But before doing so, we desire to know definitely, directly from yourself, whether you will execute such a contract and, if so, in what time do you propose to complete the road."

Colonel Donahue replied on the 14th. "Your proposition is not such a one as would guarantee me to build the road from Cloverdale to Ukiah, from the fact that it would be difficult for me to collect the amount subscribed, viz. $60,000. Your better way is to get together and have the senator from your county, Mr. McGarvey, bring a bill through the Legislature authorizing and subsidizing of at least $5,000 per mile, which is low enough to build a road through such a rugged country as that between Cloverdale and Ukiah. If such a bill be passed, and this amount authorized, I will build a road with all reasonable dispatch and guarantee to make it as good a one as that now running to Cloverdale."

The *Ukiah Democrat,* noting that even if a subsidy were possible, nothing could be done for a year, added that Donahue's proposal would raise not $60,000 but $160,000. "The connection would be immensely useful to our town, and the eastern side of our county, making the former fairly jump into prominence and prosperity, and handsomely developing the resources of the latter. The connection, too, would be largely beneficial to Mr. Donahue, sending up and down over his lower road trade and travel that would not otherwise go that way, and may be alienated, permanently, in another direction."

Alas, the time again was not ripe. Cloverdale remained the end-of-track for the SF & NP for seventeen years after Donahue's rails reached it on April 18, 1872. (Peter was long dead, and his son would build the connection as almost the last business of his own railroading career before his untimely death in 1890.)

Petaluma continued to dream of its future self as a sort of Chicago in the tules. The *Courier* ran a letter to the editor on September 7, 1881 that raised the possibility of the Northern Pacific Railroad's transcontinental line being led down the Pacific Coast through the "redwood counties" from Portland to San Francisco Bay. And the letter-writer chose as the Northern Pacific's ideal terminal the very spot that Peter had his eye on for the end of his Marin County extension, Point Tiburon (Shark Point). The writer described it as "a point opposite Angel Island, on Raccoon Straits, which is only about five miles from the metropolis of the Pacific, which can be traversed by first-class ferryboats in twenty minutes. . . . Sonoma and Marin will have one of the great overland trunk lines of railways running through their borders."

According to the letter-writer, Donahue and the Northern Pacific had already been dickering, in fact, but "Donahue won't sell this great Northern Pacific his road. Have not negotiations between Donahue and [Henry] Villard been broken off because of the pure stubbornnesss of the former? Those of us who know Colonel Donahue know that he is headstrong, but we also know [that] as a businessman he has been a success, and that if he should give the railroad he now owns to Villard, or to anyone of us here in Petaluma, he would not suffer for the necessaries of life."

The editor was not in perfect agreement with his correspondent.

> But to the question of breaking of negotiations with the Northern Pacific, our opinion is (and it *is* ours) that negotiations ceased because the Northern Pacific did not put up the coin. . . . "Donahue stands in his own light," says the friend across the way. . . . Suppose you owned the SF & NP Railroad; it is paying a fair interest on the investment. Would you sell it to the great Northern Pacific and take stock and bonds of that corporation in payment? This we suspect to be the cause of breaking off of negotiations. . . . Do you, my friend, want to force Colonel Donahue to sell his road without obtaining its value? We may find fault with Colonel Donahue for not running his road to suit each one of us, but we may never know how much injury it has inflicted upon us until an earthquake or some other great calamity destroys it.

> We are willing to judge Colonel Donahue by the standards we would be judged by. We would be glad to see the SF & NP railroad a part of the great overland system, but don't believe in forcing a man to part with his own against his will, without giving him an equivalent therefor. We hope to live to see cottages dotting every eligible location between Raccoon Straits and Petaluma, with hourly trains between the latter point and San Francisco. Such results are among the possibilities of the future; and a great overland route is one of the great forces for its accomplishment.

Peter knew what he was doing. Completing the Northern Pacific was so costly that Villard was driven into bankruptcy in 1883 and had to resign the presidency.

But Donahue still felt walled off from San Francisco up in San Rafael, with Sausalito and Point San Quentin closed to him. So, on October 21, 1882, he organized the San Francisco and San Rafael Railroad to build from the county seat to Raccoon Straits. Some have said that the pioneer of that area, Dr. Benjamin Lyford, persuaded him to locate his terminal near Hygeia, or Lyford's Hygeia, at Reed's Point or Point Tiburon. When the Petaluma *Courier* on November 1, 1882 picked up a *Marin County Journal* story, it gave the terminus, incorrectly, as California City, an anchorage short of the tip of the peninsula and on its east side. But the rest of the story was true; the company had just been incorporated with $500,000 of capital stock, and its principal office was in San Francisco. Peter was president (and a director), of course; the secretary was Arthur Hughes; and the treasurer T.I. Bergin. Peter's younger brother, Tom, popped up again as a director of the SF & SR. The Colonel announced that he would build a magnificent double-end ferryboat to carry a thousand passengers from Point Tiburon to the city. (This would be the *Tiburon.*) He also told the press that the contract for the roadbed had already been signed and a bond filed, and that work was scheduled to begin on November 30. The cost of Peter Donahue's nine-mile extension to Raccoon Straits would be high. He estimated half a million dollars. It came to $677,772.50 This was because of the need for three tunnels totalling 3,500 feet, plus 5,000 feet of approaches through the hills of the Coast Range, plus trestles across the pickleweed and tules of marshes and sloughs, and a dramatic high trestle, like those of Sierra railways, across Trestle Glen.

Surveys were made and contracts let in 1882, but progress, because of the laborious tunneling and trestling, was slow for the usually fast-paced Peter, who brought in one of the first new-fangled steam shovels from Bucyrus, Ohio.

There were "paper" delays, too. The *Marin County Journal* reported on a right-of-way conflict held up in court from October 25 till December 27, 1883, but finally decided by Judge Bowers in favor of plaintiff Donahue. It gave the SF & NP the right to cross the North Pacific Coast tracks about two miles below San Rafael. Peter was delighted, of course, with the decision, though he had to pay court costs.

By October 25, a *Journal* reporter found poles scattered along the road, ready for the telegraph line to San Rafael. By November 29, work on the road was so far along that the paper could report that "This Point [Tiburon] has made one great advance. Its grand waterfront has a fine ferry slip, a long wharf, a railroad track, depot, machine shops, store, boarding houses, etc., part of which are already built, and all will be by spring." The dock was 320 feet long and 300 feet wide, with a single track leading onto it for San Francisco-bound trains. Another track, parallel to it, brought box car floors even with its surface to facilitate loading and unloading of transshipments. Passenger trains moved directly to the ferry slip. On February 28, 1884, the *Journal* described the most prominent building on old Shark Point as the long and well-built train shed sheltering six beautiful, yellow-painted passenger coaches from New York, worth $30,000, now "on the iron" and ready to roll.

Peter had to flatten Point Tiburon considerably in order to make room for all of his improvements. Back in late 1883, when only four miles of track had been laid, the *Journal* was already noting "The high point, or bluff, composed of rock and good macadam, is rapidly receding and making acre after acre of level ground to be covered with iron track, platforms, buildings, sheds, depots, freight rooms, offices, roundhouses. . . . The shovels, picks, and drills of 400 men are busy in the transformation. Colonel Donahue was present when the writer was there, counseling in every detail, suggesting, advising or approving, as the case might be."

The April 19, 1884 *Weekly Argus* carried a short item on the driving of the last spike of the SF & SR. Donahue ran cars over the road by the 23d, though the completion is usually dated April 28. Everything looked good for a May Day opening, as long planned.

Petaluma expected that the shortening of the commutate time would permit San Francisco businessmen to build homes as far north as Sonoma County, to greatly increase the population with what the paper called "a desirable class" of citizens. Then the writer indulged in some prophecy that turned out to be right on target. "This new road probably brings us as near the metropolis, in point of time, as the present generation will ever realize, as the day will come when all the roads on this side of the Bay will cross through a tunnel or over a bridge into San Francisco."

Excavating of the point for railroad yards and buildings was continuing when the *Argus* ran its April 1884 account. But the pier, bulkhead and ferry slip were all completed, having used up 1,280 piles and a half-million board feet of ordinary lumber. The new road crossed the NPC track more than a mile south of Peter's large union depot at Fourth and Tamalpais streets. Thanks to his expensive tunnels, nowhere did the SF & SR rise more than fifty-four feet above the Bay. The first tunnel, either 900 or 1,097 feet long, depending on who was measuring it, ran under the base of Point San Quentin Ridge south of San Rafael. The road then made a leap over Corte Madera Creek via a ninety-foot drawbridge. It allowed small craft to ascend to Kent's Landing (Kentfield). The track then rolled over 800 feet of marshland on a trestle before finding really solid fill (said to be fifty feet deep!) and then solid ground again. About four miles north of the point, the SF & SR plunged into the main tunnel. It lay under Alto Hill, really the base of massive Ring Mountain, and ran due south, paralleling today's Redwood Highway (101) below Corte Madera. The bore was 1,850-1,900 feet long, depending on whose figures you accept. When the roadbed emerged into daylight again near modern Reedland Woods School, it hooked to the east for a spell beyond today's Bel Aire School before disappearing into the last (600-630 foot) tunnel where the Belveron Gardens district is today. After reemerging, it crossed Trestle Glen on a lofty trestle (finally dismantled in the summer of 1968) before coasting the last three miles to the point.

The *Argus* approved of the pains that Peter took with his last railroad line. "The work has been well done, the tunnels being timbered with redwood supports in a thoroughly substantial manner." (But Peter was still having problems in Sonoma County. In January 1884, the Board of Supervisors finally passed a resolution directing a compromise settlement in tax suits against his SF & NP. Peter was delinquent, not because he was a debt dodger, but because he contested the $17,597.79 bill. And he won. First, a debris tax (unconstitutional) was deducted from the sum, then a judgment against a Mr. Dinwiddie reduced it further. Peter offered to settle for $15,115.40, which was less than the county's offer, since the latter included 5 percent interest which Peter, naturally, resented. But he finally settled for $15,430.80.

Peter Donahue gave his May Day party although, technically, the extension was not quite finished. He had just discharged one hundred Chinese track layers; but a hundred of their compatriots, and eighty white trackmen, were still at last-minute chores along the line. He first ran fifty Sonoma County folk, and some Marinites, down to Tiburon to witness "the grand entrée." They used Peter's comfortable new coaches, and a *Courier* correspondent who was along reported (May 7) "And they are beauties, too; so neat and tasteful!" After the conductor shouted his "All aboard!," the travelers were whirled through the countryside in its most beautiful season. The *Courier* enthused, "Nature has done its work so well that no brush can do the scene justice. The earth is one vast carpet of verdure, dotted with myriads of wildflowers. Cattle and horses, sleek and fat, are browsing from the meadows and a thousand hills."

Some of the visitors toured the Tiburon peninsula, with its fine views of Angel Island and Alcatraz. Others went to San Francisco by ferry to join Peter Donahue's party. The *James M. Donahue* took only twenty-three minutes from the giant new slip to the Clay Street Wharf, such was its hurry to get the celebration really under way.

At 10 a.m., the *James M. Donahue* began her recrossing of the Bay and the group took Peter's spanking new yellow coaches, behind the gleaming *Ukiah,* to San Rafael. Accompanying Peter and Mervyn were Whiting, Zook, Hughes, Corbaly, W.T. Johnson, Baron and Baroness von Schroeder, Edward Martin and his family, Ryland Wallace, the Board of Harbor Commissioners, Dan Callahan, W.H. Barnes, and Arthur Hawkins. Colonel Bean was conspicuous by his absence. Peter's SF & NP superintendent had gone on to bigger and better things, first for the S.P. in Arizona and New Mexico, then (by 1884) in Washington, D.C. as Arizona's Territorial Delegate to Congress.

The travelers arrived at Peter's depot at 11 a.m. Although it was unfinished, with some men putting zinc on the roof while eight painters touched up its light grey walls and stone-colored trim, the

Journal was so impressed that it called the station "the finest, except one [San Jose?] in California." Willie Singley, of Petaluma, was station agent and telegraph operator. He and Colonel Whiting occupied offices in the upper part of the building.

As a railroader, Peter was used to more jeers than cheers in Sonoma County. But he received a very warm ovation in San Rafael, plus band music and an eloquent speech by Mayor Colonel John H. Saunders. His Honor reviewed Donahue's career from the days of '49 in the Union Iron Works, expanding on his part in making possible such a happy day for Marin. Completion of such a grand enterprise, he said, "evinced, and would reward, the pluck and faith of a far-seeing businessman, Colonel Donahue." He added that, at the same time, "It paid merited tribute to the welfare and beauty of the peerless country and villages through which it ran."

The *Journal* echoed Saunders's sentiments. "It is a consummation which speaks of thrift, progress and prosperity which will be a source of profit to its owner and of benefit and accommodation to us. . . . God speed to Colonel Donahue, the owner!"

The popular Judge Bowers made a few remarks. Referring to the traditional differences—"constant quarrels and bickerings"—between railroads and the people of California, he said, "We didn't understand them and they didn't understand us." (The *Courier* observed, "There is more truth than fiction in this.") But he also said that he believed "There will never be any but the most cordial feelings between this road and the people. The mutual admiration which exists between this new road and our people will continue unbroken." The Judge closed by saying, "Colonel Donahue has built a lasting monument to his name. Long may he wave!"

The *Journal* commented that the reception for Donahue "but feebly expressed the joy of our citizens at the successful organization of an enterprise which will double our facilities of communication with the metropolis, and confer upon us the countless substantial benefits which must follow that consummation."

Colonel Donahue was called for by the crowd and made what the *Journal* called "a very happy speech." Uncomfortable in the public role of benefactor, and as no-nonsensical as ever, Peter protested all of the hullaballoo.

I feel deeply the complimentary things you have said in reference to myself and the enterprise we are now inaugurating, and I scarcely know how to thank you and the people of your town and county who are now present.

But I desire to say that I entered upon this enterprise in a business point of view. I thought, and I think now, that there is something in it for me, and I am fully convinced that the best way to make it remunerative to me is to do that which will be pleasing and satisfactory to you. And so I propose to carry you safely, speedily and pleasantly to and from your handsome little town, and I propose to do it cheaply. I want you all to ride with me, but I want you to pay your fare. As business increases, as I think it will, I will reduce rates, because, while I wish to live, myself, I am willing that you shall live also.

We had intended to have a little collation here today, but our depot is not completed, and in this we are disappointed. But if you will get aboard of the cars, we will take you to Petaluma and bring you back. We have sandwiches and wine enough for the ladies and whiskey enough for the men. Get aboard—quick!

The celebrants needed no urging. The 25-year-old newlywed, Mervyn Donahue, was master of ceremonies. He had laid on some champagne in addition to the still wine and spirits, to make the party even gayer. After an hour in Petaluma, Peter whisked his guests back to San Rafael—and still more (liquid) refreshments. "Bacchus would have felt flattered at the liberal flow of his favorite beverage," said the *Journal.* There were a couple of thankfully short speeches, by Mark L. McDonald and Colonel Byington of Santa Rosa, followed by a second visit to scenic Point Tiburon. The *Courier* correspondent called it "a very healthy place . . . . sheltered from the fog and winds by the surrounding hills." Finally, the Sonomans made the final run back to Petaluma, arriving at 7 p.m. It had been a very long day but a glorious one.

On May Day 1884, Peter really began regular Tiburon service. He ended speculation over fares with 35 cent tickets from San Rafael to "The City," 50 cent round-trip. Commute tickets were $5.00, $8.00 per couple. School children paid $3.00. The first week saw only two round-trips a day, but when the Colonel inaugurated his summer schedule, there were five a day, except Sundays. By May 4, all trains were operating via the Tiburon terminal rather than isolated Donahue.

The first passage from Tiburon took the *James M. Donahue,* the aging Queen of the San Francisco ferries, fifty minutes. But the brand-new *Tiburon* made the crossing in jig time, and the *Donahue* was tied up at Tiburon as a back-up boat, pressed into service when the traffic was too heavy for the double-ender alone. (She was still, technically, in service till 1909. In 1920 or 1921 she was towed to Point San Quentin and beached. Her forty-foot flagpole survives at the home of Mr. and Mrs. Howard Lisle, overlooking Lyford's Cove in Tiburon. It was salvaged by a Paradise Drive neighbor, Burt Frochen, when the old *James M. Donahue* was lying at Tiburon and expected to be wrecked. His father had helped build her, he said, and he had worked on her, and other ferries, as a maintenance man for many years.)

The *James M. Donahue* had been built in 1875 in the Potrero district, at the foot of Humboldt Street, by shipbuilder William E. Collyer. (Union Iron Works did not go into the ferry-building business until 1898, but then it did so in a big way.) The *Tiburon*, which superceded the *James M. Donahue*, was designed by naval architect Patrick Tiernan and built by the Fulton Iron Works at North Beach, actually the Gas House Cove of today's Marina. She was 245 feet long, thirteen feet longer than her predecessor, and her wooden hull was thirty-eight feet wide and thirteen-and-a-half feet deep. The sidewheeler's weight was 1,284 gross tons. The remarkable thing about the *Tiburon* was her power plant. Her vertical beam engine (50-by-132 inches), delivering 1,225 horsepower, had been built in 1860! The powerful walking beam, with a five-foot bore and eleven-foot stroke, was one of the first marine steam engines built on the Coast. It was so far ahead of its time that, after exhibiting it at the Mechanics Fair in Union Square (1864), where it was a popular attraction, Peter stored it in a warehouse for more than twenty years before reconditioning it for the 1884 *Tiburon.*

The *Alta* covered the *Tiburon's* launching in the presence of 1,500 spectators. Said the paper, "The vessel is beautifully modelled and will be an ornament and acquisition to our line of bay steamers." Colonel Donahue now expected her to be ready for service by late April, in time for the route to open on May 1. When the last block was knocked out from under her hull, the *Tiburon* glided down the ways to enter the water "as gracefully as a swan." Annie Donahue then christened her by breaking the traditional bottle of champagne over her bow. The tug *Sea Witch* took her in tow for her first voyage, a short one made jolly by the countless toasts drunk by her passengers to the success and prosperity of both vessel and owner, Colonel Donahue.

Finishing of the *Tiburon* must have encountered some delays. It was not till July that the *Marin County Journal* reported on her trial run. "The steamer demonstrated that she will be very fast, in fact, faster than her most sanguine friends had anticipated, and will be the first craft in these waters to put the [NPC's] *San Rafael* on her mettle. The model [i.e., design] of the *Tiburon* will make her a favorite with travelers, being roomy, convenient, and in every way comfortable. . . . Being a double-ender, she will have a great advantage, saving several minutes which the other [ferry] boats must use in turning." Even though she was eventually upstaged by the *Ukiah,* built right at Tiburon (1890), the *Tiburon* did yeoman service on the Bay till retired in 1924.

Competition remained strong—intense—between the North Pacific Coast Railroad and the Colonel's line as they fought for commuter traffic with their ferries. As Donahue's men were struggling with the trio of tunnels leading down to Point Tiburon, the NPC was building a parallel tunnel under the steep Corte Madera Grade (Collins's Summit) and shifting its terminal, permanently, from Point San Quentin to Point Sausalito. By February of 1884, both lines were ready except for their tunnels. It was a neck-and-neck race. Peter's steam drills broke through to daylight on the last bore on March 10. The NPC's tunnel was not completed until the 16th, but it won the race, routing trains over the new route on April 26, just two days before Donahue got to Tiburon.

The power behind the NPC in 1884 was no longer Latham, who died in 1882. In command now was a fellow Irishman, John W. Doherty. Unlike Peter, he was no party-giver. There was no champagne victory celebration in Sausalito. However, the public was pleased as punch when Doherty set his rates low to compete with the Colonel.

The May 1, 1884 *Journal* observed that "Both lines are on their mettle, making the best possible time, and, as we have been a sleepy people so long, a good many passengers have been nervous at the rate of speed, though it is, no doubt, safe enough as long as due care and vigilance are exercised by all employees. The Donahue is an entirely new line and great interest is felt, all around, to try it. Everybody wants to go over it. But this is probably offset by the new route of the North Pacific Coast, which all are curious to ride over." But the shorter and faster Tiburon route soon stole 40 percent of the NPC's commuter patronage, hurting the company badly and almost ruining Doherty.

Donahue's Tiburon ferry offices were first at the terminal at the foot of Clay Street, next to the Oakland Ferry headquarters, and also at 222 Montgomery. But when the new Ferry Building opened in 1898 at the Embarcadero base of Market Street, the SF & NP was its first tenant, moving in on June 15.

Racing between ferryboat skippers of the two rival lines was natural. It was also strictly forbidden. However, it must be noticed that the NPC, while assessing a captain five demerits for racing, raised it to ten if he lost to a Donahue boat! On January 16, 1886, the inevitable happened. The *Tiburon* and *San Rafael* collided in one of their unsanctioned races to San Francisco. Peter's boat got off easy, with only a broken window. But the *San Rafael* lost her front railing and her life boats. (She would later, in 1901, be sunk in a collision which Jack London used in his novel, the *Sea Wolf.*)

Peter Donahue was a sharp businessman, perhaps because he took care of the small details of running railroads and ferryboat lines. Even the critical Petaluma *Argus-Courier* had to hand it to him (November 1, 1882) for his business acumen. "Those who have traveled, of late, between Petaluma and Tiburon must have noticed the hundreds of tons of railroad iron piled up alongside of the track at the different stations. It was supposed that Mr. Donahue intended to use these rails in extending the road, but it now transpires that the rails were bought because they were cheap at the time. Mr. Donahue has just sold 500 tons of these rails for just twice what they cost him. . . ."

IX

LAST YEARS

NORTH BAY RAILROADING dominated the last years of Peter Donahue's life, but not to the exclusion of everything else. Even though he was slowing down from age and declining health, he continued as a director of the Hibernia and National Gold banks and the State Investment Insurance Company. However, he did resign as president of the latter in favor of former mayor A.J. Bryant. And he sold his controlling interest in the Omnibus Line to Daniel Callahan, C.D. O'Sullivan, and Adolph Sutro.

Peter kept an eye on the cable road planned for his old Montgomery-Union Street omnibus route. The December 4, 1880 *Argonaut* reported that the road was anxiously looked for and that work already done would be completed as soon as the consent of the Supreme Court—and Peter Donahue—could be secured.

The Colonel was also an interested observer of the progress of his disciple, Irving Scott. The latter made an eleven-month tour of shipyards on the East Coast and in Europe. Donahue favored Scott's plans to make San Francisco into a national shipbuilding center based on an enlarged yard of Union Iron Works, newly incorporated (1883) and relocated to the Potrero district. The nine-block, twenty-odd acres of plant was finished in 1884, to become the nucleus of later Bethlehem Shipyard.

Frank Pixley still poked at the Colonel, from time to time, with his vitriol-dipped pen. On August 7, 1880, the *Argonaut* scolded the *Bulletin* for trying to defeat a new rival gas company which promised to sell better gas for less than Donahue's concern. Pixley told his readers that the other paper's proprietors had been thick-and-thin friends of the monopoly. He wondered if they were, perhaps, stockholders as well. He also wondered if any of them lived between Larkin, Green and Scott streets and the Bay. If they did, they would have to write their editorials with the aid of candles or oil students' lamps, as the gas usually gave out in that neighborhood. Did they walk, perchance, where the street lamps threw barely a glimmer of light in the fog for lack of gas pressure? If they but knew, as he said that he did, that the gas company was robbing the city treasury, they would not open their columns to false and cheeky letters like that of the writer who signed himself "One of the Burnt." Nor would they run unanswerable editorials favoring the gas monopoly—unanswerable because they contained (said Pixley) neither reason or argument.

"One of the Burnt" had written that Donahue's company would simply buy up the new competitor's stock, or underbid the outfit till it should go bankrupt. Pixley had his own terms for the Donahue stockholders, described by the letter-writer as the city's wealthy, influential—and best—businessmen. He called them "financial highwaymen and bandits." As for the letter-writer, himself, Pixley had this to say. "The hireling who wrote this mendacious and insolent threat ought to be one of the eternally burnt in a special hell organized for those who do the dirty work of the soulless rich."

Pixley, who claimed that the quality of Donahue gas could deteriorate no further, asked rhetorically if the Gas Light Company should be allowed to prevent competition, forever, by its corrupt practices. He predicted that, should the new firm be bought off or destroyed, another and another would surely take its place until the old company should become impoverished and swamped. He pointed to other cities where the competition of several companies insured a supply of gas of superior quality. He described the *Bulletin* as being unfair in comparing Donahue's Gas Light Company only to the two rival firms it had already conquered. He called the defunct City Gaslight Company and Metropolitan Gaslight Company "nefarious combinations," one of which in a cut-throat transaction had cost Donahue's company $1,800,000—which was, of course, passed on to consumers to pay. Donahue's company was long enough in coming out to the suburbs, and was neither very polite or accommodating, recalled Pixley, but the "scandalous"

Metropolitan Company had made contracts to avoid tearing up the streets, then had ripped them open and failed to properly repair them.

However, the *Argonaut* was sure that the new company, with $3,000,000 of capital, would correct the abuses of a quarter-century and provide better gas, via improved processes, than Peter's $10,000,000 company. Pixley concluded, "It has the sympathy of almost the entire community . . . . It is the fight of 230,000 people against a family [the Donahues] and a clique composed of less than a score of 'individuals.' "

The *Argonaut* kept up its sniping at the gas company. On New Years Day 1881, it quibbled, "They put out lamps when the moon is out . . . . We confess it would be more gratifying if the corporation and the moon came to some definite understanding . . . . Moonlight is a very pretty thing, and more poetical than gaslight, but for the sake of comfort, justice, protection, let us have one or the other . . . ."

However, by 1881, Peter had again weathered all competition—and all of Pixley's ravings—and was employing four hundred men at the gas works to deliver 1,000,000 cubic feet of gas a day, compared to the mere 70,000 feet when he had started in 1854.

In his later years, Peter managed to relax a tiny bit and to engage in social activities, though he still maintained an office at 430 Montgomery to transact gas and railroad business. He and Mervyn were among the 140 select guests at a July 4, 1880 party at the new Hotel Del Monte. This posh Monterey Peninsula caravansary was quickly adopted by San Francisco society. The Donahues arrived in "Little" Peter's yacht, *Nellie*, part of a smart flotilla that included J.D. Spreckel's *Lurline*, C.A. Spreckel's *Relief*, Harry Tevis's *Halcyon* and Dr. Samuel Merritt's *Casco*. (Robert Louis Stevenson would charter the *Casco* in 1888 for a cruise to the South Seas.)

The Colonel was back at the Del Monte on September 18, attending a reception for President Rutherford B. Hayes. Peter's daughter, Mamie, was the cynosure of all eyes. She wore a beautiful dress and train of white grosgrain silk, with white lace and pearl trimmings. The Society of California Pioneers described her, in its *Pioneer Record* as "one of our society belles, brilliant yet unaffected, and most conspicuous by her manifold and unostentatious deeds of charity."

The same volume described Mamie's stepmother as presiding with grace and dignity over "the hospitable homestead." Annie Donahue liked to ride through Golden Gate Park in her "glass coach," presumably a carriage with many glazed windows. It was the only one of its kind in the city. But as a socialite, Annie had to take a back seat to her sister, Eleanor Martin. The *grande dame* came to absolutely dominate San Francisco society—like, it was said, an "Eleanor Martinet." And she did so until her death at one hundred and one years of age in 1928.

Thanks to her dear friend and social arbiter, the plump Baltimore "Terrapin," Ned Greenway, who was the city's equivalent of New York's Ward McAllister, she became a counterpart of Mrs. Vincent Astor, leader of New York's "400." That Greenway was a charming fellow and a smooth dancer pleased ladies like Annie and Eleanor. But the Coast representative of Mumm's champagne was also respected by the menfolks. Not because he could tell, while blindfolded, the brand and vintage of any sparkling wine served him, but because of his sheer capacity. He had once polished off twenty-five bottles of champagne in a single day. The handle-bar moustached Marylander, who wore evening clothes day and night, taught Eleanor and Annie and the rest of "Eleanor Martin's crowd" all that they needed to know about etiquette and protocol.

But Colonel Donahue was never as comfortable in high society as his wife and her sister. He had been a skilled workman too long for that. But secretly, as he mellowed with age, he must have enjoyed the fact that increasing age brought him paeans as well as pains. The 1880 *Pioneer Record*, for example, stated that "From his ancestors he inherited those positive traits of character which belong to the Hiberno-Celtic race. . . . The dignity of labor has never been more exemplified than in the life of the intelligent and industrious mechanic. . . ." As if recalling the tribute to Sir Christopher Wren in St. Paul's Cathedral—"*Si monumentum requiris circumspice* (If you would seek his monument, look around you)"—the Pioneers volume went on, "He has need of no written or spoken eulogium. His *works* are his mute eulogists and the monuments of his genius. . . ."

(The compiler of *Representative Men of the Pacific* touched upon this point, too. "The evidence of his actual usefulness is diffused throughout the community; it is as difficult to enumerate or catalogue his many works as to segregate the atoms of the sunbeam that fills a room with light.")

The *Pioneer Record* continued,

Skill, toil and perseverence proclaim his victories and confirm the truth of the proverb 'Labor is King' [*sic. Labor Omnia Vincit,* Peter's motto, is more correctly translated "Labor conquers all."] He is in the highest and broadest sense of the term "a representative man" of this enlightened community and in this thriving metropolis, which is so deeply indebted to his busy brain and sturdy sinews for the present proud position it enjoys amongst the cities of the land. . . . It were [*sic*] impossible in the limits prescribed to this historiographer to fully, or even imperfectly, review all of the public-spirited enterprises in which Mr. Donahue has either been principal or participant. He is still in the vigor of mental strength and physical manhood, and his work is not yet done. It remains for the future biographer to write the history of his busy and useful life. . . . If Mr. Donahue commands, as he certainly does, the respect and confidence of the business community, so is he, in equal degree, esteemed and admired as one who is the true type of the urbane and Christian gentleman. Courteous, affable, companionable, his presence lends a charm to the social circle, and his society is ever agreeable.

Alonzo Phelps, in his *Contemporary Biography of California's Representative Men*, really rolled out the accolades for the poor and unknown Irishman who came to California in 1849.

He has lived to see his name carved upon the solid industries of the state and to witness the success, and enjoy the fruits, of the enterprise he has founded. He came as a pioneer to make this his home and has never wandered in his devotion to San Francisco and California, the city and state of his adoption.

His great wealth is not the result of brilliant speculations or lucky strikes, but the gradual accumulation of industry and business thrift. Among all the excitement, turmoil and ill-will of recent years, when the now-famous Sand Lot hurled its anathemas at the rich bond holders, land grabbers and railroad monopolists, the name of Colonel Donahue was respected. . . .

Without his ever having indicated any particular interest in political or social questions, or having assumed any prominence as an advocate of American, as against coolie, labor, he had, nevertheless, become noted for his steadfast adherence to the principle of employing none but white laborers. Among the thousands of men who are at this time employed by him directly or indirectly in the various enterprises with which he is connected and actively engaged, there is not one Chinese laborer on his payroll, and there never has been. He has risen from poverty to wealth not by impoverishing, but by enriching, his fellowman. His gains have not been wrung from cheap and half-paid laborers, but are the result of judiciously-invested accumulations which have contributed alike to the wealth of the laborer and the prosperity of the state. . . .

"Without any assumption of superior knowledge or business sagacity, he, nevertheless, impressed all who came in contact with him as a man of singularly keen insight into human nature, and almost unerring judgement in business affairs. Scorning the pretense of superior morality in others, and making no profession of philanthropy, himself, he is yet known to be one of the most charitable of givers, kindest of benefactors, and most generous of friends . . . ."

Phelps's view of the gas company diverged 180 degrees from that of Pixley. "It is justly regarded as one of the largest and richest corporations in the state and, as a consequence, under such judicious management, is known to be a safe and profitable, permanent investment for capitalists . . ."

In concluding, Phelps perpetuated the errors made by earlier writers. "The most astonishing feature of all this history is that the entire road [SF & NP], with all its branches, has been built exclusively by white labor, and that the rolling stock and engines have been built in San Francisco in Mr. Donahue's own foundry and machine shop. This has been done by Mr. Donahue in adherence to the principle to which he has conformed through life, of spending his money where he has accumulated it and refusing to avail himself of the benefits and advantages of cheap labor." (Actually, of course, the Union Iron Works had long been gone from his hands; not all engines and cars, by any means, were made there; he finally *did* hire Chinese for his North Bay railroad.)

Thus it will be seen that Mr. Donahue is eminently entitled to the appellation of Founder. He has not been content to merely copy or enlarge upon the ideas of others, but he has, himself, inaugurated the schemes which his energy, coupled with his great executive ability, has uniformly brought to a successful conclusion.

Like Stephen Girard of Philadelphia and Cornelius Vanderbilt of New York and, indeed, like all men who have secured the highest prizes in business life, Mr. Donahue is peculiarly a self-made man. Denied the advantages of a classical education, he has, nevertheless, acquired by experience a vast range of knowledge concerning men and things.

Mr. Donahue is not merely a man of active brain and strong purpose, he is a man of generous impulse. It has been the rule of his business life to overlook the minor offenses of his employees and, while exacting from them a strict performance of duty, to reward honesty and faithfulness by continuous employment and final promotion. So far has this rule been carried that he has continued in employment old and faithful servants long after their days of usefulness were ended. He is distinctly a friend to those who have been friendly and faithful to him and is unswerving in his devotion to his friends.

On July 18, 1881, the golden wedding anniversary of Martin Murphy, Jr. and his wife Mary, *neé* Bulger, was celebrated with a great barbecue in the grove of liveoaks on the couple's Bay View Farm in the Santa Clara Valley near Mountain View. The party was covered not only by the San Jose *Herald* but by the San Francisco *Call*, which described it as an event of historical importance. An architect cleared away underbrush and built an eighty-by-one-hundred-foot dance platform with a bower at its head, ornamented with flowers and canopied by an American flag. He then added hundreds of feet of long stables for feasting.

The *Call* reported that the most striking characteristic of the gathering was the predominance of pioneers. Among the crowd on the dance floor, besides Colonel Donahue, were Thomas Parrott, former Senator William Gwin, and the Honorable Phil Roach. "A gentleman remarked to us that, in all his residence in this country, he had never seen so many of the 'old-timers' together in one assemblage, nor so large a proportion of the prominent men of the Coast . . . who had dropped business and affairs of state to run down and shake hands with their old friends of pioneer days."

By the time that dinner was called, there were 5,000 guests. Colonel and Mrs. Donahue sat with the "bride and groom" being honored at the head table. Following speeches, one by Peter, and toasts, J.J. Owen of the San Jose *Mercury* read the chapter of his book *Sunday Talks* titled "The Sunset of Life," after which Colonel Donahue formally presented the book to Mr. and Mrs. Murphy.

Probably, Peter's sense of humor allowed him to chuckle over the humorous deflating of his latest honor. An article titled "Comosiama" in the May 11, 1881 *Petaluma Courier* reported that "Colonel Peter Donahue has been made by the Pope of Rome a '*Cameriere Segreto di Spada e Capa.*' Hoopa mula! What this all means we can't yet cipher out. *Spada capa*, we know, means that spades are trumps, but whether *Cameriere Segreto* means a hay rake or threshing machine we are not positively certain. But we do know that the Colonel will require a coat of arms as long as a pig's tail to emblazon his title upon. *Hoc signo vincet.* Plenty of *signo*, but we are rather suspicious about the *vincet*. Now we shall expect an improvement in the SF & NP all along the line. We congratulate Colonel Donahue on his-his-his comosiama." [Comosiama—Como se llama?, What do you call it?]

A big event for the Donahue clan was the April 1882 marriage of James's daughter, known to all her friends as Maggie, to an Irish barrister of Clonmel, Richard Burke. The ceremony took place at Old St. Mary's Cathedral, which was magnificently but tastefully decorated with flowers, palms, and smilax, a delicate and decorative trailing green plant of the asparagus and lily family; the April 29 *Argonaut* called the church "a veritable bower of enchantment." The main and side altars were almost hidden by massed blooms and buds. The cathedral's interior was packed with friends and guests by 10:30 a.m. At precisely 11, the bridal couple entered the church, preceded by ushers Sullivan, Gilman, Archer, and Thompson; and bridesmaids Mamie Donahue, Jennie Maguire, and Minnie and Lizzie McNally. The bride walked down the aisle on the arm of her brother, Peter J. ("Little Peter") Donahue, followed by the Colonel and Annie, and Mr. and Mrs. J.R. O'Kane. Mervyn was best man and the Colonel gave the bride away. The elaborate vocal and instrumental music created a very effective ceremony, celebrated by Archbishop Joseph Sadoc Alemany, assisted by Fathers Prendergast and Gallagher, and other priests.

The bridal party was driven to Mervyn's residence at 346 First Street—James's old home; and at a reception and breakfast there they accepted congratulations. Said the *Argonaut*, "The house was brilliantly lighted and ornamented throughout, the floral decorations being a marvel of artistic handiwork." The city's society families were well represented—Tobin, Casserly, Donohoe, O'Kane, Phelan, and McNamara. The ladies were beautifully dressed, the men formally attired. Among the most elegant were sisters Annie Donahue—in garnet velvet with a court train—and Eleanor Martin—in black velvet, also with a court train.

As for Maggie Donahue Burke, "the bride was dressed in a robe of white duchesse satin, the front of which was exquisitely embroidered with seed pearl clusters of field flowers; the tablis was fringed with seed pearls which fell over a knife pleating like foam; the handsome court train was a triumph of the modiste's art, the corsage was cut square and pointed; she wore a directoire collar; long sleeves with embroidered cuffs. She also wore a necklace of diamonds and pearls; her bridal veil was of tulle."

After the wedding reception, the entire party went to Menlo Park by private railroad car. There a dinner awaited them. The numerous and costly presents on display included a set of solitaire diamonds from the groom. Mervyn presented Maggie with a berry bowl, pitcher and sugar bowl, all of beaten gold. Peter James gave his sister a fruit stand, also of beaten gold, while the Colonel and Annie contributed a gold-lined silver set of one-hundred-fifty pieces.

The Burkes honeymooned in Menlo Park and, after two receptions at the Occidental Hotel (May 23 and 25, 1882), departed for the East and Ireland.

Peter now accompanied his sociable son to parties, such as the luncheon on opening day of the 1882 sailing season at Sausalito's Pacific Yacht Club. According to the *Argonaut's* notice of May 13, opening day that year was even more exciting than usual—"Little Peter's" yacht, *Nellie*, collided with Mervyn's *Annie*. When Francis J. Sullivan married Alice Phelan that same month, both Mervyn and his father were ushers. Also present at the wedding breakfast and reception was the newlywed Maggie Burke.

Soon both Mervyn and his sister Mamie would be engaged to marry. When Mamie and Annie attended a "kettledrum" reception at the California Street home of the Leland Stanfords in May of 1882, Mamie was already "more or less" engaged, but her father objected to her suitor.

"Title-hunting" was being carried on in San Francisco as well as in the East. San Francisco's eligible, wealthy, and often pretty young ladies had little trouble landing a *graf* or a baronet if they chose. (Rudyard Kipling, visiting California in 1889, would describe San Francisco as a "mad city, inhabited by perfectly insane people—whose women are of a remarkable beauty.") William Sharon's daughter, Flora, married Sir Thomas Hesketh. Mrs. William Crocker's sister, Beth, married the Polish Prince Andreé Poniatowski. As for Annie Donahue, she found a seemingly suitable life partner for her stepdaughter, Mamie, in Baron Heinrich (Henry) von Schroeder. He seemed quite a catch—a war hero, titled, wealthy, and handsome. Nevertheless, Peter Donahue balked at the match.

Von Schroeder was the grandson of an important German banker, Baron John Henry von Schroeder; and the son of Baron Charles von Schroeder, who maintained princely estates in Mecklenburg. As the eldest son, young Henry was heir to it all, but he wanted to make a life of his own. Although only eighteen years old at the outbreak of the Franco Prussian War, 1870-71, he served as an under-lieutenant of Prussia's 17th Hussars, or Dragoons. He remained in the army for a dozen years, transferring to the crack Cuirassiers of Berlin's palace guard for several years before joining the 13th Hussars and becoming a first lieutenant in that regiment. He left the Army in 1880 for reserve status and began two years of travel. In a voyage to the South Seas, he saved a sailor from drowning by jumping overboard to his rescue. He was said to have been awarded a medal for this act of courage.

Henry came to the United States and met Mamie Donahue in San Francisco. They fell in love. But, in the words of the *Chronicle*, "the parental blessing was withheld. The millionaire refused to part with his daughter, even for a title. To overcome this objection, the Baron became a ranchman, purchased a large land grant, and swore he would become a good American." Henry had fallen in love again, this time with the Eagle Ranch near San Luis Obispo, while on a hunting expedition to the Santa Lucia Mountains. He almost certainly had in mind no more than a country retreat, not a working ranch, but the gesture satisfied Colonel Donahue. "Such persistence must, of course, meet with its rewards," wrote the *Chronicle* and, at last, the long deferred consent was reluctantly given.

In 1883, Peter cut back further on his business activities. He resigned the presidency of the gas company (in favor of Eugene Murphy) so that he might take his family on a tour of Europe. Unfortunately, he was injured in an accident and Mervyn had to cut short his education, leaving Stonyhurst College in England to return home to help his ailing father manage his multitudinous business affairs.

Plans were for Mervyn's and Mamie's weddings to take place on the same day in San Francisco upon the return of the family, plus the Baron, from its 1883 European tour. On the voyage home, however, a violent lurch of the ship threw the Colonel from his chair. Peter broke two ribs. The party spent a fortnight in the Windsor Hotel, where a New York wedding for Mary Ellen was decided upon.

The *Chronicle* for November 30, 1883 carried the story of one of New York's notable weddings. It took place in the Madison Avenue residence of Cardinal John McCloskey, America's first cardinal and the principal builder of New York's St. Patrick's Cathedral. Among the score of guests were Mr. and Mrs. D.O. Mills, Mr. and Mrs. Whitelaw Reid, Mrs. James Flood and Mrs. Mark Hopkins, plus a half-dozen unidentified millionaires. Vicar General Quinn officiated at the nuptials. There were no bridesmaids, and Mervyn was the only usher. The Baron was supported as best man by the German Consul General. The blonde bride wore a costume by Worth—"one of his masterpieces"—a heavy white satin gown, with a train, with a veil of petit lace and orange blossoms. She carried a bouquet of lilies of the valley and, noted the *Chronicle*, "Her diamond jewels were especially elegant." The tall, good-looking groom wore on his chest the Iron Cross. Some wrote that he had received it from Field Marshal Helmuth von Moltke himself for conspicuous and gallant services for the Fatherland before Metz; others that he had won the medal for twelve years of distinguished army service.

After the wedding, the Donahue party continued on to California, but without the Colonel. Peter followed when he was sufficiently recovered from his accident and consequent illness.

According to the author of *The American Irish,* William V. Shannon, the Donahues' contribution to the tradition of "titled marriages" was almost unique—it was a happy match, and it lasted.

Mervyn's fiancée was Belle Wallace, daughter of Superior Court Judge (later State Supreme Court Justice) William T. Wallace. Her grandfather on her mother's side was California's first governor, Peter H. Burnett. Belle and Mervyn were married on January 16, 1884 at Old St. Mary's. The *Morning Call* devoted many inches of small type to a description of the fashionable social event—"one of the grandest and best attended weddings on this coast." (One of the ushers was James D. Phelan, later the great reform mayor of San Francisco, and U.S. Senator.)

Of the groom, observed the *Call*,

> . . . it is but necessary to say that he is to the manner born, a young Californian full of the buoyant hopefulness of the Golden State and quick with the frank abundance of vitality that he has breathed in from the breezes of the chosen city by the sea. Travel and foreign education have

left him still a Californian, and he holds as closely to the traditions of the rough old days over which his father has triumphed, with good result, as any grizzle-bearded pioneer of them all. Colonel Peter Donahue's name is a household word in San Francisco. His brave struggle for position and wealth, successful only from his indomitable energy, is one of the best-known stories of the Pacific Slope. Enterprising, cautious, and yet generous beyond the carping criticism of the meanest enemy, it may be said of him that he has peopled a city with friends, and it is not without grounds believed that the young bridegroom of last evening will be a worthy son to a worthy sire.

Frank Pixley was no friend of the Irish in general or of the Donahues in particular, but his *Argonaut* always kept a finger on the city's social pulse and dutifully covered the marriage. Its January 12 issue lamented that the general anticipation of many parties for the popular couple would be disappointed. There would "only" be the family banquet for the bride and groom at the Colonel's home; the bridal ball, also to be held at Peter's place; Judge Wallace's wedding reception; and a possible reception by Mrs. Con O'Sullivan and a dinner at Marquis Oliver's Pine Street home. (The bride's thoughtful mother also hosted a theater party for the bridesmaids and groomsmen, taking two boxes at the Baldwin Theater before an elaborate supper at her Van Ness Avenue home.)

A week later, the *Argonaut* story read, "Society can draw a long breath! The long-awaited, much talked-of Donahue-Wallace wedding is an accomplished fact." The writer, who used the *nom de plume* of Bavardin, reported that the large and fashionable throng in evening dress that besieged the cathedral was lucky. For the night air was pleasant, not chilly, and they were corraled in the street outside of St. Mary's "in a struggling, surging, mass, pushing and grumbling, a singular mixture of gas costumes, waving feathers, and policemen's stars." Once they were admitted, pews and aisles filled quickly, and latecomers had to take standing room where they could.

The church still wore its Christmas decorations—garlands of greens hanging from galleries and entwined around pillars, and delicate smilax vines running through the chandeliers. The main altar was ablaze with the light of tall wax candles and brightened further by vases of flowers. At the entrance of the chancel, a bridal arch was erected with spiral columns of smilax supporting a long green scroll with "Faith and Love" spelled out on it in white and red carnations; from the scroll's center rose a double heart of white flowers bearing a read "W" and a "D" in violets, between the hearts hung a marriage bell in violets and tuberoses, surmounted by twin doves, beak to beak. The scroll also bore a cross of Irish green with a camellia blossom (japonica) at each of its points.

Mamie, the Baroness von Schroeder, wore a robe of white brocaded satin embroidered in pearls, its long train borne by a young lad dressed in black velvet. Mrs. Peter Donahue was in gray satin brocaded with velvet flowers. Most notable, as usual, was Eleanor Martin, in black velvet and point lace with a coiffure of white ostrich feather tips.

Belle, the bride, wore a wedding gown of d'Alençon lace over white satin, with a garniture of white feathers and orange blossoms; and solitaire earrings, gifts of the groom. The *Argonaut* noted that "Everyone remarked her graceful, modest, bearing."

Ballenberg's full society band was in the organ loft, but mute till the strains of the wedding march announced the approach of the participants. Mervyn's best man was Ryland Wallace, the bride's brother.

From the cathedral, the guests repaired to a reception at Judge Wallace's home. The bridal party took up a position to receive guests under a floral arch in the large bay window of the mansion's drawing room. All evening, a constant stream of visitors called, and many of the young people remained to dance to Ballenberg's music till the "wee, sma' hours."

When the crowd diminished, the entire house was thrown open and supper served upstairs, a veranda-like enclosure off of the library being used as a punch and refreshment room. In another room, presents were displayed. Besides numerous floral offerings, they seemed (in the words of the *Argonaut's* society reporter) "to comprise everything conceivable in silverware."

The Mervyn Donahues resided temporarily at the Occidental Hotel, joining the young Burkes and von Schroeders who were also staying there.

The von Schroeders, who were to sail from the East coast to the Baron's home in Berlin after a stay at their Eagle Ranch, held two successive Monday *receptions d'adieu* while "at home" in their own elegant Occidental apartments. There were both afternoon and evening sessions, and many chose the latter in order to say goodbye in jolly parties lasting from nine till midnight. Some five hundred invitations were sent and four hundred attended, making the affairs, again in the *Argonaut*'s words, "almost an ovation."

Callers on the Baron and Baroness, Mervyn Donahues, and Richard Burkes at the Occidental in 1884, (now under the management of George H. Arnold) found the hotel to be aging, but still attractive and popular. Its central location pleased businessmen and their wives, the latter intent on visiting the nearby dry goods emporiums. The large plate glass windows of the marble-paved lobby looked out on an ever-moving panorama of humanity on Montgomery Street; and the dozen tables in the well-appointed billiard hall probably had more to do with the hotel's popularity than its Aubisson carpets and grand piano. The *Industries of San Francisco* noted that one marked feature of the Occidental was the fact that "a number of the best families have handsome suites which they have occupied for years past, a silent but eloquent tribute to the excellence of the management . . . and its advantages as a home."

From the Occidental, the Mervyn Donahues moved to San Rafael, settling in a large, three-story mansion, with murals, carved mantels, wood paneling, and crystal chandeliers. (It later became the Paloma Inn, a boarding house. In 1951, the property was bought by the First Baptist Church, Southern. The building was torn done and replaced by the church now standing behind the old bluestone walls.)

Mervyn became active as a Town Trustee of San Rafael. On May 8, 1884, the *Marin County Journal* reported that he spoke of the need for a sewer for the city; if San Rafael did not have sufficient funds for sanitation, he would advance the money and let the Board of Supervisors pay him back at its convenience. That same day, the *Journal* also reported that a Susan Crooks had sold Mervyn 14.72 acres of "Peninsular Island, Sausalito" (perhaps Silva's Island?) for $150, and two tideland lots for $10.

(Unfortunately, it had been with unconscious irony that the *Call* had opined on Mervyn's wedding day that "The young groom had, verily, drawn a prize in what is termed the 'matrimonial lottery,' " for it turned out to be a sad marriage. Mervyn and Belle had already separated before his untimely death just six years later in 1890.)

* * *

Meanwhile, back in Davenport, Iowa, Michael Donahue was now a much-praised senior citizen. However, his health was poor. Michael was suffering from a liver complaint. He kept on working ("bravely" in the words of the local paper) and refused all urgings that he rest. In the summer of 1884, his health had so worsened that he was forced to remain in his home under a doctor's care. Once in a while, he insisted on a ride down to the water works office, or to one of the pumping plants.

In September, it dawned on his family that he would not survive for long, because he now suffered from asthma and dropsy as well. Michael seemed improved as the month ended, but this was only because his spirits were lifted by visits from his niece, Mamie von Schroeder and her husband, who were on their way to Europe; and from nephew Mervyn and his wife.

On Wednesday afternoon, October 1, Michael heard the fire alarm bell sounding and, with the habit of many years, he counted the strokes. It was Fire Box No. 28. He smiled and said, "It is downtown. Well, we have a big basin full of water for them on the hill." The next day, he even talked of getting down to the office; he wanted to attend a company meeting. That evening, when Mervyn handed him a memorial to his brother, James, he read it with great interest. "Who wrote that, Mervyn?," he asked. When he was told (it was probably James O'Meara's tribute in—of all journals—the anti-Irish *Argonaut*), he said, "Well, it is well done. . . ." Reading the sketch reminded him of his old California friends, and he eagerly inquired, "How is old Phil Roach, now?"

Michael then read the newspapers and chatted with his wife and children, Mamie [Peter's daughter, Mary Ellen von Schroeder, was also called Mamie.] and James; with Mervyn and Belle; and with another nephew, Nicholas Kuhner, Jr. The Davenport Water Company, of which he was so proud because of its fine drinking water and fire protection, was never far from his mind, When some topic of the day touched on it, he remarked, "One thing, the water works are a complete success in every way; the new machinery is perfectly satisfactory." Then he turned to his son, James, who had taken over operations since his illness, and reminded him, "You had better commence that main to St. Katherine's Hall [a favorite school of his]. We will give them the hydrant as soon as we can."

Michael continued to speak, but his voice grew lower. He then coughed a little and, as James rushed to help him, he let his head fall forward. It was 9:20 p.m. Someone summoned Dr. Preston. James determined that his father had neither pulse nor heartbeat, but the family's hope of a miracle did not end until the doctor sadly informed them that Michael was dead.

The *Davenport Daily Democrat* used the term "peaceful departure" to describe Michael's death during a pleasant evening in the bosom of his family, "all suddenly and unexpectedly, with his family all about him, with mind bright, heart cheerful, and while in the midst of genial conversation.... It was a death such as one might pray for.... He passed away so gently and easily that the loved ones with him did not know that death was near him until after all was over."

Michael's death was not entirely unexpected. Although business was always on his mind, he had recently begun to take care of his soul, too. Several times in the last few days he had sent for a priest to confer with him and to direct him. The obituarist wrote, "It was known that he could not survive many weeks longer but, all day yesterday, he was feeling so much better that his family was encouraged, after all, as to his condition."

Michael's death made headlines in Davenport—"A Sorrowful City. Loss of One of Its Foremost and Best Citizens." The local paper eulogized the former mayor as a good and honored citizen who had done as much, if not more, to advance Davenport's growth and prosperity than had any other resident. "Today the hearts of our people—the professional and business men of all classes, the mechanics of all trades, and the laborers—are filled with sadness because of his departure. The city bids farewell to Michael Donahue, but not to the memory of Michael Donahue and the respect which is felt for him. The memory and respect will abide in this town so long as the city shall stand."

In sketching Michael's adventurous life, the journalist described him as a moulder, sailor, soldier, machinist, master mechanic, employer, manufacturer, municipal executive and city benefactor. "From the day he passed out of boyhood until the day his fatal ailment came to him, he was industrious, and after infirmity confined him to his home, his mind was [as] busy as ever with his business as president of the water works company, an enterprise which blesses the city through his influence and nearly all the means he possessed."

The obituary spoke of Michael's good mind, his iron constitution, his wit and genial humor, as well as his acute perception. But it stressed his determination ("Once his mind was made up, nothing could move him.") and his kindliness." "How kind he was! He was honorable and upright in all his business relations, as he was in private life. Well may Davenport lament the loss of such a citizen."

Ten members of the Davenport city council met in special session at 4 p.m. on October 4 with Mayor Ernest Claussen in the chair. His Honor felt that it was eminently proper for that body to meet and to formally express its feelings on the death of the city's former mayor, since he had been one of the city's most generous, public-spirited and enterprising citizens, besides, as Claussen noted, "giving us water works which will benefit the city forever."

A three-man committee drafted resolutions expressing the council's sorrow, adding "We not only recognize the distinguished merits of the lamented dead when he filled the position of chief executive officer of this city for two consecutive terms to the fullest satisfaction of all citizens, but we also feel that this community has lost a citizen foremost in generosity, liberality and public-spiritedness who, by the erection of munificent public works, has conferred lasting and enduring benefits to our city."

The front page of the *Daily Democrat* carried a story on the Sunday, October 5, funeral, "a demonstration of respect, esteem and regret that is not frequently witnessed in a city like this." Long before the cortege from Michael's family home reached St. Marguerite's Cathedral, all seats in the church, except for those reserved for mourners in the funeral procession, were filled with bank officers, members of the bar, the medical profession, prominent manufacturers, merchants and their wives, and "a multitude of mechanics and laboring men" of all denominations.

Officers and employees of the water company and former workers at Donahue's foundry and machine shop joined the mayor, aldermen, other city officials and the police force in accompanying Michael's family. Among the pallbearers were three former mayors, one of whom had since become a congressman. Michael's heart would have warmed to the sight of forty-odd representatives from the old volunteer fire companies. He had been an active member of Liberty Company for ten years, and an honorary member until the day he died.

The church was decorated with flower tributes and, at the curb, a carriage was laden with floral devices too big to carry inside. On the sanctuary rail near the lighted candles and the coffin was a broken wheel and a harp, done in flowers, above a cushion inscribed "Our Father." On the casket itself rested a floral cross and, nearby, a crown of flowers. Reverend D.J. Flannery conducted the office for the dead, with Bishop Cosgrove and Reverend A. Trevis present in the sanctuary.

A lengthy procession made its way to St. Marguerite's Cemetery, where services were conducted at the tomb by Father Flannery, assisted by Father Trevis. The mound of earth beside the grave was entirely covered with flowers. These, with several of the floral emblems from the carriage, were placed atop the casket. The *Democrat* concluded its story with these words—"It was a beautiful hour in the sunshine and mild air. And so the mortal body of the worthy citizen and good man was left in peaceful sleep; but his memory will be treasured in this city for many generations."

Peter was saddened, of course, by Michael's death; and with two brothers gone, he probably began to think about his own mortality. That year, 1884, he posed for a bronze bust by sculptor R. Schmid. (Ten years later, the artist made a similar sculpture, from life, of Annie; both are now in the Marin County Historical Society.)

In August 1885, Peter in one of those quiet, and generally unacknowledged, gestures of charity (like his funding of the Astronomical Society of the Pacific's bronze medals, awarded to discoverers of comets), Peter transported Grand Army of the Republic members—indeed, all interested old soldiers—to San Francisco, free, for General Grant's funeral obsequies.

Peter began to think of his planned Union Foundry Block as his monument, his memorial. He razed the old, scarred, and patched Union Iron Works buildings at Mission, First, and Fremont streets. (When he excavated for foundations, he turned up the old iron tank in which Michael had kept his moldings safe from the tides.) He put his trusted SF & NP engineer, Frank K. Zook, in charge of construction. William Patton was his architect. He would build the biggest structure in the city except for the Palace Hotel and the notorious, graft-ridden new City Hall, which Alfred Bates described as "an architectural threat."

The September 19, 1885 ceremonial laying of the cornerstone of the Union Foundry Block was attended by a large crowd of spectators, attracted by the sight of a huge crane, topped with an American flag, suspending the cornerstone in the air. W.T. Garratt opened the exercises with a speech pointing out how proper it was for the Mechanics' Institute to assist in the ceremony. He called Donahue "the father of the mechanical art" on the Coast, and quoted an 1884 Senate Committee in describing the current Union Iron Works as the most perfectly appointed shipyard in the country. Nor did he neglect to mention James, "toiling across the plains from Mexico" in 1849 to the Montgomery Street smithy.

The motto of sturdy mechanics James and Peter Donahue, said Garratt, was fair work for fair wages, and the honest miners of the day were not slow to appreciate their work. Pointing to the site that was for thirty-five years the center of industry in San Francisco, he cried out, dramatically, "I tell you, my friends, this is historic ground!" He saw it as a symbol to all young mechanics, showing them the possibilities of wealth and renown that were open to them if they followed the lead of the Donahue brothers.

A copper box containing a Bible, Garratt's speech, copies of local papers, and a biography and photo of the Colonel, was given to Peter. He inserted it into its receptacle, sealed a slab over it with a trowel and mortar, and directed workmen to lower the corner stone on top of it.

Calls for a speech by their "fellow mechanic" led to a few off-the-cuff remarks by him, almost certainly Peter Donahue's last public words.

Ladies and gentlemen, officers and members of the Mechanics Institute, and fellow mechanics. You must not expect me to say much on this occasion. My feelings are too great to tell all that I would like to say. I can only thank God that I have lived to see the day when this work was accomplished. I want to thank the Mechanics Institute for their cooperation in my enterprise. I want to thank the mechanics who have carried out my intentions for building a magnificent edifice that is to be on this very spot that, in early days, the tides used to wash, the spot on which lighters used to land, lighters which were then worth nearly as much as ships themselves, for without them no trade with this port could be carried on. In those days, there were no wharves and piers as we have now, extending along the waterfront of our fair city. In those days, when I first acquired possession of this land—the first I ever owned in the city—I could scarcely believe that there would ever be erected upon it this gigantic and substantial edifice.

Once more, let me thank the worthy mechanics who have carried out my ideas; let me thank the members of the Mechanics Institute; let me thank God that I have lived to see this day.

This was not the oratory of a politician, or the bombast of a "capitalist," but the simple and well-felt words of an artisan. They were greeted with three enthusiastic cheers and Peter was besieged by congratulating friends. A nice touch, though it made his talk and Garratt's impossible to hear by many, was the chorus of whistles saluting Donahue. Practically every foundry and factory in the city joined in the din.

The building would hold six stores on its ground floor, around an open courtyard (*a la* Palace Hotel) covered by a glass roof and entered by a sixteen-foot wide driveway from Mission Street. Peter planned to use brick, iron, terra cotta, and new-fangled glazed brick (the first in the West) on his $400,000 building.

* * *

On November 14, 1885, a chill blustery day of raw winds, Peter Donahue inspected his Tiburon railroad shops. He caught a cold. At first, Peter tried to shrug off his illness. As San Francisco's *Monitor* put it, "With his customary hardiness, he would not confine himself to the house, but insisted upon attending to his business, as usual." Mervyn told the *Alta*, "His life has been so active that he could not bear confinement and kept constantly at work until finally incapacitated by loss of strength."

When his condition deteriorated on Wednesday, the 18th, Peter finally allowed himself to be cared for. He was attacked by what the *Monitor* called "an inflammation of the bowels." Confined to his bed, he was attended constantly by doctors Lane and Plummer, but now suffered a painful partial paralysis. The doctors announced that they were hopeful of recovery. Peter bore his pain smilingly and said that he also was sure that he would recover. The doctors diagnosed his trouble, not very helpfully, as a combination of ailments, the least of which they called "inactivity of the stomach." (The *Chronicle* and *Monitor* later described his illness as diabetes.)

On Wednesday night, November 25, 1885, Peter suffered a relapse. Doctors Lane and Plummer called in Dr. Rivers for a consultation the following noon. They warned the Donahues that their patient's life was ebbing away, although, as the *Argus* put it, "A fatal termination was not anticipated until within a few hours of his death."

Donahue lost consciousness within an hour of the doctors' meeting. All day long, friends called at the house to hear the sad news that all hope was gone. He died around 11 p.m. on Thanksgiving Day, November 26, 1885, aged sixty-five years, ten months, and fifteen days.

According to his June 30, 1888 anonymous memorialist (almost certainly Alfred Bates), Peter's health had "become impaired by too constant application to business. . . . His mental activities remained unimpaired to the last, but his originally rugged constitution had been impaired by overwork in the eager pursuit of business." In *Iron Industries,* H.H. Bancroft paraphrased his employee Bates, by saying of Peter, "His zeal for industrial undertakings hastened his death."

The *Bulletin* stated on November 27, "He had been in feeble health for some time." On the same day, the *Chronicle* observed in writing of Peter's resignation as president of the gas company, "He did not feel strong enough to [any] longer perform the onerous duties of office."

Peter's passing, like Michael's, was a peaceful one. He just slipped away after twelve hours of unconsciousness. He was surrounded by his family—Annie, Mervyn, Mamie and the Baron (back from Europe and up from Eagle Ranch to their Harrison Street residence), as well as by the doctors and an old friend, Dan Callahan. The *Examiner* observed, "There was nothing special that indicated that the last moments had arrived, as the sufferer seemed to be deep in refreshing slumber." Mervyn, afraid that his sobs of grief might awaken his father, went to the end of the room. When he returned and took up Peter's hand, he found that it was cold. "Looking up into his face, he burst out in an agonized cry which announced to all within hearing that the worthy man had passed away in death." (By a sad coincidence, in 1890 Mervyn would also catch cold while inspecting the SF & NP, and die suddenly.)

The King of Spain and Vice President Hendricks of the United States had died the day before Peter, but local papers found plenty of room for obituaries of the pioneer industrialist. (They recalled John Hittell's comment, three years before, in his *Commerce and*

Industries of the Pacific Coast, "His work has left a permanent impress in California, and especially in San Francisco.")

The *Examiner* called Peter a representative citizen and one of California's most noted pioneers, and "the only man in California who ever ventured to build a railroad without the aid of a land-grant," adding, "Mr. Donahue was eminently entitled to the appellation of Founder."

The *Bulletin* described Donahue as "a courteous and companionable gentleman who well represented the dignity of labor as an intelligent and industrious mechanic."

The *Alta's* November 28 story, "The Death of Peter Donahue a Sad Loss to California," was a carefully crafted obituary. "The typical Californian is of kin to the high-spirited men of all ages who have been cast by circumstances face to face with the difficulties of isolation and the untamed wilderness, and having conquered in a contention with all the barriers that nature and time and distance have builded to challenge the lofty qualities of body and mind. Such a man was Peter Donahue. . . . He and his brothers did not go out into the world by divergent paths in search of adventure, but to find work. They were not soldiers of fortune, but they were captains of industry."

The *Alta* explained Peter's early shift from mills to locomotives—"His forcible nature needed something sturdier to subdue than a textile." The paper did not apologize for his wealth (estimated to range between $8,000,000 and $13,000,000). "His millions of honestly earned money went to the development of this state [and] the enlargement of the comfort and profits of thousands by investment in the building and operation of railroads. . . ." The paper described the lives that both Peter and James had led as being not just "pioneer enterprises and constructions of utility," but "triumphs worked for and won in the field of honest toil, which put no man's bread nor business in jeopardy but, while profitable to them, made profits and suggested opportunities to others, who also grew rich in the atmosphere of good example which was around the lion-hearted blacksmith. . . . Here, coffined for final rest in the kindly, consecrated bosom of the earth is the founder of the creative industries of a commonwealth greater in area than many kingdoms, and in riches surpassing the treasury of an empire. Upon his labors was the blessing of the gods of good fortune. . . ."

But the *Alta* stressed Peter's role as benefactor as well as businessman. "The home of solid luxury where he was the ever-generous host, the steamers riding the tide like palaces afloat . . ., his passing trains and the buildings which he added to the garniture of our busy streets"—all these (sometimes-envied) evidences of his fortune, said the paper, were but shadows cast by the substance of his philanthropy, especially his concern for orphans.

The *Mining and Scientific Press* referred to the deceased as "a man who lived a very useful life and whose work contributed largely to the industrial progress of this coast."

The *Marin County Tocsin* wrote, "As a mechanic, as manufacturer, as founder of the gas works, as railroad builder, as conductor of the San Francisco Omnibus Railway, as banker, as a leader in insurance circles, as the owner and builder of some of the most stately piles in the Empire City of the West, Peter Donahue has left behind him a greater monument than the sculptor's cunning could design. When such men drop from the procession of life, humanity suffers a genuine loss."

The *Monitor* copied the *Chronicle*'s appraisals of Peter. "In manner, he was courteous, affable and companionable, and his presence lent a charm to the social circle. The dignity of labor has never been more practically exemplified than in the life of this intelligent and industrious merchant."

The *Mining and Scientific Press* referred to Peter again on December 5. "He was one of those to whom San Francisco owes much. Having made his fortune here, he continued his investments or undertakings in the state, most of them tending towards our industrial advancement."

Back in December 1878, the Petaluma *Argus-Courier*, impatient with the non-completion of the Colonel's railway, had made jokes about his future demise. "One day, Peter Donahue will depart for an unknown world. Unless he can make better time with wings than he has done with steamboats and railroad, he will never reach his destination. Eternity will catch him in a half-way house, laid up for repairs. Delay caused by lack of decision to obtain terminals and failure to secure right-of-way." But on November 28, 1885, the *Argus* praised as "a most enterprising and valuable citizen" the man whom it had earlier described as having "imperiousness that would well become the Czar of Russia." The paper now spoke of the Colonel's remarkably active and useful life, adding "Peter Donahue was eminently the architect of his own future. The foundation of his future was laid with his own brawny arms while toiling at the forge. With far-seeing sagacity, he made investments and inaugurated enterprises that not only brought himself rich returns, but gave lucrative employment and prosperity to thousands of others. With all his vast accumulation of wealth, Peter Donahue never forgot, or looked down superciliously upon, those occupying the walks of life he once trod." On December 5, the *Argus* followed up with a long obituary, cribbed from the *Bulletin.*

For Petaluma's December 4 *Courier,* Peter's SF & NP attorney, E.S. Lippitt, composed a long "obit." "True greatness belongs not only to the conquerors, the philosophers, the scientists or the statesmen. The workshop also has its heroes, and greatness may be achieved by energy, industry and enterprise in every walk of life. In this respect, Peter Donahue is a bright example for American youth. His success has not been obtained by any turn of the wheel of fickle Fortune, but has been the legitimate result of industry and enterprise." Of the early careers of both James and Peter Donahue, Lippitt wrote, "Every branch of mechanic arts felt the touch of their master minds."

The *Courier* writer noted particularly Peter's splendid achievement in Marin County, bridging marshes and tunneling stony mountains to Tiburon. But also his survey for an extension to Ukiah, and his laying of foundations for his huge business block. (Of course, Lippitt had to add, in regard to the latter, "Alas, his oft-repeated fear that he should not live to see it completed has proved too true.")

Lippitt appraised Peter. "He was a generous man. Not alone to kindred did he exhibit a kindly spirit, but all good enterprises in San Francisco were the recipients of his favor, while hundreds of poor but deserving men have received aid at his liberal hand; quiet and unostentatious in his benefactions, he was a constant giver. . . . He was a warm personal friend, and those that have known him longest loved him most. The tears of strong men, his life-long friends, told how strong were the ties of affection that bound him to them."

Lippitt knew Donahue well, his habits and his thoughts. "His duties were onerous beyond his strength. Any one of his many enterprises—gas works, banks, street railroads, his personal estate—was enough to employ all of his time without the supervision of the system of railroads he had projected north of the Bay; and yet to these he gave his personal attention, visiting the line of road, the shops, the steamers, and directing all projected improvements and repairs."

Donahue's attorney concluded. "His faults will be forgotten, but the memory of his virtues will be precious, while his life and achievements will be a constant incentive to the young men of California who bring vigor of intellect and muscle to life's great task."

There is an old Latin saying—*Mortu leoni et lepores insultant*—"Even rabbits insult a dead lion." One journal took advantage of Peter's death to criticize him and all Irishmen. Naturally, it was the *Argonaut.* "Peter Donahue dies worth ten millions of dollars and, excepting ten thousand dollars left to two Roman Catholic orphan asylums, and a few small bequests to family relatives, does nothing for the community in which he has lived for thirty-six years and from which he has accumulated his immense fortune. . . ."

Then, wrapping himself in the flag and donning a Mandarin skull cap and slippers, the bitter and bigoted Pixley lashed out at Donahue's nationality in general. "May we not remember that this successful gentleman was of the race that furnished us with the great majority of discontented laborers, who reproach us for their poverty by riotous demonstrations against the lives of another foreign [i.e., Chinese] immigration, which is among us by invitation of national treaty, and entitled to the protection of the law . . .?"

But Pixley wallowed alone in his bile. The scholarly H.H. Bancroft was far more typical in his notes for his history of California. He wrote that all of Peter's enterprises, though undertaken primarily for personal profit, were to the great advantage of the community. "He was an acknowledged chief among those bold spirits whose schemes have been instrumental in developing California's marvelous resources. . . . He always found time to take an interest in public affairs and to assist his friends whose ambition led them into public life. He was a man of most genial and affectionate nature; he never forgot a friend or an act of kindness. . . ."

Even in the East, news of Donahue's death had an impact. The *Bulletin* of November 27 noted that his passing caused a sensation among ex-Californians on Wall Street, even though Peter had no close business connections with New York. Banker Eugene Kelly expressed something of their feelings. "I'm greatly grieved to learn of Donahue's death. He was a quiet man in tastes and inclinations and would not have liked any demonstration made over his death. So no action will probably be taken by his friends in the East. I know Donahue to have been a man of pure business habits. He made his enormous fortune by honest, legitimate business transactions. He was always foremost in assisting worthy charities."

Bret Harte was leery of California's filiopietism. He felt that the less said about many pioneers the better. Their motives were not always the best. Some were more concerned with getting away from where they were than in getting to California, or any other place. But such was not the case with Peter Donahue. His death was a real loss, a public calamity, seen (in Bates's words) as "a bereavement not only to the family but to the world at large."

Messages of sympathy flooded into the mansion on the northeast corner of Bryant and Second streets. The boards of directors of the Gas Light Company, the First National Gold Bank and the State Investment Insurance Company called special meetings to pass resolutions of respect and sorrow at Peter's passing. All stressed his marvelous energy, physical vigor, his force of character and strength of will, his personal integrity and wisdom. Although Alex S. Keenan, Jr. once wrote Richard J. Burke "I have been told that Peter Donahue was not an easy man to work with," the insurance men also mentioned his generosity, his "genial and kindly disposition and his kindly nature [which] gave him a warm and abiding place in the regard of his acquaintances."

The employees as well as the officers of the gas company met. They stressed the fact that Peter always treated them "with justice, courtesy and urbanity . . . having himself risen from the position of employee. . . . He was ever mindful of, and attentive to, those who render services."

Flags on many buildings, both private and public, were dropped to half-staff, and the same token of regard was paid him by ferry steamers and other shipping in the Bay, by the lowering of their flags to half-mast.

The 1885 volume, *Representative Men of San Francisco,* praised the late industrialist. "He can eminently claim the title of Founder.

He inaugurated his own schemes, and his energy brought them to a successful conclusion . . . in every enterprise proving himself fit to be a leader and a far-seeing counselor. . . . Firm and self-reliant, with the will to dare and judgment and business experience, joined to the command of capital, he was able to carry out to a successful termination any project upon which he might enter."

Hugh Quigley, in his *Irish Race*, tied Peter's and James's careers together, quite properly. "He [Peter] acquired his wealth by hard, honest industry and his property has grown by a gradual and natural, though a rapid, accumulation. It was by no sudden advance in stock or other ephemeral speculations that the Donahues became independent, but by the exercise of the most prudent care and calculation and the most strict integrity. . . . In addition to the profit they brought their proprietors, [they] also contributed to the improvement of the city and the state. . . . No ruined fortunes, no wild speculations or fraudulent contracts have contributed to the monument to Irish-American enterprise and prosperity which Peter Donahue has erected in this city and coast."

Quigley guessed that perhaps fifty Irishmen, in all, eventually became California millionaires by his day. "But the enterprise by which they acquired their princely fortunes were not so various, so difficult, or so useful as those of Peter Donahue." He was pleased, too, that James and Peter never changed their religion or the spelling of their name, or "denied their ancestral principles." Neither James or Peter ever forgot his origin, nor played the "nob" or nabob.

Professor Quigley admitted that there were richer Irishmen on the Coast than the Donahues. But,

> . . . as an example of persevering, honest enterprise, he [Peter] stands unrivaled. It may be said that he is the most successful man of our race on this coast, if not on the continent. . . . It requires no genius to become rich through stock speculations or the discovery and development of rich mines, but to build up institutions such as gas works, foundries, lines of steamers and railroads requires a genius of no common kind, and to carry out these improvements to a successful issue under difficulties and opposition indicates abilities and statesmanship of the highest order. A fool may become wealthy by inheritance, or a laborer or a peasant may discover a "bonanza" by a stroke of a lucky pick-ax, but it takes a man of genius, of integrity, of honesty, as well as of sound sense, to carve out a

princely fortune by the exercise of his faculties, and that in a community and in an age where the most vigorous competition had to be encountered.

Peter was survived by Annie, Mervyn, Mamie, his brother Thomas, his sisters, Ellen Dougherty and Annie Fanning (both residents of Petaluma) and nieces and nephews. Mervyn had been groomed with great care by Peter to take his place. For several years before his death, he had been delegating more of the general superintendency of the SF & NP, and his other businesses, to his son. In 1883, Alonzo Phelps had written, "It would seem as though his [Peter's] last days were destined to be his best days. His only son Mervyn, to whom the bulk of his fortune will descend, and the care and management of his estate will be necessarily transferred, has already exhibited unmistakable evidences of possessing the spirit and genius of his father, in perhaps as marked a degree as the younger Vanderbilt and Bennett of New York, and Mr. Donahue has wisely chosen to gradually impress on him the responsibility, and shift upon him the burdens, of the business while he may still direct and control the young pilot until he becomes accustomed to the wheel."

At the time of Peter's death, the *Examiner,* for one, expressed confidence that his heir would carry on in good style. "Colonel Mervyn Donahue was liberally educated and, by residence and culture abroad, and experience in responsibilities entrusted to him by his thoughtful father, is splendidly equipped for management of the great fortune and important interests which now fall to him."

The *Mining and Scientific Press,* on December 5, 1885, noted that Peter Donahue's funeral was one of the largest ever seen in San Francisco, at least for a private citizen. Ceremonies began at 10:30 Saturday morning, November 28, with Archbishop Reardon officiating at the requiem mass. St. Mary's Cathedral was jammed from altar to portal long before the cortege arrived. Thousands had called at the Donahue home, where two priests said prayers for the repose of Peter's soul, to pay their last respects. The pallbearers were SF & NP employees, the honorary pallbearers were a Who's Who of San Franciscans—Charles Mayne, R.P. Hammond, Joseph Donohoe, Dan Callahan, C.D. O'Sullivan, James Phelan, former mayor A.J. Bryant, George W. Prescott, William T. Coleman, Joseph Eastland, and others of that prominence.

Behind the coffin marched three hundred employees of the San Francisco Gas Light Company, two by two. A delegation from the Society of California Pioneers preceded carriages conveying the family and kin—Annie and Mervyn; Mamie and the Baron; Little Peter and Mervyn's wife; Tom Donahue (now the last surviving brother of the four); Ellen Dougherty; Mr. and Mrs. Cullen; Mr. and Mrs. P.E. Dougherty; the aged first governor of California, Peter H. Burnett (Mervyn's wife's grandfather); Amy Wallace; Mr. and Mrs. O'Kane; Thomas G. Maguire; Mr. and Mrs. Alexander Keenan; Mrs. Edward (Eleanor) Martin; Miss W. Martin; and Messrs. J. Martin and J. Fitzpatrick.

Five ushers met the coffin at the church door and escorted it to the front of the altar as the organist began the musical prelude to Wilcox's solemn requiem mass. Father Cottle was celebrant, assisted by Father Kirby as Deacon, Father Connelly as Sub-Deacon, and Father Montgomery as Master of Ceremonies. Father Prendergast said that it was useless to speak of the good life of the departed or to lament his death. Instead, he preached an eloquent sermon. Archbishop Reardon delivered the benediction. The newspapers noted the number of Sisters of Charity present, from St. Vincent's Orphan Asylum, and complimented the choir on its beautiful and solemn singing.

So numerous were the floral tributes that they had to be moved from the Donahue's house on Friday night to the sacristy at St. Mary's. When they began to overflow, the larger pieces were placed before the altar. But, in the morning, so many wreaths and floral crosses arrived that their cards were collected and the pieces placed along the inside walls of the church. The press noted a six-and-a-half-foot high anchor in rosebuds, white eucharist flowers, maiden hair ferns and richly-colored foliage plants, a tribute to Donahue the steamboatman. The Sonoma Valley Railroad contributed a piece in the form of gates, ajar, surrounded by anchors and with shocks of ripened grain—oats—suggesting the rural county of Sonoma to which Peter had brought modern transportation. The finest floral piece of all, perhaps, was a miniature train, a locomotive and cars, in white and dark flowers, with the card of a James Youriz attached.

The cortege moved to Mount Calvary Cemetery and the Donahue family vault as Peter Donahue finished his last journey on earth (until his remains had to be shifted to Colma when the cemetery was closed to make room for the living in crowded San Francisco).

The memorialist (probably Alfred Bates) who prepared the limited-edition volume on Peter Donahue for Annie in 1888 characterized the industrialist and his brothers Michael and James. "They were, in the best sense, builders of the Commonwealth, leaders, counselors." Peter, himself, was reticent and no great shakes as either speaker or writer. But he, at least, sketched his life, briefly, in his own words for a New York *Sun* reporter in Paterson in 1876.

It is true that I began life [*sic*] as a poor boy in Paterson. I had no hope of a great inheritance, and I knew that I must learn to work. I became, when a good-sized lad, an apprentice to the Rogers Locomotive Works here and faithfully endeavored to learn all that I could of a machinist's work during my apprenticeship. Soon afterward, I became a journeyman and in 1848 I determined to seek my fortune in California.

I had no luck in the search for gold and, going to San Francisco, I set up a forge in a tent. I prospered, gradually, and my tent forge became a substantial machine shop and that, in time, changed into my engine- and car-making establishment. I was the first man who ever melted iron in California. I built the first steam-powered engine set up in the state and the original gas works of San Francisco. I also had the honor of laying the first eighty miles of the Southern Pacific Railroad and the entire San Francisco and North Pacific.

The only thing wrong with Peter's statement, perhaps abridged by his interviewer, is the excessive use of the "vertical pronoun"—or, rather, the lack of any mention of his co-pioneers, James and Michael Donahue.

Alfred Bates was not guilty of exaggeration when he summed up Peter's role in California.

The results of his enterprise have left on the city and state of his adoption an impress for good that can never be entirely effaced, and in the lives of such men consists all that is best worth recording in the annals of our Western community . . . . He had no advantage of high birth, elaborate education or pecuniary fortune, nor was he possessed of any of those shining gifts which have distinguished great discoverers or inventors. His successful . . . career may be cited as an example and encouragement to every young man who will set out in life resolved to depend solely on industry, perseverance, and good conduct. He undoubtedly exhibited great sagacity in recognizing business opportunities, but his uniform success was due less to that than to his courage in undertaking and perseverence in pursuing enterprises of importance, and a discretion, founded on integrity, which always kept his undertakings within the limit of available means.

Others have achieved greater ultimate success; he never knew failure.

* * *

A monument (sculpted by Douglas Tilden) in memory of Peter Donahue, stands on Market at Battery Street in San Francisco. Dedicated to Mechanics, this monument can remind those who pass of the remarkable brothers Donahue. Mechanics all. *Labor Omnia Vincet.*

POSTSCRIPT

ANNIE DOWNEY would outlive Peter by eleven years, dying suddenly at age sixty on December 12, 1896 in her 2112 Pacific Avenue home. Her funeral was at St. Mary's Cathedral and she, of course, left "a vast estate." The anonymous author of *A Sketch of the Life of Peter Donahue of San Francisco,* which she commissioned three years after her husband's death, stated that she was "a lady of intelligence and education who appreciated his manly worth and whose practical good sense aided his own judgment in affairs of intricacy and importance. She still [1888] resides in the old mansion that was their home through many years of an exceptionally happy married life."

The children of Peter's son, Mervyn, both died comparatively young. His daughter Isabel was tragically killed when she was thrown while riding in Virginia with the Warrington Hunt of which her husband, Henry Poole, was Master.

Peter's older sisters died the year after their famous brother. Ellen Donahue Dougherty died at the Donahue's Landing home of her daughter, Mrs. Alexander Keenan, on April 7, 1886. Anne Fanning died on November 30, 1886 and was buried in the Donahue plot of San Francisco's Calvary Cemetery at Lone Mountain. When this graveyard was closed, all the family remains were transferred to Holy Cross Cemetery in Colma, south of San Francisco. Thomas, the youngest Donahue brother, died in California on March 11, 1899.

ACKNOWLEDGMENTS

ESPECIALLY HELPFUL to me in the research and writing of this collective biography of the brothers Donahue—and, incidentally, the history of pioneer industry in the west—were Richard J. Burke and Patricia Keenan, the archivist of the Donahue-Keenan clan. Others who helped include Susie Beichman; Adair and James Heig; Don Baxter and Ted Fuller of the Pacific Gas & Electric Co.; Robert Hawley of Ross Valley Books; Ferol Egan; Ralph Morena and Mary Minton of the Mill Valley Public Library; Peter Hanft of Bancroft Library; the reference staff of the Petaluma Library; Gladys Hansen at the San Francisco Public Library; Bruce Johnson of the California Historical Society; Ted Wurm; David Myrick; Kevin Starr; Ed Manion; Ed Fratini; Scott Martin; Cliff Hollander; Gary Kurutz and Tom Fante of the California State Library; Eleanor Capelle and staff of the Sutro Library; Louise Teather; Clyde Arbuckle; The Marin County Historical Society; James Delgado of the Golden Gate National Recreation Area; The State Division of Mines Library; Grace Baker of the Society of California Pioneers; Egon Weiss; Janet Dillon Leonard; Dan Kilgore; Al Lowman; Fred Stindt; Karl Vollmayer; Bob Allison, and Sue Shauver of the Scott County, Iowa, Genealogical Society.

Richard Dillon

INDEX

An asterisk preceding an entry indicates a primary or secondary source consulted and/or quoted by the author.